Raniero Cantalamessa

COME, CREATOR SPIRIT
Meditations on the *Veni Creator*

Translated by Denis and Marlene Barrett

THE LITURGICAL PRESS
Collegeville, Minnesota

www.litpress.org

Cover design by Ann Blattner. Cover art: *The Spirit of God Hovering Over the Waters,* miniature from the Bible de Sens (XIV c.), Turin, Biblioteca Reale.

1   2   3   4   5   6   7

Library of Congress Cataloging-in-Publication Data

Cantalamessa, Raniero.
    Come, Creator Spirit : meditations on the Veni Creator /
  Raniero Cantalamessa ; translated by Denis and Marlene Barrett.
      p. cm.
    Includes bibliographical references and index.
    ISBN 0-8146-2871-0 (alk. paper)
      1. Veni Creator Spiritus. I. Veni Creator Spiritus. II. Title.
  BV469.V462 C36 2003
  242'.7—dc21   2002029842

Contents

Abbreviations

AHMA	Analecta Hymnica Medii Aevi, ed. C. Blume
CC	Corpus Christianorum
CinSS	*Credo in Spiritum Sanctum,* Acts of the International Theological Congress of Pneumatology, 2 vols. (Libreria Editrice Vaticana, 1983)
CM	Corpus Christianorum, Continuatio Mediaevalis
CSCO	Corpus Scriptorum Christianorum Orientalium
CSEL	Corpus Scriptorum Ecclesiasticorum Latinorum
Dict. Spir.	Dictionnaire de Spiritualité (Paris, 1936ff.)
DBSuppl.	Dictionnaire de la Bible Supplément
DS	Denzinger, Schönmetzer, *Enchiridion Simbolorum* (Herder, 1967)
ED	Francis of Assisi, *Early Documents,* 3 vols. (New York: New City Press, 1999–2001)
GCS	Griechische Christliche Schriftsteller
JAWG	Jahrbuch der Akademie der Wissenschaften zu Göttingen
PG	Patrologia Graeca
PL	Patrologia Latina
PLS	Patrologia Latina Supplementum
PS	Patrologia Siriaca
SCh	Sources Chrétiennes

ThWNT   Theologisches Wörterbuch zum Neuen Testament

WA   Weimar Ausgabe (Luther's Opera omnia)

N.B.: The works of the Fathers, of which there are several editions, equally reliable, and all of which follow a commonly-accepted division, are cited without reference to any particular edition. References to more than one book of the Bible are given in footnotes in order to interrupt the reader as little as possible. Quotations of the Vatican Council II are taken from *Vatican Council II: The Conciliar and Post Conciliar Documents,* ed. A. Flannery (New York: Costello Publishing, 1988).

Introduction

In the Christian churches of the West, the year 2000 began with the solemn chanting of the hymn *Veni Creator*. Ever since the early decades of the second millennium, every new year, every century, every conclave, every ecumenical council, every synod, every meeting of any importance in the life of the Church, every priestly ordination, every consecration of a bishop, and in years gone by, every coronation of a monarch, began in exactly the same way. This hymn was composed in the ninth century, and it has resounded unceasingly ever since then, wherever Christianity has used Latin as its spoken language. It has been especially the hymn of Pentecost, like a most solemn and extended invocation of the Holy Spirit over the whole of humanity and over the whole Church.

As with everything that comes from the Holy Spirit, the *Veni Creator* is not "worn out," but enriched with use. If Holy Scripture, as Gregory the Great said, "grows by the fact of its being read,"[1] the *Veni Creator* has grown through the centuries by virtue of the fact that it has been sung. It has become charged with all the faith, the devotion, the ardent desire for the Spirit of all the generations that have sung it before our time. And now, thanks to the communion of saints, when even the most modest of little choirs of believers sing it, God hears in it the whole of that majestic "orchestration."

Today it is held most probable that the author was Rhabanus Maurus, Abbot of Fulda and later Archbishop of Mainz, who was born in about 780 and lived until 856. He was one of the greatest theologians of his day, and had a profound knowledge of the writings of the Fathers of the Church. The first evidence of an official

---

[1] Gregory the Great, *Commentary on Job,* XX.I (CC 143A, p. 1003).

use of the hymn is found in the Acts of the Council of Rheims (held in 1049), in which we read, "as the Pope entered the aula, the clergy, with deep devotion, sang the hymn *Veni Creator Spiritus*."[2] But it must already have been in use for some time in certain local churches and monasteries. The hymn had gained, and from that time onward it held, a fixed place in the liturgy of the whole Church.

The *Veni Creator* is an eminently ecumenical text, and this too helps to make it particularly suitable for the epoch in which we are living. It is the only ancient Latin hymn that has been adopted by all the major churches born of the Reformation. Luther himself undertook a German translation of it. From the very beginning of the Anglican Church, the hymn was included in the rite of ordination of a bishop. In the churches that have developed in the Calvinist tradition, it occupies an honored place in the collection of hymns for Pentecost. Hence it is that the *Veni Creator* makes it possible for all Christians to be united in their invocation of the Holy Spirit, who is the one who will lead us to full unity, as the Spirit is the one who leads us to the fullness of truth.

But the *Veni Creator* has enjoyed extraordinary success even outside of Church circles. Goethe produced a splendid German translation of it, as did the poets and mystics Tersteegen and Angelus Silesius. Composers showed their interest in it. Bach set Luther's translation to music; Gustav Mahler chose the hymn as libretto for his choral work *Symphony of a Thousand*, to say nothing of the many other authors of lesser note. Yet none of them so far has managed to equal the simple fascination of the Gregorian melody that seems to have come to birth in the same creative act as produced the words. To listen to this melody at the beginning of a retreat or at a priestly ordination is, as it were, to enter without further ado into an atmosphere charged with mystery and with the presence of the Spirit.

Nevertheless, this book is not on the *Veni Creator*, but on the Holy Spirit! The hymn is just the roadmap we will use as we move along exploring the territory. These days, if you want to learn a foreign language quickly, you use the method called "full immersion." For a space of time you avoid using your own native tongue or any other language. You speak, you hear, and you think only in the lan-

---

[2] See Mansi, *Sacrorum Conciliorum Collectio*, XIX (Venice, 1774) 740.

guage you want to learn; you immerse yourself totally in the culture and the customs of the people who speak it. That is what we need to do if we want to learn the language of the Holy Spirit, a foreign language to us who are flesh and speak the language of the flesh!

On the one hand, the words of the *Veni Creator* condense the very essence of biblical revelation and patristic tradition concerning the Holy Spirit. On the other hand, precisely because they are derived from the Scriptures, the words of the hymn provide us with an "open structure" capable of receiving each new awareness the Church has discovered and experienced concerning the Spirit. We will follow the same procedure in our reflections. We will start every time from the rich biblical and theological base provided by the hymn, in order then to open ourselves to new perspectives and above all to draw, from the doctrine, inspiration for our life. The words of our hymn are like honeycombs full of honey: our job will be like that of the beekeeper extracting the honey from the comb.

The *Veni Creator* is not only a beautiful hymn providing a wealth of inspiring suggestion. It contains within its poetry a grandiose vision of the Holy Spirit in the history of salvation that will emerge little by little as we progress through the reading. It has the advantage of being theology at prayer, sung in the key of praise, the only way in which we can adequately speak of the Holy Spirit.

What sources was the author able to consult in writing his hymn, and what sources are we able to turn to today as we comment on it? As to the Father, besides the Scriptures we have at our disposal *philosophy,* for it too has some things to say about God. As to the Son, besides the Scriptures we can turn to *history,* because he was made flesh and entered into our history. But as to the Holy Spirit, to what can we turn apart from the Scriptures? The answer: to *experience*! We can turn not only to the experience of every single individual believer, but also, and especially, to that collective experiencing of the Spirit through the course of the centuries that has been the life of the Church and which we refer to as *Tradition*. If, as the Fathers say, "the Law was pregnant with Christ," the Church is pregnant with the Holy Spirit! We need delicate hands, midwife hands, to bring to light the fruits of the Spirit that are ripening in her.

Again, we can turn not only to the Church's experience of the Spirit in the past, but also to the Church's experience of the Spirit today. A movement has arisen, in the last century, that has come to be called "a reawakening of the Spirit, of greater proportions than any other in all the history of Christianity." This has created a new situation, in which it is more advantageous than it ever has been before, to speak of the Holy Spirit. We hope that these pages will make ample use of this advantage. To remain faithful to the ecumenical character of the *Veni Creator,* we will try to draw not only from the Catholic tradition, but also from the Orthodox and Protestant traditions. It will, as a consequence, be a kind of "canto in three voices."

When we try to speak of the Holy Spirit, symbol, image, song, poetry, and prophecy are perhaps more suitable media than concepts and reasoning. For this reason we will give a great deal of space, especially in the texts quoted at the end of each chapter, to the hymnography of the various Christian traditions where all these forms of expression are much in use. We will, however, be giving even more space to the testimonies of the saints, sure, as Basil says, that "the Spirit is the place of saints, and saints are the place of the Spirit."[3]

This commentary on the "song of the Spirit," the *Veni Creator,* aims to be in its own small way a song of gratitude and of praise to the Paraclete at the beginning of a new millennium. "Sing to the Lord a new song" is something the Scripture often tells us to do (Ps 149:1). Is it possible, today, to sing a "new song" to the Holy Spirit? What can we say of the Spirit that is new, that has not already been said? Yes, it is indeed possible, because the Spirit himself makes all things new. The Spirit is the ever-new song in the heart of the Church! The Spirit "rejuvenates" all that he touches, including the ancient words that human beings invented as they struggled to say what they had discovered of his person.

And so it is that I make my own the words with which Gregory Nazianzen opens his canticle in honor of the Holy Spirit: "And now, my heart, what are you waiting for? What you must do is sing the glory of the Spirit."[4]

---

[3] Basil the Great, *On the Holy Spirit,* XXVI.62 (PG 32.184A).
[4] Gregory Nazianzen, *Dogmatic Poems,* III (PG 37.408A).

Here, in side-by-side columns, we copy the critical Latin text of the *Veni Creator* and a fairly literal English version. The commentary will take the hymn more or less line by line, a chapter on each line. At the beginning of each section a more literal translation will be given, and on that the commentary will be based.

Veni Creator Spiritus,	Come, Creator Spirit,
mentes tuorum visita,	visit the minds of those who are yours;
imple superna gratia	fill with heavenly grace
quae tu creasti pectora.	the hearts that you have made.
Qui Paracletus diceris,	You who are named the Paraclete,
donum Dei altissimi,	gift of God most high,
fons vivus, ignis, caritas	living fountain, fire, love
et spiritalis unctio.	and anointing for the soul.
Tu septiformis munere,	You are sevenfold in your gifts,
dexterae Dei tu digitus,	you are finger of God's right hand,
tu rite promissum Patris	you, the Father's solemn promise
sermone ditans guttura.	putting words upon our lips.
Accende lumen sensibus,	Kindle a light in our senses,
infunde amorem cordibus,	pour love into our hearts,
infirma nostri corporis	infirmities of this body of ours
virtute firmans perpeti.	overcoming with strength secure.
Hostem repellas longius,	The enemy drive from us away,
pacemque dones protinus,	peace then give without delay;
ductore sic te praevio	with you as guide to lead the way
vitemus omne noxium.	we avoid all cause of harm.
Per te sciamus da Patrem,	Grant we may know the Father
	through you,
noscamus atque Filium,	and come to know the Son as well,
te utriusque Spiritum	and may we always cling in faith
credamus omni tempore.	to you, the Spirit of them both.
Amen.	Amen.

I

Spirit, Come!

The Holy Spirit, mystery of strength and tenderness

1. Ruach, *the Spirit's Name*

The literal translation of the first verse of the *Veni Creator* says:

> Come, Creator Spirit,
> visit the minds of those who are yours;
> fill with heavenly grace
> the hearts that you have made.

The theme of this introductory meditation will be two words of the first line of the *Veni Creator:* "Come, Spirit," especially "Spirit." Normally, the first thing we learn about a person is his or her name. We use the name to call that person, and the name sorts that person out in our mind from all the other people we know. The Third Person of the Trinity also has a name, even though, as we shall see, it is a very special kind of name. He is called "Spirit."

Spirit, however, is a translation of his name. When you really love someone, you want to know everything about that person, including his or her "baptismal" name, the real name. The real name of the Spirit, the name by which the first recipients of revelation knew him, was *ruach*. It is so good, at times, to call on the Spirit by this name that was pronounced by the lips of the prophets and the psalmists, of Mary, of Jesus, and of Paul! Before the name of the Spirit came to us it went through yet another stage, as *Pneuma*. This is the name given to the Spirit in the pages of the New Testament.

For the Jews, the name was so important that it was identical with the very person. To hold the *name* of God holy meant to recognize and honor the very person of God as holy. The name was never simply a conventional way of referring to someone, as it often is with us today; it always said something of the origin or function of the one named. The name *ruach* is this kind of name. It contains the very first revelation concerning the person and the work of the Holy Spirit. That is why it is so important to start with the name of the Spirit on our journey of discovery into the reality of the Spirit.

What is the meaning of the Hebrew word *ruach*? Its first meaning is the space, the air between heaven and earth, a space that can be sometimes calm, sometimes turbulent, a space like the open prairie where it is easy to see how the wind blows. By extension, *ruach* means the life-space in which we human beings move and breathe. This original meaning of the word has left traces in the theological understanding of the Spirit. Especially in the New Testament, the mention of the Spirit is usually linked to words referring to place. The typical preposition in speaking of the Spirit is *in*, as for the Father it is *from,* and for the Son, *through*: "From the Father, through the Son, in the Holy Spirit." The Holy Spirit is the spiritual space, the life-sustaining ambience, in which we are able to be in touch with God and with Christ.

But let us now leave these remote roots of the meaning of the name, which at an early stage were bypassed even in Hebrew language, and turn to the usual significance the word has in the Bible.

Ruach means two things, closely linked to one another: wind and breath. This is true also of the Greek name *Pneuma* and the Latin *Spiritus*. English also has words from the root *spirit,* like inspire and respire, and from the root *pneuma,* like pneumatic, and all of these retain the link with breath and blow. This same link is present in the term *ghost,* which, like the German *geist,* derives from *gast,* breath.

And so it is that wind and breath are more than just symbols of the Holy Spirit. Here we have symbol and reality so closely linked that they share the same name. It is difficult for us to grasp the influence of the fact that wherever we read "wind" in the Scripture, people of biblical times also understood "spirit," and wherever we read "spirit," they also understood "wind." It was not the Holy Spirit that gave his name to wind, but wind that gave its name to the Holy Spirit. In other words, the sign came before the reality signified, because in human experience, we do not come to know spiritual reality first, but on the contrary, we know material reality first and only then do we come to know what is spiritual (see 1 Cor 15:46).

So it is that we start our study of the Spirit in the open air. As we go through the *Veni Creator* we shall be encountering other natural symbols of the Holy Spirit: water, fire, oil, and light. The Bible loves to teach us about the most spiritual realities by using as symbols the simplest of ordinary things found in nature. God "wrote two books": creation, made up of things and elements in themselves mute, and the Bible, made up of letters and words. These "books" explain one another and throw light on one another. The sacraments work in the same kind of way.

As I mentioned, there were two root meanings of the word *ruach* that God used to reveal to us the ineffable reality of the Spirit: wind and breath. In this connection we recall several of the more significant passages from the Bible, not simply to show that what we are saying is supported by texts, but because each one of these passages is a pearl for us to treasure.

The opening lines of the book of Genesis speak of the "Spirit of God" hovering over the waters. The closeness between Spirit and Wind is here so strong that modern translators are often uncertain whether to translate the expression as "Spirit of God," or "Wind of God," or "freely-blowing wind." A little later in the text we read: "the Lord God formed man from the dust of the ground, and *breathed* into his nostrils the *breath* of life" (Gen 2:7), and later the Bible sees in that "breath" an early, embryonic manifestation of the Holy Spirit (1 Cor 15:45).

Here, then, we see the beginnings of the two basic images destined to become more and more explicit as revelation continued to unfold. When the Holy Spirit is given in the Acts of the Apostles, the sign is that of a strong wind (Acts 2:2); in John's Gospel the same Spirit is conferred by the Risen Christ in the sign of breathing, in a gesture that deliberately recalls the Genesis account: "He breathed on them and said, 'Receive the Holy Spirit'" (John 20:22).

For John, the moment on the cross when Jesus "gave up his spirit" (John 19:30) was also the moment in which he gave the Holy Spirit. Neither is John unaware of the other image, the free-blowing wind: "The wind blows where it chooses, and you hear the sound of it, but you do not know where it comes from or where it goes. So it is with everyone who is born of the Spirit" (John 3:8). (Here, as on so many other occasions, Jesus manifests himself as the "great poet of the Spirit.")

The image of the free-blowing wind and of the whirlwind both help to convey the power, the freedom, and the transcendence of the divine Spirit. Wind, in fact, in the Bible as well as in nature, is par excellence the embodiment of a sweeping force, a force that cannot be tamed, "splitting mountains and breaking rocks in pieces" (1 Kgs 19:11). It can lash up towering waves, fling them to the sky, and plunge them to the depths (see Ps 107:25-26). What is there that can stir up the ocean as powerfully as the wind?

On the other hand, the images of breath and breathing and gentle breeze serve to express the goodness, the gentleness, the peacefulness and the immanence of the Spirit of God. Breath is that which is most "inward" and intimate, most vital and personal to a human being.

Those who study religious phenomenology have brought to light a fact that can be verified in all the higher forms of religion, but especially in the Bible: the divine is perceived as a mystery, "awesome and fascinating," able at the same time to inspire fear and love, to terrify and to attract.[1] Augustine writes that, at the moment when for the first time he saw closely the mystery of God, he trembled "for love and in terror," and that the thought of God made him at once "shiver and burn with desire."[2] The Bible gives us ample confirmation of these observations. "You indeed are awesome! Who can stand before you when once your anger is roused?" (Ps 76:7) is speaking of the same God that elsewhere is exalted for his "abundant goodness" and his tender-hearted "compassion . . . over all that he has made" (Ps 145:7-9). It is not as though God were complicated or changeable (God is simplicity itself), but it is we ourselves who cannot quite take in, at a single glance, God's reality which is both most simple and utterly infinite. We need to come at it from two different points of view in order to know God, just as we need two eyes in order to enjoy any perception of depth or distance.

Well now, the Holy Spirit is the personification of this mystery of God who is, at the same time, absolute power and immeasurable tenderness, irresistible movement and infinite rest. Let us look a little more closely at these two characteristics. They will help us to understand a great part of the biblical revelation concerning the Paraclete. At this point, the symbols of wind and

---

[1] Cf. R. Otto, *Das Heilige* (München, 1947).
[2] Augustine, *Confessions,* VII.10.16; XI.9.11.

breath do not help us: they have served their purpose, which was to help us lift our perceptions from the natural level to the supernatural. It would be a great pity if we could not make this very clear distinction between symbol and reality. We would be stuck in the philosophy of the Stoics who, never having made the qualitative leap from breath to spirit, ended up thinking of the divine Spirit as "a subtle breath permeating all things," or as "a creative fire," that is, something material.[3] This kind of thinking leads us to fall into pantheism and materialism and so to destroy the very notion of spirit as we understand it today.

2. The Holy Spirit Comes to Help Us in Our Weakness

We are reflecting, therefore, on the Spirit first as mystery of power and transcendence. The Spirit represents the "numinous" (that is, the wholly other, the transcendent) in its pure state. The Sequence for Pentecost very fittingly applies this concept to the Spirit when, praying to the Spirit, it says: "Without your divine presence (*numen*) there is nothing in man, nothing at all of innocence."[4]

The Old Testament often speaks of the Spirit of God who "assails" like a hurricane, or who "bursts in upon" certain people, like Samson, conferring a supernatural strength on them.[5] This revelation of power grew by the addition of the appellative "Holy," *qadosh,* which from Isaiah 63:10 and Psalm 51 onward is more and more closely associated with Spirit and eventually comes to form one single, composite name with it, the Holy Spirit.

But what does the Hebrew word *qadosh* mean? The word "holy" has become more circumscribed, but also somewhat emptied of power, in modern usage. It has taken on an almost exclusively moral meaning, signifying good, dutiful, pure. It has become a reassuring sort of word. But for Isaiah, who heard the Seraphs cry out this word three times while "the pivots of the threshold shook . . . and the house filled with smoke," it was anything but reassuring, so much so that he himself cried out, "Woe is me! I am lost" (Isa 6:3-5). In fact, "holy" is a term utterly

---

[3] See J. von Arnim, *Stoicorum Veterum Fragmenta,* I.108; II.246; II.1027.

[4] *Sine tuo numine, nihil est in homine, nihil est innoxium.*

[5] See Judg 6:34; 13:25; 14:6.

full of the "numinous," that is, loaded with the divine; it expresses
a sense of the complete separateness of the transcendent, of absolute otherness, and in consequence it demands adoration, silence, purification of any who dare remain in its presence. "Who
is able to stand before the Lord, this holy God?" (1 Sam 6:20). To
say that God is holy is the same sort of thing as saying that God is
a "consuming fire." "Holy," *qadosh,* becomes closely associated
with "terrible" or "awesome": "Holy and awesome is his name"
(Ps 111:9). The term doesn't refer only to the moral sphere but to
the very being of a person. "I am God and no mortal, the Holy
One in your midst" (Hos 11:9). Holy is something that belongs to
the divine as opposed to the human sphere. All of this is attributed
to the Spirit when we call him "Holy."

In the New Testament, this "sweeping unstoppableness" of the
divine breath is brought out by the frequent joining of the names
"Spirit" and "Power." God anointed Jesus of Nazareth "with the
Holy Spirit and with power" (Acts 10:38). After his baptism in
the Jordan, Jesus returned to Galilee "filled with the power of the
Spirit" (Luke 4:14). The Spirit is equated with "the Power of the
Most High" (Luke 1:35) or the "power from on high" (Luke
24:49). The old "terrible" or "numinous" character of the Spirit,
too, shows up here and there, as when Ananias lied to the Spirit
and fell down dead (Acts 5:3ff.).

The coming down of the Holy Spirit at Pentecost is deliberately
described using the same signs which accompanied the theophany on Mount Sinai at the giving of the Law (Exodus 19–20).
In an indirect way this affirms that the mystery of the Spirit is no
less, nor is it in nature different, from the mystery of God. The
same mystery, the same effects: those who witness it are "dis-
mayed," "amazed," "beside themselves with amazement." Before
the Church came to attribute to the Spirit in an explicit way the
same honor and the same absolute sovereignty attributed to God,
Scripture had already done it in that way—indirectly, but perhaps
for that very reason more effectively.

But let us now come to the practical aspect of our reflection.
What is it that the Bible wants to impress upon us with this revelation of the Spirit as strength and power? What can we deduce from
it, for our life of faith? This, I think, above all else: The Holy Spirit
is the one and only true strength and real power that keeps the

Church alive! Just as the individual believer, the Church itself cannot live by its own strength. Its strength is not in "armies," nor in "horses and chariots" or in any other things of that kind. "Not by might, nor by power, but by my Spirit, says the Lord of hosts. What are you, O great mountain? Before Zerubbabel you shall become a plain!" (Zech 4:6). Neither does the strength of the Church consist in "the arguments that belong to philosophy," or in intelligence, diplomacy, Canon Law, or wise organization. Paul says: "Our message of the gospel came to you not in word only, but also in power and in the Holy Spirit and with full conviction" (1 Thess 1:5).

It is therefore from the Holy Spirit that the Church, and every preacher of the Gospel, has the power to convince and to lead to conversion, to get through to the very heart of a culture, and to destroy within it all the bulwarks erected against Christ, and to lead people to the obedience of faith.[6] It follows, then, that the Holy Spirit is the source and the secret of the courage and the daring of all believers. Of the apostles, at a very difficult juncture in their mission, we read: "They were all filled with the Holy Spirit and spoke the word of God with boldness *(parrhesia)*" (Acts 4:13, 31).

The Holy Spirit is the strength of the prophets, the apostles, and the martyrs. As Micah exclaimed, "I am filled with power, with the spirit of the Lord, and with justice and might" (Mic 3:8). Paul said, "God did not give us a spirit of cowardice, but rather a spirit of power" (2 Tim 1:7). Writing of the Christians who had to face wild beasts in the arena, Tertullian called the Holy Spirit the "coach of the martyrs."[7] In his turn, Cyril of Jerusalem writes, "The martyrs bear their witness, thanks to the strength of the Holy Spirit."[8]

It is not then entirely true that "one cannot give oneself courage." On the spiritual level, at least, it is possible to "take courage," because "the Spirit helps us in our weakness" (Rom 8:26). Therefore, our very weakness itself may be a privileged occasion for us to experience the power of the Spirit. Every single thing, in the life of the Church or in the life of an individual believer, takes its power from the Spirit, or is without any power whatsoever.

---

[6] See 2 Cor 10:3-5; Rom 15:18-19.

[7] Tertullian, *To the Martyrs*, 3.3 (CC 1, p. 5).

[8] Cyril of Jerusalem, *Catecheses*, XVI.21.

3. The Holy Spirit Fills Our Loneliness

Let us pass on to the second characteristic: the Holy Spirit as a mystery of goodness, gentleness, indulgence, closeness, and as a mystery of quietness and rest. Western Christianity has attempted to express this bouquet of qualities using the verse from the Bible that, in the Latin Vulgate, said, "Oh, how good and how sweet, Lord, is your Spirit in all things" (Wis 12:1). In a sermon on Pentecost, Pope Innocent III exclaimed: "Oh, how agreeable is this Spirit, how peaceful, how gentle! Those alone know him who have tasted him!"[9]

In Semitic languages, the noun "spirit" is feminine, and this has certainly made its influence felt, so much so that (particularly among the ancient Syriac authors) there has been a rich development of doctrine on the Holy Spirit as "mother," which stresses these "gentle and tender" characteristics of the Spirit. In one of these authors, we read that Adam's disgrace after the Fall was that "he no longer saw the true Father of the heavens, nor the benign, good Mother, the grace of the Spirit, nor the agreeable, desirable Brother, the Lord."[10]

Because of the way the Gnostics abused this theme in the early days, the mainstream of Church Tradition left it almost entirely aside. One thing, however, is sure: Of the three divine persons, the Holy Spirit is certainly the one that, in revelation and in language, is least characterized as masculine (the first person is "Father" and the second is "Son," and he became "man").

Though they avoided any speculation on the Spirit as "mother," Church writers did not hesitate to make use of this title while speaking of the functions of the Paraclete. When teaching us to cry "Abba," the Spirit behaves "like a mother teaching her own little baby to say 'daddy,' repeating that word along with the baby until it becomes so much the baby's habit that it calls its daddy even in its sleep."[11]

We need only to look at the position of women through the stages of our history to see that, in every facet of life, women have

---

[9] Innocent III, *Sermons*, XXV (PL 217.427A)

[10] *Spiritual Homilies*, attributed to Macarius, 28.4 (PG 34.712–3).

[11] Diadochus of Fotike, *On Spiritual Perfection*, 61 (SCh 5, p. 121).

been marginalized. In every domain, except that of family, the position of women in history appears to be inferior to that of men: in philosophy, literature, art, politics. There is only one area of achievement in which, most fortunately for us all, women have maintained a footing of absolute parity with men, and that is in holiness. In the history of the Church it is very difficult to make out whether the greater saints have been men saints or women saints. The Holy Spirit sanctifies both men and women, and in so doing always preserves total respect for the differing sexual nature of each, but the sanctity he creates in men and in women is always one and the same sanctity. In women it shines out as feminine, and in men as virile. Thus we see that in men the Spirit has tended to manifest its presence as power, strength, and courage, and in women as tenderness, loving care, and gentleness.

We said that *ruach,* meaning breath, indicates that which is most intimate and secret in God, just as it indicates what is most intimate and unrevealed in human beings: the very principle of life, the soul. This is the sense in which it is used where we read that no one knows the secret thoughts, the depths, of a person but that person's own spirit and no one knows the secret depths of God but the Spirit of God (see 1 Cor 2:11).

The Scripture begins at a relatively late stage to speak of the divine Spirit as one who enters into human beings in order to dwell or remain with us in an uninterrupted way. This was in fact a remarkable achievement, a significant advance in relation to the way the Spirit acts in his charismatic manifestations. Isaiah spoke of the Spirit that God caused to dwell within Moses (Isa 63:11), and also of a Spirit that can be saddened and grieved (Isa 63:10). However, only in the New Testament does this aspect come fully to light. When Jesus promised the Spirit he said, "You know him, because he abides with you, and he will be in you" (John 14:17). The Spirit is in you to stay, and no longer simply passing by. We become the Spirit's temples (1 Cor 3:17; 6:19). This is the idea behind another of the lines of the Sequence for Pentecost, *dulcis hospes animae,* "sweet guest of the soul."

We have looked at the way the Spirit shows himself, first as "causing us dread" and next as "fascinating." What does this second "agreeable" mode say to us? Saint Basil, in one simple and stupendous phrase, says it all: the Holy Spirit is the one who creates

"intimacy *(oikeiosis)* with God."[12] This image is biblical; in the
letter to the Ephesians we read:

> Through him both of us have access in one Spirit to the Father.
> So then you are no longer strangers and aliens, but you are citi-
> zens with the saints and also members of the household of God
> *(oikeioi)*. . . . In him the whole structure is joined together
> and grows into a holy temple in the Lord; in whom you also are
> built together spiritually into a dwelling place for God (Eph
> 2:18-22).

The term used has a whole range of meanings that make the concept all the more significant: it conveys the notions of appropriation,
attraction, affection, and familiarity. In the Holy Spirit God becomes
ours, he draws us lovingly to himself, he takes away from us the fear
and the sense of unease that, as heirs of Adam, we would feel in
meeting him. Through the Spirit we are "at home" with God! John,
in his turn, writes: "We can know that we abide in him and he in us,
because he has given us of his Spirit" (1 John 4:13).

This, stripped of all metaphor and human imagining, is what
intimacy with God means: God in us, and we in God, due to the
presence of the Holy Spirit. (The Latin word *intimus,* intimate, is
the superlative form of *intus,* inside.) Augustine, then, was perfectly right when he said that God is "more intimate to me than I
am to myself."[13]

Intimacy is one of the very few words in human language that
always and everywhere is used only in a positive sense: the intimacy of a loving couple, the intimacy of the home, between
friends. In intimacy with another person we experience a reconciliation of identity with otherness, of *I* with *thou.* In every moment of honest intimacy the Holy Spirit is at work in some way.
Just as all fatherhood comes from God the Father (see Eph 3:15),
all intimacy too comes from the Holy Spirit. In fact, intimacy does
not arise out of being together in a place; it is created by love, and
love comes from the Holy Spirit. In every experience of genuine
human intimacy, including the conjugal embrace, what people are
seeking is intimacy with God, intimacy that is absolute. In fact

---

[12] Basil the Great, *On the Holy Spirit,* XIX.49 (PG 32.157A).
[13] Augustine, *Confessions,* III.6.11.

what we are seeking, though perhaps we may not know it, is that center of being, that point at which all melts into one, that place of perfect rest apart from which we know there is nothing more profound and nothing that can give greater happiness.

This, too, has a practical consequence for us. The Holy Spirit is the answer to loneliness, which, along with fear and weakness, is the greatest cause of human suffering. What really overcomes loneliness? Certainly not finding yourself in the midst of a great crowd, but rather having a friend, someone to share thoughts with, a companion. If we are open to him, this is what the Holy Spirit wants to be to us. It is again Saint Basil who says that the Holy Spirit was "the inseparable companion"[14] of Jesus during his life on earth, and that the Spirit wants to be the same for us. John Chrysostom adds that Jesus "always had the assistance of the most agreeable Spirit, consubstantial with him," just as he seems to suggest that Moses, all his life long, had his brother Aaron as companion and counselor.[15]

If it is possible for weakness to provide an occasion for us to experience the strength of the Spirit, it is possible for loneliness to be the occasion and also the stimulus for us to experience the Spirit as "sweet guest." By faith we know that no one is ever truly alone in this world. If we need to speak with someone about something, and it is simply not possible to find anyone to speak to, we can learn, little by little, to talk it over with that guest, who is discretion itself and who also is "perfect consoler" and "wonderful counselor."

As mystery of *rest*, the Holy Spirit is also the answer to our *restlessness.* Our heart is restless, searching, dissatisfied; the place where our heart finds rest is the Holy Spirit, in whom our heart quiets and finds peace.[16] The Sequence for Pentecost has us call on the Holy Spirit as *in labore requies,* "rest in the midst of labor." One of the things one sees most often in Pentecostal and charismatic circles is the phenomenon called "resting in the Spirit." It is something that calls for much discernment, but in many cases its authentic spiritual character cannot be denied. The one who is "touched" by the Spirit falls, but gently, as if lying

---

[14] Basil the Great, *On the Holy Spirit,* XVI.39 (PG 32.140C).

[15] John Chrysostom, *Baptismal Catechesis,* III.26 (SCh 50, p. 166).

[16] Augustine, *Confessions,* I.1.1; XIII.9.10.

down on the ground; all thought ceases, and if afterward that person tries to describe the experience, the only words to be found are, "Peace, such profound peace!"

It is not necessary, nor may it even be possible, to experience the Holy Spirit as power at the same time we experience the Spirit as tenderness and intimacy, or to experience the Spirit simultaneously in his dynamism and his rest. The Spirit reveals himself at various times under one or the other form, and we experience him sometimes in one way and sometimes in another, depending on our need, our disposition, and the grace of the moment. On Sinai Moses perceived God in the thunder and the stormy wind (Exod 19:18-19); Elijah, on the same Mount Horeb, perceived God in the gentle breeze (1 Kgs 19:12).

4. In the School of "Brother Wind"

Now we can go back to the symbols of wind and breath because they help us get a visual image of the content of our contemplation. The symbols are "functional"; they tell us what the Spirit *does,* and this is what makes them so useful to us at this time. Let's go to the school of "brother wind," as Saint Francis of Assisi called it. The wind will remind us of many things, if we look at it with new eyes washed clear by the word of God. The language of words changes; the language of things is unchanging. Brother Wind speaks today exactly as in the time of Ezekiel and at the very beginning of the world.

Look, for instance, at what happens when a strong, blustery wind blows. Trees bend and sway; if they try to resist the wind, like mighty cedars of Lebanon, they break. This reminds us of the Church's prayer: "Bend our wills, however rebellious they may be, to you." Look now at the little green leaves that stream out lightly in the wind and suffer no damage as they allow it to pass (at least, as long as they are still green). Our souls are to be sensitive and docile to the Spirit as the young green leaves are to the wind. A Christian text dating from the second century says that the human soul is like an Aeolian harp that sounds as the wind passes through it, and that the Holy Spirit is the wind that strums on the strings of the soul to draw from it sounds of sweet harmony.

> As the wind passes through the lyre
> and the strings speak,
> in the same way through my inward being
> sounds the Spirit of the Lord, and I speak in his love.[17]

What effort it takes to walk or to row against the wind! What joy to do the same thing with the wind in your favor! Try to go about doing what you do without the Holy Spirit: how heavy that is! Work with the Spirit; how very much lighter everything becomes!

Fruitfulness is the wind's gift; the wind makes plants fecund. It carries pollen from flower to flower and seeds ripen; it carries seeds to the earth and they germinate. This is what the Holy Spirit does for the seed that is the word of God.

The Fathers were the first to be eager to learn the doctrine of the Spirit in the school of Brother Wind. One wrote that when the warm spring wind, called Favonius, blows, flowers of every kind and color burst open and the fields are sweet with their perfume. The same happens in the soul when the Holy Spirit blows.[18] Another writes of "the breath of the Spirit blowing to fill the sails of our faith and of our praise."[19]

Years ago I spent some time in a retreat house in the northernmost part of Ireland, right by the sea coast. The place is the kingdom of the gulls. It was there that I began to think of writing a commentary on the *Veni Creator,* and for a time it was the gulls that were my masters, teaching me the doctrine of the Spirit. From the cliff tops of that wild and lonely place I would spend many an hour watching them. They would glide from the high rocks and hover motionless over the sea. There, before my eyes, was the very image the holy writer had in mind when he said that, in the beginning, the Spirit of God "hovered over the waters." What impressed me most of all was the way the gulls excelled in the art of making the wind work for them! They fly on the wings of the wind (see Ps 18:10); they let the wind carry them. That is why they are able to remain in the air for long hours, hovering still or moving faster than the eye can follow, and yet not grow tired. Does that not tell us something?

---

[17] *Odes of Solomon,* 6.1-2 (*The Old Testament Pseudepigrapha,* 2 [New York, 1985] 738).

[18] Zeno of Verona, *Treatises,* I.33 (CC 22, p. 84).

[19] Hilary of Poitiers, *The Trinity,* I.37 (CC 62, p. 35).

Wind is the one thing that it is utterly impossible to bridle. It cannot be bottled or canned and distributed for use at need. We can do that with water. We even do it with electricity, storing up power in batteries. But there is no way we can do it with wind. Wind, bottled, is no longer wind, air in free motion; it is still, confined, dead. The rationalism of our day has pretended to circumscribe, to enclose the Spirit in concepts or definitions, texts or tracts, more or less as though the Spirit can be packed in cans or sachets, like milk. But all that this achieves is that the Spirit is lost, rendered trivial and vain.

Yet there is a temptation, somewhat similar, though contrary, to the rationalistic, and it is to want to shut up the Spirit in milk bottles of an ecclesiastical kind: in canons and institutions and definitions. The Spirit calls institutions into being and breathes life into them, but the Spirit himself cannot be institutionalized. The wind blows where it will; in the same way, the Spirit pours out his gifts where he will (see 1 Cor 12:11). It is simply impossible to "canalize" or rigidly control the Spirit, even in the so-called "channels of grace," as if the Holy Spirit were not at perfect liberty to act outside of them. The Second Vatican Council recognized that the Holy Spirit "offers to every human being the possibility of becoming linked to the Paschal mystery in a way that is known only to God."[20] Wind is surely the most eloquent symbol of the Spirit's freedom.

The other symbol, breath, reminds us of many things. What happens if, for whatever reason, we have to hold our breath for a while? We have a tremendous sense of asphyxiation: "I can't breathe. I'm suffocating!" If we only knew how to hear the cry of our own soul when we have neglected to pray for too long a time and so been deprived of the Holy Spirit, we would hear the same cry: "I can't breathe. I'm suffocating!" If someone is about to faint, we usually hold them and say, "Breathe. Breathe deeply!" We need to say the same to those about to shrug their shoulders and give up the struggle against evil: "Turn to prayer, and take deep breaths of the Holy Spirit!"

On Easter evening Jesus breathed on his disciples. In baptism he has repeated this gesture on every one of us. In the rite in use

---

[20] *Gaudium et Spes* 22.

until recently, at a certain point the minister spoke the words, "Go out of this child, unclean spirit, and give place to the Holy Spirit." So saying, he breathed three times over the face of the child. Jesus is ever willing to repeat his paschal gesture for anyone, anywhere, who is open and ready to receive it.

There is a passage in the Bible where we find, brought together, all three meanings of *ruach* that we have been considering in this meditation: wind, breath, and Holy Spirit. It is the prophecy of the dry bones in Ezekiel 37. Symbol and reality are here interwoven and, so to say, run together. "There was no breath in them" (v. 2); that is, they had no life, they were not breathing. "Come from the four winds, O Breath, and breathe upon these slain, that they may live" (v. 9); that is, Wind, come from north and south and east and west and blow. "The breath came into them, and they lived, and stood on their feet" (v. 10). So far the symbol; now the spiritual reality. "I will put my Spirit within you, and you shall live" (v. 14). The Spirit spoken of is the Spirit of God, the Holy Spirit; the life that the Spirit brings is no longer ordinary physical life.

"Spirit, Come!" This is the primordial epiclesis, the root of all prayers of invocation. This is where the opening invocation of our hymn *Veni Creator Spiritus* comes from, as well as the opening line of the Sequence for Pentecost: *Veni, Sancte Spiritus.* It is the first and only prayer to the Holy Spirit recorded in Scripture, and it is the only prayer to the Holy Spirit that the Church has made its own and continued to pray through the centuries. It is the *Marana-tha* of the Spirit, equal to that "Come, Lord!" that the early Christians used to cry out to Christ when they gathered for worship. "Then he said to me, 'Mortal, these bones are the whole house of Israel. They say, "Our bones are dried up, and our hope is lost; we are cut off completely"'" (Ezek 37:11).

We are now this "house of Israel." Among us too in the Church there are those who go about saying, "Our hope has gone; we are as good as dead. Everything is falling to ruin." The promise of the blowing Wind is made to us too: the coming of the Holy Spirit, and the experience of being raised to life again. We hope that our meditations, in this book, will serve mainly to help us to become acutely aware that the "powerful wind" of Pentecost is still blowing, that Jesus is still breathing on his disciples today, that the Upper Room is wide open to us, and that the angel is even now stirring the waters in the pool of Bethesda. Those who want to be healed have only to jump in.

May we resolve never to get tired of joining in this unceasing prayer of invocation that is the constant overtone to the history of the Church, and may we too repeat:

> *Come, oh Holy Spirit!*
> *Come, power of God and tender sweetness of God!*
> *Come, you who are both motion and rest!*
> *Renew our daring,*
> *Be our companion so that we will not feel lonely in this world.*
> *Create in us intimacy with God!*
> *We do not say any longer, as the Prophet said,*
> *"Come from the four winds"*
> *as though we did not yet know where you come from.*
> *We say, "Come, Spirit, from the pierced side of Christ on the*
>   *Cross!*
> *Come on the breath blowing from the lips of the Risen Jesus!"*

II

Creator

The Holy Spirit changes chaos into cosmos

Veni Creator Spiritus, Come, Creator Spirit! The title "Creator" is new and unusual. Our hymn is perhaps the only liturgical text in which the Spirit is called by this name instead of by the other "canonical" name, Holy. It is the strongest word, not only in the first verse but in the whole hymn. Using "Creator" in this way is like throwing open the window to a view of the Bible and Tradition. A window is a small opening, but looking through it one can see an immense panorama; the closer one gets to the window, the wider the panorama he can see. In a similar way Creator is just a little word, but the deeper we dig into its history, the more it reveals profundities we never would have anticipated.

Toward the end of his life the composer Gustav Mahler set out to write a choral symphony. He asked himself what words would be able really to express "the unheard." He reviewed all the world's literature, including the Bible. Ultimately, he decided upon the *Veni Creator,* and for it he assembled the greatest vocal and instrumental "ensemble" ever attempted. The work has come to be known as the *Symphony of a Thousand.* The first line, *Veni Creator Spiritus,* contains the theme of the whole work; it is a kind of cosmic paean rising wave upon wave as the various voices and instruments take up the cry. The composer wrote to a friend, "Try to imagine the universe itself beginning to sing and let its own voice resound. What I want us to hear are not simply human voices, but whirling planets and suns."

1. The Spirit as Creator in Tradition

If we analyze the title "Creator," we come to understand very quickly that the word was not chosen because it slotted nicely into the meter. On the contrary, it is the firm, precise footing of a long series of biblical revelations and Church Traditions and the one point in which all of them come together.

At the Council of Nicea (325), the concept "Creator" played a decisive role in the definition of the divinity of Jesus Christ. It was the point on which the Arian view diverged from the Orthodox. The Arians, following Middle-Platonic philosophy, distinguished three levels of being: ungenerated being, which belongs to God; intermediate being, which belongs to the Demiurge or lesser god; and produced or created being, in which all creatures exist. Against this threefold division the Council of Nicea upheld the new Christian perception that there are only two orders of being: Uncreated Being, and created being. Whatever exists is either Creator or creature, and there is no possibility of any in-between kind of existence.

The struggle of the Orthodox party all turned on this point, and on the need to show that God the Son was not some kind of creature and that, consequently, he was of the same order of being as the Creator, uncreated, like the Father. The Nicene Creed formulates a distinction, *genitum non factum,* "begotten, not made," and in that way overcomes the Arian dilemma. The Creed provides the distinction between generating and creating; though *generated* of the Father, the Son is nevertheless *not created* but coequal with the Father as Creator.

Once the divinity of Christ had been firmly established, the council could go ahead to resolve the problem of the divinity of the Holy Spirit. It was again Athanasius, the champion of orthodoxy at Nicea, who was first to put forward the force of this argument in support of the divinity of the Holy Spirit. His reasoning is quite straightforward:

> The Son, who is in the Father, is not a creature but of the very substance of the Father. For the same reason it is not permissible to count the Holy Spirit a creature and so do violence to the Trinity, since the Holy Spirit is in the Son and has the Son in him.[1]

This argument rests upon and alludes to a fundamental Christian experience: Christians know that contact with the Spirit transforms and deifies them.

---

[1] Athanasius, *Letters to Serapion,* I.21 (PG 26.580C).

> If the Holy Spirit were a creature, we would not have any partaking in God through him. . . . But if, by partaking in the Spirit, we become sharers in the divine nature, one would be senseless to say that the Holy Spirit belongs to the created nature and not to the uncreated nature of God.[2]

All the Fathers who write in defense of the divinity of the Holy Spirit follow Athanasius on this point.[3] Ambrose brings this discussion to the Latin-speaking world: "The Holy Spirit is therefore not a creature, but Creator!"[4] The very phrase *Creator Spiritus* is used by Saint Augustine, who writes: "They judge badly who confuse the creature with the Creator, and think that the Creator Spirit of God is one of the creatures."[5]

The Council of Constantinople in 381 did not explicitly add the title "Creator" in the article of its Creed on the Holy Spirit, possibly in order to avoid repetition, as it had already used it for the Father. Instead, the council used the title "Lord" ("I believe in the Holy Spirit, who is Lord . . ."). However, the difference between servant and Lord (or King) is simply another way of expressing the distinction between creature and Creator. Gregory Nazianzen says that those who say that in God there is a Creator (the Father), a collaborator (the Son), and a servant (the Holy Spirit) are wrong.[6] And Saint Basil writes: "If he is created, the Holy Spirit is clearly servant, but if on the other hand he is above creation, then he must belong to Royalty."[7]

To us today it must appear a little strange that the problem was not once and for all radically resolved by clearly and simply attributing the title "God" to the Holy Spirit. But up to that time, that was the policy of orthodoxy. It avoided any direct application of the term "God" to the Holy Spirit in its determination to remain faithful to the Scripture that speaks of "one God and Father of all" (Eph 4:6), and to express belief in the absolute divinity of the Spirit by in fact according it the same *isotimia*, that is, the same honor and veneration as accorded to the Father and the Son. This is why the

[2] Ibid., I.24 (PG 26.586B).

[3] Gregory Nazianzen, *Sermons*, XXXI.6 (PG 36.140).

[4] Ambrose, *On the Holy Spirit*, III.139–40.

[5] Augustine, *Commentary on the Psalms*, 32.II.2 (CC 38, p. 259).

[6] Gregory Nazianzen, *Sermons*, XXXI.5 (PG 36.137D).

[7] Basil the Great, *On the Holy Spirit*, XX.51 (PG 32.161C).

article of faith defined by the Council of Constantinople in 381 does not say that we believe in the Holy Spirit "who is God," but "who with the Father and the Son is adored and glorified."

Later on the belief in the Holy Spirit as Creator was deepened and anchored theologically in the doctrine of the Trinity. Whatever God does outside the Trinity is a work of all three Persons together,[8] and hence the Holy Spirit is Creator along with the Father and the Son. Augustine develops this idea saying that "in God everything is common to the three Persons, except what belongs to a single person in virtue of his relationship to the others."[9] Hence, the act of creation is common to all three Persons.

It is in this definitive form that the patristic notion of the Holy Spirit as Creator was taken up in the *Veni Creator*. In another of his writings Rhabanus Maurus says:

> Very fittingly, saying that "God, in the Beginning—which is like saying 'the Father, in the Son'—created heaven and earth," the Scripture inserts a mention of the Holy Spirit, adding: "and the Spirit of God hovered over the waters." Thus the text shows that the power of the whole Trinity worked together in the creation of the world.[10]

Later, Thomas Aquinas was to say that "the Holy Spirit is the very principle of the creation of things."[11] In all of this, we have just begun to take account of what there is behind the word that proclaims the Holy Spirit "Creator."

2. The Creator Spirit in Scripture

The Fathers, attributing the role of Creator to the Spirit, are taking the Bible as their base. A great deal of their argument is negative in character; in other words, they intend to show that the Spirit is "not a creature." However, in doing so they also affirm that the Holy Spirit is in fact "Creator." They were not mistaken in the substance of their teaching. The Scripture contains the idea of the "Creator" Spirit. The difference is that the Fathers accentuated the

---

[8] See Gregory of Nyssa, *Against the Macedonians*, 13 (PG 45.1317).

[9] Augustine, *The City of God*, XI.10; see DS 1330.

[10] Rhabanus Maurus, *Commentary on Genesis*, I.1 (PL 107.447).

[11] Thomas Aquinas, *Contra Gentes*, IV.20, n. 3570, ed. Marietti, vol. 3 (Turin, 1961) 286.

ontological meaning of the word, understanding "Creator" as a designation of the essence or the nature of the Holy Spirit (the Holy Spirit *is* Creator and hence he is God), whereas the Bible is usually interested in expressing the functional and dynamic significance of the word (the Holy Spirit *creates;* the Holy Spirit *acts as* Creator).

We find two types of affirmation concerning the Spirit in the Bible. We find, first of all, words that qualify the Spirit in such a way that the creative function is explicitly attributed to him, and there are also moments or instances in which the Holy Spirit is represented as associated in God's creative action and represented implicitly as the principle by which new life comes into being. In the majority of this second group of texts, the Bible is speaking of "the new creation," that is, the spiritual creation in Christ, but the two creations, the old and the new, relate to one another. Just as the Spirit is the author of the new creation, he was also the author of the old; the Spirit re-creates what the Spirit has created. Ambrose had already remarked: "How could one deny that the creation of the earth was the work of the Holy Spirit, if it is the Spirit's work to renew it?"[12]

Yet it was the New Testament that first established this link, often representing the interventions of the Holy Spirit in the work of redemption in counterpoint with parallel moments in the work of creation. Thus, the dove that descended over the waters of the Jordan recalls the Spirit who in the beginning hovered over the waters (Gen 1:2), the more so as the verb "hovered" in the Hebrew text actually suggests the action of a bird covering or nestling over its brood. Jesus, breathing on the face of his disciples on Easter evening, recalls the moment when God breathed "the breath of life" into Adam.[13]

The point of departure for all of these developments is, clearly, the text of Genesis 1:2, which, following tradition, I translate: "God's Spirit hovered over the waters."

If we interpret the Hebrew expression *ruach 'elohim* in the light of certain analogous expressions in Babylonian poetry, it could be translated "wind of God," "storm of God," or "terrifying wind." However, in that case the subject (wind of God) would not

---

[12] Ambrose, *On the Holy Spirit,* II.34.
[13] See Gen 2:7; 1 Cor 15:45.

make appropriate sense when used in conjunction with the verb that has always been understood, in the Hebrew and in ancient translations, as "hovered," "rested," or "brooded," that is, as a verb expressing peace and not fury.

If we were to exclude the possibility of any reference, however embryonic, to the reality of the Holy Spirit, we would have to read the text exclusively in the light of what went before it and not at all in the light of anything that came after it in the Bible; in the light of the influences it has undergone, and not at all in the light of the influence it has had. As we read on through the Bible, here and there we find allusions that become more and more explicit to a creative activity of the *pneuma* that clearly hark back to this text. "By the word of the Lord the heavens were made, and all their host by the breath of his mouth" (Ps 33:6).

"Breath" in this verse is certainly not natural wind, because it is called breath of the mouth of God. Nor may one think that the Psalmist puts the two, breath and word, together in a parallelism, one to be taken as belonging to the divine order and the other to the natural order. Another psalm says: "When you send forth your spirit, they are created; and you renew the face of the ground" (Ps 104:30).

This line of development becomes abundantly clear in the New Testament, which describes the intervention of the Holy Spirit in the new creation, making use of the very images we find in Genesis concerning the creation of the world. The idea of the creative *ruach* cannot simply have been snatched out of the void. In one and the same commentary on the Bible, there could be no valid argument for translating Genesis 1:2 as "a wind of God blew upon the waters" and then referring to this same text to throw light on the dove at the baptism of Jesus![14]

It is not wrong, therefore, to continue to refer to Genesis 1:2 and to the evidence of the later texts in order to find in them a biblical foundation for the Creator role of the Holy Spirit, as the Fathers have done. As Saint Basil said, "If you accept this explanation, you will draw great advantage from it."[15] And it is true: acknowledging a first, veiled allusion to the Holy Spirit in Genesis 1:2 ("the Spirit

---

[14] See *The New Jerome Biblical Commentary* (Englewood Cliffs, N.J.: Prentice Hall 1990) 10 and 638.

[15] Basil the Great, *Hexaemeron,* II.6 (SCh 26, p. 168); see also Luther, *On Genesis* (WA, 42, p. 80).

of God hovered over the waters") is a key that opens up many other passages of the Bible to our understanding.

3. The Title "Creator," an "Open Structure"

What does the title "Creator" mean to us today, first of all from the point of view of theology and faith? The fundamental point is still the same as was brought to light by the Fathers: The Holy Spirit is God! Using the title "Creator," the author of the hymn wanted to put a solemn profession of faith in the divinity of the Holy Spirit at the very start, ahead of everything else. The title "Creator" is like the clef placed at the beginning of a symphonic score, determining how the whole symphony and every note in it is to sound: this hymn is about God himself, and not about God's attributes or about a nebulous kind of "divine energy." A beautiful thing about the hymn is that it is written in the form of a prayer. In the Creed we speak *about* the Spirit; in the *Veni Creator* we are speaking *to* the Holy Spirit.

However, the words of the hymn are "open structures." We shall see very soon how the title "Creator" truly stands out as a bulwark and unbreakable embankment preventing any attempt to divert the current of Tradition, an antibody that springs into action to defend the body against any return of the malady that caused the body to produce it long ago. The rationalistic idealism of the eighteenth century brought about a popular revival, in a new and more radical form, of an idea that had been refuted in the fourth century: the idea of the Spirit as creature. In those ancient times the adversaries of the Holy Spirit (followers of Macedonius, also called Tropici and Pneumatomachi) considered the Spirit to be an entity, a hypostasis, midway between God and man, but the more recent deviation looked on the Spirit as the spirit of humanity pure and simple. The Spirit was said to be not a divine Spirit, but the spirit of man, intellect, or reason.

All such new "reductions" are shut out by that simple invocation in the first line of the hymn: "Come, Creator Spirit!" If one sings these words along with the Church, what is it that one is affirming? That the Spirit, of his very nature, is not within one, is not oneself. The one who makes the invocation is not the one who is invoked. Those who say, "Come, Creator Spirit!" at the same time profess themselves a creature and give recognition to the infinite difference between Creator and creature. They position themselves in the truth. They do not try to put the creature in the place of the Creator (see Rom 1:25), nor do they try to put the Creator on the level of the creature.

Yet the significant impact of the title "Creator" is not wholly accounted for in this negative function. It has a positive function too, of the greatest importance. The fact that the Spirit is Creator is the very foundation of Christian universalism and of the possibility of carrying on a meaningful dialogue with other religions.[16] For what in fact does it mean, to proclaim that the Holy Spirit is Creator? It says, clearly, that the Holy Spirit's sphere of activity is not confined to the Church or to the history of salvation, but reaches as far and as wide as creation itself. It also shows that it is not possible to uphold the view of those authors of ancient times who taught that there were three kinds of dominion: the Father's dominion, extending over all beings; the Son's dominion, extending only over the order of rational creatures; and the Spirit's dominion, extending only to sanctified creatures.[17] None of these three spheres of action—that of creation, that of redemption, and that of sanctification which comes to realization in the Church—is foreign to the Spirit. No period of time was ever or will ever be without the active presence of the Spirit. The Spirit is at work apart from the Bible and within the Bible; the Spirit was at work before Christ, in the time of Christ, and after Christ, though of course never without reference to him. Maximus the Confessor rightly says:

> The Holy Spirit is not absent from any creature whatever. . . . He is present simply *in every thing* in that it is he who keeps every thing together and who vivifies all; he is present in a special way in those who are *under the Law;* he is present in all Christians in a new and different way, making them children; he is present as the author of wisdom *in the saints* who, through a divinely inspired tenor of life, have been worthily disposed for his indwelling.[18]

[16] See H. Schwarz, *Reflections on the Work of the Spirit Outside the Church,* in CinSS II, pp. 1455–71.

[17] See Origen, *On the Principles,* I.3.5 (PG II.150–1).

[18] See Maximus the Confessor, *Various Chapters,* I.73 (PG 90.1209).

Truly, "The spirit of the Lord has filled the world, and that which holds all things together knows what is said" (Wis 1:7). No one can remove him- or herself from the beneficent light of the Spirit, just as no one can remove him- or herself from the warmth of the sun. "Where can I go from your Spirit?" asks the psalmist (Ps 139:7). From this it follows that not only supernatural charisms but also natural gifts and secular and lay activities all come, each in its own way, from the Holy Spirit.

In one of its documents the Second Vatican Council teaches that the Spirit of God is at work in the heart of every human being, to bring everyone to ask himself or herself the basic religious question. And then, speaking of the evolution of the social order, the council affirms that "the Spirit of God that, with wonderful providence, directs the course of the ages and renews the face of the earth, is present in that evolution."[19]

Certainly, the manner in which the Spirit is at work in the sphere of creation is qualitatively different from the manner in which the Spirit is at work in the sphere of redemption and of the Church. Between the one and the other there is the same kind of relationship that we find between "seeds of the Word" and the "Word in its totality" revealing itself in Jesus Christ. It was Thomas Aquinas who wrote, "Every truth, no matter what its source is said to be, comes from the Holy Spirit."[20]

It is not true, therefore, that the Bible, by teaching that material things are not to be treated as sacred beings, has opened the way for exploiting creatures and looking on them merely as serving man's purposes. In those cultures that embrace animism and idol-worship, creation is protected by the belief that in every being—tree or grove or rock—a spirit dwells. The Christian view does not see a distinct animistic moving principle in each individual being, but only one authentic, spiritual moving principle through which every creature is taken up into that harmony and order that is the work of the Creator Spirit. The key difference is that in the Christian view the Spirit remains transcendent, while in the pantheistic view, such as that of the Stoics, it is part of nature itself.

---

[19] *Gaudium et Spes* 26.

[20] Thomas Aquinas, *Summa Theologiae*, I-II, q. 109, a. 1 ad 1; Ambrosiaster, *On 1 Corinthians*, 12:3 (CSEL 81, p. 132).

Saint Ambrose already opposed the biblical view of the Creator Spirit to the pagan one, even though his point of view was different from that of modern ecology. Referring to Virgil, he writes:

> Some of the pagan poets have said, in their verses, that "heaven and earth, and also the moon and the starry spheres, are nourished in their inmost being by the Spirit." They do not deny that thanks to the Spirit there is power in creation, and we, who read that very thing in the Scripture—should we deny it?[21]

The title "Creator" therefore represents a huge opening up of our understanding of the Holy Spirit, a 360-degree enlargement of our perspective. It would not have been possible to achieve this result with any other title. "Holy" itself would have tended to restrict the Spirit's activity to the sphere of sanctification and grace. The work of the Creator Spirit transcends these specific salvational activities and should not be identified with them only; the Spirit is active in every field, in the inspiration of poets and in every form of artistic creativity. Goethe, who was the author of a beautiful German translation of the *Veni Creator* and wanted to hear it sung every Sunday in his own home, saw it as "a work of genius, a brilliant invocation that speaks powerfully to every spirited and great-hearted person."[22]

4. Experience of the Spirit as Creator

The most important thing, also in the matter of the Holy Spirit as Creator, is not to understand or explain what this might mean, but to *experience* the Spirit as Creator. In the strictest sense, to create means to draw forth being out of nothingness. How, then, can someone who already exists invoke the Spirit as Creator? If you invoke, you must exist, and if you exist, how can you still experience being created?

This point has a profound religious implication. To invoke the Creator Spirit upon oneself is to carry oneself back, in faith, to that moment when God still retained all power over you, when

---

[21] Ambrose, *On the Holy Spirit*, II.36.

[22] J. W. Goethe, *Translations*, in *Gedenkausgabe der Werke*, vol. XV (Zürich: Artemis-Verlag, 1948–64) 131–2 and 1103.

you were only "a thought in God's heart," and God could have made of you whatever God willed without infringing on any liberty of yours. To invoke the Creator Spirit is to give back to God that total freedom in your regard. It is to cast yourself, by a free and spontaneous decision, like clay into the hands of the potter, saying to God the words inspired for this purpose: "O Lord, you are our Father; we are the clay, and you are the potter, we are all the work of your hand" (Isa 64:8).

To invoke the Creator Spirit upon us is, therefore, to abandon ourselves to the sovereign action of God, with complete confidence; it is determinedly to take on what is called the "creaturely" attitude before God, and that is the very basis of all authentic religious belief and practice. It is to remove all reservations, all conditions, and to be open to everything. It is to give God *carte blanche,* total freedom to do as God wills, as Mary did when she said, "Here am I, the servant of the Lord; let it be with me according to your word" (Luke 1:38). The Fathers saw, in Mary in that moment, the supreme manifestation of the Spirit as Creator: "The creative power of the Most High formed the body of Christ at the moment when the Holy Spirit descended upon the Virgin Mary."[23]

To invoke the Holy Spirit as Creator upon oneself is to open oneself to a newness, and it is also to enter into an awesome silence.

But let us return to the text that lies at the start of all of these reflections on the Creator Spirit, Genesis 1:2, in order to grasp the significance of the fact that in the *Veni Creator* we invoke not the divine creative action in general, but the creative action of the Spirit. What, specifically, does the "person" of Spirit bring to the work of creation? That is determined, as always, by the relationships within the Trinity itself. The Holy Spirit is not at the commencement of the creative act, but at the conclusion, just as the Spirit is not the origin, but the completion, of the Trinitarian process. In creation, wrote Saint Basil, the Father is the principal cause, from whom all things come; the Son is the efficient cause, through whom all things are made; and the Holy Spirit is the perfecting cause. This is not to say in any sense that the operative power of the Father might be imperfect, but that the Father desires

---

[23] Didimus of Alexandria, *On the Holy Spirit,* 31 (PG 39.1062).

to bring creatures into being through the Son and to bring them to perfection through the Spirit.[24]

Hence, the creative action of the Spirit is the primary source of the perfection of all that exists; the Spirit is, we might say, not so much the one through whom the world is brought into being out of nothingness, but rather the one who transforms all that is, making it grow from its unformed initial state of being to its final perfection. In other words, the Holy Spirit is the one who makes creation pass from chaos into cosmos, and makes of it something beautiful, orderly, and clean. (The Greek *kosmos* and the Latin *mundus* both mean clean, beautiful). "When the Spirit began to hover over it, creation had no beauty as yet. But, when creation had experienced the action of the Spirit, it received all that splendour of beauty that makes it shine forth as the *mundus*."[25]

We know that the creative action of God is not limited to the initial moment only, which is how creation is seen in the deist or mechanist view of the universe. We cannot say that God "was" Creator at one certain moment only. God "is" always Creator. And this, not only in the watered-down sense that God "keeps things in being" and in God's providence governs the world, but also in the fullest meaning of the word: God continually communicates being and energy; God moves, stimulates, enlivens and renews creation. "To create is continually to make new."[26]

What does all this mean in relation to the Holy Spirit? It means that the Spirit is always the one that brings about the change from chaos to cosmos, from disorder to order, from confusion to harmony, from deformity to beauty, from oldness to newness—not, of course, in a mechanical way and all of a sudden, but in the sense that the Spirit is at work in all of this kind of change for the better, guiding its evolving progress until it reaches its fulfillment. The Spirit is always the one at work, "creating and renewing the face of the earth."

---

[24] Basil the Great, *On the Holy Spirit,* XVI.38 (PG 32.136).

[25] Ambrose, *On the Holy Spirit,* II.32. This extends to the Holy Spirit the prerogative of taking the universe "from disorder to order," which Plato had attributed to the Demiurge (see Plato, *Timaeus,* 30a) and which some of the Fathers attributed to the person of the Logos (see Clement of Alexandria, *Stromata,* V.14).

[26] Luther, *Resolutions on Indulgences* (WA 1, p. 563).

> If it were possible to remove the Spirit from creation, all beings would become confused and the life in them would appear to have no law, no structure, no ordered purpose whatever.[27]
> Without the Spirit, the entire creation would be unable to continue in being.[28]

This holds true at all levels, for the macrocosm as for the many microcosms of which every human being is one. Let us consider, first of all, the grand scenario of the world and its history. At the moment Christ died, the Gospel writers note that "darkness came over the whole land" (Mark 15:33). This is a veiled allusion to the primordial chaos into which humankind, because of sin, had fallen back—a darkness that reached its paroxysmal climax in the killing of Christ. A writer of the second century wrote:

> The universe was on the point of falling back into chaos and would have melted away for sheer dismay at the sight of the Passion, had not the great Jesus sent forth his divine Spirit, crying out, "Father, into your hands I commit my Spirit" (Luke 23:46). And suddenly, as the divine Spirit was poured out, the universe found itself becoming steady again, as if reanimated, enlivened, and made solid.[29]

Once again, in this grand vision, it is the Holy Spirit who makes the world pass from chaos to cosmos. This time, however, it is not a question of a vaguely understood "spirit of God," but the Spirit that comes from Christ on the cross; "chaos" is no longer the primordial physical confusion and darkness, but the moral darkness of evil and of sin, and "cosmos" is no longer the material universe but Church, "the cosmos of the cosmos,"[30] that is the ornament of the world.

This vision finds a continuity in the way in which the coming down of the Holy Spirit at Pentecost is described. The Holy Spirit transforms the Babel chaos of many languages and draws out of it many voices speaking in harmony. Thanks to the Spirit, "all tongues together, of one accord, then raised up a hymn to God,"[31]

---

[27] Basil the Great, *On the Holy Spirit*, XVI.38 (PG 32.137B).

[28] Ambrose, *On the Holy Spirit*, II.5.33.

[29] *Ancient Paschal Homily*, 55 (SCh 27, p. 183).

[30] Origen, *Commentary on the Gospel of John*, VI.59.301 (SCh 157, p. 360).

[31] Irenaeus, *Against the Heresies*, III.17.2.

as when the conductor steps up to the podium and suddenly the clamor of all the instruments of the orchestra being tuned is silenced, and in its place one hears a magnificent symphony.

5. *Come, Creator Spirit*

Now, let us apply all of this to that "little world" which is our own heart. The Fathers, in fact, do not reserve to the Church the title of "cosmos of the cosmos," the crown of creation, but sometimes speak also of the individual human being in the same terms.[32] This can have an extraordinary influence on the way we grasp the Holy Spirit in our mind and cooperate with the Spirit in our lives as believers. "Darkness covered the face of the deep" (Gen 1:2). But the human heart too, says the Scripture, is an abyss, a place of hidden depths (Ps 64:7). There is an outward chaos, but there is also the chaos within. Our chaos is the darkness that is in us, the whirlpool of desires, intentions, undertakings, and contrary regrets all in conflict with one another. A spiritual writer of the Middle Ages (he was a Carthusian monk who lived a life of profound contemplation!) described his own spiritual state in these words:

> I become aware, Lord, that the world of my own spirit is still formless and void and that darkness still covers the face of this abyss. It is truly in a state of confusion, a kind of dark and terrifying chaos, knowing nothing of its own end or of its own origin or of what sort of being it is. That is how my soul is, my God! That is how my soul is! A wasteland, empty and formless, and darkness is upon the face of the abyss. But the abyss that is my spirit cries out to you, Lord, asking you to make a new heaven and a new earth of me too![33]

There is a current in modern literature that simply takes up and continues, but in a psychological key, the theme of humankind, the prey to chaos, rushing headlong into the morass of its own contradictions: man "in the underground."[34] Or else, it chooses to

---

[32] *Apostolic Constitutions*, VIII.12.16 (SCh 336, p. 184); Methodius of Olympus, *On the Resurrection*, XXXV (GCS 27, p. 275).

[33] Guigo II, *Meditations*, V (SCh 163, pp. 148–50).

[34] See F. Dostoyevsky, *Notes from the Underground* (New York: Dover Publications, 1992).

rerun, but in reverse, the creative journey: starting this time from being and ending in nothingness; from light to darkness. This is the path of nihilism.

What a light faith in the Creator Spirit throws on this universal experience of chaos! The Spirit of God, that was working upon and within the primordial chaos, is still at work in this world. Intoning the *Veni Creator,* we are saying, "Come, Holy Spirit, hover over my chaos too and breathe upon it and put light again into my darkness (see Ps 18:28), make of me too a microcosm, a real little world, something beautiful, harmonious and pure: a new creation."

See here what a person writes who has spent a long time meditating on the opening words of the *Veni Creator:*

> *Come, Creator Spirit!* Confronted with these words, we cannot remain as we are—not kneeling, not sitting, not on our feet. We are stunned, we need to fall to the ground, bowed low, overcome, and powerless like a paralytic: more accurately, like the clay before God breathed into it the breath of life. And silent, absolutely silent. The protagonist of the universe, the author of life: God is that! And the invocation spreads around me, like a spot of oil on the water, covering all my family, my friends, my neighbours, all those I know and all those I do not know. How many millions inhabit the earth? On every one of them all, *Veni, Creator Spiritus!*
>
> New heavens, new earths, new Adams, new Eves! Politicians, governors, the poor, the unhappy, prostitutes, homosexuals, the depraved, all sinners who know not what they do, the whole earth and all that is in it, all under the creative power of God. To this Creator Spirit, who has created the human model in the perfection of every single one of its cells, I entrust this tangle of muscles, nerves and ganglia, synapses, hypothalamus, and all that works together for the orderly functioning of the life of my body and my mind and my emotions, so that in his hands it will all be able to be brought to new birth in harmony, in beauty, in truth and in purity. In the sanctity of children of God. *Come, Creator Spirit!*

We carry within ourselves a vestige of the primordial chaos, our own unconscious. What modern psychoanalysis has outlined as the passage from the unconscious to the conscious, from the Id to the Superego, is an aspect of the creative work that needs to continue in us until it is fully accomplished. We need to progress, from unformed to fully formed. The Holy Spirit also wants to hover over the chaos of our unconscious where obscure forces are at play and contrary impulses arise, this depth in us that is the hatching-place of anxieties and neuroses, but that is also a source of unexplored possibilities. "The Spirit reaches the depth of everything" (see 1 Cor 2:10).

To one who has problems with his or her own unconscious (and who does not?), it is not possible to give better counsel than to foster a special devotion to the Holy Spirit and to call often on him, particularly in his function as Creator. The Spirit is the very best psychoanalyst and the very best psychiatrist in the world. Devotion to the Holy Spirit does not necessarily mean that we make less use of the human resources we have in this field, but the Holy Spirit certainly completes them and far surpasses them.

Besides that, there is a particular time of our day when it is even more necessary for us, and when we are more ready to experience the creative power of the Spirit, and that is the time of waking up in the morning. Each morning we have a vivid reminder and a symbol of the emergence of the world from the primordial chaos. The wonder is renewed. The liturgy itself suggests this association, particularly in some of the hymns for Morning Prayer:

> At the dawning of the day,
> robed in light and silence
> all things emerge from the darkness,
> just as when time began.[35]

Night is like a temporary falling-back into chaos. "The sun goes down and there comes the frightful chaos."[36] Anguish, dreams, nightmares; good and evil; reality and fantasy: all is mixed up and confused in the darkness of night. All is vague; dreams have no timeframe, no color. There are times when we wake up with the feeling that we have to start all over again, from the very beginning, as if we were atheists who had never known anything of God and have no idea of what faith or hope or love might be. That is why it is important to start every new day with the Holy Spirit, so

---

[35] See P. Beltrame Quattrocchi, *Psalms, Christian Prayer* (Sorrento, 1986) 424.

[36] Prudentius, *Cathemerinon*, 5.3 (CC 126, p. 23).

that the Spirit may transform our nighttime chaos into the light of faith and hope and love. I have found that the loveliest words with which to begin a new day are in fact the first two lines of our hymn, "Come, Creator Spirit, visit the minds of those who are yours!" I feel an almost physical need of them as I face the task of shaking off the heaviness, the inertia, and the oblivion of the night.

All the rest of our reflections, in this book, are intended to help us to come to a meaningful insight into this mystery on which we are meditating: to pass anew from chaos to cosmos, to emerge as a "new creation" by the grace of the creative action of the Holy Spirit.

We close this chapter with a hymn that is used in the Liturgy of the Hours in English-speaking countries:

> *Spirit of God, on the waste and the darkness*
> *hov'ring in power as creation began,*
> *drawing forth beauty from clay and from chaos,*
> *breathing God's life in the nostrils of man,*
>
> *Come and sow life in the waste of our being,*
> *pray in us, form us as sons in the Son.*
> *Open our hearts to yourself, mighty Spirit,*
> *bear us to life in the Three who are One.*[37]

---

[37] From the Stanbrook Abbey Hymnal, England.

III

Fill with Heavenly Grace the Hearts that You Have Made

The Holy Spirit renews the prodigies of the first Pentecost

The last two lines of the first verse of the *Veni Creator* say, "Fill with heavenly grace the hearts that you have made."

In the New Testament we find three words and three images that are used to express the coming of the Holy Spirit to us: to be *baptized* in the Holy Spirit,[1] to be *clothed* with the Holy Spirit (Luke 24:49), and to be *filled* with the Holy Spirit. This last is the one that is most frequently used. We are told that Jesus left the Jordan "full of the Holy Spirit" (Luke 4:1); John the Baptist, Elizabeth, and Stephen are all said to be "filled with the Holy Spirit."[2] But this word "filled" is above all the word used to describe the miracle of Pentecost: "All of them were filled with the Holy Spirit" (Acts 2:4).

So it is that this particular line of the *Veni Creator* evokes the Pentecost event. The word "grace" in this line refers to the Holy Spirit in person. The author of our hymn says in another place that the Paraclete is called grace "in as much as he is given freely, not for any merit of ours, but simply because God wills it so."[3] Thus, what we are asking the Holy Spirit to do is to fill us with the Spirit's own self, not with one or another of the Spirit's gifts, however wonderful they may be. In an ancient hymn attributed to Ambrose, the Holy Spirit is asked "to pour himself out and fill our hearts with himself."[4] Through the influence of the *Veni Creator,* this manner of speaking became quite common in later times. The Sequence of Pentecost addresses this prayer to the Spirit: "Light

---

[1] See Matt 3:11; John 1:33; Acts 1:5.

[2] See Luke 1:15, 41; Acts 6:5; 7:55.

[3] Rhabanus Maurus, *On the Universe,* I.3 (PL 111.25); see Isidore of Seville, *Etymologies,* VII.3.20 (PL 82, 269).

[4] See Ambrose, *Nunc Sancte nobis Spiritus,* in *Opera Omnia,* vol. 22, Bibliotheca Ambrosiana (Milan, 1994) 88.

immortal, Light divine, visit thou these hearts of thine, and our inmost being fill." An antiphon dating from the tenth century, still in use in the liturgy, says: "Come, O Holy Spirit, *fill* the hearts of your faithful and enkindle in them the fire of your love."

The author of the *Veni Creator,* too, could have said, quite explicitly, "fill with your own self the hearts of your faithful," but by using the word "grace" he introduces a whole new dimension to the message and enriches it tremendously. He has drawn all the work of Christ into the orbit of the Spirit. He has pointed out the unbreakable bond between Pneumatology and Christology. Grace is in fact the point where the work of Christ and the work of the Spirit converge: Christ is the *author* of grace; the Spirit is, so to say, its *content.* "What does it mean, to say that Christ gives *grace* to humankind? It means that he gives *the Holy Spirit.*"[5]

Therefore, what we are asking for in these lines of the hymn is nothing less than this: that there should be, for us, a whole new outpouring of the Spirit, a whole new Pentecost. Here we see again how the hymn is able to draw on an immense biblical and theological background and with scintillating clarity reveal its practical application, bringing theology and spirituality, doctrine and experience, together for us in a way that is most telling. We ought to try once again, therefore, to be clear about the underlying theological insights, in order fully to make our own the decision expressed, in crescendo, in the three words, "Come, visit, fill!"

1. The Holy Spirit and the Creatures' Return to God

After he had written of the Holy Spirit's part in the work of creation, Saint Basil started the next chapter of his book with these words:

> As far as concerns the matter of the salvation of humankind by the work of our great God and Saviour Christ Jesus (Titus 2:13) brought about by the goodness of God, who could deny that it is put into effect by means of the grace of the Holy Spirit?[6]

---

[5] Augustine, *Sermons,* 270.6 (PL 38.1243).
[6] Basil the Great, *On the Holy Spirit,* XVI.39 (PG 32.140B).

These words contain the first glimmerings of one of the great developments of our faith-understanding concerning the Holy Spirit, an understanding that little by little came to be formulated with greater and greater precision. Diachronically, that is to say, in relation to *time,* the Holy Spirit was at work first in creation and then in redemption; synchronically, that is to say, in relation to *space,* the Spirit is at work in the Church and also in the world.

This insight was taken up by the Latin world, where it was given further precision. Ambrose, after he had written on the Creator Spirit, devoted a whole section of his work to the Spirit in the economy of salvation. There we read: "The Spirit is the author of spiritual regeneration, by which we come to be created on the divine level, in order to become children of God."[7]

By the first creation we are God's *creatures;* by the second creation we are also God's *children.* The new creation, therefore, is nothing other than the new birth "from on high" or "of the Holy Spirit" of which Jesus speaks in the Gospel (see John 3:3-5). Augustine says that by the first creation we are *human beings;* by the second we become also *Christians.* The very gift of being created is itself already grace, insofar as it is gratuitously given, but the grace by which we are Christian is a very different grace. In the first case we have no merit by which we might have *deserved* the gift, but in the second we do indeed have many demerits that make us *unworthy* of the gift. This is why we do not refer to creation as a grace, or if we do, we use the word only in a generic sense, and we reserve the term grace in the strict sense for redemption.[8]

The Spirit, then, is at work both in the order of nature and in the order of grace. This patristic view was taken to the peak of its development by the medieval theologians. On the subject of creation and redemption Saint Bonaventure writes: "Both of these works are suffused with the power of the Holy Spirit: the works of creation are kept in being by him, and the works of redemption are brought to perfection by him."[9]

Saint Thomas Aquinas put together the whole of his *Summa Theologiae* on the schema "how all creatures come from God,

---

[7] Ambrose, *On the Holy Spirit,* II.62–9.

[8] See Augustine, *Sermons,* 26.5 (CC 41, p. 351–2).

[9] Bonaventure, *Sermons on the Saints,* I (Quaracchi IX, p. 468).

and how all creatures return to God." He writes: "It is fitting that for the reasons that creatures came from God in the first place, they should for the same reasons return to God. . . . Thus, just as we were created through the Son and the Holy Spirit, through them too, we are taken to our final end."[10]

If, in this context, a certain distinction ought to be made between the Son and the Spirit, it must consist, according to one of the first Latin theologians to write on the Trinity, in the fact that the coming *(progressio)* of all creatures from God is attributed more particularly to the Son, and their return *(regressus)* to God more particularly to the Spirit.[11]

Thus, the Holy Spirit's activity extends through all of the stages and events of salvation. Like the sun, of which it is said that "its rising is from the end of the heavens, and its circuit to the end of them; and nothing is hid from its heat" (Ps 19:6). "The Holy Spirit was at our side from the very beginning, in every one of God's plans for us, foretelling the future, showing forth the present and recalling the past."[12]

There is no question of linking only certain special areas of competence to the Spirit, seeing the Spirit's work as confined to them alone, as some have tried to do in the past. On the contrary, the whole cosmos and all of history belong to the Spirit, and everything falls within the Spirit's sphere of competence, just as the whole extent of reality falls within the ambit of the Father and of the Son. The aim, rather, is to discern the special "imprint" of each of the three Persons on each of the works of God.

There is simply no basis for the thesis, commonly attributed to Joaquin of Fiore, that the Spirit's concern is the third and last epoch of history. The notion of a third era would seem to be justified only if it is applied not to the *reality* and activity of the Spirit, but to his revelation and the way he has been manifested to humankind. This is how Gregory Nazianzen applies the idea. In fact, Nazianzen distinguishes three phases in the revelation of the Trinity: in the Old Testament the Father is fully revealed and the Son is promised and announced; in the New Testament the Son is fully

---

[10] Thomas Aquinas, *On the Sentences,* I d., 14, q. 2, a. 2.

[11] See Marius Victorinus, *Hymns to the Trinity,* 3.72–3 (CSEL 83.1, p. 295).

[12] Irenaeus, *Against the Heresies,* IV.33.1.

revealed and the Spirit is announced and promised; and in the final era the Church at last knows the Holy Spirit fully and rejoices in the Spirit's presence.[13]

2. What Did the Spirit Bring at Pentecost that Was New?

All of this grand vision re-echoes in the words of our hymn: "Fill with heavenly grace the hearts that you have made." In praying these words we are saying, "You who are the principle of our creation, be for us also the artificer of our sanctification!" It would surely have been impossible to find words more clear or more concise to affirm that the Spirit of the creation is also the Spirit of the redemption. The word grace is the window that opens wide to the view of this new horizon. This word refers to Christ, to the Church, to the sacraments, to the theological virtues of faith, hope, and love. The word grace moves us to a new plane, different from the one evoked by the word Creator in the first line of the verse. Grace, in the language of Christians, is always "grace of Christ." Quite distinct from its secular use, the word grace in the New Testament is never used to signify any natural or creaturely gift, but always one or more of the supernatural gifts. The second part of this verse, then, says very precisely that the Creator Spirit, the Spirit "of God" in the first part of the verse is none other than the Spirit "of Christ."

Yet we must not see this as a kind of substituting one Spirit for another, or withdrawing attention from the work of creation and placing it in parenthesis in order to affirm the work of redemption. Nature is not supplanted by grace. We are concerned, rather, to see that grace and nature are linked, as are the supernatural gifts of the Spirit and the natural gifts. That is why we call on the Spirit as Creator and at the same time as grace, and say "Come!" to the Spirit as creating and simultaneously as engracing. For grace does not destroy nature but "presupposes" nature and builds on nature. This remains true even after sin because, though sin has "wounded" nature, it has not corrupted it entirely. From this viewpoint the new creation is a restoration, a renovation, an elevation, and not a creation *ex nihilo,* out of nothing, like the first creation.

[13] See Gregory Nazianzen, *Sermons,* XXXI.26 (PG 36.161–2).

The Spirit "fills with divine grace" the hearts that he himself, not another, has created. What the Fathers, speaking of Christ, have maintained against Marcion and the Manicheans is equally true of the Holy Spirit: There are not two diverse and opposed economies each arising from a different spirit, but there is only one God, only one Word, only one Spirit. Continuity is affirmed at the same time as newness.

If, then, it is not necessary to deny the Spirit of creation in order to receive the Spirit of grace, neither is it permissible any longer to be content simply with the Creator Spirit while making little of the Spirit of Christ. It is one and the same Holy Spirit that spurs us on to follow through and make the leap forward. To refuse to do that is to resist the Spirit (see Acts 7:51).

However, we need to say right away that the distinction between the Creator Spirit and the Redeemer Spirit is not at all the same as the distinction between the Old and the New Testaments. The Spirit of grace was in fact already at work in the Law, preparing the way for the Gospel. The one who spoke through the prophets was already the Spirit of Christ (see 1 Pet 1:10-11). Also in regard to the reality of the Spirit, there is a link with Israel that is different from and much more profound than our link with any other people or any other religion.

Neither is the distinction between the Creator Spirit and the Redeemer Spirit exactly the same as the distinction between *world* and *Church,* as if outside of the Church the Spirit acts only as Creator and not also as Spirit of Christ. The Second Vatican Council affirmed that "the Holy Spirit, in a way known only to God, offers to every human being the possibility of becoming linked to the Paschal Mystery."[14]

And so, just as it is now no longer possible to say that "outside of the Church there is no salvation" (at least in the sense in which this used to be maintained), neither is possible any longer to say that "outside of the Church there is no Holy Spirit." Outside of the confines of the visible Church (but not without reference to the Church), and in a mysterious way, the Holy Spirit is active also as the Spirit of Christ, making present the salvation that the Spirit has brought about (the paschal mystery!).

[14] *Gaudium et Spes* 22.

In what the Spirit brought about in the coming of Christ and in Pentecost, what was new? The answer to this question about the Spirit is the same answer Irenaeus gave to the same question about Christ: "He brought about all newness by bringing himself."[15] The Spirit, who at various times and in various ways used to come to the prophets, is now among us personally and enduringly in Christ:

> For this the Spirit came down upon the Son of God who had become the son of man: with him he became accustomed to dwelling with humankind, to resting upon human beings (see Isa 11:2; 1 Pet 4:14) and to making his home in God's creatures; in them he brought about the realization of God's will, and he renewed them, making them pass from their old condition to the newness of Christ.[16]

For as long as the Word had not yet become "flesh and lived among us" (John 1:14), neither was the Spirit able to dwell among us. Before the Spirit had descended on Jesus and rested on him (John 1:33), the Spirit was not able to descend on us and remain with us. Consequently we can say, in language that is somewhat more developed, that before Pentecost the Spirit was present in the world through the Spirit's gifts and power, but since the time of Pentecost onward the Spirit has been *hypostatically* present, that is, present in person: "The Prophets enjoyed a profound illumination by the Holy Spirit. But the faithful enjoy more than only this illumination; the Holy Spirit himself dwells in us and remains with us. We are called temples of the Holy Spirit, something that was never said of the Prophets."[17]

So it is that we pass from the ambit of creation to the ambit of conversion. By sin, humankind transformed the *coming forth* from God into an estrangement and an aversion from God, and for that reason the movement of the return of creatures to God could continue only in the form of a *conversion* to God. The coming forth and the return are two objective movements that are

---

[15] Irenaeus, *Against the Heresies,* IV.34.1.

[16] Ibid., III.17.1.

[17] Cyril of Alexandria, *Commentary on the Gospel of John,* 5.2 (PG 73.757A).

universal and that do not depend on humankind at all. Whether we want to or not, we come from God and return to God, either to God as goal and reward, or to God as judge. Estrangement from God and conversion to God, on the other hand, are two subjective movements, two decisions made by free human choice. Since humankind turned their coming from God into a turning their back on God, they now need to turn their simple return to God into a conversion to God. And it is in this process of conversion that the Holy Spirit is now seen in action.

The role of the Spirit in the return of creatures to God also comes to light in and through the theme of *jubilee*. The Bible speaks of a "fiftieth day" or "day of Pentecost," but it also speaks of a "fiftieth year" or a "year of Pentecost." This is the year when the ground is left to lie fallow, to rest; the year when slaves are given their freedom, and when each person gets back what belongs to him and returns to his ancestral home (see Lev 25:10-13). Medieval theologians found inspiration in this text to see Pentecost as the sign of the entry into ultimate rest, the remission of all debt, the loosening of all bonds, and as the sign also of the moment in which humankind would regain possession of that state that we enjoyed before our sin caused us to become enslaved. "Keep this day as Jubilee / if its mystery you would see."[18]

3. The Spirit of Grace

By now it must be clear: the message of this part of the *Veni Creator* is all contained in the little word "grace." This is the "honeycomb" from which we need to "draw all the honey"; this is the key that will open for us the door to a whole new chamber in the treasure-house of revelation concerning the Holy Spirit. Grace is one of the words that we need to revive and restore to its original splendor, because it has been spoiled just as a fresco is spoiled

---

[18] Adam of Saint Victor, *On Pentecost,* AHMA 54, p. 243: *"Typum gerit jubilaei / dies iste, si diei / requiris mysteria"*; see also Rupert of Deutz, *On Leviticus,* II.41 (CM 22, p. 907); Rupert of Deutz, *Book of the Divine Office,* 12 (CM 7, p. 347–8); Hermann of Runa, *Sermons for Feast-days,* 34.1 (CM 64, p. 142). The idea was first expressed by Origen, *Homilies on Numbers,* 5.2 (GCS 30, p. 28).

by too many attempts at restoration, each imposing traces of the transient taste of the moment.

The first thing that jumps out at us when we read the New Testament, especially Paul, is the close similarity, not to say equivalence, between the Holy Spirit and grace. The two realities are actually linked together in one text, "the Spirit of grace" (Heb 10:29). But the principal test rests in the often identical prerogatives attributed to each of the two realities, Spirit and grace. At times, where "Holy Spirit" is written we could read "grace," and likewise for "grace" we could read "Holy Spirit," without in the least altering the meaning of the text.

The identification of grace as Holy Spirit and of Holy Spirit as grace is explicit in the Fathers from the very earliest reflections on the divine nature of the Paraclete: "Just as it is of the Father and of the Son, so grace is of the Holy Spirit. For how could there be grace at all, without the Holy Spirit, since every divine grace is in the Spirit?"[19]

What is it about the Holy Spirit that brings this close relationship with grace to light? The first thing is the *gratuitousness* of grace. In as much as the Spirit is grace, the Holy Spirit is an absolutely gratuitous gift, totally unmerited, that God gives to humankind. The second thing is the *historicity* of grace, that is, its arising from the redemptive event of the death and resurrection of Christ. The Holy Spirit, by whom and in whom we live, is not some vague, atemporal reality that enwraps the believers' world more or less like the atmosphere enwraps the earth. The Spirit came into history with Christ and comes into the life of each Christian at the moment of that person's baptism.

And in its turn, what is it about grace that brings its close relationship with the Holy Spirit to light? First, grace is not simply a benevolent disposition, a disposition of "good will," in God toward us; it is not merely a matter of intention, but something real. Second, grace is an event, a very specific act, a new and personal intervention by God, of a sort comparable to God's initial act of creation. Grace, according to the basic meaning of the word, is not something that God finds in a human being, or some

---

[19] Ambrose, *On the Holy Spirit,* I.127; see Didimus of Alexandria, *On the Holy Spirit,* 16 (PG 39.1048–9).

kind of entitlement that would make a human being pleasing to God, but more radically still, it is that specific act of God that justifies this particular human person and so makes this particular person pleasing to him. Grace is, above all and before all, "God's" grace, "divine grace," and not our grace, not "human grace." Once received by a human being, grace is then not merely a kind of juridical title to salvation, a sort of certificate of safe conduct, a passport; grace is a power that is real, in the same sense as the Holy Spirit is a power that is real.

Grace is an experiential reality. We do not merely have an idea or a concept of grace, or even a belief in grace (if we take belief to mean only an assent of the mind), just as we do not merely have an idea or a concept or a belief in the Holy Spirit. Grace is something we *experience,* and it is normal that we should experience it. Scripture makes this very clear.[20] One day Jesus "rejoiced in the Holy Spirit and said . . ." (Luke 10:21): the action of the Spirit was the wellspring of the joy that flooded the heart of Jesus and spurred him at that moment to bless and praise and thank the Father. We find the same sort of thing in Paul. When he writes, "hope does not disappoint us, because God's love has been poured into our hearts through the Holy Spirit that has been given to us" (Rom 5:5), or when he says, "it is that very Spirit bearing witness with our spirit that we are children of God," or "the Spirit helps us in our weakness" and "intercedes with sighs too deep for words" (Rom 8:16, 26), Paul is not making abstract statements about some principle. Rather, Paul is seeking to find words to convey something that he has experienced and that moves him to the very heart. Nor is this merely the experience of an individual; it is a shared experience. Expressions such as "God has given us his Spirit" or "you have received the Spirit" or "the Spirit dwells within you" lead us quite clearly to see that these texts speak of an evident fact of which all were aware, and of which all were convinced.

Hence, the apostle speaks of the Spirit and equally of grace as a reality that we are able to experience, in a spiritual way of course and not in a material sense. It was precisely the experience of the Holy Spirit, as attested by the Christian community in its meetings for worship, in martyrdom, and in Christian life in gen-

[20] See J.D.G. Dunn, *Jesus and the Spirit* (London: SCM Press, 1975) 201.

eral, that moved the ecumenical Council of Constantinople in 381 to proclaim and define as an article of faith the divinity of the Holy Spirit. Athanasius was fond of repeating the argument: If the Holy Spirit makes us divine, there cannot be any doubt that the Spirit is God.[21] First comes the experience, "the Spirit makes us divine" or "the Spirit sanctifies us," and then follows the dogmatic proclamation, "the Spirit is God."

Now, where does the *Veni Creator* stand in relation to this view of the Holy Spirit and of grace? I have already referred to what the author of the *Veni Creator* wrote in another of his works on the matter of calling the Holy Spirit "grace." The Holy Spirit, he says, is called grace insofar as the Spirit is given gratuitously *(gratis datur)*. Later, in scholastic theology, there was a marked change in the way these things were understood. The grace of the Holy Spirit came to be called grace insofar as grace is *gratum faciens,* that is, what makes us pleasing to God, while the specific quality of being *gratis data,* that is, gratuitously given, came to be applied to the charisms. In that way, charism, and not grace, would come to convey the initial idea and the strongest expression of grace. Thomas Aquinas writes:

> The grace that makes us pleasing to God makes the soul ready to have the divine Person, and when we say that by grace the Holy Spirit is given, that is what we mean. However, the Holy Spirit is also the source of that same gift of grace, and when we say that "the love of God is poured into our hearts by the Holy Spirit," that is what we mean.[22]

It is clear that he holds firmly to the teaching that was formulated earlier by Augustine, who says that in grace we possess not only a gift distinct from the Holy Spirit, but also the very person of the Holy Spirit. From Thomas we have the pregnant phrase, "the grace of the Holy Spirit," meaning, "the grace that is the Holy Spirit."[23]

[21] Athanasius, *Letters to Serapion,* I.22–6 (PG 26.581ff.).

[22] Thomas Aquinas, *Summa Theologiae* I, q. 43, a. 3: ". . . *gratia gratum faciens disponit animam ad habendam divinam Personam: et significatur hoc, cum dicitur quod Spiritus Sanctus datur secundum donum gratiae. Sed tamen ipsum donum gratiae est a Spiritu Sancto: et hoc significatur, cum dicitur quod 'caritas Dei diffunditur in cordibus nostris per Spiritum Sanctum.'"*

[23] Thomas Aquinas, *Summa Theologiae* I-II, q. 106, a. 1; see Augustine, *The Spirit and the Letter,* 21.36.

The fact that the Holy Spirit had come to be seen as grace "that makes us pleasing to God" would, however, lead to a growing emphasis on "created" grace: that is, on grace as that "quality" or "habit" inherent in the human soul that determines whether a person is in "the state of grace." For it is in fact not possible to define sanctifying grace as "that which makes us pleasing to God" without necessarily including in that reality both the conferring of grace and what follows upon it, both *God's act* and also *that which we possess* as a result of God's act. And so it happens that interest becomes focused on the created effect of justification, and not so much on the divine act of justification. All of this came very much to the fore in the polemic against the teachings of the Reformation. The Council of Trent says that the grace of justification is above all a created gift, that is, a supernatural effect produced by God in the human soul; a gift "the efficient cause" of which is God, and which for that very reason cannot be identified with the Holy Spirit.[24]

We know that the difference is really a difference of perspective, or of one's point of departure, because it is clear that the Council of Trent did not intend to deny that, in another sense, grace is identified with the Holy Spirit who indwells the soul. This notwithstanding, however, we have to admit that the polemics of the moment severely narrowed the general appreciation of the New Testament message. Whenever Christians allow divisions to separate them, something of their patrimony is fragmented, divided, and lost. It is as if a mosaic were to end up part in one museum and part in another: no one would any longer have the opportunity to see it and appreciate it as a whole in all its original beauty.

The arguments with the Pelagians had restricted the appreciation of grace to "healing" or "aiding" grace; the arguments with the Protestant Reformers restricted the field further, to "created" grace. The gift given to us, to live in the new climate brought about by ecumenical dialogue, is the gift of at last being able to put together again the various fragments of our heritage and to rediscover the original "whole" without having to forgo any of the great gains and clarities of perception that have come out of the many controversies on grace.

[24] See DS 1529.

The *Veni Creator* is a great help to us on this road of rediscovery. It was written before the time of Scholastic theology and the subsequent controversies, and so it takes us very close to the biblical basis and starting point. In the way it expresses the essentials, and in its conciseness, it allows us to appreciate the "original whole" in which Holy Spirit and grace appeared as it were fused together as one, yet not *confused*. And it allows us to appreciate and embrace the Holy Spirit and grace, not in a static way as something that happened once and for all and is now over, but as a coming-to-us, perennial and unceasing.

4. The Baptism of the Spirit

The first verse of the *Veni Creator* is given muscles, so to say, by the three verbs positioned strongly at the beginning or at the end of a line: "Come, visit, fill!" They give the verse a rhythm of tremendous energy, like a musical crescendo. But these three verbs, if you think carefully about it, also pose a problem for our theology. How can the Church now invite the Holy Spirit to "Come, visit, and fill!"? Does not the Church believe that she has already received the Holy Spirit at Pentecost, and that we have already received the Holy Spirit in our individual baptism? What sense can it make to say, "Come, visit, fill!" to someone who is already present?

The problem is there in Scripture as well. On the day of Pentecost all were filled with the Holy Spirit, but just a few days later we find a kind of second Pentecost when all over again "all were filled with the Holy Spirit," and among them were some of the apostles who had been present at the first Pentecost (see Acts 4:31). Paul recommends to certain Christians, who at the time were already baptized and active in the community, that they be filled with the Holy Spirit (Eph 5:18), almost as though up to that moment they had not been "filled" in that way.

What appears to be a contradiction is, in fact, a very valuable clue that can lead us to a deeper understanding. Thomas Aquinas has this theological explanation to offer concerning the new "comings" of the Holy Spirit upon us. He notes, first of all, that the Holy Spirit "comes" not in the sense of moving from that place to this place, but "because *by grace* he begins to be, in a new way, in those whom he makes temples of God."[25] He writes:

> There is an invisible sending of the Spirit every time any progress in virtue or increase in grace takes place . . . when someone enters upon a new activity or into a new state of grace: for example, when a person receives the grace to work miracles, or the gift of prophecy, or when spurred by the fervour of love a person risks martyrdom or gives up possessions or undertakes some difficult or exacting task.[26]

But more important than the explanation he gives of it is the fact itself. The new Pentecost is actual and it is happening now. It always was so, but in the last century it has taken on new proportions of a scale never known before. At the beginning of the twentieth century the Pentecostal phenomenon emerged, and later, around mid-century, through various charismatic movements it began to appear within the traditional churches. Many seriously believe that this is the greatest spiritual upsurge in all the history of the Church: in a mere eighty years, from zero to about four hundred million people.

In this context we need to take note of what is called the baptism of, or in, the Holy Spirit, which is the special grace at the core of all of this vast spiritual revival. It occurs as a rite of very simple gestures, shared in an attitude of humility and repentance and personal readiness to become little children, "for of such is the kingdom." It is a renewal and a reactivation and actualization, not only of baptism, but of all that Christian initiation involves. Those who want it prepare themselves, not only by confessing and repenting sincerely of their sins, but also by taking part in meetings where they receive teaching and where they come into a living and joyous contact with the great truths and realities of the faith: the love of God, sin, salvation, new life, transformation in Christ, charisms, and the fruits of the Spirit. And all of this in an atmosphere marked chiefly by a profound sense of belonging and being loved and cared for.

---

[25] Thomas Aquinas, *Commentary on the Gospel of John*, XV, n. 2061.

[26] Thomas Aquinas, *Summa Theologiae* I, q. 43, a. 6 ad 2; see F. Sullivan, Dict. Spir. 12, col. 1045.

At times, on the other hand, it all happens unexpectedly, without any intention or forethought or planning, and comes as a "surprise" of the Spirit. One man tells how it happened to him:

> I was in an aeroplane, on a journey, and I was reading the last chapter of a book on the Holy Spirit. Suddenly it was as if the Spirit came out of the page and entered into my body. Tears began to stream from my eyes. I began to pray. I was overcome by a Power much greater than I.[27]

The most common result of this grace is that the Holy Spirit, who before was the more-or-less abstract object of a person's intellectual assent of faith, becomes a fact of experience, as we have seen that of the Spirit's very nature the Spirit should always be. A well-known theologian has written:

> We cannot doubt that in this life we can *experience* grace in such a way that it gives us a sense of freedom and opens up horizons that are entirely new, making a profound impression on us, transforming us and moulding in us, even over a long period of time, a more inward Christian attitude. There is nothing that prevents us calling that kind of experience a *baptism in the Spirit*.[28]

Through what aptly has come to be called the baptism in the Spirit, we experience the Holy Spirit, the Spirit's anointing in our prayer, power in our apostolic service, consolation in our trials, light upon the choices we make. More basic than any manifestation of the Spirit in the charisms, this is the first way we perceive the Holy Spirit, as transforming us from within, giving us a desire to praise God and a taste for praise, leading us to discover a new joy in life, opening our mind to understand the Scripture, and above all teaching us to proclaim Jesus our "Lord." Or perhaps giving us courage to take on new and difficult tasks in the service of God and neighbor.

This is the description of the effects of the Spirit given by a person who took part in the retreat in 1967 that was the start of the charismatic renewal in the Catholic Church:

> Our faith has come alive, our believing has become a kind of knowing. Suddenly, the world of the supernatural has become

---

[27] In "New Covenant" (Ann Arbor, Mich.) June 1984, p. 12.

[28] K. Rahner, *Erfahrung des Heiligen Geistes,* in *Schriften zur Theologie,* vol. 13 (Zürich: Einsiedeln-Köln, 1978) 232.

more real than the natural. In brief, Jesus Christ is a real person to us, a real person who is our Lord and who is active in our lives. We read the New Testament as though it were literally true now, every word, every line. Prayer and the sacraments have become truly our daily bread instead of practices which we recognise as "good for us." A love of Scripture, a love of the Church I never thought possible, a transformation of our relationships with others, a need and a power of witness beyond all expectation, have all become part of our lives. The initial experience of the baptism in the Spirit was not at all emotional, but life has become suffused with calm, confidence, joy and peace. . . . We sang the *Veni Creator Spiritus* before each conference and meant it. We were not disappointed. We have also been showered with charismata. This also puts us in an ecumenical atmosphere at its best.[29]

How could we explain the extraordinary efficacy of this simple little gesture in making Pentecost alive and present to us? One explanation we find in the words of Thomas Aquinas quoted earlier. In a person's spiritual life or ministry, every time the person is faced with a new need or a new task that calls for a new level of grace, there is a new sending of the Spirit. In the normal course of events, this "stepping up the pace" in the life of grace is linked to the reception of the sacraments, but not always, as Thomas Aquinas himself pointed out.

Saint Ambrose too, speaking in that special style of his that was more poetic than conceptual, expresses the same conviction. He says that, besides the Eucharist (the cup of salvation) and the Scriptures, that is, besides the sacramental signs, there is another way we can become "soberly drunk" on the Holy Spirit: the Pentecostal way, free, unanticipated, not linked to the institutional signs, but arising wholly in God's sovereign and free initiative:

> The kind of inebriation that comes to us from the cup of salvation is a good thing. But there is another kind of being drunk that comes from drinking long and deep of the Scriptures, and yet a third kind that comes upon us when we are soaked in the dew of the Holy Spirit. It was because of this third kind of

[29] Testimony reported in P. Gallagher Mansfield, *As by a New Pentecost* (Stubenville, 1992) 25–6.

being drunk that, according to the Acts of the Apostles, those who heard people speaking in various tongues thought they must be drunk.[30]

Pentecost was the very first baptism of the Spirit. Telling of the Pentecost to come, Jesus said: "John baptized with water, but you will be baptized with the Holy Spirit not many days from now" (Acts 1:5).

John the Baptist presented Jesus to the world as "the one who baptizes with the Holy Spirit" (see John 1:33).

Not only through the sacrament of baptism that he instituted, but throughout the whole of his work, Jesus "baptizes in the Holy Spirit." His entire messianic mission consists in pouring out the Holy Spirit upon the world. The baptism in the Holy Spirit, that once again we have started to recognize and discuss in the Church, is one of the ways in which the risen Jesus continues his essential work, which is to baptize all of humankind "in the Spirit." It has been described as a renewal of the *Pentecost event* and, as importantly, also of the *sacrament* of baptism and of Christian initiation in general, even though the two realities coincide and therefore never come about separately or in opposition one to the other. The most important fruit of the dialogue between the traditional churches and the Pentecostal churches will be achieving this aim: to recognize that Pentecost does not cast sacrament into a lesser role (especially the sacrament of baptism with water), and neither does sacrament cast Pentecost into a lesser position.

5. Come, Visit, Fill!

What do we individually need to make it possible for each one of us to experience Pentecost in this way? First we need to ask the Father, consistently and persistently, to send us the Holy Spirit in the name of Jesus, and actually to expect the Father to answer! We need *expectant* faith, a faith *full* of expectancy! Saint Bonaventure asks, to whom does the Holy Spirit come? And he answers, with his usual preciseness, "He comes to the ones who love him, who

---

[30] Ambrose, *Commentary on the Psalms,* 35.19 (CSEL 64, p. 63–4).

invite him, who eagerly await him."[31] It is not possible to count the immense number of people who, in the twentieth century, have felt the thrill of the Spirit in their soul when, joined together with others, they plead for the Spirit's coming in the words of the Pentecostal chorus: "Spirit of the Living God, fall afresh on me. Melt me, mould me, fill me, use me. Spirit of the Living God, fall afresh on me."[32]

There are places where it is customary to invite whomever happens to come to the house at mealtimes to sit down and share what is on the table. But it is also taken for granted that the person you invite will excuse himself and say, "No, thank you, I am expected at home." One would be more than a little surprised and perhaps secretly irritated if, instead, the person were to answer, "Why, thank you very much. It will be a pleasure to share with you!" We tend often to make our invitations to the Holy Spirit in somewhat the same sort of vein. We issue these invitations because it is the convention, our custom, but we don't really mean what we say. However, we ought to express these three invitations, to come, to visit, and to fill, as genuine invitations, in the certain knowledge that the One we invite will take them seriously, listen, and act upon them.

We need, then, to be "of one mind" and "persevering" in our prayer. As were the apostles with Mary in the Upper Room, gathering together, whenever possible, with other people who have already known what it is to experience a new Pentecost and who are able to help us to be ready and to overcome any fear we may feel.

And next, we need to be ready for things to change in our own lives. It is just not possible to invite the Holy Spirit to come, to visit, and to fill us on condition that the Spirit leave us, thank you, just as we were before. "Whatever the Spirit touches, the Spirit changes," as the Fathers often said. Whenever you cry, "Come, visit, fill," by the same token you give the Spirit freedom to take charge and control your life: you give the Spirit the keys to the inward heart-house where you dwell. Commit your life to the Father, and the Father will commit his Spirit to you! That is the only way!

---

[31] Bonaventure, *Sermon for the Fourth Sunday after Easter*, 2 (Quaracchi, IX, p. 311).

[32] Words and music: Michael Iverson.

It is simply not possible to cry, "Come, visit, fill," and have the little secret voice of the flesh add quietly, "But watch it now: nothing strange, no excesses!" The apostles thought nothing of it that they were taken for drunkards. There should be no reason to be surprised if, now and then, when Jericho's "walls come tumbling down," they make a little noise and throw up a little dust. I mean if the coming of the Spirit provokes in some persons laughter or tears or some other "uncomfortable" reaction of the body. It is clearly not the Spirit that is directly responsible for provoking reactions of this sort; it is the flesh that, at times, is simply not ready for the impact of the Spirit and reacts like cold water to the touch of red-hot iron. Nevertheless, it is not the sort of thing that need give rise to any concern or feeling of shame. In the Mass for the feast of Pentecost, as we have it in the original Latin text, the Church prays to the Father saying: "Renew, O God, in our day, in the community of believers, the prodigies you brought about when the Gospel was first preached."

How, now, can we carry on saying these words if, as soon as the Holy Spirit begins to take us at our word and to do what we ask, we become all fearful and say, "not like that, not like that!" and if we too say, of those who openly show the effects of the Spirit's coming, "they have been drinking too much new wine"?

Let me end with the inspired words spoken by a bishop of an Eastern rite at a solemn ecumenical assembly:

> *Without the Holy Spirit:*
> *God is far away,*
> *Christ stays in the past,*
> *the Gospel is a dead letter,*
> *the Church is simply an organization,*
> *authority a matter of domination,*
> *mission a matter of propaganda,*
> *liturgy no more than an evocation,*
> *Christian living a slave morality.*
>
> *But with the Holy Spirit:*
> *the cosmos is resurrected and groans with the birth-pangs of the*
> *   Kingdom,*
> *the risen Christ is there,*
> *the Gospel is the power of life,*
> *the Church shows forth the life of the Trinity,*

authority is a liberating service,
mission is a Pentecost,
the liturgy is both memorial and anticipation,
human action is deified.[33]

---

[33] Ignatius di Latakia, Discourse given at the Third World Assembly of Churches, July 1968, in *The Uppsala Report* (Geneva, 1969) 298.

IV

You Whom We Name the Paraclete

The Holy Spirit teaches us to be paracletes too

Saint Seraphim of Sarov said to one of his disciples:

> We need to keep praying up to the moment when the Holy
> Spirit comes down upon us and grants us heavenly grace in a
> measure known only to him. As soon as he visits us, we should
> stop calling upon him to come. For indeed, what purpose could
> it serve to keep on pleading, "Come, you who are goodness it-
> self, make your dwelling in us, purify us of every stain and
> save our souls," if he has already come?[1]

To behave differently would be like inviting someone to your
house, and when he arrives meeting him at the door and letting
him stand there while you repeat over and over with monotonous
insistence, "Do please come and visit me!" People who behave
that way merely show that they are paying no attention to what
they are saying.

For us too, the time has come to be done with saying to the
Spirit, "Come, visit us, fill us with heavenly grace!" and to believe that in a way and in a measure known only to him, the Spirit
has come and is in each one of us. In fact, from this point onward
in the *Veni Creator,* the place of *invocation* of the Spirit is given
over to *contemplation* of the Spirit. If we can think of the *Veni
Creator* as a symphony, this would be the beginning of the second
movement, which is usually *adagio* or *largo,* a calm, peaceful
melody following on the *mosso* or *impetuoso* mood that pervaded
the opening verse of the hymn played *fortissimo.*

---

[1] Conversation with Motovilov, in G. P. Fedotov, *A Treasury of Russian
Spirituality* (London: Sheed and Ward, 1950).

1. The Sanctifying Work of the Spirit

The second verse of the *Veni Creator* literally reads:

> You whom we name the Paraclete,
> are gift of God most high,
> living fountain, fire, love
> and spiritual anointing.

This is the start of a long and moving contemplation of the Holy Spirit in the Church. The hymn now speaks, intentionally, of the Spirit who is the Spirit of grace, of the return to God, the Spirit of the redemption who in fullness is at work in the Church.

Even from a literary point of view the hymn changes its key signature. First came the *epiclesis* or invocation (Come, visit, fill!); now follows the *eulogy,* the formal praise-song to the Spirit. In the traditional form the eulogy starts with the words "you who . . ." and is made up of a list of the titles and the good qualities and the achievements of the person addressed, that as praise-singers we put forward as the grounds on which we are confident that we will be heard. At the same time these titles and qualities are mentioned in recognition and acknowledgement. That is, we do not recall them in an attitude of adulation, simply to try to get the godhead to see us in a good light, but rather, as moved by a genuine impetus of grateful admiration, praise, and enthusiasm. It is certainly so in the case of this hymn.

The eulogy in our hymn is made up of a series of titles or symbols of the Holy Spirit taken, without exception, from the Bible. And it is in this that their power lies. The *Veni Creator* is like a large-meshed net thrown into the great ocean of Scripture and drawing out of it only the "big fish," that is to say, the most precious pearls. All that the author does with them is string them together on the unobtrusive thread of the meter in a precise theological pattern. In this sense, there is a close affinity between the *Veni Creator* and Mary's canticle, the *Magnificat.* With its titles and expressions also drawn almost without exception from the Scripture, Mary creates a prayer so fresh, so new, so personal that no one other than Mary herself will ever be able to make it her own. It is the inimitable quality of the Scripture, to say new things with old words, and to express, with few short words, truths of infinite depth.

The contemplative part of the *Veni Creator* takes up its second and third verses. Yet there is a most important difference between these two verses, and simply to point it out will be enough to show how profound is the theology and how exquisite the biblical inspiration of this hymn.

In the Bible two lines of action emerge, one after the other, concerning the manifestation of the Spirit. The first, which we could call the *charismatic* line, is the one that presents the Spirit as a power that on certain occasions breaks in upon special people, giving them the ability to do things and to explain reality in a way that is not humanly possible. The Spirit comes upon someone and fills that person with wisdom or artistic giftedness for the embellishment of the Temple (Exod 31:3; 35:31); the Spirit fills another with the gift of prophecy (Mic 3:8) or gifts of extraordinary ability in governing (Isa 11:2) or supernatural physical strength to use in saving the people (Judg 13:25).

On the other hand the second line, that of *sanctification,* began to be seen in the prophets and the Psalms after the Exile. For example see Ezekiel, where God announces: "A new heart I will give you, and a new spirit I will put within you. . . . I will put my spirit within you, and make you follow my statutes and be careful to observe my ordinances" (Ezek 36:26-27).

Or again in Psalm 51 where, for the first time, the Spirit is given the title "Holy," associating him with the process of being made clean and renewed in heart (see Ps 51:12f.).

The fundamental difference is that the *charismatic action* of the Spirit passes through, without remaining in, the person who receives it; its aim is not the betterment of the particular person but rather the good of the community as a whole. The particular person may not be made any better through the charism he has received; he may even abuse the gift and turn it into reason for his own reprobation. On the contrary the *sanctifying action* of the Spirit remains within the person who receives it, who is renewed by it and transformed from within.

The first line will again come to the fore in the New Testament revelation concerning the charisms, the gifts and the works of the Holy Spirit that are seen first in Jesus of Nazareth and later, after Pentecost, in the Church. The second line finds its apex in what will be called "the sanctifying action of the Spirit,"[2] consisting in new life in the Spirit and, more concretely, in charity. Paul would make a synthesis of these two lines of action of the Spirit, speaking in order first of the charisms and then of charity (see 1 Corinthians 12–14). He stresses the superiority of charity, but recognizes that both lines are necessary to the Church, as coming from the same Spirit and intended for the same purpose, which is the building up of the body of Christ.

These general remarks will help us better to understand the two verses of the hymn that we are setting out to ponder. The titles we read in the second verse, starting with "Paraclete," all refer without exception to the sanctifying and illuminating work of the Spirit, and it is clear, right from the start ("You are sevenfold in your gifts"), that the third verse is dedicated wholly and exclusively to the Spirit as the one who distributes the gifts and charisms.

2. A Name Born of Experience

We come right away to the first line of this verse and to the first title: "You whom we name the Paraclete" *(Qui Paracletus diceris)*. For those who have any familiarity with a computer, it provides a comparison that may help to grasp what happens at the simple mention of the name Paraclete. I am thinking of what we call a file, or the name we give a document, and what that represents. I sit at the computer and write a whole book, this one, let us say, on the *Veni Creator,* and I put it into memory, giving it a name of no more than eight characters. In this case the eight-letter name was in fact "paraclet." The whole book is there, stored in the computer's memory, but there is no way to draw it out to read it, or to print it, if I do not key in that word. But, no sooner have I tapped the keys for that word "paraclet" on the keyboard and punched "enter" than the whole content of that memory surges marvelously out and appears on the screen before me, page after page, and I can read it, write some more into it, and change it. Something of the same sort happens with each of the titles of the Holy Spirit that we find in this verse: Paraclete, Gift of God, Fire, Love, and spiritual Anointing. Each one, on its own, works a wonder of unlocking floods of revelation and of doctrine concerning

[2] See 2 Titus 2:13; 1 Pet 1:2.

the Holy Spirit from those great stored memories that are the Bible and Tradition.

From what source did John the evangelist draw this title "Paraclete"? He uses it four times in the short space of chapters 14 through 16 of his Gospel. We cannot prove that he had it from the living lips of Jesus himself, but neither can we prove the opposite. Jesus spoke many times about the Holy Spirit, both before his death and after his resurrection. Can we exclude, a priori, that he may once have used a word, an image, a comparison, and that the evangelist knew it or remembered it and gave it a central place in his reflections? Luke is the only one of the evangelists who uses the title "finger of God" in referring to the Holy Spirit, but can we conclude on that account that the title is not authentic?

The name and the concept Paraclete applied to the Holy Spirit, then, is not something strange or far-fetched. On the contrary, it is in keeping with a whole line of biblical thought. In the Old Testament God is the great consoler of the people; God is the one who proclaims, "I am your consoler," or in a literal rendering of the Greek text of the Septuagint, "your paraclete" (Isa 51:12), the one who comforts with maternal affection: "As a mother comforts her child, so I will comfort you" (Isa 66:13).

This "God of all consolation" (Rom 15:5) is made incarnate in Jesus Christ who is in fact the first Advocate or Comforter (see John 14:15). In this, as in every aspect of God's activity. The Holy Spirit is the one who continues the work of Christ and brings the shared work of the Trinity to completion, and so the Spirit could not fail to be described with the same title.

Yet there is another source from which this title surely takes its origin and importance. That source is the *experience* of the evangelist and of the Church. The whole Church, after the Resurrection, had a lively and powerful experience of the Holy Spirit as consoler, defender, and ally in inward difficulties and in those that came from the outside, in persecutions and trials and in the details of everyday life. We read in the Acts of the Apostles that the churches were building themselves up, "living in the fear of the Lord and in the comfort *(paraclesis)* of the Holy Spirit" (Acts 9:31). The evangelist himself alludes to this experience as the source of his own knowledge, when he relates what Jesus said of the Paraclete: "You know him, because he abides with you, and he will be in you" (John 14:17).

We cannot not be amazed at what took place between the disciples and the Holy Spirit after the resurrection. What we know of the Spirit of God from the Old Testament is absolutely not enough to explain all that we are now told of him. At every level, the Church was vitally aware of the Spirit as a presence, a familiar reality, someone with whom they were "at home." For them to speak of Jesus in that way was normal; they had seen him, they knew him, there were the things he had left, signs that he had been there, a "memorial" of him, the Eucharist. But who had ever seen the Holy Spirit? Nevertheless, everybody was speaking about him as a reality, taking for granted that the others would know very well what they were talking about. They saw everything that happened as linked to him, from the littlest things to the greatest events.

What could ever be the reason for a fact so evident, if not the revelation that the Church had received from Jesus himself coupled with the living experience of the community? In this we are face to face with the mystery of the Holy Spirit. The Paraclete is quite simply carrying out, point by point, all that Jesus said he would do.

3. Advocate, Consoler, and Spirit of Truth

If we take account of the various contexts in which the word is used, in the Bible and elsewhere, Paraclete can mean *intercessor* or *advocate* (as when it is applied to Christ in 1 John 2:1), or else *consoler,* as is clear from the verb and the corresponding noun that in fact mean to console and consolation: "Console [*parakaleite*] my people, console them, says your God" (Isa 40:1).

Tradition has accepted the polyvalence of the term, its multifaceted meaning, and interpreted Paraclete sometimes as advocate and sometimes consoler. This becomes clearer when we move to the Latin world, where the translators, tackling the Greek word, had to pick one meaning or the other. Some translated Paraclete as advocate, others as consoler, and still others used both terms together.[3] This last strategy was the one in common use at the time when the *Veni Creator* was composed.[4]

---

[3] Tertullian, *On the Fast,* 13.5 (CC 2, p. 1272), Hilary of Poitiers, *On the Psalms,* 125.7 (CSEL 22, p. 610), Augustine, *Commentary on the Gospel of John,* 94.2.

[4] See Isidore of Seville, *Etymologies,* VII.2.31; VII.3.10; Rhabanus Maurus, *On the Universe,* 1.3 (PL 111.24).

In its early years when the Church was subjected to persecutions and trials and death-sentences were an everyday experience, Christians saw the Paraclete above all as the divine advocate and defender who stood by them. At Lyon in the second century, at the trial and sentencing of a group of Christians, one of the onlookers stood up "on fire with the Holy Spirit" to object to the way the whole process had been conducted. He was promptly arrested and sentenced along with the group on the charge of being "the Christians' advocate." "And properly so," comments the author of the account, "because he had in him the Paraclete, the great Advocate who is the Holy Spirit."[5]

The role of advocate in human affairs was also seen as just one aspect indicative of an assistance of much deeper import: the defense the Paraclete provides before the judgment seat of God, against "that persecutor who accused our brothers day and night before our God" (Rev 12:10). It was of this role of the Holy Spirit that Saint Irenaeus was thinking when he wrote that God has given the Paraclete to the Church, "so that, where we have an accuser, there too we should have a Defender."[6]

We notice that when the Church emerged from the era of persecution there was a change of accent. The usual sense of the word Paraclete was now consoler. Saint Bonaventure draws the contrast between the consolation offered by the world and the consolation of the Spirit:

> The Spirit brings consolation that is true, perfect, and in proportion. It is true, because he brings consolation where it is more in place, that is, in the soul, and not to the flesh as the world does. The world, in consoling the flesh, actually afflicts the soul, like an incompetent innkeeper who stables the horse well but neglects the rider. It is perfect because, whatever the tribulation, it is effective, unlike the consolation of the world that for every way it soothes brings two new sorts of trouble, like someone who sews up a rent in an old cloak and causes two new tears on either side of it. And it is in proportion, because the greater the tribulation, the greater the consolation,

---

[5] See Eusebius, *Church History,* V.1.10.

[6] Irenaeus, *Against the Heresies,* III.17.3.

unlike the world that consoles and flatters when one is prosper-
ous, but ridicules and condemns when one falls on hard times.[7]

The same sentiment is revealed in the Sequence for Pentecost,
composed in the thirteenth century, where it calls the Holy Spirit
consolator optime, "the very best of consolers."

The words of the *Veni Creator,* as we have already said, are an
"open structure," able without difficulty to take in anything new
that the Church discovers regarding a particular theme in Scripture. This is truer than ever as to Paraclete. For this is in fact a title
that expresses not what the Holy Spirit is as a person in the Trinity (this will be declared only in the last verse of the hymn), but
what the Holy Spirit is and what he is doing for us in the history
of salvation. There is nothing to be surprised at, therefore, if the
title carries a meaning that appears with different emphases and
that is enriched over time and through the successive situations
that believers encounter as history proceeds.

However, the terms advocate and consoler, whether we take
them singly or together, do not draw out the whole of the meaning
that the fourth Gospel gives the word Paraclete. In many verses of
the Gospel the title Paraclete that John chooses to signify the Holy
Spirit is similar to the title Logos that he uses to signify the Son. In
both of these instances the evangelist has made use of terms in
common use in the language of the day and has "supercharged"
them with such a new range of meaning that he has inaugurated a
new phase in the history of these words. From that moment onward
it is no longer possible to define them in terms of their etymology
or their previous usage. In other words, it is not possible to explain
the meaning of Paraclete by reference only to the *name;* it is necessary also to take into consideration the *functions* that are attributed
to the one who bears the name. "The Paraclete *is* what the Paraclete
does."[8] The functions stretch the sense of the name boundlessly, so
that at times they seem to give the impression that there is conflict
between the name and the prerogatives it tries to convey.

If we want to get to know what these functions are, there is no
more effective way than to read, one after another, all the state-

---

[7] Bonaventure, *Sermons: Sunday in the Octave of Ascension,* II (Quaracchi,
IX, p. 329).

[8] See E. Cothenet, *Esprit Saint,* DB Suppl., fasc. 60, 364.

ments that are made about the Paraclete in the fourth Gospel.[9] Two things stand out clearly from such texts: the Paraclete is in function of the truth, and the Paraclete is in function of Jesus. The various activities attributed to the Paraclete—to teach, to recall, to witness, to convince, to lead to the truth, to announce—indicate that his principal role is doctrinal, that is, an instructive or teaching role, and that his domain is principally the domain of knowledge. John seems to want almost to equate Paraclete with "Spirit of truth."

Yet all of this does not mean that we are dealing with two distinct "centers"—Jesus and truth—but with one only, because the evangelist sees truth as nothing else than the revelation brought into the world by Jesus Christ. "Spirit of truth" is to all intents and purposes the same as "Spirit of the Son."[10] From one section to the next in the fourth Gospel, the role of the Holy Spirit is to bring us to accept, to interiorize, to comprehend, and really to live all that is revealed to us in the Son. It is above all in this sense that the title "Paraclete" belongs to the Spirit in the Spirit's role as the one who sanctifies and enlightens—the role summed up in the second verse of the *Veni Creator.*

4. The Paraclete, a "Person"

"Paraclete" is the title that most clearly expresses the personal character of the Holy Spirit. Using that title, the author of the hymn takes us a decisive step forward in contemplating the Holy Spirit. If by the term "Creator" he affirmed that the Spirit was by *nature* divine, now by the term "Paraclete" he affirms that the Spirit is also a divine *person.* The other titles and symbols of the Spirit—water, fire, love, and the very name Spirit—might of themselves at the very most convince us that there is "something divine" about the Holy Spirit. Paraclete, however, is in itself a personal title: it can be attributed only to a person, because it implies both intellect and will. Grammatically, it is not a neuter like *pneuma,* "breath," but masculine, and the corresponding pronoun is "he," not "it." In the text where John is referring to the neuter

[9] See John 14:16-17, 26; 15:26-27; 16:7-15.
[10] Cyril of Alexandria, *Commentary on the Gospel of John,* IX.14, 16–17 (PG 74.257B).

pneuma, he writes, "He [*ekeinos*] will glorify me" (John 16:14), so showing that he would rather disregard the rules of Greek grammar than be untrue to his notion of the Holy Spirit.

By this we do not intend to imply that John had clearly in mind our own concept of the divine Persons or of the Trinity; all we want to say is that what he had in mind was enough to justify the future faith of the Church. This is an absolutely crucial point on which we cannot allow any uncertainty to remain unresolved. Otherwise, we will simply not understand anything at all of the *Veni Creator,* for the whole of the hymn is a cry to a real person, a someone, who is truly able to hear, to "come," and to "visit."

In John, the relationship of the Spirit to Jesus is modeled on the relationship of Jesus to the Father. The Father is the one who testifies to the Son,[11] and the Holy Spirit is the one who testifies to Jesus (John 15:26); the Son does not speak simply on his own account, but says what he has heard from the Father;[12] neither does the Spirit speak simply on his own account, but says what he has heard from the Son (John 16:13). Jesus glorifies the Father (John 8:49; 17:1) and the Spirit glorifies Jesus (John 16:14).

On this point Paul is in total agreement with John, and we cannot afford not to listen to his testimony as well. For him too, the Spirit is not merely an *action* but also an *agent,* that is, a principle endowed with intellect and will, who knows what he is doing and chooses freely to do it. Paul says that the Spirit teaches, bears witness, groans, intercedes, is made sorrowful, knows, desires. This clear evolution toward a subjective rather than an objective conception of *pneuma* is confirmed by Paul's use of triadic formulas like the following: "The grace of the Lord Jesus Christ, the love of God, and the communion of the Holy Spirit be with all of you" (2 Cor 13:13).

Read, as it is right to do, in the light of Matthew 28:19 (". . . baptizing them in the name of the Father and of the Son and of the Holy Spirit . . .") and also of the later unfolding of the faith, the triadic formulas[13] indicate a new orientation in the understanding of the revelation concerning the Holy Spirit, linked with revelation concerning the Father and the Son, that is, with the revelation of the Trinity.

---

[11] See John 5:32, 37; 8:18.

[12] See John 8:28; 12:49; 14:10.

[13] See 1 Cor 12:4-6; Rom 5:1-5; Gal 4:4-6.

There are some who would explain the Holy Spirit in Saint Paul as "a power that is to be identified with the Lord in Glory considered, not as he is in himself, but insofar as he is active in the community."[14] This view, however, does not take account of the fact that in the Bible the Spirit is there before the resurrection of Christ, and even before his very incarnation. Paul calls him "Spirit of God," and not simply "Spirit of Christ" (see 1 Cor 2:11-14). If, then, the Holy Spirit is to be identified with the risen Lord "insofar as he is active in the community," how would it be possible to attribute the resurrection itself to the work of the Spirit?[15] And what could be the meaning of phrases like "the Spirit of him who raised Jesus from the dead" (Rom 8:11), or "no one can say 'Jesus is Lord' except by the Holy Spirit" (1 Cor 12:3)? Do not these expressions presuppose a certain clear distinction between the Spirit and the risen Christ?

Surely enough, there is a very close relationship between the Spirit and the risen Lord. Paul also uses expressions like "the Lord *is* the Spirit" (2 Cor 3:17, immediately followed, however, by "the Spirit *of* the Lord") and "the last Adam became a life-giving Spirit" (1 Cor 15:45). Nevertheless, these affirmations cannot be taken in isolation from the rest, as if to suggest that Christ is no more than *the Spirit incarnate,* and the Spirit is no more than *Christ spiritualized.* To do this would be to wind theology back to the time of *The Shepherd of Hermas* and the writings of other authors of the second century that are in fact characterized by a sort of binitarian view that takes account only of two realities: God and God's Spirit.

The same author states, in the same work:

> The metaphysical question concerning the inward relationships between God, the Spirit and Christ was not of any concern to Paul, and because Paul often uses the term *pneuma* in a clearly impersonal sense, it would be wrong to take *pneuma* as Paul's first choice for referring to the third person of the Trinity.

It is true that Paul often uses *pneuma* in an impersonal sense, but it is also true that at least as often he uses the term to indicate

[14] E. Schweitzer, *Pneuma,* ThWNT, VI, pp. 431ff.
[15] See Rom 1:4; 1 Pet 3:18; 1 Tim 3:16.

someone *personal,* and that is enough to allow us to say that for Paul the Spirit already figured as a personal reality, that is, as someone who is active and who acts with knowledge and in freedom. How would it be possible, for instance, to deny the personal character of the Spirit in this text: "All these are activated by one and the same Spirit, who allots to each one individually just as the Spirit chooses" (1 Cor 12:11)?

The Spirit is not merely a gift, or all the gifts taken as a whole, but the one who distributes gifts "just as the Spirit chooses" and knows what he is doing and that he is doing it.

The same author objects that "the problem of the personality of the *pneuma* is mistakenly raised, as shown by the simple fact that the term 'person' did not exist, either in Hebrew or in Greek."[16] This objection is itself "mistakenly raised," for taken to its logical conclusion it would mean that for Paul neither the Father nor the Son could be said to be "persons," since Paul did not have access to the concept to be able to apply it to them either. When we are dealing with something new, hitherto unknown, the lack of a term does not necessarily mean the absence of the corresponding reality. To maintain the contrary would be tantamount to saying that it was not possible to invent the telephone until we had the word "telephone" and knew what it meant. This holds true in a special way as far as the concept "person" or "hypostasis" is concerned because, insofar as these terms mean something distinct from "substance," they did not exist in any culture until Christian thinkers began reflecting on what Jesus had revealed of the Father, the Son, and the Holy Spirit and discovering what this revelation implied. If this fact is not recognized, it is simply not possible to explain how or why the new concept "person" ever arose or why it was developed.

We can therefore say that in Paul, and in the New Testament, we do not yet find the concept or the term "person" applied to the Holy Spirit (as, for that matter, we do not find it applied to the Father or to Jesus Christ), but the corresponding reality is clearly there. *Pneuma* is no longer seen merely as a principle or sphere of action, as was the case in Hebrew thought, and neither was it any longer seen as a kind of fluid substance, as was the case for the

---

[16] E. Schweitzer, *Pneuma,* ThWNT, VI, pp. 431ff.

Greeks, but it was now also seen as an agent, as one, distinct from any other, and who acts on his own account. The Greek Fathers would later give expression to this discovery of faith, saying that the Holy Spirit was not merely a "divine energy," but an "active substance" or a "substantial agent" possessing will and intellect.[17]

"It is one who generates and another who is generated; one who sends and another who is sent."[18] This principle that serves as basis for holding that Father and Son are distinct persons holds true also of the relationships between the Spirit and the Father, and the Spirit and the Son: "It is one who proceeds and others from whom he proceeds; those who send are other than the one who is sent."

However, one thing is true. When we use the term "person" of the Father, the Son, and the Holy Spirit, we have to be careful to free the word of the meaning we commonly give it. Applied to the Holy Spirit, the term "person" does not mean a center of action complete in itself, an agent independently conscious of self, in the modern sense; it signifies only the relationships-of-origin that "contrast" or distinguish the Father, Son, and Holy Spirit as among themselves. This, however, does not allow us to come to the conclusion that, "concerning the notion of person in Trinitarian theology, it makes no difference whether the Spirit is represented as a person who speaks and who acts (in the usual sense), or as an impersonal force."[19] On the contrary, it is precisely the fact that the Spirit speaks and acts that allows us to be sure of the kind of relationship the Spirit has with the Father and the Son. On the other hand, if a person in the Trinity is not simply an autonomous center of action and of will, he does participate nevertheless in that unique center common to the Three Persons, and in that sense is capable of acting and willing: "The creative will . . . and the activity of the divine being are common to all three Persons, but they belong to each one in a way that is special to each."[20]

---

[17] See Origen, *Fragment 37, on John* (GCS IV, p. 513); Gregory of Nyssa, *Catechetical Discourse,* 2 (PG 45.17C).

[18] Tertullian, *Against Praxeas,* 9.2 (CC 2, p. 1168).

[19] See F. J. Schierse, in *Mysterium salutis,* II.2.2 (Einsiedeln/Zürich: Köln, 1967) 121–2, 125.

[20] Cyril of Alexandria, *Dialogue on the Trinity,* VI (PG 75.1056A).

From the time of Athanasius, one thing has been clear and commonly accepted in the Christian understanding of the Trinity: Either it is homogeneous or there is in fact no Trinity. It cannot possibly be made up of two *persons* and one *thing*, or (in the language of the Greeks) of two *hypostases* and one *energy*. For then there would be no Trinity but only a complex of beings of different kinds.

5. Be Paracletes

So it is that in the term Paraclete we reach in a certain sense to the apex of revelation concerning the Holy Spirit. He is not merely "something," but "Someone." The Spirit is one who dwells in us, a presence, one who speaks on our behalf, a defender, a friend, a consoler, the "sweet guest of the soul," as the Sequence for Pentecost says. The Spirit was the "inseparable companion" of Jesus during his earthly life,[21] and now wants to be just that to each one of us. All that one person might hope for of another, of what is best and of what is delightful, we can find, and infinitely more, in the Spirit. What "Paraclete" conveys to us opens up for us an inexhaustible field for our reflection on the Holy Spirit. One of the great contemplatives of the Middle Ages wrote:

> To the children of grace and the poor in spirit, he is their advocate in the exile of this present life, their consoler, their strength in adversity, their aid in hardship. It is he who teaches them to pray as they ought, who keeps them firmly close to God, who makes them pleasing to him and worthy to be heard.[22]

It remains for us to draw something practical and workable from our contemplation of the Paraclete. It is not enough to study the meaning of the word Paraclete; we need to become paracletes ourselves! If it is true that a Christian ought to be *alter Christus,* another Christ, it is equally true that a Christian ought to be "another Paraclete."

By the Holy Spirit, the love of God has been poured into our hearts (Rom 5:5), and this love is both the love with which God

---

[21] Basil the Great, *On the Holy Spirit,* XVI.39 (PG 32.140C).
[22] William of St. Thierry, *The Enigma of Faith,* 100 (PL 180.440C).

loves us, and also the love that makes us able in our turn to love God and our neighbor. Applied to consolation—that is, to the form love takes when confronted with the suffering of a loved one—this word from the apostle tells us something of supreme importance: The Paraclete comes not merely to console us, but also to prompt us to console, and to empower us to console. The same apostle Paul writes: "Blessed be the God and Father of our Lord Jesus Christ, the Father of mercies and the God of *all consolation,* who *consoles* us in all our affliction, so that we may be able to *console* those who are in any affliction with the *consolation* with which we ourselves are *consoled* by God" (2 Cor 1:3-4).

In this passage the Greek word from which Paraclete is derived is used five times, sometimes as a verb, sometimes as a noun. We have here all that is needed for a complete theology of consolation. Consolation comes from God who is "the God of all consolation." It comes to those who are in sorrow. But it does not stop there; its purpose is achieved when the one who has experienced consolation gets up and in turn brings consolation to others. What kind of consolation? This is where we come to the most important point. We console with the consolation we have received from God, that is, with divine and not with human comforting. We cannot be content simply to repeat empty words ("have courage," "don't let it get you down," "you'll see, everything will turn out all right") that really do nothing to change the situation. We need to offer the authentic comfort that comes from the words of Scripture, words that are able to keep hope alive (see Rom 15:4). This is the explanation of the miracles that come about at the bedside of someone who is sick, when a simple word is spoken or a gesture is made with faith and in a prayerful way, and in the presence of the Holy Spirit. God comforts and consoles through us.

In a certain sense, the Holy Spirit has need of us in order to be Paraclete. The Spirit wants to console, to defend, to exhort and encourage, but the Spirit does not have lips or hands or eyes to "embody" consolation. Let us say, rather, that the Spirit does have hands and lips and eyes: ours. As the soul within us acts and moves and smiles by means of the members of our own body, so the Holy Spirit works through the members of "his" body, which is the Church. Paul recommends to the first Christians that they should "give encouragement to each other" (1 Thess 5:11), and if we go to his original Greek text and translate literally, what he says is "make yourselves paracletes" or "be paracletes" to each other. In one of his sermons Cardinal Newman said:

> Instructed by our own sorrows and our own sufferings, and even by our own sins, we will be trained in mind and heart for every work of love for those who are in need of love. To the measure of our ability, we will be consolers in the image of the Paraclete in every sense that this word implies: advocates, helpers, bringers of comfort. Our words and our counsel, our manner, our voice, our glance, will be gentle and tranquil.[23]

If the consolation we receive from the Spirit does not pass from us to others, if we want to cling to it selfishly for ourselves alone, it very soon rots away. That is why a lovely prayer attributed to Saint Francis of Assisi says:

> Let me not seek so much
> to be consoled as to console,
> to be understood as to understand,
> to be loved as to love.

There is a psalm that the evangelists applied to the suffering Christ, and that Jesus once made his own. It says: "I looked for pity, but there was none; and for comforters, but I found none" (Ps 69:20).

In Gethsemane, Jesus looked for someone to console him but found nobody. May he not have to say these words about me too. Jesus is in agony until the very end of the world. He is in agony above all in his mystical body, in those who suffer and are desolate. The Paraclete is called "father of the poor"; one can never be more sure of being a paraclete than when one reaches out to the poor, the humiliated, and those who suffer, offering consolation freely, unsought.

Let us ask this grace from Mary whom Christian piety honors as "*consoler* of the afflicted" *(consolatrix afflictorum)*. She most surely has made herself "paraclete" to us! A document of the Second Vatican Council says this: "The mother of Jesus shines as a sign of sure hope and *consolation* for the people of God on their way."[24]

---

[23] J. H. Newman, *Parochial and Plain Sermons*, vol. V (London, 1870) 300–1.
[24] *Lumen Gentium* 68.

We end this chapter with this invocation to the Paraclete, taken from the Office of Solemn Vespers of Pentecost in the Orthodox liturgy (the same prayer to which Seraphim of Sarov is alluding in the passage quoted at the beginning):

> *Heavenly King, Consoler, Spirit of truth,*
> *who are present everywhere and fill the universe,*
> *treasure of graces who give life:*
> *come and dwell in us,*
> *purify us of all that is vile*
> *and save our souls, oh God of all goodness.*[25]

---

[25] See *Pentecostaire,* translated by D. Guillaume (Parma, 1994) 400.

V

Most High Gift of God

The Holy Spirit teaches us to make our own life a gift

This meditation will focus on a title of the Holy Spirit that, as we have it in the version of the hymn now in common use, is "gift of God most high" *(donum Dei altissimi)*. I think, however, that a copyist's error has crept in at this point in the text: the original would probably have read *donum Dei altissimum,* that is, "Most high gift of God."

The difference is not insignificant. In the phrase "gift of God most high" the adjective "most high," in the specific context of this hymn, would appear superfluous if it is to be taken simply as referring to God, or else it would seem to be a kind of "filler" tucked in to pad out the meter. Now, in a hymn every word of which has been chosen with great care and precision, that is very unlikely, for in that case "most high" would be saying nothing whatever about the Holy Spirit in particular, but merely recalling an attribute of divinity in general. However, if "most high" refers to "gift," it is making a very precise observation about "gift" that, from Augustine onward, was frequently repeated by Latin writers: "there is no more excellent gift than love," that love which is the Holy Spirit. Consequently the Holy Spirit is "the greatest gift that God can give."[1] We find the concept in the very text from which the author of the *Veni Creator* drew inspiration for many of the titles he chooses and applies to the Holy Spirit.[2] It is significant that one of the ancient commentators on this hymn, after having cited the title in the form in which we traditionally have it—"gift of God most high"—carries on to interpret it in the sense of "most outstanding gift."[3] On this point there are

[1] Augustine, *The Trinity,* XV.18.32; 19.37.

[2] See Isidore of Seville, *Etymologies,* VII.3.16; Rhabanus Maurus, *On the Universe,* 1.3 (PL 111.25).

[3] Dionysius the Carthusian, *Exposition on the Veni Creator,* in *Opera Omnia,* vol. 35, (Tournai, 1908) 54 *("donum praestantissimum").*

variations even in the ancient manuscripts of the hymn, showing that there was some uncertainty about the correct reading.[4]

However, the uncertainty on that point does not have any bearing on what is fundamental to the message carried by the line we are looking at; that is conveyed in the substantive, "gift," rather than in the adjective, "most high." The title gift throws light on an important aspect of the person of the Paraclete, and it carries a message of very special significance for Christian spouses and also for people in religious life. This title expresses the reality in which they can feel the Holy Spirit closest to them; it would be no surprise to me if for many of them it were to become their favorite title for the Holy Spirit. But before we come to look at the ways we can apply these things to our own lives, we ought, as always, to lay the doctrinal foundation, because our devotion to the Holy Spirit must not become something snipped away from our faith, but must rather grow from it as its most exquisite fruit.

1. The Holy Spirit's Very Own Name

In many passages of the New Testament the Holy Spirit is presented, directly or indirectly, as the gift of God. "If you knew the gift of God," said Jesus to the Samaritan woman (John 4:10), and he goes on to speak of the living water. It has always been understood that in this context Jesus is alluding to the Holy Spirit (see John 7:38-39.). Whatever the case, the Acts of the Apostles clearly defines the Holy Spirit as "gift of God": "Repent . . . and you will receive the *gift* of the Holy Spirit."[5] "Gift *of* the Holy Spirit" signifies either that the Holy Spirit is the giver of the gift, or that the Holy Spirit *is* the gift. "He is given as the gift of God, in such a way that he, as God, is himself the giver giving himself."[6]

In this case, the gift of the Holy Spirit is nothing else than the Holy Spirit. In other texts, however, the subject, giver, and the object, gift, are distinct, and the Holy Spirit appears as the gift that the Father, or Christ, gives to believers. "By this we know that we

---

[4] One manuscript has *"altissimus"*; see A. S. Walpole, *Early Latin Hymns* (Cambridge, 1922) 375.

[5] Acts 2:38; see also 8:20; 10:45.

[6] Augustine, *The Trinity*, XV.19.36.

abide in him and he in us, because he has given us of his Spirit" (1 John 4:13). The Spirit is also called "the heavenly gift" (Heb 6:4), or quite simply the "gift" that God gave to the apostles at Pentecost (Acts 11:17).

Irenaeus was the first to adopt and make use of this biblical title of the Holy Spirit: "The gift of God was given to the Church, as once the breath was given to the creature newly formed, in order that all the members, partaking of that gift, should be enlivened."[7]

The title "gift of God," however, found its greatest acceptance in Augustine and, following him, in the Latin Church, in the evolving doctrine of the Spirit, which to a large extent was a development of Augustine's work. This appears also in the differences between the Latin and the Greek Fathers; on the Greek side "gift" played a much more modest role as a personal title of the Spirit.

Augustine saw "Gift" as the precise and proper name of the Holy Spirit: the name that expressed the Spirit's relationship with the Father and the Son and that causes us to recognize that the Spirit is a distinct divine person. Neither "Spirit" nor "Holy" can support the same conclusion, for the Father is also "Spirit" and "Holy," and the Son too is "Spirit" and "Holy." The name "Holy Spirit" could also be used of the other two persons; it is given especially to the Third Person of the Trinity because it expresses "the ineffable communion between Father and Son." As Augustine points out, "The relationship itself, however, is not indicated by this name, but it is indicated when we call him the gift of God." It would in fact be possible to call the Holy Spirit "Spirit of the Father" and "Spirit of the Son," but the converse would be quite incorrect: we cannot call the Father "Father of the Spirit" nor the Son "Son of the Spirit." We cannot indicate the reciprocity of the relationship when we use the names Father, Son, and Spirit, but the reciprocity is clear in the terms "Gift" and "Giver." We can in fact call the Holy Spirit "gift of the Giver" (that is, of Father and Son together), and we can also correctly look on either the Father or the Son as "Giver of the gift."[8]

How does all this that is said of the Holy Spirit as gift accord with all that is said of the Spirit as love? This is the answer Saint Thomas Aquinas gives, following Augustine's lead:

[7] Irenaeus, *Against the Heresies*, III.24.1.
[8] Augustine, *The Trinity*, V.11.12; 12.13.

> The first gift we give to someone we love is love itself, which makes us long for the good of that person. Thus it is that love itself is the primary gift, in the strength of which we offer all other gifts that we are able to give. And so it is that from the moment the Holy Spirit proceeds as love, he proceeds as the primary gift.[9]

From all of this it follows that the Holy Spirit, by pouring the love of God into our hearts, infuses into us not only a virtue, even though it is the greatest of all virtues, but pours his very own self into us. The gift of God is the Giver himself. We love God by means of God himself in us.

In this same line of development, insights gained in the theology of gift would lead to significant advances when applied to the doctrine of *grace*. Grace is nothing other than the Holy Spirit who, given to us as gift, is the "new law" written on living hearts, the principle of the new life in us.[10] Sanctifying grace is not merely a "created quality" infused into us, and neither is it merely an uncreated "energy" accorded us; it is the indwelling of the Holy Spirit, himself in person and, with the Holy Spirit, the whole Trinity, in the soul. "Through grace which disposes us to have God in us, the soul is given the uncreated gift of the Holy Spirit himself."[11] This does not exclude the "created" gift, that is, grace understood as a habit or disposition toward God that is distinct from God himself, which readies us for the indwelling of the Holy Spirit and, at the same time, is caused by this indwelling.[12]

2. The Holy Spirit, God's "Gift" and God's "Self-Giving"

This is the rich significance contained in the line that defines the Holy Spirit as "most high gift of God." Rhabanus Maurus uses expressions taken word-for-word from Augustine to explain the title "gift of God." In fact, he calls the Holy Spirit "giver of the gift and gift of the giver," and "ineffable communion of Father

---

[9] Thomas Aquinas, *Summa Theologiae* I, q. 38, a. 2; see Augustine, *The Trinity*, XV.18.32.

[10] See Thomas Aquinas, *Summa Theologiae* I-II, q. 106, a. 1.

[11] Bonaventure, *Breviloquium*, V.1 (Quaracchi, V, p. 253).

[12] See W. Kasper, *Der Gott Jesu Christi* (Mainz, 1982) 279.

and Son." He too says that "gift of God" is the title that "expresses his relationship."[13]

But Tradition and progress did not come to a halt when the hymn was written. The Church does not lose the ability to carry on pondering what is revealed, and to find less and less inadequate ways to express it. What has subsequent reflection been able to bring us concerning the title "gift of God"? I believe that the most recent developments in the theology of the Trinity have laid the groundwork for a more profound understanding of this title. According to the classical Western view, Father, Son, and Spirit are all three gift, but not gift in the same sense. The Father is gift in a purely *active* sense, inasmuch as the Father gives without receiving from anyone; the Son is gift in an *active* and at the same time in a *passive* sense, inasmuch as the Son receives love from the Father and gives it to the Spirit; and the Holy Spirit is gift only in the *passive* sense, inasmuch as the Spirit receives but does not pass on to another person in God what the Spirit has received, and thus the Spirit closes the Trinitarian circle.[14]

This explanation gives rise to a certain reserve today, especially in the dialogue with the Orthodox, because it seems to assign only a passive role to the Holy Spirit in the Trinity and not to recognize any active part that the Spirit might play. The position changes if to the word "gift" we attribute a significance that is not merely static but dynamic, as we must to all concepts regarding the Trinity, because the Trinity is wholly "act." The Father gives to the Son not merely the gift, but his own self-giving (just as he shares with the Son not only his love, but also his infinite capacity for loving). In this self-giving the Holy Spirit is in a certain sense already present.

Hence, within the Trinity the Holy Spirit is not simply gift in a passive sense, as the one that is given, but also, actively, the self-giving that prompts the Son to give himself back to the Father. This paints a picture of what happens in the economy of salvation. It is the Spirit that prompts the Son to cry, in an outburst of joy, "*Abba*, Father!" (Luke 10:21), just as the Spirit will do later in the members of Christ (Rom 8:15f.). Again, it is the Spirit who

---

[13] See Rhabanus Maurus, *On the Universe,* I.3 (PL 111.23–4).
[14] See Richard of Saint Victor, *The Trinity,* V.8 (PL 196.954–5).

gives rise to the determination of Jesus on earth to offer himself as sacrifice to the Father: "Christ, who through the eternal Spirit offered himself without blemish to God" (Heb 9:14).

If what happens in the economy of salvation is a reflection of the life and inmost relationships of the Trinity, all of this must be saying that the Holy Spirit is the very principle of the self-giving; the Spirit is both "gift" and "self-giving" together.

When we come to look at the last two lines of the hymn, we will have occasion to see more clearly what this contributes to our understanding of the inner relationships of the three persons in the Trinity. For the present it is enough that we keep in mind that the Holy Spirit infuses in us not only "the gift of God," but also the ability and the need to give ourselves. From the Spirit we "catch," so to say, the very qualities of what he is in himself. The Spirit is "self-giving," and in whomever he touches, the Spirit creates a dynamism that leads that one, in turn, to be a self-giving gift to others.

"God's love has been poured into our hearts through the Holy Spirit that has been given to us" (Rom 5:5). The word "love" could indicate either God's love for us or the new capacity in us to return God's love and to love our brothers and sisters. It signifies "the love by which we become *lovers* for God."[15] It follows, then, that what the Holy Spirit brings about in us is not only *love* in the substantive sense, but also that *we actively love* God and others in the verbal sense. The very same observation must be made concerning "gift": Coming to us, the Holy Spirit not only brings us the *gift* of God, but also God's *self-giving*. The Holy Spirit is in very truth the fountain of living water that, once received, "wells up to eternal life" (John 4:14), which is to say that it squirts up and splashes onto anyone who happens to be near.

3. Make Yourself Gift

This truth has direct impact on our life. If the Holy Spirit is the one who, so to say, makes the act of self-giving of the Three-in-One God present in our world and prolongs it in our history, it

---

[15] Augustine, *The Spirit and the Letter*, 32.56.

must follow that he is the only one who can help us to make a gift of our own life and live it as a "living sacrifice." This one truth gathers together and sums up the entire scope of the Christian life and purpose; it is, for Saint Paul, the only adequate response to Christ's Passover: "I appeal to you therefore, brothers and sisters, by the mercies of God, to present your bodies as a living sacrifice, holy and acceptable to God, which is your spiritual worship" (Rom 12:1).

The Old Testament laid down that no one was to appear before God "empty-handed."[16] However, the need to make oblation was given expression by means of the offering of things: Offerings were made to God of fruits or animals, external gifts and sacrifices, even though the inward disposition of the giver was considered vital (see 1 Sam 15:22). Jesus brought about a new kind of offering and a new kind of sacrifice: the offering and the sacrifice of self. He went to the Father "not with the blood of goats and calves, but his own blood" (Heb 9:12), offering himself as "a fragrant offering and sacrifice to God" (Eph 5:2). Saint Paul recommends that we should all "try to imitate God" and follow Christ's example in this (see Eph 5:1). God says to every one of us what Paul says to his disciples: "I do not want what is yours but you" (2 Cor 12:14).

It is in this that the whole purpose of the existence of human beings on earth is realized. Why would God have given us the gift of life, if not that we in our turn should have something great and beautiful to offer him as gift in return? Saint Irenaeus writes:

> We make an offering to God, not as to one who needs what we are able to offer, but in order to thank him by means of his very own gifts to us and in so doing to make creation holy. It is not God who has a need for something that we can offer to him, but we ourselves who have a need to offer something to him.[17]

When the moment of our death is upon us, all that will remain to us is what we have given, for in being given it is transformed into something eternal. One of Tagore's poems is about a beggar telling his story:

---

[16] See Exod 23:15; Deut 16:16.
[17] Irenaeus, *Against the Heresies,* IV.18.6.

I had gone a-begging from door to door in the village path, when thy golden chariot appeared in the distance like a gorgeous dream and I wondered who was this King of all kings!

My hopes rose high and methought my evil days were at an end, and I stood waiting for alms to be given unasked and for wealth scattered on all sides in the dust.

The chariot stopped where I stood. Thy glance fell on me and thou camest down with a smile. I felt that the luck of my life had come at last. Then of a sudden thou didst hold out thy right hand and say, "What hast thou to give to me?"

Ah, what a kingly jest was it to open thy palm to a beggar to beg! I was confused and stood undecided, and then from my wallet I slowly took out the least little grain of corn and gave to thee.

But how great my surprise when at the day's end I emptied my bag on the floor to find a least little gram of gold among the poor heap. I bitterly wept and wished that I had had the heart to give thee my all.[18]

Whatever is not given is lost because, as we ourselves must one day die, all that we have clung to, to the very end, will die with us, but what we have given away will escape corruption for it has been sent ahead into eternity.

This holds true for every Christian. In a special way it holds true for people who live consecrated lives. What is the very soul of religious consecration, if not to offer one's life as a gift and a living oblation to God? This is how one of the ancient Fathers explained religious vows:

The Fathers were not content simply to keep the commandments; they also offered gifts to God. Let me tell you how. Christ's commands were given to every Christian, and every Christian is obliged to keep them. One might say that they are like the taxes that we owe to the king. If someone were to say, "I will not pay the king's tax," would he be able to escape punishment? But there are in the world some great and famous people who not only pay their taxes to the king, but who offer him gifts over and above, and they are accorded great honour, great reward and dignity. So too the Fathers: they not only kept the commandments but also offered gifts to God. Virginity and poverty

---

[18] R. Tagore, *Gitanjali*, 50.

are gifts given to God, freely and not out of obligation. For nowhere is it written, "Do not take a wife. Do not beget children."[19]

When speaking of offering one's life as a gift and a living sacrifice, we must be careful not to forget the basic law of sacrifice. In the Christian way there are always two considerations in any gift or sacrifice: to whom is it addressed, and whom will it benefit. The *addressee* is always God and the *beneficiary* is always one's neighbor. Christ "gave himself up for us, as a fragrant offering and a sacrifice to God" (see Eph 5:2). He gave himself "to God," but "for us." We too ought to offer our life to God, but for the sake of the brethren (see 1 John 3:16).

God has no need of our gifts and sacrifices. It is possible for us to offer our life to God and to renew the offering every morning, and to live all the time in the expectation that God would come and take to himself what we have offered, even perhaps in a special way, like martyrdom. All, however, to no avail: God accepts our offering as genuine, and sends a needy brother to "take delivery" of the gift we have promised, but that is what we least expect and we do not recognize the needy one at all.

We ourselves are not, however, in a position to make a gift of our life to God for our brothers and sisters, unless we have the special help of the Holy Spirit. Jesus, as we have seen, offered himself to the Father "in the eternal Spirit" or *"cooperante Sancto Spiritu"*—with the cooperation of the Holy Spirit—as one of the ancient prayers of the Mass expresses it. Neither can his members offer themselves in any way but that. This is the reason why the liturgy insists on this very aspect, when it invokes the Holy Spirit on the assembly after the Consecration: "May he make us an everlasting gift to you."[20]

Christ has given us the Mass as a way that provides every believer with the opportunity to offer himself or herself to the Father in union with him. Jesus, lifted up on the cross, "draws us all to himself" (see John 12:32) not in the sense of a general attraction of glances and drawing of hearts to him, but in the sense that he unites us most intimately with himself in his very own offering, so that we all together make one single offering with him. We are like the drops of water

---

[19] Dorotheus of Gaza, *Instructions,* 1.11–12 (SCh 92, p. 164).
[20] *Roman Missal,* Eucharistic Prayer III.

that become indistinguishably one with the wine in the chalice and are consecrated to become the one cup, one unique drink of salvation. That way, the humble offering that we make of ourselves is given an immense value. A very simple way to give ourselves a real sense of participation in all of this is to repeat aloud with the celebrant, or at least in our heart, the doxology at the end of the Eucharistic Prayer, savoring the full meaning of each word: "Through him, with him, in him, in the unity of the Holy Spirit, all glory and honor are yours, Almighty Father, forever and ever. Amen."

4. The Holy Spirit Gives New Life to the Mutual Self-Giving of Husband and Wife

All that we have said about the Holy Spirit as gift takes on a very special importance for those who are married. Marriage is a state of life that occupies a singularly important place in the great processes of creation, "creatures flowing forth from God" and then "creatures returning to God." For that reason, the Holy Spirit occupies a very special place in marriage.

What makes a marriage a marriage is the reciprocal self-giving of the spouses, the gift of their bodies to each other that, in biblical language, means the gift of their whole selves. And so it is that, as analogously in any act of donation, the one who has given is no longer master or owner of what is given. It is no longer the husband who has sole ownership of his own body, but his wife, and vice-versa (see 1 Cor 7:4). John Paul II, in one of his Wednesday catecheses, said:

> The sexual nature of the human body, in its masculinity and femininity, is not only the root of fruitfulness and procreation as in all the rest of the order of nature, but from the very beginning has implied that special attribute of partners in marriage which is to express love: that love precisely by which human persons become gift, and by means of this gift, give actuality to the very purpose of their essence and existence.[21]

As the sacrament of gift, marriage is by its very nature open to the action of the Holy Spirit. How does the Holy Spirit sanctify

---

[21] John Paul II, *Catechesis,* 16 January 1980, in *Insegnamenti di Giovanni Paolo II* (Libreria Editrice Vaticana, 1980) 148.

marriage? Not from the outside, but from within the marriage itself, in the very inmost core and essence of marriage that is the self-giving of the spouses, as we have just seen. It is the sanctifying presence of the Holy Spirit that makes marriage a sacrament. The Holy Spirit, who as the "Creator Spirit" is active in every human couple through the desire for each other, is active in every Christian couple also as the "Redeemer Spirit," the Spirit of grace, expressing himself in the generous self-giving of the spouses which is the likeness of the mutual self-giving of Christ and his Church (see Eph 5:32).

Thus, the Holy Spirit is intimately present not only in the "celebration" or the rite of marriage, but also in the living and continuing reality of the marriage. The Spirit is present not only at the moment when the marriage is contracted, but in every moment and every gesture of mutual self-giving of the spouses, and therefore in a very special way in the conjugal act which is the most intense realization of mutual self-giving. In ancient times there were some who, influenced by the Rabbinical prescriptions regarding ritual purity, wanted to prevent married people from approaching the sacraments after conjugal intimacy, assuming that in such moments the Holy Spirit could not be present to them. A canonical source contains a very forceful rejection of this view and practice: "Through baptism the spouses receive the Holy Spirit, who is ever with those that work righteousness, and does not depart from them by reason of natural issues and the intercourse of marriage, but is ever and always with those who possess Him, and keeps them."[22]

If we look now to what Tradition can show us, in the light of these developments, we find them very strongly confirmed. The theologians of the Latin Church were well aware of this very close link between the Holy Spirit and conjugal love, although they developed it in only one direction. They started from the *symbol*—human conjugal love—in order to illustrate the *reality*, that is, the Holy Spirit. Saint Hilary, for a start, drew the connection between the two concepts of "gift" and "enjoyment" and wrote: "Immensity is realised in the Father, manifestation in the Son, and enjoyment [*fruitio*] in the Holy Spirit."[23] Augustine took up this intuitive insight and developed it:

---

[22] *The Didascalia*, XXVI, ed. R. H. Connolly (Oxford, 1969) 242.
[23] Hilary of Poitiers, *The Trinity*, II.1 (CC 62, p. 38).

> The ineffable embrace of the Father and the Likeness is not without fruition, without love, without joy. In the Trinity, all that delight, pleasure, happiness, beatitude—if only we had a human word able to express these things—that Hilary has called "fruition," is the Holy Spirit who is not generated but who is the sweetness savoured by the One who generates and the One who is generated, and who in his immensely abundant generosity floods out into all creatures according to their capacity, to preserve them in their order and to bring them back in their proper place.[24]

The implication of this wonderful text is that whatever delight and joy there is on the face of the earth is nothing else but a kind of echo, or the shining glow, of the Trinity's embrace. After this, it became quite usual for Latin writers to speak of the Holy Spirit in images reflecting the relationship of spouses: embrace and kiss. Saint Ambrose writes that "in the kiss, there is more than just the contact of lips; there is the desire of each to share their very breath with the other."[25] And Saint Bernard exclaims, "What is the Holy Spirit if not the mutual kiss of Father and Son?"[26] As to the embrace, a medieval author comments:

> This mutual delight, this sweet love, this happy embrace, this beatifying love through which the Father rests in the Son and the Son in the Father; I say, this rest that nothing can disturb, this incomparable goodness, this inseparable unity, this making of two one only, this finding again of self in that one unity; everything that we can say that is good and joyous and sweet; all of that is the Holy Spirit.[27]

This symbolism, as we can see, has been used only as leading from the symbol to the reality, inasmuch as it attempts to throw light on the person of the Holy Spirit, taking as its starting point the nuptial gestures of the embrace and the kiss. But it is possible to follow the line in the other direction too, taking as starting

---

[24] Augustine, *The Trinity,* VI.10.11.

[25] Ambrose, *On Isaac and the Soul,* 3.8 (CSEL 32, p. 648).

[26] Bernard of Clairvaux, *Various Sermons,* 89, ed. Cistercense, VI.1, p. 336; see Isaac of Stella, *Sermons,* 45.12 (SCh 339, p. 104).

[27] Aelred of Rievaulx, *Mirror of Charity,* I.20.57 (CM 1, p. 36).

point the Holy Spirit, gift of God, in order to throw light on the profound significance of human conjugal love. The author just quoted on the matter of the divine embrace called it happiness, love, rest, sweetness, full satisfaction, perfect coming together in unity. But is that not exactly what spouses desire with all their heart, when they come together in true love for each other?

The carnal embrace, of itself, is totally unable to achieve any of this, as the poet Lucretius was able to show in terms that were crude but nonetheless quite efficacious.[28] It is only when this dark, aggressive, and possessive kind of loving is raised up to become love in self-giving (and this is the very thing that the Holy Spirit comes to teach) that intimacy between spouses can be the realization of that sweet unity in peace that is a pale reflection on earth of the divine embrace in the Holy Spirit.

The Holy Spirit, as gift of God, provides the basis for a theology of "pleasure" that, at least in principle, can set human experience of this kind free of the weight of ambiguity that presses upon it today. The pagan poet Lucretius, to whom we have just referred, made note of a characteristic of every kind of pleasure, and especially of carnal pleasure: "Something of bitterness springs up at the heart of every delight / and sows anxiety among its flowers."[29]

Pleasure and pain follow one another in human experience, joined like the links in an iron chain. But in the light of the Trinity, pleasure comes to us as the inseparable companion of gift and therefore, as long as we live this life, as the companion of the sacrifice that gift implies. In that light, pleasure *follows* suffering as its *fruit;* it does not come before suffering as its *cause;* hence pleasure has the last word, not suffering or anxiety. The joy that comes in the reciprocal self-giving of spouses should be of this kind, a small reflection of the joy shared in the Trinity, where the Holy Spirit is "the enjoyment in the gift."

What I have tried to outline here is not just a pretty theory of marriage. In this case too experience has preceded theory, and it is theory's most valid confirmation. The Holy Spirit, who makes all things new, has shown that he knows how to make marriage new

---

[28] Lucretius, *De rerum natura,* IV.1104ff.

[29] Ibid., IV.1129–30.

too, marred as it often is by weakness and by sin. One of the most visible fruits of the coming of the Spirit is the revival of dead or dried-up marriages. Matrimony, says Saint Paul, is a charism (1 Cor 7:7) and, as with all the charisms, it is fired up anew by contact with the flame from which it comes. It is important to listen to living testimonies, because they speak more clearly than any reasoned argument. First, one from a husband:

> My wife and I recognize that the Holy Spirit is the soul of our marriage; it is he, that is, who gives our marriage life, in exactly the same way as he is the soul of the Church. When we became engaged, we promised each other that we would pray the Pentecost sequence together every day, "Come, Holy Spirit," and for twenty-two years, with very few exceptions, we have tried every day to do that, and we hope to continue to do so until death separates us.

For her part, the wife has this to say:

> For me, the moment of conjugal intimacy is not different, as a moment of following the Spirit, from any other moment in our lives. In our life as a couple it has become natural to pass from moments of intimacy to conversation, from prayer to silence; there is no break between one and the other. Instead of considering certain moments, for example the Sunday Mass, "for God," and other moments, for example our sexual intimacy, "for us," all is for God, and we do it all freely and deliberately in his presence. The Holy Spirit is not only the source of the tendernesses we show each other when it is "time for embracing"; he is also the one who helps us grow in mutual love when it is "time to refrain from embracing" (Qoh 3:5), especially now when we are by no means as young as we used to be.

There is a wealth of hope for Christian couples in this kind of meditation on the Holy Spirit as "most high gift of God." Not only for some, like the couple quoted, but for all couples. The times we live in, human impoverishment, and above all the inability to love tend to reduce spouses and their marriage to "dry bones." It is to them, therefore, that God addresses his promise in a very special way: "O dry bones [withered hearts in withered marriages!], hear the word of the Lord. I will put my Spirit within you, and you shall live" (Ezek 37:4, 14). The Holy Spirit wants to repeat for every couple the miracle of the wedding at Cana: the Spirit wants to transform the water into wine; the water of routine, of lowered expectations, of coldness, into the heady wine of newness and of joy. Important to know, the Spirit *is* the new wine.

However, the most important thing that the Holy Spirit teaches Christian spouses is not how they can realize the full the value of their marriage, but rather, how to transcend it. "All that passes is only a symbol"; it is only in heaven that "the unattainable becomes reality."[30] Marriage is in point of fact one of the things that is passing: "The present form of this world is passing away" (1 Cor 7:31). It would be a huge mistake to make marriage an absolute upon which one depends and against which one measures the success or the failure of one's very life. If this is what we are doing, we are overloading marriage with demands that it cannot possibly meet and therefore condemning it to inevitable failure. It is only in God that complete togetherness, perfect unity, utter self-giving, "the unattainable," will become reality, and remain reality forever.

Let us entrust to the Holy Spirit all human couples, confident of the Spirit's ability to lead them to a renewal of their mutual self-giving. Let us do this in the words of a hymn that is sometimes sung in the Anglican Church when marriages are blessed:

> *The voice that breathed o'er Eden*
> *that earliest wedding day,*
> *the primal marriage blessing,*
> *it hath not passed away.*
> *Be present, Holiest Spirit,*
> *to bless them as they kneel,*
> *as thou for Christ the Bridegroom*
> *the heavenly spouse dost seal.*[31]

---

[30] W. Goethe, *Faust,* Part 2, Finale.

[31] *Hymns Ancient and Modern* (London, 1924) hymn 350, by J. Keble, pp. 286–7.

VI

Living Water

The Holy Spirit communicates the divine life to us

God is revealed to us in two ways: by means of things and by means of words, in creation and in the Bible. Saint Augustine says that these are like two books:

> Let your book be the divine page to which you ought to listen; let your book be the universe that you ought to observe. Only those who know how to read and write can read the pages of Scripture, while everyone, including the unlettered, can read out of the book of the universe.[1]

There is no question of there being two "books," separate and distinct and without connection, because the Bible itself very often listens to and reflects the voice of things, interpreting it and using it as a vehicle for its own more explicit revelations.

In the voice of creation we have a kind of primordial and universal sacrament. "Join the word to the element and you have a sacrament," says Saint Augustine.[2] For instance, join the formula of baptism to the pouring of water and you have the sacrament of baptism, or join the words of consecration to the bread and the wine and you have the sacrament of the Eucharist. In a wider sense the same applies to all the elements of creation. In this way, the entire universe is "sacrament." What makes the seven sacraments different is that they are channels of the grace of God, while created things are a means by which we come to *knowledge* of God. Contemplating the works of creation, we are able to come only to an intellectual appreciation of the invisible perfections of God (see Rom 1:20).

"Signs are those things that, besides the impression they make on the senses, evoke in the mind a notion of something other than

---

[1] Augustine, *Exposition on the Psalms,* 45.7 (CC 38, pp. 522).

[2] Augustine, *Commentary on the Gospel of John,* 80.3.

themselves."[3] The efficacy of a sign in conveying knowledge is based upon the psychology of knowledge itself. In the passage from the symbol to the signified reality, the soul is lit up and inflamed, like a torch in motion. As long as we remain fixed on things and material signs, nothing happens, no light illumines the soul. It is the same when the intellect lingers on invisible and abstract things. But in *the passing* from one to the other, in the movement and the thrust, the soul is set aflame and hidden meanings are disclosed to the mind.[4]

I started out with these observations, because the Bible uses material things to speak of spiritual realities, and applies this principle above all in opening up to us that greatest of all "spiritual" realities which is the Holy Spirit. It has, so to say, enlisted the service of the simplest and most common of things to speak to us of the Spirit of God: wind, water, light, fire, oil, new wine. Three of these classical symbols of the Holy Spirit are listed in the verse of the *Veni Creator* that we are looking at now. The verse calls on the Holy Spirit first as living water *(fons vivus)*, next as fire *(ignis)*, and then finally as ointment *(spiritalis unctio)*. We have already studied the course on the Pneuma in the school of "Brother Wind" when we were speaking of the name of the Spirit. We are now invited to do the same in the schools of "Sister Water," "Brother Fire," and "Precious Ointment." In this, as on every other point, we will see that our hymn is a most faithful mirror of the biblical revelation on the Holy Spirit.

1. Water, Life, and the Spirit

If we can say, by analogy, that the whole of creation is sacrament, that is, sign of God, we can also see that certain elements of creation have become sacramental signs of the Holy Spirit also in a stricter sense: water in baptism as a sign of rebirth in the Spirit; oil and chrism in confirmation as signs of the Spirit anointing. Water, then, is more than a mere symbol of the Spirit; it is an efficacious sign of the Spirit: it not only calls the Spirit to mind, but renders the Spirit present and active.

---

[3] Augustine, *On Christian Doctrine,* 2.1 (CSEL 80, p. 33).
[4] See Augustine, *Letters,* 55.11.21 (CSEL 34.2, p. 192).

From what source is the title of the Holy Spirit, "living fountain," derived, and what does it signify? The author of the hymn tells us, in another of his writings:

> The Holy Spirit was called water in the Gospel itself, in the passage where the Lord cries out, "If any man is thirsty, let him come to me. Let the man come and drink, who believes in me! As Scripture says, from his breast shall flow fountains of living water." And the evangelist immediately explains what he meant, adding, "He was speaking of the Spirit which those who believed in him were to receive" (John 7:37-39). But the water we use in the sacrament is one thing, and the water that is the Holy Spirit is something else. The former is a visible kind of water, the latter, invisible; visible water washing the body is a sign of what happens in the soul, but the Holy Spirit washes and nourishes the soul directly.[5]

As usual, the patristic Tradition, and in this case particularly Saint Ambrose, provide the link that connects Scripture and our hymn:

> By *fountain,* we do not mean the kind of water that was created, but the source-fountain of divine grace, that is, the Holy Spirit: it is he who is the living water . . . . So it follows that the Holy Spirit is a river, and how great and strongly-flowing a river . . . . If a river rises above its banks, it floods. How much more the Holy Spirit, who stands higher than all creatures . . . . The fountain of life, then, is the Holy Spirit himself.[6]

What, then, is the exact meaning of the expression *fons vivus,* living fountain, in our hymn? In the first place it has the meaning of "living water" (fountain here stands for water, as the container for the contained), and also the meaning of "fountain of life." This is how a medieval writer paraphrased the expression we find in our hymn: "He is at the same time fountain of life, living fountain, fountain that enlivens, fountain that wells up from life itself and fountain that gives life to those to whom it comes."[7]

---

[5] Rhabanus Maurus, *On the Universe,* I.3 (PL 111.25); see Isidore of Seville, *Etymologies,* VII.3.27 (PL 82.270).

[6] Ambrose, *On the Holy Spirit,* I.153–60; see Hilary of Poitiers, *Treatise on the Psalms,* 64.14–15 (CSEL 22, pp. 245–6).

[7] Walter of Saint Victor, *Sermons on the Holy Spirit,* 8 (CM 30, p. 69).

Three linked pairs are interwoven in this symbolism: the association water/life; the association water/Spirit, and the association Spirit/life. In passing from the level of the first of these to the third, the meaning of the word "life" changes, or perhaps we should say it becomes loaded with new significance: It moves from indicating only natural and physical life to indicating also the life of the spirit.

The association *water/life* is so universal and so widely used that there is no need to explain it. It is a particularly telling association in a culture such as that of the Bible which developed on the edge of the desert, in a region where the dependence of animal and plant life on rain was a matter of daily experience. One of the ancient Fathers asked, "Why do we use the word water to indicate the grace of the Holy Spirit?" He goes on to answer, "Because water is a necessary element in the make-up of all things: whether we talk of animal life or plant life, it is water that gives rise to life."[8] In this symbolic role water very soon came to be associated in the Bible with the Spirit of God: "For I will pour out water on the thirsty land . . . . I will pour my Spirit upon your descendants" (Isa 44:3).

The association *water/Spirit* is present, implicitly, in every reference to the Spirit making use of terms like "pouring" (see Joel 3:1; Zech 12:10), "flowing," or "washing," and in expressions like "baptize in the Spirit"[9] and "born again of water and the Spirit," not to mention the expressions recalled earlier in which Jesus refers to the Spirit using the image of "living water" and "fountains of living water."

This symbolism finds its culmination in John's Gospel. John sees the water that issued from Christ's pierced side as a sign and associates it with the gift of the Spirit given by Christ on the cross (see 1 John 5:6-8). In doing this, he is tacitly saying that it is to Christ that Ezekiel's grand vision applies—the vision of the water flowing from the temple, causing life to flourish wherever it flows until finally it runs into the Dead Sea and transforms it into a sea teeming with life (Ezek 47:1ff.). In fact, for the evangelist, Christ on the cross is the new and definitive "temple" of God (John 2:19)

---

[8] Cyril of Jerusalem, *Catecheses,* XVI.12.
[9] See Matt 3:11; Acts 1:5.

and the water flowing from his side is the fulfillment of the promise of "fountains of living water." The Holy Spirit is that "river of the water of life, flowing from the throne of God and of the Lamb," on whose banks flourish the trees of life that, like the trees in Ezekiel's prophecy, "bear fresh fruit every month," the leaves of which are medicinal.[10]

The Holy Spirit is therefore the water that flows from the Redeemer, which transforms the face of the desert of this life, and flows finally into the great "Dead Sea" that is this world of sin and into the little "dead seas" which are all the human beings in need of grace, transforming them all into places full of life.

At a certain point in the New Testament we notice that the symbol of water has disappeared, and only the reality symbolized remains, which is life. And so we have the third association, *Spirit/life,* without any intermediary: "It is the spirit that gives life . . . . The words that I have spoken to you are spirit and life" (John 6:63). "The law of the Spirit of life in Christ Jesus has set you free from the law of sin and of death" (Rom 8:2). "The letter kills, but the Spirit gives life" (2 Cor 3:6).

At the Council of Constantinople in 381, when the Fathers needed to sum up their belief in the Holy Spirit in a short phrase that would be added into the Nicene Creed, they found no more essential or more important thing to say about the Spirit than this: that the Spirit gives life, that the Spirit is a "life-giving Spirit": "I believe in the Holy Spirit, Lord and giver of life."

The Bible gives us a whole series of interventions by the Spirit of God, and times when the Spirit was present, that trace out a kind of "history of the Spirit" within the history of salvation. Every time we come to a point where there is a "leap forward" in the quality of life, we find the Holy Spirit there at work producing it.

> The breath of the Spirit
> came upon Adam at the creation and he became a "living being";
> It came upon the Virgin at the Incarnation, and the Savior started living in her.
> It came upon Jesus in the Resurrection and made of him a "Spirit, giver of life."
> It came upon the apostles at Pentecost, and the Church came into being.

[10] See Rev 22:1-2; Ezek 47:12.

It comes upon the waters of baptism, and human beings are born
to a new life.

It comes upon the bread and the wine in the Eucharist, and they
are changed into the Body and Blood of Christ.

It will come upon us at the end of time, and "give life to our
mortal bodies."

In the Latin tradition, the prerogative of the Spirit to give life is
expressed in the adjective *almus.* *"Alme Spiritus"* is one of the
titles of the Paraclete that Medieval authors preferred to use; we
find it in many hymns, including some by the author of the *Veni
Creator,* perhaps more often than "Holy Spirit."[11] *Almus* comes
from *alere;* it means generous, abundant, friendly, nourishing,
life-sustaining. At times it was used of the earth *(alma tellus),* of
the sun, of mothers *(alma mater),* and in every instance we see
that it is associated with life. John Paul II entitled his encyclical
on the Holy Spirit *"Dominum et vivificantem,"* words taken from
the Creed, where the Holy Spirit is proclaimed "Lord and giver of
life." In it he proclaims the Spirit, "The one who gives life, the
one in whom the inscrutable God who is One and Three communicates himself to humankind, establishing in us the wellspring of
eternal life."[12]

2. What Life?

But now it is time to ask ourselves about what kind of life are
we speaking when we say that the Spirit gives life. The faith of
the Church has never had any hesitation or doubt in answering
this question. We are talking of divine life, that is to say, the life
that has its source in God the Father, which in Christ "was made
visible" (1 John 1:2) and in baptism is given to the believer. Between this life and the natural life that we have from our human
birth there is no *real* opposition (both come from God who is the
absolute master of all life, physical as well as spiritual); yet the
two are diverse and in contrast on the *moral* level, as we see in the

---

[11] See Arator, *On the Acts of the Apostles,* I.226 (CSEL 72, p. 25); Rhabanus
Maurus (PL 112.1596C); Adam of Victor (AHMA 54, p. 239); Rupert of Deutz
(CM 29, p. 380).

[12] John Paul II, *Dominum et vivificantem,* n. 1.

well-known antitheses: nature/grace, flesh/Spirit, old life/new life, earthly life/eternal life.

The *diversity* is due to the fact that this new life according to the Spirit is the fruit of a new intervention by God, different from the creation; the *contrast* is due to the fact that sin has caused natural life to be closed in, "bent back" upon itself, and so of itself resistant to receiving the life that is according to the Spirit.

The reason for the contrast, however, is not found only in human sin, that is, in an event that came about in the course of history. Its roots are sunk deep in the very composition of human nature which is made up of two elements, one material and the other immaterial, one tending to carry it toward multiplicity and the other tending toward unity. There is no need whatever to think (as some Gnostics, Manicheans, and many others have thought) that these two elements derive from two rival "Creators," a good one who created the soul and an evil one who created all things material, the body included. The one and only God created both together, in a profound, "substantial" unity. He did not, however, create human nature to remain static, as if human beings should be content to remain in this intermediate position, the two forces within them nicely counterbalancing and canceling each other out. On the contrary, God created human beings so that in the actual exercise of their own freedom, each should decide freely in which direction to develop and come to self-realization: either "upward," toward that which is "above" them, or "downward," toward that which is "beneath" them. "The soul finds itself between these two things: at times it follows that Spirit, and thanks to the Spirit, is able to fly; and at times it obeys the flesh, and falls into desiring earthly things."[13]

Human dignity lies precisely in this ability to choose and determine one's individual goal freely. One of the philosophers of the Renaissance said that it was as if God, by creating humans as free beings, was saying to them:

> I have put you halfway in the universe, so that you may best perceive what there is in you. I have not made you beings of heaven only or of earth, nor mortal or immortal, because you by yourselves, like free master-builders, will mould and sculpture

---

[13] Irenaeus, *Against the Heresies,* V.9.1.

> yourselves according to the pattern you have chosen. You could degenerate and become something inferior, a mere animal; you could, if you will, regenerate yourself and become something higher than yourself, divine.[14]

This explains the struggle between flesh and spirit and hence the dramatic quality that characterizes a Christian's existence in the world. If "to choose is to renounce," it is not possible to choose to live according to the Spirit without sacrificing something of life according to the flesh.

> Those who live according to the flesh set their minds on the things of the flesh, but those who live according to the Spirit set their minds on the things of the Spirit. To set the mind on the flesh is death, but to set the mind on the Spirit is life and peace. For this reason the mind that is set on the flesh is hostile to God; it does not submit to God's law—indeed it cannot, and those who are in the flesh cannot please God (Rom 8:5-8).

The contrast between the two ways of living eventually emerges as the contrast between life and death. "If you do *live* according to the flesh, you will *die;* but if by the Spirit you put to death the deeds of the body, you will live" (Rom 8:13).

The relationship between death in the flesh and life in the Spirit is not to be understood as a relationship in the order of time: We need first to die to the flesh, and to ourselves, in order next to experience the new life and resurrection. Rather, it is a relationship of simultaneity and of cause and effect. It is in the very act of dying to the flesh that one experiences and grows in the new life of the Spirit; it is in the measure of one's conformity to the crucified Christ that one shares in the life of the risen Christ, while we are awaiting that ultimate outcome when there will no longer be any contrast.

This is not a question of sacrificing one of the elements of human nature in order to save the other, but of preserving both. The flesh itself cannot be saved except through the spirit, as long as the spirit itself is saved. In her *Dialogue Between the Soul and the Body,* Saint Catherine of Genoa shows how it is simply not

---

[14] G. Pico della Mirandola, *On the Dignity of Man,* ed. Tognon (Brescia, 1987) 4–6.

possible to satisfy all the demands of the body and all the demands of the soul at the same time. Either the body will enslave the soul for the sake of its bodily goals, or the soul will subject the body for the sake of its spiritual goals. In this dialogue the soul says to the body: If you do what I tell you, we will both be saved eternally, but if I do what you want, we will both be lost for ever.[15]

This contrast provides the basis for all asceticism which, for that matter, is not a specifically Christian thing, but in various forms is found in all great religions, almost without exception. Whatever the case, it is unfair to lay at Augustine's door the "blame" for what came to be called "hatred of the body" because that (if one can speak of it as "hatred") was there in full measure in the Christianity of the East, starting with the Desert Fathers, quite apart from Augustine or any influence he may have had.

It cannot be denied that asceticism was at times taken to excess. But one saint like Francis of Assisi is enough to show how "mortification" and the most radical forms of renunciation can accord very well with a tremendous love of life and for things, and with ecstatic delight in God's creatures.

3. Supernatural Life, or Natural Super-Life?

In the course of the late nineteenth and early twentieth centuries something changed in the significance given to this aspect of Christian life, following the emergence of a philosophy that exalted the notion of vitalism. In various forms, this philosophy was the central message of biological evolutionists like Darwin, of the positivists, of the historicists, of the pragmatists and of the intuitionists like Bergson with his seductive theory of the *"élan vital."* But it was Nietzsche who made a religion of this vitalism. He put forward the theory of a superior form of well-being as the essential means by which the course of history, as he conceived it, would be realized. He spoke of Christians as "tuberculotic of soul, no sooner born than they begin to die, following their doctrines of weariness and resignation."[16] In the introduction to her edition of

[15] Catherine of Genoa, *Spiritual Dialogue,* 40, in *Opere,* II, Marietti (Genoa, 1990) 54.

[16] F. Nietzsche, *The Gay Science,* n. 382; *Thus Spoke Zarathustra,* I (Of the Preachers of Death).

her brother's works, Nietzsche's sister gives this summary of his thought on this point:

> He supposes that, because of the resentment of a weak and fallacious Christianity, everything that is beautiful, strong, proud and powerful—like the virtues that arise out of strength—would have been rejected and forbidden, and that, for that reason, the power of those things to promote and elevate life would have been greatly diminished. But it is now time for a new scale of values to be held up to mankind, values of strength and power and man the magnificent, until its most exalted point is reached, that of the superman, and proposed to us with driving passion as the purpose of our life and will and hope. . . . This new and wholly different scale of values . . . should hold before us a model, vigorous, healthy, eager for life, an apotheosis of life.[17]

In place of the Christian idea of supernatural life this substitutes a notion of a natural super-life; in place of the new man this proposes a superman. Quality has been turned into quantity. Life holds only the potential of a linear evolution in intensity and "power," but not of any qualitative leap. In the light of these developments, there seems to be a prophetic quality in the words written by Kierkegaard some decades earlier:

> There is nothing to which man clings more than he clings to life; there is nothing for which he yearns with greater intensity and force than to feel the pulsation of life within himself, and there is nothing that makes him shudder more than death! But see what an enlivening Spirit has to tell us here. Let us then cling to him: who would hesitate? Let him give us life, abundant life, and may the feeling of being alive seethe in me, as if life in all its entirety were contained within my breast. . . . But this enlivening that the Spirit brings is not a direct sublimation of the natural life of man in an uninterrupted continuity and coherence. . . . It is a new life, in the strict sense of *new* life. In fact, you have only to make sure that death intervenes here, that you mortify yourself, and a life that, from another aspect is death, is most certainly a new life.[18]

---

[17] F. Nietzsche, *Also sprach Zarathustra* (Lipsia, 1919).

[18] S. Kierkegaard, *For Self-Examination,* III, First Day of Pentecost (Samlede Vaerker, XIII, pp. 337ff.).

Nietzsche's thought has to some extent been taken up by certain theologians and given rise to a new way of understanding what is meant by "life-giving" Spirit. In place of the traditional notion of *spirituality,* they propose that we substitute the idea of *vitality,* understanding that to mean "love of that life that makes humankind one with all other living beings," a vitality taken to be "true humanity."[19]

Our hymn, in the title "Creator," also evokes a universal action of the Holy Spirit, also beyond the confines of the Church. But, as we have seen, the hymn draws a clear distinction between the two ways in which the Spirit acts: as "Creator" Spirit and as Spirit "of grace." In the view we have just been considering, between the two spheres of the Spirit's action there is a difference more of degree than of quality. Every trace has disappeared of that almost infinite distinction that Pascal places between the three "orders" of life: material, intellectual, and spiritual.[20]

The new interpretation of "Spirit of life" arises from the desire to find a theological foundation for the effort to come to the defense of life, especially life that is seen as weak, "impeded," and threatened. This divorces it radically from Nietzscherian vitalism which, on the contrary, is expressly conceived as propagating the notions of the strong, the *Übermensch,* of superior well-being. I believe, however, that this very worthy effort can find no better foundation than in the traditional perspective, drawing its inspiration from the biblical principal of death to self as engendering life for others. Paul expressed it all when he wrote of the tribulations of the apostolic mission: "So death is at work in us, but life in you" (2 Cor 4:12).

Mortification should never be an end in itself; it should always serve the purpose of promoting life in others, whether physical life or spiritual life. The ultimate model here is Christ, who died in order to give life to the world, and gave up his own joy in living so that others might know joy to the full.[21] Truly "spiritual" Christians are those who have followed Christ in this. Often those who are most rigid in their asceticism, imposing the strictest discipline on their own body, are the very ones who are most ready to reach out and alleviate the physical sufferings of their brothers and sisters,

---

[19] J. Moltmann, *Der Geist des Lebens* (München, 1991) 95–101.

[20] B. Pascal, *Pensées,* 793, ed. Brunschvicg.

[21] See Heb 12:2; Rom 15:3, John 15:11.

whatever form those sufferings might take: disablement, sickness, hunger, leprosy. . . . No one has ever shown greater respect for life than they, or done more to assist and defend it. And finally, experience shows that no one is able to say "yes" to a brother or sister in need without being ready to say "no" to self.

The two lives engendered by the Spirit—the natural and the supernatural—are therefore never to be separated one from the other, and still less opposed to one another, but neither must they be confounded and put on the same level. It is the Spirit who gives and enlivens life in all of its manifestations, natural or supernatural, but each in its own order. The Spirit promotes natural life, making it an apt recipient of the form for which God intended it, which is "conformity" to Christ. He supports physical life in everything that ennobles human beings and orients them toward their eternal end, and he "mortifies" physical life in everything that stands in the way of their achieving that end.

To deny the radical "newness" of the life of the Spirit would mean to eliminate any relevance of the coming of Jesus Christ. Life in Christ, or in the New Adam, would not be any different in kind from life in the old Adam. It would mean also that we would have to accept that the life-engendering work of the Spirit would be heading for a checkmate, doomed to failure, because we know very well where our "vitality" on the natural level will lead us: to death. The ultimate success of the Spirit is founded on the possibility that decline and death on the natural level can be "raised up" and transformed into success on another level. The apostle writes: "So we do not lose heart. Even though our outer nature is wasting away, our inner nature is being renewed day by day" (2 Cor 4:16).

4. The Life of the Spirit

Now all that the reading of certain texts of the New Testament will tell us about the Spirit "who gives life" will afford us a better understanding of what we have seen so far. Paul writes: "There is therefore now no condemnation for those who are in Christ Jesus. For the law of the Spirit of life in Christ Jesus has set you free from the law of sin and of death" (Rom 8:1-2).

Let us leave aside for the present the theme of the "new law," as we will be considering it at another time. The principal point that we gather from the text is this: The Spirit is the Spirit of life, and the life that the Spirit gives is none other than life in Christ, the life that flows from his paschal mystery. To live according to the Spirit therefore means to have a share in the very life of Christ, to share Christ's own inward dispositions, to be "of one spirit" with him (1 Cor 6:17). For all practical purposes, to be or to live "in the Spirit" is the same as to be or to live "in Christ."

The same basic juxtaposition appears in another form in Paul, when he writes, "The letter kills, but the Spirit gives life" (2 Cor 3:6). In this light the Holy Spirit stands out as the very principle of the new covenant, the Christian norm, and the power of Christian living, source of a new life and a new activity that derives directly from the work of Christ.

Turning to John we find the same link between the Spirit and life, and between the life of the Spirit and the work of Christ. For John too the "fountains of living water" of the Spirit spring forth from Christ's glorified body. The paschal mystery and the Incarnation, however, are placed differently within the relationship to Christ which is common to both. The life that the Spirit confers is basically the life of the Father, the Trinitarian life, that in the Incarnation "was made visible" (1 John 1:2). The entry of eternal life into the world was already accomplished in the coming of the Word "in whom was life" (John 1:4). Jesus himself is "the life" (John 14:6). Just as he lives by the Father, so those who depend for nourishment on him will live by him (see John 6:57). For John the cross and the Passover are not so much the moment in which this new life first comes into being, but rather the moment in which sin, the obstacle preventing human beings from receiving this life, is removed. In this sense John could say that "there was no Spirit as yet, because Jesus had not yet been glorified" (John 7:39).

Although from different approaches with different emphases, John and Paul both present the life of the Spirit as one and the same with the divine life that, in Christ, is offered to humankind as a new possibility. New not only because it had not existed before, but also because it is of a totally different kind: divine, not human; eternal, not temporal.

Seen from the viewpoint of the one who receives it, the life of the Spirit is *voluntary,* received freely, and in this quite different from natural life, in receiving which the recipient has no option. No one can decide whether to be born or not, but everyone is free to decide whether to be reborn or not. In fact, the new life presupposes the act of faith; one comes to the new life "through sanctification by the Spirit and through belief in the truth" (2 Thess 2:13). There is thus a sense in which faith makes us our own parent.

How does one actually enter into this new life? By two means: the Word and the sacraments. The words of Jesus are "Spirit and life" (John 6:63). The Word is not only "inspired" by the Holy Spirit, it also "breathes" the Holy Spirit, inspires the Holy Spirit into those who receive it. Without the Holy Spirit it is a dead letter, but with the Holy Spirit it gives life (see 2 Cor 3:6). It is a fact of experience: Read the Scriptures "spiritually," that is, in the light of the Holy Spirit and under the Spirit's anointing, and you find them bursting with light and comfort and hope; in a word, with life.

And alongside of the Word, the sacraments. In baptism we are reborn in the Spirit (John 3:5); it is the moment when we begin to "live a new life" (Rom 6:4). But baptism is not only the *beginning* of the new life; it is also its model, its *form*. In the very way in which the original and basic rite of baptism is carried out, that is, by immersing into and rising out of the water, baptism indicates a burial and resurrection, a dying and coming to life again. Saint Basil writes:

> Regeneration, as the very word indicates, is the beginning of a second life. But, to begin a second life, it is necessary to lay down the first. . . . The Lord, in offering and giving us life, has entered with us into the covenant of baptism, figure of death and of life: the water provides the image of death, and the Spirit provides the input of life.[22]

Cyril of Jerusalem says, in a poetical way, to the newly-baptized: "The saving water was both tomb and mother to you."[23]

The life inaugurated in baptism is a life that nourishes itself on death. It is a dying in order to live: exactly the contrary of natural life, which is by definition, inescapably, living-for-death.[24] On the

---

[22] Basil the Great, *On the Holy Spirit*, XV.35 (PG 32.129A).

[23] Cyril of Jerusalem, *Mystagogical Catecheses*, II.4 (PG 33.1080).

[24] M. Heidegger, *Being and Time*, II.1.51.

natural level, every second of a lifetime is a second closer to death; it is space subtracted from life and added to death. On the supernatural level, every little mortification of the flesh is transformed into life according to the Spirit; it is space subtracted from death and added to life.

5. Water the Thirsty Soil

Now, to apply what we have seen in a practical way, let's call again to our help the symbol of "Sister Water." Water is something that always runs down, never up. It is always trying to find the lowest place. So it is with the Holy Spirit: the Spirit loves to visit and fill the lowly, the humble, those who know their own emptiness. Francis of Assisi, in his *Canticle of Brother Sun,* makes water a symbol of humility: "Praised be You, my Lord, through Sister Water, / who is very useful and humble and precious and chaste."[25]

One of the most disquieting phenomena of the physical world in our time is the creeping menace of desertification. Scientists calculate that hundreds of thousands of hectares of arable ground are engulfed every year by encroaching desert. The absence of vegetation causes the precipitation of atmospheric water vapor to diminish, and the lower precipitation causes the remaining vegetation to disappear. The cycle is "mortal."

From the time of Isaiah, people have understood that the same sort of thing can happen on the spiritual level. In other words, there is also a desertification of the heart, and the Holy Spirit is the only one who can turn the process around and transform spiritual desert into a place of life:

> I will pour out water on the thirsty land,
> and streams on the dry ground.
> I will pour my Spirit upon your descendants (Isa 44:3).

John's image of fountains of living water flowing from Christ (John 7:38) also fits into this symbolism of dryness and thirst. Saint Irenaeus writes: "As the dry ground, if it receives no water, will not bear crops, neither will we . . . ever bear the fruit of life without the rain that falls generously from above."[26]

---

[25] Francis of Assisi, *Canticle of Brother Sun* (ED, I, p. 114).
[26] Irenaeus, *Against the Heresies,* III.17.2.

Tauler used the example of a real river, the Rhine (he lived all his life on its banks), to illustrate what Saint Ambrose had said in the passage we quoted earlier, about the "strong-flowing stream" that gives joy to the City of God:

> This precious Holy Spirit has entered into the disciples and into all who are open to him, bringing well-being, abundance and plenty in such measure as inwardly to submerge them. It is as though the Rhine were to be dammed up and its floodgates opened, so that it fills every valley and every low-lying place. In such a way the Holy Spirit came down on the disciples and on all who are open to him. And so he continues to do even today, without ceasing. He fills and floods the depths of our souls and hearts and minds, every place he finds. He fills them with great well-being, with grace and love and gifts beyond telling. He fills the valleys and the depths that are open to him.[27]

The last few words suggest a practical program we might follow: Open the canals and the valleys to the Holy Spirit. In one of the earliest hymns to the Trinity the Father is called "spring," the Son "stream," and the Holy Spirit "watering."[28] The same image was the inspiration for the beautiful prayer in the Sequence for Pentecost: *riga quod est aridum,* "water what is dry."

Sometimes one will see, on a farm where an irrigation channel follows the upper contour of a sloping field, people hurrying to open up little furrows, little channels, to lead the water little by little into every planted row and to every little seedling. It is a happy kind of work, especially in summertime. It is the kind of work that makes people sing while they are doing it, and everyone can take part in it, even the little children. It is an image of what needs to be done in the vineyard of the Lord. Trace out a little furrow to lead the water of the word of God, or faith or praise or consolation, to someone: the water of the Spirit. We need not merely trace out these furrows; we can become ourselves channels of the Spirit to others.

Let us conclude with the words of a hymn to the Holy Spirit written a few years after the *Veni Creator,* which sings of the mystical connection between water and the Holy Spirit:

---

[27] Johannes Tauler, *Predigten,* 25, vol. 1 (Einsiedeln, 1987) 170.

[28] Marius Victorinus, *Hymns to the Trinity,* 3.30–4 (CSEL 83.1, p. 295): *"Fons, Flumen, Irrigatio: o beata Trinitas!"*

When God by his Word created
the great rolling engine of earth,
you hovered, oh Spirit, o' er the water
sending forth rays of your warmth.
Keep making fruitful the water
that makes holy the soul in rebirth.
Breathe on us now, Holy Spirit:
make us live by the life in your breath.[29]

---

[29] Notker Balbulus, *Hymn of Pentecost* (PL 131.1013).

VII

Fire

*The Holy Spirit frees us from sin
and from lukewarm half-heartedness*

1. He Will Baptize You with the Holy Spirit and Fire

After wind and water, fire *(ignis)* is another natural phenomenon that takes its turn as a symbol of the Holy Spirit. The Scriptures readily make use of antinomies, that is, of opposites, to speak to us of divine realities. Jesus is called lion but also lamb. It is not surprising, then, that two symbols that are themselves diametrically opposed, water and fire, should both be used to refer to the Holy Spirit. Opposites, because they stand at the extremes, have the advantage of creating a limitless space between them and opening up our horizons to the infinite, and this is exactly what we need if we are to speak of divine realities.

In this case the contrast is invested with a significance that is more profound than usual. Water engenders life; fire destroys it. Placing the two symbols together, one after the other, the author of the hymn reinforces the teaching we have already seen in the symbol of living water: the Spirit indeed creates new life, but does this by putting the old life to death. The Spirit, at the same time, both creates and destroys, breaks down and builds up. So it is that in the *Veni Creator* we cannot isolate the title "living water" from the title "fire" that follows it without compromising our understanding of what the hymn is telling us.

As always, the words of the *Veni Creator* lead us back to the Bible as it is read and as it is lived in Tradition. We see right away where the Holy Spirit is represented as fire, or at least associated with fire, in the New Testament. Speaking of Christ, John the Baptist says: "He will baptize you with the Holy Spirit and fire" (Matt 3:11). (In this text itself note the contrast between water—"he will *baptize* you"—and fire.) This promise finds its visible and external fulfillment in Pentecost: "Divided tongues, as of fire, appeared among them . . . . All of them were filled with the Holy Spirit" (Acts 2:3-4).

The words of Jesus, too, "I have come to bring fire to the earth," refer to the giving of the Holy Spirit, or at the very least they include it. Paul also implicitly compares the Holy Spirit to fire when he tells us not to "quench" the Spirit (1 Thess 5:19).

If we want really to grasp the message, we need to discover what was symbolized by fire in the Bible. We will see that it has many meanings, some positive, some negative. Fire gives light, as was the case with the pillar of fire in Exodus. Fire warms, it sets alight, it destroys enemies, it is the eternal punishment of the wicked . . . .

But of all the meanings attached to fire, one is singled out and stands out above the rest: Fire purifies. Water also often symbolizes purification, but there is a significant difference that the Bible often brings out in bold relief: "Gold, silver, bronze, iron, tin, and lead—everything that can withstand fire, shall be passed through fire, and it shall be clean. . . . Whatever cannot withstand fire, shall be passed through the water" (Num 31:22).

Fire symbolizes a deeper, more radical purification. Water washes the surface, the outside; fire cleanses through and through. The Psalmist sings, "Prove me, O Lord, and try me; test in fire my heart and my mind" (see Ps 26:2). Precious things—gold among material things, faith in the realm of the spirit—are tested by fire (see 1 Pet 1:7). Hence the imagery of the crucible, the smelter's furnace: "I will smelt away your dross as with lye and remove all your alloy" (Isa 1:25).

The idea and the symbolism of purifying fire are found especially in the texts that foretell the work of the Messiah who is to come. "I will put this third into the fire, refine them as one refines silver, and test them as gold is tested" (Zech 13:9). "But who can endure the day of his coming, and who can stand when he appears? For he is like a refiner's fire and like fuller's soap; he will sit as a refiner and purifier of silver" (Mal 3:2-3).

In this light we ought to understand what is meant when God is called a "devouring fire." The holiness of God and his absolute simplicity will tolerate no compromise, no admixture of any kind, but will strip all evil naked and burn it away. Only the one who rejects every last trace of evil can live with this devouring fire, can exist in everlasting flame (see Isa 33:14). In a certain sense, the title "fire" does nothing more than explain the meaning of the adjective "holy" as we use it along with the noun "Spirit" in naming the Holy Spirit. The Spirit is *fire* because the Spirit is *holy.*

I have said that the *Veni Creator* gathers together and sums up the biblical revelation of the Spirit as it has come to us through the Tradition of the Church. A few texts will show just how faithfully the Bible's teaching has been received and experienced in the Church. Saint Cyril of Jerusalem writes that at Pentecost the apostles received "the fire that burns away the thorns of sin and gives glory to the soul."[1] Speaking of the glowing coal that cleansed Isaiah's lips, Ambrose writes: "This fire was a figure of the Holy Spirit who was to come down after the Lord's ascension, to forgive the faithful all their sins and as with fire to inflame their souls and minds."[2]

There is an ancient responsory that used to be recited in the Office for Pentecost. It reads: "There came on them a divine fire, not burning but enlightening, not consuming but causing to glow; it found the disciples' hearts pure receptacles, and it filled them with the gifts of its charisms."[3]

How can it be said that this fire does not *consume,* if it is written that our God is a consuming fire? A medieval author answers, "This divine fire does consume the thorns and the knots of vice and the corruption of sin; it does not consume, but rather purifies, our nature."[4]

One of the great poets of our own time has summed up this tradition of the creative and destructive fire of Pentecost:

> The Dove descending breaks the air
> with flame of incandescent terror
> of which the tongues declare
> the only hope, or else despair
> lies in the choice of pyre or pyre
> to be redeemed from fire by fire.[5]

[1] See Cyril of Jerusalem, *Catecheses,* XVII.15; cf. Origen, *Homilies on Exodus,* VII.8 (SCh 16, p. 183).

[2] Ambrose, *On Duties,* III.18.103 (PL 16.174).

[3] Response at Matins for Pentecost: *"Advenit ignis divinus, non comburens sed illuminans, nec consumens sed lucens, et invenit corda discipulorum receptacula munda, et tribuit eis carismatum dona."*

[4] Walter of Saint Victor, *Sermons,* III.1–2 (CM 30, pp. 27–8).

[5] T. S. Eliot, *Four Quartets,* in *The Complete Poems and Plays* (London: Faber & Faber, 1990) 196.

We "choose" to pass through the redeeming fire in order not to have to undergo, one day, the consuming fire of judgment. Our reflection on the Spirit as fire will be a kind of penitential liturgy, a paschal exodus from sin, under the inward guidance of the Holy Spirit. As usual, we will look first at the biblical and theological principles, and then at how we may apply them in a practical way.

2. The Holy Spirit Is the Remission of All Sins

At this point, "Brother Fire" also has carried out his duty and is ready to stand back. He has raised our minds to the spiritual reality that he symbolizes. The reality is this: The Holy Spirit is the one who carries out the work of purification on us from deep within our inmost being. He is the one who melts our stony-hard heart, who destroys "this body of sin" (Rom 6:6) and re-moulds us in the image of God.

This has been the Church's conviction from its very earliest beginnings, and it comes to the fore in all kinds of situations. An ancient variation of the text of the Our Father, in place of "your kingdom come," has "let your Holy Spirit come upon us and purify us."[6] In one of the liturgical prayers of reconciliation used in the Syriac Church, the priest prays these words of absolution over the penitent: "May the Lord, by the inrushing of the Holy Spirit, destroy and utterly wipe out of your soul every fault, every blasphemy and every kind of injustice by which your soul has been made unclean."[7]

So we see that the Holy Spirit forgives sin; moreover, the Spirit *is* the remission of sin! An ancient liturgical prayer expresses it this way: "We pray you, Lord, may your Holy Spirit make healthy and whole again our souls through the divine sacraments, because he himself is the remission of all sins."[8]

The boldness of this statement finds its inspiration in Saint Ambrose who taught that, in the forgiveness of sins, "human beings perform a ministry, but do not exercise any power of their own, because it is by the Holy Spirit that all sins are forgiven."[9] The au-

---

[6] See Gregory of Nyssa, *On the Lord's Prayer,* 3 (PG 44.1157D).

[7] In PS 43, p. 452; quoted in E.-P. Siman, *L'experience de l'Esprit par l'Eglise, d'apres la tradition Syrienne d'Antioche* (Paris: Beauchesne, 1971) 121.

[8] *Roman Missal,* Tuesday after Pentecost.

[9] Ambrose, *On the Holy Spirit,* III.137.

thor of the *Veni Creator* was fully aware of all this liturgical and theological background because he too states that "sins are not forgiven without the Holy Spirit."[10]

Here, again, Church Tradition has done no more than take and bring to light a truth that was present all along in the Scripture. According to the New Testament, in fact, the action of the Holy Spirit is seen to be precisely at the very heart of the work of justification from sin. Paul affirms this again and again: "For through the Spirit, by faith, we eagerly wait for the hope of righteousness" (Gal 5:5). "You were washed, you were sanctified, you were *justified* in the name of the Lord Jesus Christ and in the *Spirit* of our God" (1 Cor 6:11).

On Pentecost day Peter said, "Repent, and be baptized every one of you in the name of Jesus Christ so that your sins may be forgiven; and you will receive the gift of the Holy Spirit" (Acts 2:38). This does not mean that first there should be the forgiving of sins and only after that, the giving of the Holy Spirit. It means that in the forgiveness of sins the Holy Spirit is involved, from the very first moment, as *agent* (the forgiver), and, forgiveness given, the Holy Spirit is there also as *gift* (possession, indwelling). Our mind thinks of two moments, first forgiveness, then giving the gift, but in fact there is but one moment; the two are simultaneous. The Acts of the Apostles prefers to attribute to Jesus himself the act of forgiving sins but this was always understood in the light of the general principle of the Scriptures, that *everything* is done for us and given to us *by* the Father, *through* Christ, *in* the Holy Spirit.

The Holy Spirit, therefore, is not merely the effect of justification, but also its cause. Saint Basil writes, "Purification from sin comes in the grace of the Holy Spirit."[11] Augustine drew the following conclusion: "The love that is poured into our hearts by the Holy Spirit is its very self the forgiveness of sins."[12]

The forgiving of our sins and the infusion of grace into our hearts are not two operations, one taking place after the other, but one unique action, although we look at it from two different aspects.

---

[10] See Isidore of Seville, *Etymologies*, VII.3.17 (PL 82.269); Rhabanus Maurus, *On the Universe*, I.3 (PL 111.25).

[11] Basil, *On the Holy Spirit*, XIX.49 (PG 32.157A).

[12] Augustine, *Commentary on the Gospel of John*, 121.4.

In cleansing us from sin, the Holy Spirit is not one who comes along once the job has been done; it is the Spirit who actually cleanses us. In any case, how would it ever be possible to carry out a work as infinitely great as the forgiveness of sin, if God himself is not the one who carries it out? Sin is "annihilated," done away with entirely. This is possible only to the creative power of God, working, so to speak, in reverse: not a creation of something out of nothing, but an obliteration of what was once there so that nothing remains (and this annihilation, just as the act of creation, is something that only God can do). The sins of humankind are not merely "covered" or "not imputed" or "ignored" by God. They are truly done away with, destroyed, cancelled. If we look into the most intimate depths of our heart, the sanctuary of God's dwelling, it is simply not possible that we should find there, at one and the same time, both sin and grace, both death and life. Two masters, the spirit of evil and the Holy Spirit, cannot share that sacred place. The Messalians, a heretical sect active from late in the fourth century, as Diadochus of Photike recalls, "imagined that in the baptised were hidden together, in the intellect, both grace and sin, that is, the Spirit of truth and also the spirit of error." But that cannot be. Rather,

> Before a person comes to be baptised, grace is at work, from without, encouraging the soul towards the good, while Satan is at work, from within. After baptism, the contrary is the case. Grace works from within and the demons from without. These continue their work, and work even more evilly than before, but not as present together with grace. The only way they can work is through the promptings of the flesh.[13]

It follows that, when Jesus gave the Holy Spirit to the apostles in the supper room (John 20:22-23), he did not merely give to the Church a juridical "competence" or external empowerment, a simple "authorization" to go and forgive sins; rather, he gave the Church a real power, a power intrinsic to its very being as Church, and that power is the Holy Spirit. The Church, then, has the power to forgive sins, but only in the sense that the Church has the Holy Spirit who has the power to forgive sins. As Saint Ambrose points

---

[13] Diadochus of Photike, *On Spiritual Perfection,* 76 (SCh 5, p. 134). See also Augustine, *On the First Letter of John,* 4.1 (PL 35.2005).

out, when the Church forgives sins, she is not exercising a power, but only carrying out a ministry, though a ministry which cannot lightly be bypassed by the sinner:

> In fact, the Church *cannot* forgive any sin without Christ, and Christ *does not intend* to forgive any sin without the Church; the Church *cannot* forgive a sinner unless that person is repentant, which is to say, unless Christ by his grace has touched that person; and Christ *does not intend* to hold anyone forgiven who scorns the ministry of the Church.[14]

We should have an understanding of the Church that is very different from the way the world sees it. The Church is the furnace where the Spirit "burns" in order to destroy sin—a kind of "incinerator" always alight, always at work to do away with the refuse of the soul and to keep the city of God clean. There is a hidden hearth, with welcome fire burning, in the inner privacy of our home which is the Church, and blessed are those who know where to find it and who make a habit of staying close to it, until it becomes their heart's favorite spot, to which they hurry back every time they feel burdened by guilt and in need of a fresh breath of life.

3. A Penitential Pathway with the Holy Spirit

We have looked at the theological foundations. It is time for us to draw the practical implications we can apply in our own life. How is it possible to pass through this fire that purifies and creates anew? Fire affects the one who touches it, not someone who talks about it or who merely listens to someone talking about it. There was a time, once, when surgery was nearly all a matter of cauterizing. Doctors in days gone by would treat a wound or a diseased part of the body with fire, that is, by burning it with a red-hot iron. We still have the prayer that Saint Francis of Assisi prayed to "Brother Fire" when the healers told him that his eyes needed to be treated in that kind of way.

> My brother Fire, your beauty is the envy of all creatures, the Most High created you strong, beautiful and useful. Be gracious to me in this hour; be courteous! For a long time I have

[14] Isaac of Stella, *Sermons,* 11.14 (SCh 130, p. 246).

> loved you in the Lord. I pray the Great Lord who created you to
> temper now your heat that I may bear your gentle burning.[15]

We might make this prayer our own when the need is upon us
to face, and persevere through, some kind of spiritual "cure by
fire" for the good of our own soul. The Holy Spirit is a "gentle
cautery."[16] The Bible gives us a description in the book of Isaiah
of this kind of "fire-treatment":

> Then one of the seraphs flew to me, holding a live coal that had
> been taken from the altar with a pair of tongs. The seraph
> touched my mouth with it and said: "Now that this has touched
> your lips, your guilt has departed and your sin is blotted out"
> (Isa 6:6-7).

To whatever extent it is possible for us, we ought to make Isaiah's
experience our own, allowing God to do for us what he did for his
prophet.

For God, the elimination of sin is the simplest of things and it
takes only an instant, but in us it is a complicated matter and takes
the form of a process. It takes place in a number of stages that we
can list in order:

> The Holy Spirit:
> knocks at our conscience through remorse,
> opens up our conscience through confession,
> enters in through repentance,
> sets us free through absolution,
> transforms us by justification,
> inflames us with his own fervor.

Let us try to say something about each of these stages. The process of detachment from sin begins with *remorse*. Remorse is something that works like a nagging thought, a worm that will not die
(see Mark 9:48). One of the great spiritual teachers of the Orthodox
Church has called it "poison in the belly."[17] When we have been
guilty of a transgression, it will not allow us any false sense of
peace. The Bible is full of stories of great remorse. Remorse like

---

[15] Thomas of Celano, *Second Life,* 125 (ED, II, p. 355).
[16] John of the Cross, *Living Flame of Love,* B.2.1–2.
[17] See Simeon, the New Theologian, *Catecheses,* XXIII (SCh 113, p. 15).

Cain's or like David's; remorse such as Peter felt, or remorse like Judas's. These examples, however, make it clear that remorse itself is something ambiguous; it can lead to salvation or to despair.

The great works of literature give us similar examples. Macbeth felt remorse: he had murdered his king and several of the king's key men ("Methinks I heard a voice cry, 'Sleep no more!' Macbeth does murder sleep!").[18] Or there is remorse like that of the hero of Dostoevsky's *Crime and Punishment*. In the first case, remorse leads to despair and punishment, and in the other, to confession and redemption. Yet perhaps no one has described the transition from remorse to repentance with greater insight than Manzoni, in one of his characters. Suddenly he sees his past life and his crimes in a new and fearsome light; he attempts in vain to quell remorse and go back to his habitual ways of thinking; hope flashes in him that there could be a way out; and finally the tears of joy come to him as he repents and resolves to confess his crimes and begin a new life.[19]

These days remorse does not exactly enjoy "a good press." There has been a long and sustained effort, even on the part of certain philosophers, to devalue it, presenting it as "a useless burden, autosuggestion, a vain attempt to obliterate the past." All remorse is explained as a guilt-complex induced by external influences, by culture or by society, and therefore sick. This line of reasoning has helped us (and so doing has served a good purpose) to understand more clearly the difference between genuine remorse for the wrong that we have done, and the false feelings of remorse and the sense of guilt that are among the great afflictions of humankind. But all this dismissal of the value of remorse has not been able to change the widespread view that continues to look upon remorse as one of the strongest signs of the natural morality of conscience and, indirectly, of the existence of God. A contemporary author writes: "Do you know what led me to God? I can tell you in one short phrase: what we call the objection to evil. That is what led me, as you lead a little child by the hand." What he means is this. Through the millions of years of its existence on earth, humanity has learned how to get used to anything

---

[18] W. Shakespeare, *Macbeth,* act 2, scene 2.
[19] See A. Manzoni, *The Betrothed,* ch. XXI.

at all, to become immune to everything, even to the germs that cause plagues. But not to evil. Human beings continue to sense that evil is evil, and it makes them remorseful. There is no explanation for this, unless there really is a determinant of what is good: that is, unless God exists. Without God, we would long since have lost any awareness of evil.[20]

When it is genuine, therefore, remorse is a first, though still imperfect, manifestation of the Holy Spirit. For how would it be possible to experience anything like an acute sense of evil and of sin, otherwise than in the presence of the holiness of God? Our conscience is like a built-in receiver within us, letting us hear the voice of the Spirit. "It is simply not possible that anyone should accuse himself or feel displeased with himself except by the gift of the Holy Spirit."[21]

It follows, therefore, that by prompting the "accusation" and giving rise to the "conviction" of sin, the Holy Spirit must already be at work in a person who feels remorse. Remorse is like a spiritual inflammation, a kind of fever, indicating an altered state of the conscience caused by the presence in it of a "foreign body." It is clear, then, that to try to get rid of the sense of guilt and the feeling of remorse without dealing with their root cause is no less futile than to try to cool down a fever without making any effort to find out what kind of sickness is causing it. Fever is simply a providential sign that a person is unhealthy in some way. The effort to do away with the sense of remorse could well be no more than a systematic effort by modern culture to "quench the Spirit."

It was necessary to speak out in defense of remorse, because it is important that we should not gradually become so accustomed to evil that we lose the capacity to react to it. The instinctive distaste for evil is in fact one of humankind's most ennobling features. Remorse can be a powerful ally in our daily struggle against evil and against sin. For remorse is not something that arises only in the context of egregious crimes; it is concerned also with our daily peccadilloes. The Spirit uses remorse just as a father or mother teaches a little child and helps it to grow: with smiles, praise, and encouragement, but also, when appropriate, with frowns and disapproval.

[20] C. Còccioli, *Il cielo e la terra* (Heaven and Earth) (Florence: Vallecchi, 1950) 290.

[21] Augustine, *Commentary on the Psalms,* 50.16 (CC 38, pp. 611–2).

Little by little we need to grow more sensitive to these calls of the Spirit, coming to us through the voice of conscience. We need to take even the little stirrings of remorse quite seriously; for example, remembering that we forgot to pray, spoke unkindly of another, behaved unlovingly toward a poor person, that our words fell a little short of the straightforward truth, or that we dwelt with unhealthy curiosity on something we should not have been looking at. And we need, above all, to learn to act on any and every stirring of remorse and turn it promptly into repentance.

4. From Remorse to the Joy of Being Forgiven

There is a Psalm that tells of the transition from the heavy, burdened silence of remorse to the liberating confession of guilt:

> While I kept silence, my body wasted away
> through my groaning all day long.
> For day and night your hand was heavy upon me;
> my strength was dried up as by the heat of summer.
> Then I acknowledged my sin to you,
> and I did not hide my iniquity;
> I said, "I will confess my transgressions to the Lord,"
> and you forgave the guilt of my sin (Ps 32:3-5).

When we actually take notice of remorse, it leads to *confession* and to the joy of pardon. The Psalm just cited begins like this: "Happy are those whose transgression is forgiven, / whose sin is blotted out." By confession, the soul opens itself to the Spirit and becomes united with the Spirit. Think of a city that has been under siege, whose people can at last open their defenses and rush out to meet the liberating army.

It is certain that confession is something that itself needs always to be renewed. Confession can so easily degenerate into a legalistic rigmarole, but we need to keep it what it is meant to be: a personal meeting with the risen Christ who for one reason only looks forward to your coming and your confession—simply to restore to you the joy of being saved. One way to make this experience real is to avoid all the stereotypes and schemes imposed from without or taught to us when we were little children, and each time to single out what has been the real trouble, that is, what is evil "in his eyes" and not as we see it or as the world would have us judge. The criterion by which to discern healthy remorse and distinguish it from a false sense of guilt is simply this: Healthy remorse is caused by something that is evil "in the sight of God," and false guilt is caused by things considered evil only by social convention or in the worldly view.

Yet even the most perfect confession is sterile and will not "open" the conscience to the Spirit if there is no sense of *compunction,* no *repentance.* Judas confessed his sin; he said, "I have sinned by betraying innocent blood" (Matt 27:4). But though he confessed there was no real repentance in his attitude and no hope of being forgiven, and so his confession did him no good whatsoever.

The story of Pentecost is the very best illustration of how the Holy Spirit moves us to compunction and works through that. There is first of all the horrendous accusation, "You killed Jesus of Nazareth!" The three thousand hearing Peter's words "were *cut to the heart,*" and they said, "What must we do, brothers?" (Acts 2:23ff.). What was it that was taking place in them, in their very depths? The Holy Spirit was at work, "convincing the world of sin" (see John 16:8), exactly as Jesus had promised. By the action of the Holy Spirit, those people understood that if Jesus had died because of the sins of the world, and if they themselves had ever committed a sin, they had crucified Jesus, even if they personally had not been the ones to hammer the nails that day on Calvary.

Genuine compunction is not a mere matter of feeling sorry or regretting something that has been done; it is infinitely more than that. Genuine compunction means to begin to see sin against the backdrop of God the Father's infinite love and Christ's death on the cross. True compunction is in fact to see sin as God sees it, to judge as God judges. The climax of the *Miserere* comes when the psalmist, already repentant, says to God, "You are justified in your sentence / and blameless when you pass judgment" (Ps 51:4). The sinner takes responsibility for the evil that has been done, proclaims that God is not to blame. By genuine compunction, we reestablish in ourselves and in the things around us the truth that was kept imprisoned in wickedness (see Rom 1:18). Saint Simeon—called the New Theologian in reference to Gregory Nazianzen, the theologian par excellence in the Orthodox tradition—writes:

Even if one has a heart harder than bronze or iron or diamond, as soon as *compunction* enters, it becomes soft as wax. Compunction is the divine fire that melts mountains and rocks, that sweetly softens every hardness, that everywhere changes and totally transforms the souls that welcome it into a paradise. . . . All of that is brought about by the divine fire of compunction, along with tears, or let us rather say, by means of tears.[22]

When the three thousand asked Peter, "What should we do?" he answered, "Repent" (Acts 2:38). It is in repentance that the encounter takes place between grace and freedom. Human freedom freely puts itself in line with grace, and this achievement is the most delicate of all the works of the Holy Spirit.

The fact that you are not pleased with what you have done is the result of a gift of the Holy Spirit . . . . Though you are still pleading for pardon, nevertheless because you yourself do not like the evil you have done, you are already united to God, because you have come to dislike what displeases him. You are both at work to cure your fever: you yourself, and the doctor too.[23]

There are two keys to the human heart: God has one, we have the other. Neither can open the heart without the other. God in his omnipotence can do all things, with one exception: God cannot make a human heart humble and contrite alone. It is a mystery, but for this God needs our repentance. God cannot "repent" in a person's place. This is why, throughout the Bible, we find that "a humble and contrite heart" is the place of rest, a kind of paradise on earth, the place to which God feels most drawn (see Isa 66:1-2). We human beings cannot offer God any sacrifice more pleasing, more acceptable to God, than a contrite heart (Ps 51:19). And what is there to stop us burning with desire to have God find, every time God visits us, this secret place, this place of rest, that God loves so much?

From repentance we pass to absolution and to justification. It is in repentance that, strictly speaking, the part we humans can play ends and the part that belongs exclusively to God begins. In Psalm 51, the *Miserere,* there is a point at which the tone of the prayer suddenly changes. Up to that point it was all about guilt, evil, and sin. From that point on it is all about a new heart, the Holy Spirit,

[22] Simeon, the New Theologian, *Catecheses,* IV (SCh 96, pp. 348–9).

[23] Augustine, *Commentary on the Psalms,* 50.16 (CC 38, p. 611).

and the joy of being saved. From the reign of sin we pass to the kingdom of grace. The psalm speaks of a new creation, with the Holy Spirit at its center; it is all about the Spirit and the Spirit is its whole aim. "God, create a clean heart in me" is not saying anything different from "Do not deprive me of your Holy Spirit."

The Church only carries out a ministry; it is the Holy Spirit that transforms the sinner and makes the sinner justified. The ritual of reconciliation very rightly has us pray, before the words of sacramental absolution, "May God, Father of mercies, who has reconciled the world to himself in the death and Resurrection of Christ, and has *poured out the Holy Spirit for the remission of sins,* grant you, *through the ministry of the Church,* pardon and peace."

God is really doing a new thing. "There is a new creation: everything old has passed away; see, everything has become new!" (2 Cor 5:17). Justification, say the Fathers of the Church, is the Holy Spirit re-moulding us, recasting us, in the image of God.[24] Of all the characteristics that the Holy Spirit shares with fire, this is surely the most sublime. In this re-moulding, the Holy Spirit takes us back to our primordial beginnings and at the same time anticipates our final state, when "all manner of things shall be well." Quoting this well-known saying of the English mystic Julian of Norwich, and linking the ardent hope and conviction it expresses with the fire of Pentecost, the poet we quoted earlier in this chapter writes:

> And all shall be well and
> all manner of things shall be well
> when the tongues of flame are all in-folded
> into the crowned knot of fire
> and the fire and the rose are one.[25]

5. Afire with the Spirit

From the point of repentance onward, the Spirit continues to work as fire; however, not as fire that purifies and melts down, but as fire that warms and sets aflame. These two effects are almost always mentioned together when we read of fire in the Bible or in

---

[24] Cyril of Alexandria, *Commentary on the Gospel of John,* XI.10 (PG 74.541D); see also John of Damascus, *Orthodox Faith,* 4.9 (PG 94.1121A).

[25] Eliot, *Four Quartets,* 198; see Julian of Norwich, *Revelations,* ch. 27.

spiritual literature. Augustine says that Scripture uses the symbol of the dove to express *simplicity* and the symbol of fire to express *fervor*.[26] This teaching is taken up in the liturgy, where it has us say in the Mass of Pentecost, "Come, Holy Spirit, fill the hearts of your faithful and kindle in them the fire of your love,"[27] and also in the Sequence, "warm the chill."

In Syriac, the text of Genesis 1:2 is translated in the sense that the Spirit of the Lord brooded upon the waters to warm them. Taking his cue from this interpretation, common to many authors,[28] Saint Ephraem the Syrian wrote a hymn, as profoundly insightful as it is poetical, on the special capacity of the Spirit to bring warmth and fecundity, to melt the "ice of sin" that makes the soul frigid and stiff:

> It is thanks to warmth that all things ripen;
> and it is thanks to the Spirit that all is made holy:
> so clear a symbol!
> As warmth overcomes the chill of the body
> so does the Spirit overcome the impurities of the heart.
> As at the first signs of springtime warmth, baby animals begin to dance,
> so the disciples, when the Holy Spirit comes upon them.
> Wintertime stumps and branches hold flowers, fruits imprisoned;
> spring warmth breaks them open.
> Thanks to the Holy Spirit, the yoke of the evil one is broken,
> the yoke that kept grace from blossoming forth.
> As warmth brings summer again to the bosom of sleeping earth,
> so the Holy Spirit works upon the Church.[29]

Saint John of the Cross, too, speaks of the two effects of *The Flame of Divine Love:* it cleanses the soul and endows us with strength, liveliness, and ardor for God.[30] The Spirit does not merely purify us of sin, but continues to act in us in order to enable

[26] Augustine, *Commentary on the Gospel of John,* 6.3.

[27] Alleluia verse, Pentecost Sunday: *"Veni, Sancte Spiritus, reple tuorum corda fidelium et tui amoris in eis ignem accende."*

[28] See Luther, *On Genesis* (WA 42, p. 8); see also Basil the Great, *Hexaemeron,* II.1 (SCh 26, p. 142); Paschasius Radbertus, *Commentary on Matthew,* X (CM 56B, p. 1144).

[29] Ephraem Syrus, *Hymn to Faith,* 74 (CSCO, Script. Syri 73.1955, p. 195).

[30] John of the Cross, *Living Flame of Love,* B.I.3.

us to be "ardent in spirit" (Rom 12:11). The Spirit goes to work like fire when it attacks damp wood: First it causes all the dampness, all the impurities, to come hissing noisily out, and all the while it continues to heat up the wood until, eventually, the wood is transformed into fire itself, glowing and aflame.

Applied to our life this means that it is the Holy Spirit that keeps us from falling back, from growing cold again, and if it happens that we have in fact fallen, or are busy falling, growing lukewarm, it is the Holy Spirit who sets us free from that. If we have grown cold in the spiritual sense, we cannot escape from it without a new and decisive intervention of the Holy Spirit. We see it in the life of the apostles. Before Pentecost they were hardly fervent. They could not manage to stay awake even for an hour. They tended to be concerned about which of them was the most important. Danger filled them with fear. But once the tongues of fire had come upon them, they were not like that at all. From that moment onward they were the very image of zeal itself, full of courage, full of fervor. Fiery in preaching, in praising God, in setting up and organizing the churches, and eventually in giving their life for Christ. A medieval author has written:

> The Paraclete, who in tongues of fire came down on the apostles
>   and the believers
> comes on us like fire too:
> to burn out of us and destroy all guilt,
> to purify what is natural,
> to strengthen us in grace and bring that grace to perfection,
> to drive out the laziness that is ours because we are so lukewarm,
> and to kindle in us the fire of his love.[31]

Some say: The remedy for tepidity is fervor, but that is like saying that health is the remedy for sickness. It ignores the fact that the sick person's problem is, precisely, the lack of health. No, the remedy for lukewarmness is not fervor, but the Holy Spirit. Fervor is the *opposite* of lukewarmness, not its *remedy*.

Yet this itself is actually cause for hope. If it seems to us that we have all the symptoms of this "dark disease" of the spiritual life, lukewarmness, and we feel worn out, cold, disinterested, apa-

---

[31] Hermann of Runa, *Sermons for Feast Days*, 31 (CM 64, p. 132).

thetic, dissatisfied with God and with ourselves, there is a remedy and it is infallible: we need a good, healthy Pentecost! With the help of grace it is possible to rise up out of our half-heartedness. There are great saints who, as they themselves tell, became full of fervor after a prolonged time of lukewarmness.[32]

As we come to the end of this chapter, this is what we need to ask of the Holy Spirit, upon whom we have been pondering, so to say, in the glow of fire. There is a hymn in the Methodist Church that gives us just the words to do it:

> *Oh, that in me the sacred fire*
> *Might now begin to glow,*
> *Burn up the dross of base desire,*
> *And make the mountains flow!*
>
> *Oh, that it now from heaven might fall,*
> *And all my sins consume!*
> *Come, Holy Ghost, for thee I call,*
> *Spirit of burning, come!*
>
> *Refining fire, go through my heart,*
> *Illuminate my soul;*
> *Scatter thy life through every part,*
> *And sanctify the whole.*[33]

---

[32] See Teresa of Avila, *Autobiography,* 8.2.

[33] J. and C. Wesley, *Selected Writings and Hymns* (New York: Paulist Press, 1981) 224.

VIII

Love

The Holy Spirit leads us to experience the love of God

1. New Wine in New Wineskins!

In this chapter we meet the Holy Spirit in the profoundest and most personal depths of the Spirit's reality and work. The natural symbols—wind, water, fire—are here no longer adequate, and we pass from the world of nature to the world of human experience. When we speak of God, all the terms we use, "love" included, are symbols, metaphors. But "love" is a metaphor of a different kind because it relates specifically to human reality, and human beings are made in the image and likeness of God (see Gen 1:27).

Salvation and the new life in the Spirit always carry two elements, inseparable one from the other, one negative and one positive. The negative element consists in the removal of sin, something taken away: "I shall cleanse you of all your defilement and all your idols. I shall *remove* the heart of stone from your bodies." The positive element consists in the gift of a new life, something given not taken away: "A new heart I will give you; . . . a heart of flesh. . . . I will *put* my spirit within you" (Ezek 36:24-27). John the Baptist, pointing to Jesus, said, "Here is the Lamb of God that *takes away* the sin of the world," but straight away added that he "is the one who *baptizes* with the Holy Spirit" (John 1:30, 33).

Imagine having a bottle that up to now you have used to hold your vinegar, and now you need something to keep some new wine. What will you do? Put the wine in on top of the vinegar? That way, both will be spoiled. No, first you have to clean out the bottle, scour it thoroughly of every trace of vinegar, and then it will serve to hold the wine and the wine will not be tainted. So it is with our human heart. "God does not fill them with his good things, without first taking out the evil we have put there."[1]

---

[1] Augustine, *Sermons*, 71.12.19 (PL 38.454).

At times there has been a tendency to separate these two elements, calling the negative one the work of Christ as fruit of his paschal mystery, and assigning the positive one to the Spirit, as the fruit of Pentecost:

> First the Son was sent, to purify the ones who were to receive, so that nothing should remain in them that would be offensive to the Spirit, and only then was the Holy Spirit sent, to fill the cleansed vessels. Thus, the Son was sent to drive out bitterness, and the Holy Spirit to fill with sweetness; the Son to take away the old, the Holy Spirit to confer the new; the Son to set us free, the Holy Spirit to make us blessed.[2]

But this is a manner of speaking, and we should not give it too much importance. Jesus, by his death and resurrection, is also author of *all that is new,* and we have already seen that the Holy Spirit as well is at work in setting us free from *all that is old.*

The positive reality, instilled in us at baptism, is designated by various terms: new life, grace, gift of the Spirit, the new creation. One of these terms, which can serve for them all, is *caritas,* love. Love is the crucial test that shows one has passed from death to life (see 1 John 3:14). And so it is that the *Veni Creator,* after attributing to the Spirit the negative element, the removal of sin— under the title of "fire"—now draws on the title "love" to lead us to contemplate in all its splendor the positive element of the new life. Our heart is like a vessel cleaned out and purified, ready to receive the "new wine" that Christ promised.

To come to grasp the immensely rich content of the title "love," we will look first of all to discover what themes the author set out to sum up and express in that term; next, we will move on to bring to light the spiritual and theological traditions he wanted to convey with that term. On the one hand this will steer us back to the Bible, the ultimate source of every authoritative statement about the Spirit; on the other hand, these same traditions will help us discover new and pertinent insights that the word "love" can open up in our present-day understanding of the work of the Holy Spirit in the Church and in human souls individually.

---

[2] Walter of Saint Victor, *Sermons on the Holy Spirit,* 3 (CM 30, p. 28).

We already know there is a short treatise on the Holy Spirit by the author of the *Veni Creator,* dependent on an earlier work by Isidore of Seville. In this work we find listed, each with a short comment, all the titles that we find again, metrically rearranged, in the hymn. This is what it has to say about "love" as a title of the Holy Spirit:

> We very properly give the name "love" to the Holy Spirit, first of all because by his very nature he is the bond between those from whom he proceeds and is revealed as of one being with them; secondly, because he brings it about that we live in God and God lives in us [see 1 John 4:13]. In fact, among God's gifts none is greater than love, and therefore there is no greater gift than the Holy Spirit. . . . And, just as the title "wisdom," by appropriation, is attributed to the Word, even though in a more general sense it belongs just as properly to the Father and to the Spirit, so it is that the title "love," by appropriation, is attributed to the Holy Spirit, even though, in a more general sense, it belongs just as properly to the Father and to the Son.[3]

The author has in fact borrowed this explanation from Augustine. Largely through the titles "love" and "gift of God," the Augustinian view finds a broad and welcome acceptance in the *Veni Creator,* and along with it, all the rich spirituality of the Latin Church that had been nourished by that view. Yet it was not Augustine who invented the title; he in his turn had borrowed it from Scripture. Paul and John are the ones who use the word "love" in speaking of the Spirit.

To understand what lies behind the title "love" we need to consider three things: First, the Spirit is love in the *Trinity,* insofar as the Spirit is the bond of unity between Father and Son; second, the Holy Spirit is love in the *Church,* insofar as the Spirit is the bond of the Church's unity; and third, the Holy Spirit is love in *each believer,* insofar as the Spirit brings the believer to a living experience of the love of God.

[3] Rhabanus Maurus, *On the Universe,* I.3 (PL 111.25); see Isidore of Seville, *Etymologies,* VII.3.18 (PL 82.269).

2. The Holy Spirit, Love of the Father and the Son

Augustine was struck in a very special way by three things that the New Testament says about the Holy Spirit: that the Spirit is *gift,* the Spirit is *fellowship* or communion, and the Spirit is *joy.*

The Holy Spirit is *gift!* Simply to look up this one word is enough to turn up, one after another throughout the whole Bible, many enlightening points that link together and call one another to mind, until together they make a great, bright highway of light.[4] We have spoken of this already in the section on the title "gift of God," so we do not need to go through it all again.

Next, the Holy Spirit is *fellowship* (see 2 Cor 13:13). First of all he is the mutual fellowship of the Father and the Son, as we will see when we come to consider the last line of the *Veni Creator.* For in fact, in the Trinity, it is only the Holy Spirit who is called by a name that belongs to all three divine Persons in common (God is wholly Spirit and God is all Holy!), while we cannot call all three Persons Father or Son.

In the third place, the Holy Spirit is *joy, gaudium.* The Scriptures bear witness to this, for so often they associate joy with the Holy Spirit.[5]

Now, all three of these facets of the Holy Spirit drawn from the Bible—gift, fellowship, and joy—hark back to one single reality: love. Gift is a sign of love: "There is no gift of God more excellent than Love; it is the only one that is the identifying mark of the children of the Kingdom. . . . Many other gifts are given through the Holy Spirit, but none of them serves any purpose if there is no love."[6]

Fellowship too is a sign of love, evidence of the love that is present. Love, so to say, is what fellowship, sharing, communion, are all about. Fellowship is the result of rational creatures meeting together in love. And finally, how would *joy* arise, if not through the experience of loving and being loved in return? There is a kind of principle in every being, like the law of gravity in material things, by which each one naturally tends toward the place where it is in balance and at rest. For rational beings that principle

---

[4] Augustine, *On the Trinity,* XV.19.32–6.
[5] Acts 13:52; Rom 14:17.
[6] Augustine, *On the Trinity,* XV.18.32.

is love: "My weight is love; wherever I am taken, it is love that takes me there."[7]

In Augustine's mind, this realization produces a sudden flare of light that makes everything clear to him. It follows, therefore, that the Holy Spirit is that God of whom the Scripture speaks when it says that "God is love!" (1 John 4:8, 16). Certainly enough, everything in God is love, but the Holy Spirit is love not only according to the Spirit's nature, but also in the personal and proper sense. We read that "love is from God" (1 John 4:7) and, following immediately upon this, the affirmation "God is love." But it is precisely the Holy Spirit that "comes," in the sense of "proceeds" from God as love. (The Father proceeds from no one and the Son is *begotten* of the Father, not simply *proceeding* from him.)

This is an enlightenment of midday brilliance to Augustine, who cries out enthusiastically:

> The Holy Spirit is therefore the God who is love! A little later, after he has repeated that God is Love, the Evangelist adds, "and anyone who lives in love lives in God and God lives in him" (1 John 4:16), indicating the same mutual presence of which he said a little earlier, "We can know that we are living in him and he is living in us, because he lets us share his Spirit" (1 John 4:13). It is therefore the Spirit of whom he is speaking when he says that "God is love." We can see, therefore, why it is that the Holy Spirit, God who proceeds from God, once he is given to human beings, sets them on fire with love for God and for their neighbour: he himself is love itself. We human beings, in fact, love God only because we have received love from God. For this reason, he states, "not our love for God but God's love for us" (1 John 4:10), and a little later, "We are to love, because he loved us first" (1 John 4:19). And the Apostle Paul too says, "the love of God has been poured into our hearts by the Holy Spirit which has been given us" (Rom 5:5).[8]

This vision throws a bright beam of light for us into the inward life of the Trinity itself; that is, it helps us to understand something of the mystery of a God who is Three in One. God is love and because of this, Augustine seems to conclude, God is Trinity!

---

[7] Augustine, *Confessions*, XIII.9.10.

[8] Augustine, *On the Trinity*, XV.17.31.

"Love presupposes one who loves, the one who is loved, and their love itself."[9] In the Trinity, the Father is the one who loves, the principle and the source of all; the Son is the one who is loved; and the Holy Spirit is the love with which they love. It is true, of course, that this is no more than a human analogy, but it is without doubt one that gives us our best means of a glance into the inscrutable mystery of God.

When the author of the hymn says that wisdom is the attribute that pertains most specially to the Son, as love is attributed most properly to the Holy Spirit, he is quoting Augustine word for word.[10] In the Latin tradition, these appropriations became classical. "The Son is Truth, the Spirit is Love, and the Father is Power."[11]

Unfortunately, this principle of appropriation has not always been applied with the necessary discretion and flexibility. It has at times come to be rigidly insisted upon and has given rise to more difficulties than it has served to solve. That which is appropriated to one Person is not so much a certain attribute or a certain area of action, as the manner of realization of that attribute or action. Wisdom and love belong, properly speaking, to all three Persons equally, but each of the three nevertheless possesses and exercises them in a manner uniquely special to the particular personality of each in the Trinity. The same holds true of the customary attribution of the work of creation to the Father, of redemption to the Son, and of sanctification to the Holy Spirit. Each of the three is actively concerned in all these operations insofar as their effect is *ad extra,* that is, in the created order of being; nevertheless, each of the three Persons is engaged in these works in his own special and personal manner. The Holy Spirit, too, as we have already seen, is *Creator!* Cyril of Alexandria says, very appropriately,

> Even when we incline to attribute some particular action that God does for the sake of us his creatures to one or other of the Three Persons in a special way, we ought always to be sure and never shaken in our conviction that everything is from the Father, through the Son, in the Spirit.[12]

[9] Ibid., VIII.10.14.

[10] Ibid., XV.17.29.

[11] See Thomas Aquinas, *Summa Theologiae* I, q. 37, a. 1; see also Isaac of Stella, *Sermons,* 44.14 (SCh 339, p. 92).

[12] Cyril of Alexandria, *Commentary on the Gospel of John,* X.2 (PG 74.336A).

Nowadays we know that we can speak of the Holy Spirit in more ways than only in terms of love. The Latin tradition itself looks upon wisdom as one of the greatest gifts of the Holy Spirit, and it has developed the themes of the Spirit as light and as truth at great length. But what compels us to be aware of this more than anything else is the renewed contact with the Eastern churches. The theme of the Spirit as love is almost entirely absent from the theology of these Churches, which prefers to relate to the Holy Spirit as the "breath" that accompanies the "word" and, even more, as "illumination." In the Greek tradition we had to wait until Gregory Palamas before we could read something analogous to Augustine's words on the Holy Spirit as love:

> The Spirit of the most high Word is as it were the unutterable love of the Father for his Word whom he generates in an utterable way; a love that this same Word who is the beloved Son of the Father has, in his turn, for the Father insofar as he possesses the Spirit who, together with him, proceeds from the Father and who rests in him and is connatural to him.[13]

From all of this, what conclusion should we draw? That the Latin tradition, which has its impetus from Augustine, is to be abandoned? In the present ecumenical dialogue on the Holy Spirit one gets the impression at times that some of those involved would, tacitly at least, want that to happen. But that is an unacceptable position and contrary to the very principle of ecumenism, the purpose of which is to make the riches of each tradition available to all, and not to achieve the triumph of one tradition over all the rest. It would be simply impossible, moreover, to reject the view we have been considering without, at one stroke, obliterating from the memory of the universal Church an essential part of its liturgical, theological, ascetical, and mystical heritage.

I am convinced, rather, that the new climate of ecumenical dialogue gives us a real opportunity to reevaluate Augustine's contribution because, although on the one hand it comes to be seen as one view among other possible views, on the other hand it comes to be even more deeply appreciated. And ultimately this dialogue helps us to rediscover, freed of all Scholastic rigidities and later

---

[13] Gregory Palamas, *Capita physica,* 36 (PG 150.1144–5).

distortions, the genuine sense of Augustine's intuitions. Nothing was further from his mind than the idea that he had discovered how to explain the Trinity or, in particular, the place of the Holy Spirit in it. He begins his treatise on the Trinity by declaring:

> Whoever reads this work will carry on with me if he shares my own certainties, search with me if he shares my own doubts, come back to me if he recognises errors of his own, and call me to account if he becomes aware of mine. And together we will set out to walk the pathways of love.

And he ends the book with the words:

> Among the many things I have said, I am sure and I declare that I have said nothing that is worthy of this supreme and ineffable Trinity, but confess rather that the knowledge of God is quite beyond the reach of my weakness. I have not been able to reach such heights.[14]

Would that all who have spoken of the Holy Spirit and of the Trinity had done so with that same humility. In our day, having moved away from the exclusiveness of this or that school of thought, we are coming to appreciate a little better the immense contribution that, in his humility, Augustine has made. As Augustine himself foresaw and wished, we are learning to integrate his into a fuller view, along with the insights others have brought us, without finding any real opposition between them. And together, Greeks and Latins, we are learning to find what riches there are for us, and what cause for joy, in the great "symphony of the Fathers" that began on the day of Pentecost,[15] without any hidden desire to see one tradition prevail against the other. "Symphony" means the togetherness of many voices, not one voice alone. "Symphony" enhances the beauty of each particular voice; no one voice is put out or diminished by the sound of the others. Orthodox brothers, reading Augustine and the Western tradition in this new spirit and linking it to the tradition that is closer to their heart, will be able to bring us to a deeper and richer understanding of their insights and help us also to discover implications still unex-

---

[14] Augustine, *On the Trinity*, I.3.5; XV.27.50.
[15] See Irenaeus, *Against the Heresies*, III.17.2.

plored in our own. And the same applies to us of the Latin tradition in their regard. We can take a lesson from musicians: Sometimes we need a German conductor to draw out the potentialities of an Italian orchestral work, and sometimes it is an Italian conductor that best manages to reveal the hidden resonances of a German composition.

The ancients, speaking of God, used to say that "no one way suffices to approach so great a mystery"; the same would hold true, to an even greater extent, of the Triune God of Christians. Jesus himself gives us an example of this in the Gospel. He uses many parables to speak of the one reality of the kingdom. Sometimes it seems that one parable is contradicting another, or at least is saying something of the kingdom that is quite different from what another says. The fact is that the parables are "discreet messengers"; each tells its own part of the message and then stands aside, leaving the next to tell its special part, and gradually the whole message is pieced together. When we speak of God and of the Spirit, the concepts we develop and the ways we find to express them work in the same sort of way.

3. *The Spirit Who Is Love, in the Church*

The Father and the Son wanted us to be united to them and with one another in the selfsame bond that unites them with each other, and that bond is the love whom we name the Holy Spirit.[16] This is the principle that allows us to pass, without breaking the continuity, from the contemplation of the Spirit of love in the Trinity to the same Spirit of love in the Church.

There is a short formula dating back to the fifth century, *in unitate Spiritus Sancti* (in the unity of the Holy Spirit), that for a long time was the only mention of the Holy Spirit in the Latin Mass. It expresses the theme that Augustine develops in each one of his sermons on Pentecost. The outline is always the same. First, the event is recalled, the coming of the Spirit and the miracle of the many languages. This leads to the question, if the apostles spoke all those languages, why now do Christians not speak all known languages even though they too have received the same Spirit? And Augustine's

---

[16] Augustine, *Sermons,* 71.12.18 (PL 38.454).

answer is that in our own day too, every Christian speaks all languages! Every Christian in fact is a member of that one body, the Church, and the Church speaks all languages and proclaims the truths of God in them all. If we look at our own body, we understand right away that not every part of it can see, nor can every part hear, nor is every part a foot for walking, yet spontaneously we say, "I see," not "my eye sees," and "I hear," not "my ear hears," and "I walk," not "my feet do the walking," because each member does what it does for the good of the whole body, and the whole body acts in each of its members.

And so it is with the Holy Spirit in the body of Christ which is the Church. The Spirit is to the Church what the human soul is to the human body. The Spirit is the principle that moves and inspires the whole. What then would be the conclusive sign that one has received the Holy Spirit? To speak in tongues? To work miracles? No, not those, but to love the unity, and to know that you are firmly committed to living in union with the Church:

> If, therefore, you want to live by the Holy Spirit, remain steadfast in love, love the truth, let your desire be for unity, and you will reach eternity.
>
> As at that time the fact that one person was able to speak various languages was a sign of the presence of the Holy Spirit, so now *the love of unity* that makes many peoples one is a sign of his presence. . . . Know therefore that you have the Holy Spirit when you adhere to the *unity* by the sincerity of your *love*.[17]

Here we have the reason why love is "the greatest" (1 Cor 13:13). Love multiplies the gifts; it makes the charism of one to be the charism of all.

Against the Donatist teaching Saint Augustine affirms that the Church is not something monolithic, either achieved in its totality or not there at all. The Church comes into being gradually, in stages. Church unity exists on two levels: the visible level of signs, called "communion in the sacraments" *(communio sacramentorum)*, and the invisible level, called "the fellowship of the saints" *(societas sanctorum)*. The latter comes into being as individuals are brought into that body that is animated by the Holy

---

[17] Augustine, *Sermons,* 267.4 (PL 38.1231); 269.2.4(PL 38.1236).

Spirit and begin, through love, to belong to it as its members. This Church in the full and inward sense consists of all those who, through love, share the same Spirit, and it is represented by the *dove* which is a symbol, at one and the same time, both of the Church (in the Song of Songs) and of the Holy Spirit (at the baptism of Christ).[18] Is it not something singularly interesting that the term love *(agapé)* in the Christian tradition became the accepted way of referring both to the Holy Spirit and at the same time to the Church? Ignatius of Antioch says that the community of Rome "presides over the *agapé,*" that is, in the gathering of the Church as a whole.[19]

This is the spectrum of doctrine that the title "love" evoked in the days when the *Veni Creator* was composed. What does it suggest to our minds today? When we sing the hymn, what is it that we are asking for when we come to this word *caritas,* love? We, especially in the Western world, live at the end of a long age, the particular mark of which has been the very sad divorce between the Church and the Holy Spirit. In the years that followed the Reformation, the Catholic side placed heavy insistence on the importance of the visible hierarchical and institutional aspects of the Church (in the words of Robert Bellarmine, "a society of men as tangible and as visible as the city of Rome or the kingdom of France or the republic of Venice"), to such an extent that the role of the Holy Spirit in the Church was lost in the shadows. This begins to come to the fore again in Pius XII's encyclical *Mystici Corporis* in which he speaks again of the Holy Spirit as the soul of the Church and the bond of its unity.

A decisive impulse came from Vatican II. The council speaks of the charisms and the all-pervasive, active presence of the Holy Spirit (the "pneumatic dimension") in the Church as well as of its hierarchical and institutional character. After the council, Catholics began to speak of the Church as "the mystery of the Holy Spirit in Christ and in Christians." As in the Trinity we may think of the Holy Spirit as a divine *"We"* in which the *"I"* of the Father is united with the *"Thou"* of the Son, so in the Church the Holy Spirit is the one who makes one unique, mystical person of the multitude

---

[18] See Augustine, *On Baptism,* VI.3.5 (PL 43.199).
[19] Ignatius of Antioch, *Letter to the Romans,* Preamble.

of believers.[20] It has come to the point where the Church may be defined as the "sacrament of the Spirit."[21]

On the Protestant side, the effects of the same divorce were seen, but in the opposite direction. Here the emphasis was on the Holy Spirit as constitutive of the invisible, inward, hidden reality of the Church, to such an extent that the concrete, visible dimension of Church was lost from sight. To sketch the situation, on the Catholic side we had the Church without the Holy Spirit, and on the Reform side we had the Holy Spirit without the Church. One ended up with the distortion of a Church deprived of the Holy Spirit, and the other, with a distortion of the Holy Spirit deprived of the Church. At a certain stage, the philosophy of idealism had so influenced Western thinking that the Holy Spirit came to be looked upon as human self-awareness: no longer the Spirit of God, but the spirit of man. The healing of the divorce on the side of the Reform began with Barth, who set in train a movement similar to the movement taking place in the Catholic Church, but in the other direction, taking the form of a renewed interest in the Church.

Although each reads its own shades of meaning in the words, both sides today find themselves in agreement on Irenaeus's ancient formula: "Where the Church is, there too, is the Spirit of God, and where the Spirit of God is, there too, is the Church."[22]

It is simply not possible to cut a formula like that in two and give serious attention only to the first half, as Catholics tried to do, or pay attention only to the second part, as was the tendency of the Reformation. The entire Church needs the Holy Spirit, and no one has given expression to the renewed awareness of this need with more passion than Paul VI:

> On several occasions we have asked about the greatest needs of the Church. . . . What do we feel is the first and last need of this blessed and beloved Church of ours? We must say it, almost trembling and praying, because as you know well, this is the Church's mystery and life: the Spirit, the Holy Spirit. He it is who animates and sanctifies the Church. He is her divine breath, the wind in her sails, the principle of her unity, the inner

---

[20] See H. Mühlen, *Una Mystica Persona* (Paderborn, 1964).

[21] See W. Kasper, "Die Kirche als Sakrament des Geistes," *Die Kirche, Ort des Geistes,* ed. W. Kasper and G. Sauter (Freiburg/Basel/Wien: Herder, 1976).

[22] Irenaeus, *Against the Heresies,* III.24.1.

source of her light and strength. He is her support and consoler, her source of charisms and songs, her peace and her joy, her pledge and prelude to blessed and eternal life. The Church needs her perennial Pentecost; she needs fire in her heart, words on her lips, prophecy in her outlook. . . . The Church needs to rediscover the eagerness, the taste and the certainty of the truth that is hers. . . . And then the Church needs to feel flowing through all her human faculties a wave of love, of that love which is called forth and poured into our hearts "by the Holy Spirit who has been given to us" (Rom 5:5).[23]

To ponder upon the Spirit as *caritas,* as love, can be a great help to us on the road toward the unity of all Christians. There is a question that arises in the minds of many Catholics today, and it is this: There is a multitude of people who are baptized into the same Church as I but who have no interest in Christ whatsoever and who are only nominal Christians. Can I, as a Catholic, see myself as more in communion with them than with the great number of those who, though they belong to other churches, believe in the same basic truths as I believe, who love Jesus to the point of giving their life for him, and who live and work in the power of the same Holy Spirit?

It will not be possible much longer to avoid this question, or to delay answering it. If we continue to give precedence to institutional communion rather than to communion in spirit wherever the two, most unfortunately, still do not in fact coincide, it will simply mean that we are scrapping our traditional principles and according a higher importance to a communion of signs than to communion in reality, which the Holy Spirit is.

If, as Augustine said, the sign of the presence of the Holy Spirit is "love of the unity," we need to say that the Holy Spirit is at work today above all where we find lively enthusiasm for Christian unity, where people work for it and where they are willing to suffer to achieve it.

At the beginning, in Cornelius's house, God gave his Spirit to pagans, and the outward signs were exactly the same as they had been for the apostles at Pentecost. God did this to persuade Peter,

---

[23] *Insegnamenti di Paolo VI,* vol. X, Tipografia Poliglotta Vaticana, pp. 1210–1 (Discourse of 29 Nov. 1972); translation in E. O'Connor, *Pope Paul and the Spirit* (Notre Dame, Ind.: Ave Maria Press, 1978) 183.

and the whole Church with him, to accept pagan Gentiles too into the communion of the one and only Church. In our own day God is giving the Holy Spirit to believers belonging to the different churches in the same way, and often with exactly the same outward manifestations, for the very same purpose: to persuade us to accept one another in the love of the Spirit and to set out together on the road to full unity. The Spirit, who was able to gather Jews and Gentiles, slaves and free, into one single body, is well able today to gather together into one body Catholics and Protestants, Western churches and Eastern, Roman and Orthodox! We need to ask the Holy Spirit to do it when, in the *Veni Creator,* we call on the Holy Spirit as *caritas,* the Spirit of Love.

4. All Were Filled with the Love of God!

We have reflected on the Holy Spirit as love in the Trinity and in the Church, and now it is time to be thinking of the Holy Spirit of Love in each believer, that is, in each one of us. For this purpose, we need to go back to the Pentecost event.

If the Holy Spirit is indeed nothing other than the love of God, love in Person, the statement in Acts that "they were all filled with *the Holy Spirit*" can mean nothing other than that "they were all full of the *love of God!*" In this light, the Holy Spirit can truly be seen as the "seal" that is stamped upon all God's creative and redemptive work (see Eph 1:13) and Pentecost as the culmination of all the works of God. Why did God create the world? Why did he send his Son to redeem the world from sin? Why would God have given us the Scriptures? For no other reason than that he wanted to fill his creatures with his love.

Pentecost, therefore, was not only an event in the objective order, bringing a profound but unnoticed change beyond any awareness; it was also an event in the subjective order, an experience. The shift, from the slave-heart full of fear to the filial heart brimming with love, is not something that can happen without the one to whom it happens being aware of it; it is not the kind of heart transplant that is done under general anesthetic! On the contrary, the experience of the love of God was one of overwhelming intensity for the apostles: to be loved by God, and to love God in return! They were literally inundated, "baptized," in love.

That was what moved them so much that they were beside themselves, to such an extent that people thought them drunk (see Acts 2:13). The sudden change in the apostles cannot be explained in any other way; it was the fire of divine love itself that flared up in them. What they did on that occasion are the sort of things that only love moves one to do. The apostles, as the martyrs would be later on, were in effect "drunk," but "drunk on love that came to them through the finger of God which is the Holy Spirit."[24] Drunk because "drenched in the torrent of divine delights; drunk with that sober inebriation that does sins to death and gives life to the heart."[25]

The fact that the sign of the coming of the Holy Spirit, on the subjective level, is an experience of love is confirmed every time there is question of a "new Pentecost." The people who took part in the retreat that proved to be the beginning of the charismatic renewal in the Catholic Church confessed later that there was a moment when they feared being loved too much and not being able to stand such love. In the words of one of them, "It was as if the God of Sinai had come into the place where we were gathered, and completely filled it and us too." Every time someone has a genuine, strong experience of the Spirit, the most vivid memory of the moment that the person retains is of an intense perception of the Father's love. Witnessing to this, someone said: "All my life long, I had felt unloved. The next day, that feeling vanished entirely. I felt myself immersed in a new experience of the love of God, and from that day it has never left me."

This is the most beautiful moment of any creature's life: to know that one is loved, personally, by God, to feel oneself lifted to the bosom of the Trinity and to find oneself in the flood of love that flows between Father and Son, enfolded in their love, sharing their passionate love for the world. And all of this in one instant, without any need to think about it or for words to say it.

> Amazing condescension of the Creator towards the creature, signal grace, inconceivable benevolence, the greatest of motives for the creature to trust the Creator, sweet closeness shared, delight of mutual knowing; we come to find ourselves clasped in the embrace and sharing the kiss of Father and Son, and that is

[24] Augustine, *Sermons,* 272.B.7 (PLS 2.527).
[25] Cyril of Jerusalem, *Catecheses,* XVII.19 (PG 33.989).

the Holy Spirit; united to God with the same love that unites Father and Son, made holy in him who is the very holiness of the Two. To rejoice in such a great good, to have the sweet experience of it, as far as it is possible in this troubled and deceptive lifetime: that is to experience what it is truly to be alive.[26]

But why this insistence on felt experience? Is it in fact necessary to have such an experience of the love of God? Is it not enough, and is it not even more meritorious, to accept it in pure faith? When we are talking of the love of God, the author we have just quoted tells us, the felt experience is itself also a grace: nature is not capable of giving rise to such a desire in us.[27] Though it is not within our abilities to have or to retain the awareness of an experience of that kind, it is nevertheless a good thing to seek it and desire it. "So we have known and believe the love that God has for us" (1 John 4:16): not only believe but also known, and in the language of the Bible *to know* means also *to experience*.

If Pentecost consists in this—a vital and transforming experience of the love of God—why is such an experience a thing still unknown to the majority of believers? How can it be made available to them? Let me suggest a way that never fails. This love of God that is poured into our hearts by the Holy Spirit has two sides; it is the love with which God loves us and the love with which God makes it possible for us to love him and our neighbor. In some texts in the Bible the first side is stressed (see John 4:10), and in other texts (see Paul's hymn to love in 1 Corinthians 13) the second side. In Tradition we find the same. Augustine gives precedence to the enabling aspect of love: the love poured into us is the new ability given us to love God and to love our neighbor; Thomas Aquinas very rightly points to both aspects, mutually united.[28]

But it is important to keep in mind that these are two facets of the same love, not two different loves. As in the Trinity the love of the Father for the Son does not end in the Son, but through the Son it continues in the Spirit, so also outside of the Trinity. The

---

[26] William of St. Thierry, *Mirror of Faith,* 111–2 (SCh 301, p. 180).

[27] William of St. Thierry, *Meditations,* XII.29 (SCh 324, p. 210).

[28] See Augustine, *The Spirit and the Letter,* 32.56; Thomas Aquinas, *Commentary on the Letter to the Romans,* chap. V, reflection 1, n. 392.

love of God comes to us but does not "end" in us; it comes, fills us, catches us up in its own vital movement, and gives rise in us to the urge to love in our turn, with the same love that God has for us. "Since God has loved us so much, we also ought to love one another" (1 John 4:11).

The love of God brings ecstasy, the experience of being lifted out of oneself. To go no further than the first movement, that is, to be the recipient of God's love but not also its conduit, passing it on in our turn, would be like trying to stop the flow of a river; it would not be a river any longer, but a marsh, a wetland. As the rain comes down from the heavens and does not return without first watering the earth, making it yield and giving growth to provide seed and bread (see Isa 55:10), so also the love of God, flowing into our hearts, should not return to God without first having achieved the purpose for which God gave it to us and borne its fruit in us.

I have stressed this point precisely because it is that "way that never fails" that I spoke of, to come to a Pentecostal experience of the love of God for us. When we were baptized we were given a new heart. Perhaps this new heart of ours has remained inactive, atrophied, because it has not been exercised. It should have been a "spring, welling up," and instead it has remained a "sealed fountain." We need to unseal it, to turn it on, set it in motion. When, for whatever reason, someone's heartbeat stops, we try by every means available to massage it back into action, until it begins again to beat of its own accord, by its own natural and spontaneous movement. We may need something of the same sort: a kind of spiritual heart-massage or artificial respiration. And this comes when we set ourselves to love, if need be by sheer act of will, without any strong feelings at all. Set yourself to love everyone, the people close to you, the people far from you, the ones who love you and, perhaps even more, the ones who do not. We should not think that we know "the love of God that is poured into our hearts by the Holy Spirit" if it has not, at least once, led us to forgive an offense, love an enemy, be reconciled with a brother or sister.

It is an observed fact that the Jordan forms two "seas" in its course, the Sea of Galilee and the Dead Sea. The Sea of Galilee receives the Jordan's water but then lets it flow out again, and that sea teems with life. The Dead Sea receives the Jordan's water and keeps it; no streams flow out of it, and it is in fact "dead"; there is no life in its waters or on its shores, but all is a salty waste. It is a symbol to us. Love has been given us, with abundant generosity, in our baptism and many, many times since. If we are still to receive it after that, we need to let it flow through us; we need to spend all the love we have received, break down the levees of our self-centeredness.

We need to follow the example of the widow of Zarepath. Elijah the prophet came to her house and asked for some water and a little bread. She answered that all she had was a handful of flour and a drop or two of oil; she planned to make a little bread for herself and her son to eat, and then they would die. But the prophet insisted, "Use all you have to make me a little loaf first, and then make something for yourself and your son." Does that not seem an unreasonable request? The widow was herself in a situation of extreme need of something to eat, and the prophet was asking her to give away all the little that she had. But we know what happened. "The jar of meal was not spent, nor the jug of oil emptied," and as often as she needed some for herself and her son, it was there for her (see 1 Kgs 17:7-16). God does the same with us. We ask of God to give us a little love, and God asks us first to give God, and our neighbor, all the little love we have, until the "jar is empty." "Give, and it will be given to you. A good measure, pressed down, shaken together, running over, will be put into your lap; for the measure you give will be the measure you get back" (Luke 6:38).

It is not a question of being the first to give, as if God is someone who only gives in return, and still less is it a question of deserving God's love, but rather a matter of allowing God to pour out gifts upon us. Every time we love, God has first loved us, and the very fact that we love someone is itself a sign that God is at that moment loving us.

Let us pray, in the words of a medieval Sequence that uses the images of river, flame, and wind to sum up all the tradition of the Western Church on the Holy Spirit who is gift and who is love:

> *Oh, love of Father and of Son,*
> *sacred source of every good,*
> *Spirit Paraclete!*
>
> *From the abyss of the Trinity,*
> *flow now, river of love, into*
> *our inmost heart.*

Sweet flame, in every corner felt
of our stony heart to melt
the ice of ill.

Breeze of gentle strength so warm
breathe all through us till we burn
with love that makes divine.

Through you are we with God at one
and linked in heart, together run
in covenant of love.[29]

---

[29] Sequence of the Holy Spirit, AHMA, 54, p. 247 (translator's English rendition):

> *Amor patris et filii, / sacer fons totius boni, / Spiritus paraclite.*
> *De thesauris trinitatis / veni, torrens caritatis, / corda nostra visere.*
> *Huc emerge, dulcis flamma, / lambe corda indurata, / fuga frigus*
> *noxium.*
> *Suavis auster, illabere, / perfla nos adustione / amoris deifici.*
> *Per te tibi uniamur, / per te nobis connectamur / caritatis*
> *foedere.*

IX

Anointing for the Soul

The Holy Spirit makes us share the fragrance of Christ's holiness

The theme of this reflection is the title *spiritalis unctio,* "spiritual anointing," that closes the second verse of the *Veni Creator.* Wind, water, and fire have each told us what they have to say of the Holy Spirit, and now it is the turn of oil, or ointment, along with the perfume that arises from it.

"Anointing" is a title attributed to the Holy Spirit from the very earliest theological treatises on the Spirit:

> The Spirit is called, and is in fact, an anointing and a seal. . . . This anointing is the breath of the Son, in such a way that those who experience it are able to say, "We are the redolence of Christ." The seal is the representation of Christ, in such a way that those who are sealed with it are enabled to take on the form of Christ.[1]

We notice that the title "seal" is used along with the title "anointing" (see 2 Cor 1:21). As an anointing, the Holy Spirit makes us redolent of Christ; as seal, the Spirit shapes us in the form or the image of Christ. In this sense, the title "spiritual anointing" serves to draw attention, yet again, to the divinity of the Holy Spirit. In fact, the text just quoted carries on to say: "If the Holy Spirit is the perfume and the form of the Son, it is clear that the Spirit is not a creature, for the same reason that the Son, who exists in the form of the Father, is himself not a creature."[2]

However, the use of the title "anointing" is not restricted to the context of dogmatic reflection; it speaks to us not only of what the Spirit is in himself, but also, and especially, of what the Spirit is for us. As anointing, the Holy Spirit is the one who makes us "smell right," causing us to share the "odor of sanctity" arising from the holiness of Christ.

[1] Athanasius, *Letters to Serapion,* III.3 (PG 26.628–9).
[2] Ibid. (PG 26.629A).

He is so to say of his very substance the living and efficacious
perfume, and he transmits to the creature that which comes
from God himself. . . . In fact, if the redolence of a perfume
transmits its own quality to garments that have come in contact
with it, in a certain sense it confers its own quality as perfume
on them too. Now if it is true that the Holy Spirit is by nature
the very Spirit of God, how could he not by his very presence
make those among whom he lives and moves partakers of the
divine nature?[3]

This anointing is a kind of outflowing of the divinity that the
Holy Spirit "receives from Christ" and communicates to the soul.
"For the Spirit indeed is the redolence of Christ and that is why
the apostles, since they are temples of the Spirit, are themselves
also the good odour of Christ."[4] On the basis of these texts we already gain some insight into the richness and the evocative beauty
of the title on which we have set out to reflect in this chapter.

1. Anointing: Figure, Event, and Sacrament

The anointing, like the Eucharist and the Passover, is one of
those realities that are present in all three of the phases of the history of salvation. It is in fact present in the Old Testament *in figure,* in the New Testament *as event,* and in the time of the Church
as sacrament. The figure anticipates and prepares for the event,
while the sacrament celebrates it, renders it present, makes it actual, and in a certain sense prolongs it.

In our context, the *figure* is found in the several kinds of anointing (of kings, of prophets, and of priests) that were practiced in
Old Testament times. The *event* is realized in the anointing of
Christ the Messiah, "the Anointed One," toward whom all the figures were pointing as to their fulfillment. The *sacrament* is found
in that ensemble of sacramental signs that make use of an anointing either as the rite of principal significance or as a complementary rite. And so it is that if we follow the development of the title
"spiritual anointing," it is possible to outline a complete theology

---

[3] Cyril of Alexandria, *Commentary on the Gospel of John,* XI.2 (PG
74.453).

[4] Pseudo-Athanasius, *The Trinity,* I.7 (PG 28.1128B).

of the Spirit. A perfumed trail goes through the entire history of salvation, reaching all the way to us!

As we consider this wide range of historical and ritual significances of anointing, we find grafted onto it another entire level of meanings in which anointing is not an act but rather a state or mode of being and behaving and, so to say, a whole style of living. When we say that someone is clearly anointed in the spirit, or that someone has spoken under an anointing, or goes about his work in an anointed way, we are using the expression within the ambit of this second level of significance. This corresponds to what Augustine calls the "spiritual anointing" (*spiritalis unctio,* the very words of our hymn!) which, he says, is the Holy Spirit himself in person, or love, as distinct from the "*visible* anointing" that is the sacramental sign.[5]

Our practical purpose is to be edified and led to understand, to love, and if possible to possess the anointing I have called "anointing as a state" or "ongoing anointing." But, if we are to achieve this purpose, we need first to speak of anointing as an event and as a rite, because anointing as a "state" flows from this as its effect. Here too, in other words, we need to lay the biblical and theological foundations from which we will then be able to draw consequences for our spiritual life. This will allow us, besides, to touch on certain problems that have contributed a great deal, after the council, to the renewal of the theology of the Spirit.

Before we go any further, notice that the two areas of significance just outlined—anointing as a christological event and as a sacramental rite, and anointing as a permanent gift in a Christian—were, in an embryonic way, both present to the author of our hymn. In fact, in the work from which he drew his choice of titles we read:

> The Holy Spirit is called a spiritual anointing on the basis of what Saint John has written. Of the Lord it is said that he was "anointed with the oil of exultation" (Ps 45:8), that is, with the Holy Spirit, and it was in fact the apostle John who called the Holy Spirit an anointing, when he said, "You have not lost the anointing that he gave you, and you do not need anyone to teach you; the anointing he gave teaches you everything" (1 John 2:27).[6]

[5] Augustine, *On the First Letter of John,* 3.5 (PL 35.2000); see 3.12 (PL 35.2004).

[6] See Rhabanus Maurus, *On the Universe,* I.3 (PL 111.25); see Isidore of Seville, *Etymologies,* VII.3.28–9 (PL 82.270–1).

2. The Anointing in Christ: The Event

Of all the wealth of material regarding anointing as a figure in the Old Testament, two elements are of interest to us: its link with the anticipation of the coming of the Messiah and the relationship between the anointing and the conferring of the Holy Spirit.

In the Old Testament we read of three kinds of anointing: kingly, priestly, and prophetic. That is to say, anointing to kingship, to the priesthood, and to the prophetic office, although in the case of the prophets the anointing was usually metaphorical, without any use of actual oil. In each of these three kinds of anointing we can trace a messianic perspective: the anticipation of an awaited king, priest, and prophet who would in very fact be the Anointed One, the Messiah.

Along with the official and juridical investiture by which a king became the Anointed of the Lord, the Bible shows that the anointing also conferred a real inward power in bringing about a transformation that came from God, and this power was more and more identified with the Holy Spirit. When he anointed Saul as king, Samuel said: "The spirit of the Lord will possess you, and you will go into ecstasy with the prophets and be turned into a different person" (see 1 Sam 10:1, 6).

David too, when Samuel anointed him, received the Spirit (see 1 Sam 16:13). "That which the king received is the *ruach* of the Lord that filled him through and through with its vital power."[7] The link between anointing and the Spirit comes to light above all in the well-known text from Isaiah: "The Spirit of the Lord God is upon me, because the Lord has anointed me" (Isa 61:1).

The New Testament unhesitatingly presents Jesus as the Anointed of God, in whom all the anointings of the old order find their fulfillment. The title Messiah, or Christ, which in point of fact means "the Anointed," is the clearest evidence of this. But we also find it quite explicitly stated, "God anointed Jesus of Nazareth with the Holy Spirit and with power" (Acts 10:38).

The historical event referred to is the baptism of Jesus in the Jordan. Which of the types of anointing of the old order took place in Jesus' baptism: the kingly, the prophetic, or the priestly anointing?

---

[7] H. Cazelles, *L'apport de l'Ancien Testament à la connaissance de l'Esprit Saint,* CinSS I, p. 723.

The prophetic interpretation is favored by the fact that the anointing Jesus received, like that of the prophets, was an anointing of a purely spiritual kind and not a physical one. Yet it is perhaps closer to the truth to see all three types of anointing fulfilled, and that is how theological tradition and the Church liturgy in fact see it.

Whatever the case, the Holy Spirit is the "content" of this anointing: "God has anointed him with the Holy Spirit and with power." And Jesus himself was to say, "The Spirit of the Lord has been given to me, for he has anointed me" (Luke 4:18).

A theological problem concerning the anointing of Jesus is, how does it relate to the incarnation? From the earliest days until the end of the fourth century no one had any difficulty in accepting the account of the Gospels. The anointing of Jesus was understood as linking with his baptism in the Jordan, and was understood as a Trinitarian event. Irenaeus writes: "By the name 'Christ' we understand the one who anoints, the one who is anointed, and the anointing itself. For in fact the Father anoints, and the Son is anointed in the Spirit who is the anointing."[8]

Moreover, this is a historical event. Because of this anointing, Jesus is named "Christ," a name that properly denotes an event, an action, rather than a person or a substantial entity. It denotes the investiture of Jesus as the Messiah, and that investiture was in fact the commencement of the economy of salvation. By the incarnation, the Word made flesh becomes "Jesus"; by the anointing of the Spirit at his baptism Jesus, who is fully human and fully divine, becomes in fact "the Christ."[9] This brings about something new in his life: a newness that is functional and not ontological. It immediately produces obvious and awesome effects in him: miracles, preaching with authority, victory over demons, the establishment of the kingdom. In our regard his anointing is an ecclesial anointing: "The Spirit of God came down upon him, so that we, sharing in the abundance of that anointing, might be saved."[10]

Two factors gave rise to a crisis in regard to this ancient theological view that placed so great an importance on the baptism of Jesus. The first was the emergence of heresies that, from all that

---

[8] Irenaeus, *Against the Heresies,* III.18.3; see Basil the Great, *On the Holy Spirit,* XII.28 (PG 32.116C); Ambrose, *On the Holy Spirit,* I.44.

[9] Irenaeus, *Against the Heresies,* III.9.3.

[10] Ibid.

we have been considering, drew false conclusions. The Gnostics held that Jesus and Christ were not the same reality. The name Jesus was taken to refer to the man born of Mary, and the name Christ was taken to mean the divinity that descended on him at the time of his baptism. In the Gnostic view, the baptism took the place of the incarnation. Later, Paul of Samosata would come to a similar conclusion and Nestorius, if we are to believe his opponents, did the same. The Arians, in their turn, held that if Jesus was subject to change and experienced progress in his life, this means that he was not God in the full and perfect sense.

The second of the two factors was the need to express the content of the faith in terms adapted to the Greek culture, for which the reality that mattered most was not the unfolding of events in history, but rather the *arché,* what is given once and for all at the beginning. We find all these concerns reflected in a text from Gregory Nazianzen:

> If anyone says that Jesus Christ came to be judged worthy of adoption as Son after he had become perfect as a result of the works he had done, or after his baptism, or after his resurrection from the dead, let him be cut off from the community of faith. For in fact, that which has known a commencement, or that which progresses, or that which grows to perfection, is not God.[11]

The outcome was that the mystery of the anointing of Jesus came to be seen as separate from his baptism, and linked instead with the incarnation. The same Gregory Nazianzen says that "in the incarnation, Jesus was anointed with divinity, and the anointing of his humanity is nothing other than this divinity itself."[12] Jesus "was anointed of the Holy Spirit in as much as he became man."[13] Augustine, in the west, says the same:

> Christ, we are sure, was not only anointed with the Holy Spirit when the Spirit descended on him in the form of a dove when he had just been baptised; on that day he had wanted to prefigure his body, that is, the Church, in which we were to receive the Holy Spirit in a special way when we receive baptism. But

---

[11] Gregory Nazianzen, *Letter 1 to Cledonius,* 23–4 (SCh 208, p. 46).

[12] Gregory Nazianzen, *Sermons,* XXX.2 (PG 36.105B).

[13] Cyril of Alexandria, *Commentary on the Gospel of John,* XI.10 (PG 74.552C).

we do need to understand that Christ was anointed with this mystical and invisible anointing in the very moment in which the Word of God became flesh.[14]

The title "Christ," which at one time had been understood to refer to an event and an action, now came to be taken as referring to the person himself.[15]

What happened as a result of this new perspective was that, by appropriation and also because of the influence of Luke 1:35, the Spirit was still mentioned, but writers more frequently used the general term "divinity." Some even began tacitly to leave the Spirit out and, when speaking of anointing or chrism, make it clear that they were referring to the Logos, the Word, and not to the Spirit. In one of the texts from this time we read, "I, the Logos, am the chrism, and man is the one who is anointed by me."[16] The mystery of the anointing becomes a Christological question in the strict sense, and no longer carries the Trinitarian quality that it had in the early authors.

It was on this foundation that all the subsequent development of systematic theology was based, right down to the beginning of the twentieth century. As a negative result of this, we came to have a watered-down appreciation of the role of the Holy Spirit, and the theology of the Spirit was reduced to a mere facet of christology. This, much more than the *Filioque,* was what led to the shriveling away of the pneumatic dimension in theology.

In recent times, the reevaluation of the baptism of Jesus, on a biblical basis, has induced us to look again, and in depth, into this impoverishment of theology. We have again recognized the need to reevaluate the more ancient perspectives which distinguished the mystery of the anointing from the mystery of the incarnation and the mission of the Spirit from the mission of the Word. The anointing achieves a specific purpose in the life of Jesus: It defines the moment in which he receives the fullness of the Spirit as Head of the Church and as Messiah. He was, of course, filled with the Holy Spirit from the moment of his incarnation, but there it

[14] Augustine, *The Trinity,* XV.36 (PG 26.524B).

[15] John of Damascus, *Orthodox Faith,* III.3 (PG 94.989). "We say that the name 'Christ' is the name of the hypostasis."

[16] Pseudo-Athanasius, *Against the Arians,* IV.36 (PG 26.524B).

was a matter of a personal grace, linked to the union of his human nature with his divine nature in him as one person both human and divine (the "hypostatic union"), and as such, the grace was not something he could share with us. Now, by the anointing, he is given a fullness of the Spirit that, as Head, he can communicate to his body. The Church lives by this "capital" grace *(gratia capitis)*. More than a prolongation of the incarnation, the Church is the continuity of the anointing in history. It is the Holy Spirit who makes "one mystical person" of Jesus and the Church, one personal reality made up of many persons. As in the Trinity, so also in the history of salvation, the role of the Holy Spirit is not to unite many natures in one person, but rather to unite many persons in one mystical personhood.[17]

The result of all this is an entirely renewed vision of christology and of the Church. The dimension of the Spirit is not something that is linked into them from the outside as an extra (stuck on, someone has said, like sugar on a cookie!), but appreciated as intrinsic to them. It was in this direction that Vatican II was moving, when the council again began to speak of the anointing, after this mystery had for centuries been ignored by the writers of the great *Summae* and given no place at all in strictly theological debate. In one of the council's documents we read: "The Lord Jesus, whom the Father consecrated and sent into the world, makes his whole Mystical Body sharer in the anointing of the Spirit wherewith he has been anointed."[18]

3. The Anointing in the Church: The Sacrament

In the Old Testament the anointing was present as a *figure;* in the New Testament it was present as an *event;* now, in the Church, it is present as *sacrament.* What is the sacrament in relation to the event? The sacrament takes its sign from the figure; from the event it takes the reality that is signified. Like the anointings of the Old Testament it makes use of the material element (oil, or chrism which is perfumed oil), and it is from Christ that it gets its effectiveness for salvation. Christ was not ever anointed with oil

---

[17] See H. Mühlen, *Una Mystica Persona* (Paderborn, 1964).
[18] *Presbyterorum Ordinis,* n. 2.

(apart from that occasion at Bethany when Mary Magdalene anointed his feet), and he himself did not ever physically anoint anyone else. In him, the symbol was replaced by the reality.

Anointing in the Church is more than a single sacrament: it is a range of related sacramental rites. As *sacraments* in their own right, we have confirmation in which the sign is an anointing with chrism and the anointing of the sick. Then there are the anointings that form *part* of other sacraments: the anointings in the rite of baptism, and the anointing in the sacrament of Holy Orders. In the rite of baptism, following the baptism itself, there is an anointing with chrism in which explicit reference is made to Christ's threefold anointing: "May he bless you with the chrism of salvation: made now a partaker in Christ priest, king and prophet, may you be always a member of his body, unto eternal life."

In the consecration of a bishop attention is drawn particularly to the relationship between the anointing and spiritual fruitfulness: "May God, who has brought you to share in the supreme priesthood of Christ, pour out upon you his mystical anointing and by the abundance of his blessing make your ministry fruitful."

And finally, let us remember, among the *sacramentals* the anointing of altars and of church buildings and the anointings practiced on many other occasions.

How do we pass from the event to the sacrament, that is, from the anointing of Christ to the anointing of Christians? In other words, how did all these anointings practiced in the Church come to be in the first place, and how did they develop? On this point two texts in the New Testament have proved decisive, one from Paul and one from John, which speak of anointing in very clear reference to the Holy Spirit: "But it is God who establishes us with you in Christ and has anointed us, by putting his seal on us and giving us his Spirit in our hearts as a first installment" (2 Cor 1:21-22). In this text we see, among other things, how in Scripture the theme of anointing comes to be intimately linked with the notion of the seal (see Eph 1:13). In his turn, John writes:

> As for you, the anointing that you received from him abides in you, and so you do not need anyone to teach you. But as his anointing teaches you about all things, and is true and is not a lie, and just as it has taught you, abide in him (1 John 2:27).

The author, the source of this anointing is the Holy Spirit, as we can clearly deduce from the fact that elsewhere (see John 14:26) the function of "teaching everything" is attributed to "the Spirit of truth." John too makes mention of the Holy Spirit as "seal," though he applies it to Christ himself where he says, "For it is on him that God the Father has set his seal" (John 6:27).

It is still an open question whether these texts, which speak of an anointing and of a seal, are indications of a liturgical praxis that had already become established in the Church in connection with the Christian initiation, or if they simply serve to encourage the establishment of such practices at a later time. Whatever the case, it is certain that as early as the second century, in the context of Christian initiation, a rite of anointing is seen, usually following baptism but sometimes, as in the Syrian Church, preceding it. From this rite of anointing *(chrio)* believers came to be called Christians *(christianoi)*, as in fact the name Christ itself had been derived.[19] (Hence also the English *christen* and *christening*.) The theme, then, of the Holy Spirit as "royal seal" that Christ imprints upon his followers, his sheep, at the moment of their baptism, recurs again and again in the ancient sources[20] and finally evolves into the doctrine of the "indelible character."

The rite of anointing stands out in particular relief in mystagogical catechesis, where it appears as a separate rite within the context of Christian initiation, coming after baptism and before the reception of the Eucharist. We find a special catechesis dedicated to it, in which the neophytes are told:

> Now that you have become partakers in Christ, it is proper that you should be called "christi," since you have been marked with the seal of the Holy Spirit. . . . After Christ had been baptised in the Jordan and conferred upon the waters the sweet odour of his divinity, he came up out of the water and the Holy Spirit in person descended upon him. Upon you too, when you came up out of the sacred baptismal pool, was conferred the chrism that is a figure of the one who anointed Christ, that is, of the Holy Spirit.[21]

[19] See Theophilus of Antioch, *To Autolicus,* I.12 (PG 6.1041C).

[20] See G.W.H. Lampe, "Sphragis," *A Patristic Greek Lexicon* (Oxford: Clarendon Press, 1961) 1355–6.

[21] Cyril of Jerusalem, *Mystagogical Catecheses,* III.1 (PG 33.1088).

At a later stage this rite of anointing came to be practiced as a sacrament on its own, the actual sacrament of confirmation, and it took on different forms and variations of content in the different churches. Let us then say something about this sacrament. Not to go into its history and the way it evolved, which are very complex issues, but only to touch on the present-day catechesis in the Catholic church concerning confirmation.

> Confirmation is for each one of the faithful what Pentecost was for the Church as a whole and what the descent of the Holy Spirit was for Jesus when he came up out of the Jordan. It strengthens our baptismal incorporation into Christ and into the Church and our consecration to a prophetic, royal and priestly ministry. It brings us an abundance of the gifts of the Spirit, the "seven gifts" that work together to bring us to the perfection of love. If therefore we can call baptism the sacrament of birth, confirmation is the sacrament of growth. For that very reason it is also the sacrament of witness, because witness is linked closely to maturity in the Christian life.[22]

The new and most delightful element in this is the stress that is laid on the link between confirmation and Pentecost and between confirmation and the charisms. If we were able to have all of this really put into practice, we would eventually no longer need to seek "baptism in the Spirit," because confirmation would then admirably fulfill its function. It would be the normal opportunity given to every Christian to ratify and renew the baptism they received as little children, so "releasing" its latent power. This spontaneous testimony given by a young woman shows what the experience of confirmation can be in a person's progress in the life of faith:

> The fact that I came back to the Church, I owe to my Confirmation which I remember as a decisive moment in my life. The day I received this sacrament, something changed in me. When the bishop anointed my forehead, I felt an unexpected thrill in my heart and a great warmth of soul, as if a fire long gone out was lit again. But what made the deepest impression on me was the joy that filled me such as I had never experienced before.

[22] *La verità vi farà liberi* (The truth will set you free), Catechism for Adults (Rome: Libreria Editrice Vaticana, 1995) 324.

4. Anointed in Spirit: A Way of Life

And now we will see how the anointing, seen as a way of life or a quality of action, is grafted onto these biblical and sacramental roots. There is a very close relationship between this anointing and the sacramental one. Nevertheless, the two are not identical, because one belongs in the *objective* order of sacraments, while the other belongs in the *subjective* order of asceticism and mysticism.

How did this second or spiritual sense of anointing come to be accepted? One of the important steps was presented, once again, by Augustine, who interprets the text of 1 John 2:27 in the sense of an ongoing anointing by means of which the Holy Spirit, within us as teacher and guide, enables us to enter into and understand what we hear from others in the outward way of hearing. Saint Gregory the Great did much to ensure that Augustine's insight on this point, as on many other points, became popularly known through all the Middle Ages.[23]

A new phase in the development of the theme of anointing opened with Saint Bernard and Saint Bonaventure. In their writings the new, spiritual, and modern understanding of anointing became firmly established, linked not so much to the theme of the knowledge of *truth* as to the theme of the living experience of the divine *reality*. At the start of his commentary on the Song of Songs Saint Bernard says: "A song such as this only *anointing* can teach, and only experience can enable you to understand it."[24]

Saint Bonaventure sees the anointing as the same as *devotion*, which he understands as "a tranquil feeling of love for God arising from the remembrance of all that Christ has done for us."[25] And in another place he defines the anointing as "that feeling of consolation given by the Holy Spirit to the soul that has reached the state of fervour."[26]

However, anointing is not something that is limited to the area of devotion; it is of interest above all in the area of contemplation.

---

[23] See Augustine, *On the First Letter of John,* 3.13 (PL 35.2004–5); see Gregory the Great, *Homilies on the Gospels,* 30.3 (PL 76.1222).

[24] Bernard of Clairvaux, *On the Song of Songs,* I.6.11, ed. Cistercense (Rome, 1957) 7.

[25] Bonaventure, *Sermon III on Saint Mary Magdalene* (Quaracchi, IX, p. 561).

[26] Bonaventure, *Sermon I on Holy Saturday,* 3 (Quaracchi, IX, p. 269).

Bonaventure distinguishes between two basic forms of contemplation: an *intellectual contemplation,* whose goal is knowledge of the truth and that is based on the gift of understanding, and a *sapiential contemplation,* whose goal is an experience of and a taste for things divine based on the gift of wisdom. The latter is what he calls "the anointing." He liked to say the Dominicans tended to experience the first kind of contemplation, and the Franciscans the second. "One Order concentrates first on speculation and secondarily on the anointing, and the other Order attends first to the anointing and secondarily to speculation."[27]

The meaning that Saint Bonaventure gives to the anointing comes across more clearly in what he writes at the beginning of his work *The Mind's Journey to God:*

> Therefore I exhort the reader, before anything else, to turn earnestly in prayer to Christ crucified, whose blood takes away the stain of our faults, and I do that lest he think that the reading alone will be enough for him, without the *anointing,* or that speculation will be enough without devotion, or study without admiration, consideration without exultation, effort without piety, knowledge without love, understanding without humility, or zeal without the grace of God.[28]

This anointing, he says finally, depends not on nature, nor on science, nor on words, nor on books, but on "the gift of God that is the Holy Spirit."[29] After Bonaventure, this was to become the usual way of understanding the anointing, especially in the Franciscan school. One of Bonaventure's disciples writes: "The anointing is as it were a beautiful dew that, as it becomes diffused through all of the soul, instructs, strengthens and comforts it, and leaves it sweetly disposed to gather to itself and to contemplate the splendours of Truth."[30]

The new understanding of the word is reflected in the interpretation given, from that time onward, to the title "spiritual anointing" in the *Veni Creator.* In a paraphrase of the hymn we read: "He is called *spiritual anointing* because he makes all the trials

---

[27] Bonaventure, *On the Hexaemeron,* XXII.21 (Quaracchi, V, p. 440).

[28] Bonaventure, *The Mind's Journey to God,* Prologue, 4.

[29] Ibid., VII.5.

[30] Pseudo-Bonaventure, *The Seven Stages of Contemplation,* in Bonaventura, *Opera Omnia,* XII (Paris, 1868) 183.

and tribulations of the world gentle and joyfully bearable, as indicated by the expressions 'rest in weariness' and 'cool refreshment in the heat' *(in labore requies, in aestu temperies)* that we find in the Sequence."[31]

If we are to understand the term "anointing" in a way that embraces the entirety of its usage, especially in the English-speaking world, following the spread of the Pentecostal and charismatic phenomenon, we need to take into account a still-later development of the term. Not only within the Catholic ambit, but outside of it as well, the terms "anointed" and "anointing" are used today to describe the way a person goes about doing something, or to describe the quality of someone's preaching or teaching. There is, however, a difference of nuance. In the traditional usage, "anointed" would first of all suggest, as we have seen in the texts we have cited, the idea of gentleness and sweetness to the point where, in the profane use of the word, a negative sense emerges suggesting "a smooth or insinuating manner of speech or attitude, often hypocritical." The related adjective, "unctuous," comes to mean "a person or attitude degradingly ceremonious or servile." However, in the Pentecostal and charismatic use of the term it suggests the idea of empowerment and persuasive power and efficacy. A sermon is said to be anointed when the listeners are moved to recognize the work of the Spirit in it: a message that moves the hearer deeply, that "convicts" one of sin, that pierces the heart. And in this we come back to an exquisitely biblical usage of the term, found for example in the text from Acts where it says that Jesus was "anointed with the Holy Spirit and with power" (see Acts 10:38).

Moreover, the term "anointing" comes back to signifying an act rather than a habit. It is not something that we possess in a permanent way, but something that comes upon us, "investing" us for the moment in the exercise of a ministry or in prayer. There was a man, a laborer, who had no knowledge whatever of this kind of anointing, but who described to perfection its effects upon him:

> For some time now, when I want to pray, I ask the Holy Spirit to come upon me. And then I feel a strength come into me, a

---

[31] Pseudo-Bonaventure, *Compendium of Theological Truth*, 10, in Bonaventure, *Opera Omnia*, VIII (Paris, 1868) 68.

sweetness (I do not know what to call it), something that goes all through me, from head to foot, soul and body, and when it has passed it leaves me in such peace, and with a desire to pray again.

This charismatic way of perceiving the anointing is not new in the history of the Church. What is actually happening is that we are seeing emerge once again the kind of experience that has been well known in spiritual and charismatic movements ever since ancient times. An author who lived in the fourth or fifth century writes:

Those who come to be anointed in mind and in the inner man with the heavenly and spiritual oil of gladness, that sanctifies and fills with joy, are receiving a sign of the incorruptible Kingdom and of the eternal power, that is, the assurance of the Spirit, and thus, they are receiving the Holy Spirit, the Paraclete himself.[32]

5. How to Receive the Anointing of the Spirit

At this stage, we have all the elements that we need to put together to apply, in our own life, all the wealth of biblical and theological content in the theme of spiritual anointing. Saint Basil says that the Holy Spirit "was always present in the life of the Lord, with him as his *anointing* and inseparable companion," in such a way that "everything that Christ did, he did in the Spirit,"[33] in the presence and under the guidance of the Spirit. This implies a certain passivity, a being put into action, moved, or, as Saint Paul says, "led by the Spirit" (Gal 5:18). The anointing is more something that the Spirit gives than anything we can do.

The outward effects of all of this are seen at times in gentle calm and peacefulness, in delicacy, devotion, or in deep emotion, and at times in authority, strength, power, or ability to take command of the situation, all in keeping with the circumstances, the character of the person concerned and also the responsibility each carries for the work that must be done. The clearest example is Jesus himself who, moved by the Spirit, showed himself meek

---

[32] *Spiritual Homilies,* attributed to Macarius, 17.1 (PG 34.624C–D).

[33] Basil the Great, *On the Holy Spirit,* XVI.39 (PG 32.140C).

and humble of heart but also, when the occasion demanded it, able to act with divine authority.

One characteristic of the anointing is that it confers a certain inward clarity that enables us to do what has to be done with ease and mastery. It is, in a way, like "being in form" for an athlete or "inspiration" for a poet: being in a position really to give of one's best. Yet the anointing itself is something more than we will ever be able to tell in words. There is no mistaking an anointing when we are in the presence of someone who is experiencing it, but though we "see" it, it is never possible to find clear concepts or definitions to say what it is that we see, for it partakes, in fact, of the very nature of the Holy Spirit and of an order of being beyond our grasp. The *Dictionary of Spirituality* says, "The spiritual teaching of Saint Bonaventure is suffused throughout with *anointing* and poetry."[34] One has an intuitive grasp of what that means, though one cannot define it with concepts and words.

But, if the anointing is something that comes from the presence of the Holy Spirit, and is in fact the Spirit's gift, what could we possibly do to experience it? Right away we need to remember what Saint John assures us, "You have been anointed by the Holy One" (1 John 2:20). That is, we already possess the anointing because we are baptized and confirmed. As the traditional teaching concerning the indelible seal, based on 2 Corinthians 1:21-22, expresses it, Christ has anointed us in these sacraments "marking us with his seal and giving us the pledge, the Spirit, that we carry in our hearts." This anointing, however, will remain inert and inactive in us, unless we "set it free." As long as perfume is sealed in the bottle, no one will be able to enjoy its lovely scent. The alabaster jar needs to be broken! (see Mark 14:3). When the woman broke the jar, says Saint John (12:3), "the house was filled with the fragrance of the perfume." The broken jar was a symbol of Christ's humanity: pure as he was, he was truly "a vessel of alabaster" to be broken in his death on the cross so that the Holy Spirit within him could be poured out, to fill the whole Church and the whole world with the Spirit's fragrance. "The Lord received a precious ointment *(myron)* on his head to exhale the fragrance of incorruptibility upon his Church."[35]

---

[34] See Dict. Spir., I, col. 1842.

[35] Ignatius of Antioch, *Letter to the Ephesians,* 17.1.

And it is here that we find where our part in the anointing comes in. The actual anointing does not depend on us, but the removal of the obstacles that prevent the anointing shining forth does depend on us. It is not difficult for us to understand what the breaking of the alabaster jar means in our own case. The jar is our own humanity, our "I," often the arid intellectualism to which we cling. To break it means to surrender ourselves to God, to become obedient to him even to death, just as Jesus did.

However, although our own effort to be surrendered, obedient, plays a part, it is not all that is needed. The anointing comes much more through believing, praying, and in humble simplicity asking for it. Notice when Jesus received his anointing: "while Jesus . . . was praying, the heaven was opened, and the Holy Spirit descended upon him" (Luke 3:21-22). "How much more will the heavenly Father give the Holy Spirit to those who ask him!" (Luke 11:13). What we need to do, simply, is ask for an anointing before we set out to do any work, any service of the Kingdom. When we priests come to get ready for the reading of the Gospel and the homily, the liturgy has us ask the Lord to "cleanse our heart and our lips" so that we may worthily proclaim his Good News. Should it not encourage us to pray, now and again, "Anoint my heart and my mind, Almighty God, so that with gentle kindness and in the power of your Holy Spirit I may proclaim your word"?

There are times when we almost in a physical way feel the anointing coming upon us. Feelings are deeply moved, the soul enjoys clarity and assurance; all trace of nervousness disappears, all fear and timidity are gone. We experience something of the tranquility and the authority of God himself. Certain songs or hymns are particularly helpful in disposing us to be open to this anointing from on high. The *Veni Creator* itself is one of them. Another very well known throughout the Pentecostal and charismatic movement is the little chorus:

> Spirit of the living God, fall afresh on me;
> melt me, mould me, fill me, use me.
> Spirit of the living God, fall afresh on me.

There is no counting the number of people who have experienced the anointing of the Spirit coming upon them while the strains of this hymn and its simple melody rose all around.

Singing in general, but especially choral singing by an assembly at prayer, is known to be very effective in this, because it makes us "change pace"; it breaks the routine of our usual human way of thinking, and puts us in a frame of mind and of feeling in which it becomes easier to soar to a level of reality higher than the human.

6. Anointed to Spread the Pure Odor of Christ

On every side we see signs of how vitally necessary it is, especially for the leaders of the Church, to live and work under this spiritual anointing in its twofold aspect of gentleness and strength. It would be a mistake for ordained ministers to count only on the sacramental anointing, received once only when they were ordained and not to be repeated, and which enables them to be appointed to lead, to preach, and to teach. Ordination provides, so to say, the *authorization* to do certain things, but not necessarily the *authority* to do them. It assures the apostolic succession, but not necessarily any apostolic success!

See how an Anglican bishop describes his experience of a new charismatic anointing at a certain stage in his life:

> I did not really know what was happening then because I wasn't expecting anything very much. But there was a wonderful tingling and a sense of the love of God, and an overpowering sense of his presence. I found myself being pressed to the ground and simply submitting to him in joy, saying the one word "yes" and not able to say another word. Later that afternoon I again found myself in chapel, and once again *the Lord anointed me* in a very deep and loving way. With incredible joy, I found myself repeating, "I am your son. I am your son." God had not just accepted me as a person, but had created me anew as his own son. Eventually I had no words left. The last word I could say with any authenticity was "God," and I just said it very lovingly. When I found myself without any words, I began to make some rather strange noises! I didn't know what they were at the time . . . . This has involved first of all submission to the Lord, sonship, praise, the fruits of the Spirit being given instead of striven after, and a wonderful sense of victory. The Lord has just taken away sins that I have been battling for years.[36]

[36] Ralph Martin, ed., *The Spirit and the Church* (New York: Paulist Press, 1976) 255–6 (the testimony of Bill Burnett), emphasis added.

This bishop goes on to describe the effect that this anointing had on his diocese. Where before he had not known what to do for priests struggling with the problem of alcoholism other than to suggest to them that they go to a clinic for treatment, he now invited them into his home and prayed with them, and a number were completely healed by the power of prayer. Where before at clergy meetings they had spoken of everything but evangelization and the real spiritual mission of the Church, they now all agreed that what the diocese most needed was renewal in the Holy Spirit. Ecumenism, which had been a kind of abstract doctrinal problem, became a living reality, and the various Christian churches in the area were drawn together in a new relationship and by new contacts. If we judge by its effects, this anointing was no different from what we described earlier as the "baptism in the Spirit."

The anointing in the Spirit is, of itself, not something confined to particular occasions or limited to certain categories of people in the Church. An ointment continuously spreads its perfume simply because it is there. And the anointing has been conferred on every believer precisely in order to make him or her "the aroma of Christ" (2 Cor 2:15). When at the Mass on Holy Thursday the bishop blesses the oil that will be used in the anointings at baptism and confirmation, he says: "May this anointing penetrate and sanctify them so that, freed from natural corruption and consecrated as temples of your glory, they may spread abroad the good odor of a holy life."

In the second century the pagan Celsus raised the objection, "How could one man, who lived in an obscure village in Judea, fill the world with the perfume of the knowledge of God as you Christians say?" Origen answered, saying that it was possible thanks to the mystery of the anointing in which all Christians share:

> Jesus received the anointing with the oil of gladness in all its fullness. Those who are partakers in Jesus, each according to his own measure, partake also in his anointing. Since Christ is in fact the Head of the Church which forms one single body with him, the precious oil poured upon the Head, runs down to Aaron's beard and all the way to the very fringes of his garments (see Ps 133:2).[37]

---

[37] Origen, *Against Celsus,* VI.79 (SCh 147, p. 378).

The Holy Spirit, according to this evocative spiritual interpretation of the Psalm, is the precious ointment that is poured out on the head of the new High Priest who is Christ Jesus; from him, the Head, it spreads "like a soaking of oil" down through his body, the Church, to the very hem of its garment, there where the Church touches the world. The liturgy puts this image before us when, in the Mass for the blessing of oils on Holy Thursday, it prays this prayer that we can make our own as we end this reflection:

> *Father, you have consecrated your only Son with the oil of the Holy Spirit and made him Messiah and Lord. Grant that we may share in his consecration and be witnesses in the world to his work of salvation.*[38]

---

[38] *Roman Missal,* Holy Thursday Mass for the Blessing of Oils.

X

Sevenfold in Your Gifts

The Holy Spirit adorns the Church with many charisms

This reflection brings us to the third verse of the *Veni Creator.* Translated literally, the verse reads:

> You are sevenfold in your gifts,
> you are finger of God's right hand,
> you, the Father's solemn promise
> giving tongues the gift of words.

From the point of view of its *form,* this verse continues the *encomium,* the solemn praise of the Paraclete consisting of a series of biblical titles used in the vocative case: "You who are called the Paraclete . . . . You who are sevenfold in your gifts . . . ."

However, from the point of view of its theological *content* a whole new horizon is opened. In the second verse the author of the hymn had us contemplate the sanctifying work of the Spirit, the Spirit's action within us, transforming us, but now the hymn invites us to contemplate the charismatic work of the Spirit which is manifested in a variety of gifts and charisms. All the titles and the themes brought together in this verse link back more or less directly to this particular activity of the Spirit: The Holy Spirit gives the seven gifts; the Spirit is the "finger of God's right hand," driving out demons, working signs and wonders; the Spirit is the promise of power from on high fulfilled at Pentecost; the Spirit is manifested through the gifts that relate to the use of speech—preaching, teaching, prophesying, the gift of tongues . . . .

We have come to make this distinction between the two avenues of the Holy Spirit's action—sanctifying and charismatic—through modern developments in exegesis. The distinction, however, was not entirely unknown to the Fathers and it is reflected in the Tradition where we find it expressed in the distinction between "the Spirit as Gift" and "the gifts of the Spirit." Augustine, making a comparison between Psalm 68:18 ("receiving gifts from people") and Ephesians 4:8 ("he gave gifts to his people"), makes this comment:

> Both of them, the prophet as well as the apostle, speak of gifts in the plural because by the work of the Gift which is the Holy Spirit who is given to all the members of Christ alike, a multitude of special gifts is distributed, each one receiving what befits each.[1]

The author of our hymn took up this idea and followed it faithfully. In the previous verse he had called the Holy Spirit "the supreme gift of God" (in the singular); now, starting from this verse, he calls the same Spirit "sevenfold in your gifts" *(septiformis munere)*.

This brings a fundamental truth to light: The Holy Spirit, who is the principle of Church unity, is also at the same time the principle of the richness, beauty, and diversity within the Church. We have here a faithful echo of the momentous message of the letter to the Ephesians. In that letter Saint Paul first spells out what is one and the same for everyone in the Church—the sacraments, the virtues of faith, hope, and love: "There is one Body and one Spirit, just as you were called to the one hope of your calling, one Lord, one faith, one baptism, one God and Father of all, who is above all and through all and in all" (Eph 4:4-6). He then goes on to spell out a list of the things that are different and particular to each individual member: "But each of us was given grace according to the measure of Christ's gift. Therefore it is said, 'When he ascended on high he made captivity itself a captive; he gave gifts to his people'" (Eph 4:7-8).

Certain writers provide an evocative image of this transition from our vision of the Spirit as one and undivided, to our vision of him as the source of limitless variety in the works he does and the special gifts he gives. Cyril of Jerusalem finds such an image in the rain. Though one and undivided as rainfall from heaven, it causes an endless variety of kinds and colors of flowers to spring up: apt image of the Holy Spirit who, "though he himself is one, confers on each whatever grace he wills."[2] An Italian poet finds another such image in light that "falls on this and that, and wher-

---

[1] Augustine, *The Trinity,* XV.19.34.
[2] See Cyril of Jerusalem, *Catecheses,* XVI.12.

ever it is at, makes myriad colours shine."[3] The relationship between light and colors is perhaps what best expresses the relationship between grace and charisms.

In the long series of works of the Spirit that has been unfolding since the creation and will continue until the end of time, we come now to the one Saint Basil calls "order within the Church":

> Now is it not clear and incontestable that the making of the Church is the work of the Holy Spirit? It is he himself who has given "the first place to apostles, the second to prophets, the third to teachers; after them, miracles, and after them the gift of healing; helpers, good leaders, those with many languages" (1 Cor 12:28). This order is arranged according to the diversity of the gifts of the Spirit.[4]

1. What Is a Charism?

If we want to define a charism, we need to take account of two elements. First of all, a charism is a gift given "for the common good" (1 Cor 12:7). In other words, a charism is not ordinarily or primarily given for the sanctification of the individual who receives it, but for "the service of others" (1 Pet 4:10). Second, a charism is a gift given "to one" or "to some" in particular, and not to all equally in the same way. This is what distinguishes charisms from sanctifying grace, from the virtues of faith, hope, and love, and from the sacraments, for these are given in the same way to all and they do not differ from one person to another.

In certain charisms the first element prevails, in others the second. But neither of these two elements, taken separately, can explain the meaning of "charism" in all the places where the word occurs in the New Testament. Paul, for instance, says that marriage and virginity are charisms (see 1 Cor 7:7), not because they are gifts given principally for the service and benefit of others (each is, rather, a stable response to a personal grace, a particular vocation), but because in this matter each one has his or her own gift.

We need to take both of these aspects of charism into account if we are to understand how the Church Fathers used the term.

---

[3] A. Manzoni, *Pentecost* (a hymn): *"Come la luce provvida / piove di cosa in cosa, / e i color vari suscita / dovunque si riposa."*

[4] Basil the Great, *On the Holy Spirit*, XVI.39 (PG 32.141A).

Where they list the charisms, their lists include wisdom, prophecy, the power to drive out demons, clarity of insight in interpreting the Scriptures, voluntary continence; that is to say, they speak of charisms given for the common good as well as of charisms destined to personal sanctification.[5] We can see too why the Church today considers the various forms of the religious life also as charisms.

Scholastic theology saw a distinction between forms of grace, defining a charism as *gratia gratis data* (grace given gratuitously) as distinct from *gratia gratum faciens,* sanctifying grace, that is, the kind of grace that makes us pleasing to God. In the context in which it arose this distinction has a certain validity, but we cannot insist on it outside of that context without creating serious problems. For sanctifying grace is in fact also freely, gratuitously given (in a deeper sense than any other), and a charism, properly put to use, also makes us pleasing to God and helps toward our sanctification, especially if it is one of the charisms in which the personal aspect of the gift is primary.

There is also the question of talents. What are we to say of them? Do we need to widen the concept of charisms, in order to include the natural giftedness that we call talent, as some modern writers tend to do?[6] It is a fact that the whole of life, lived in faith, is grace, and that life is not divided into parts, one religious or sacred and the other secular or profane. Nevertheless, we do not find the New Testament using charism to indicate an enhanced or transformed natural human ability. Charism is always "a manifestation of supernatural power."[7] Talents and charisms come to us in very different ways: talent as the result of natural birth, and charism by a free and sovereign act of God, linked to our baptism. For this reason, talent is often a matter of heredity, but charism never.

If we were to do away with the distinction between talent and charism, we would also lose the distinction between nature and grace. It may be that a charism is "supported" by a natural talent or giftedness, but the two are not the same. Saint Maximus the Confessor explains:

[5] See Cyril of Jerusalem, *Catecheses,* XVI.12.

[6] See J. Moltmann, *Der Geist des Lebens* (München, 1991) 195ff. (English trans.: *The Spirit of Life* [London: SCM Press, 1992]).

[7] J.D.G. Dunn, *Jesus and the Spirit* (London, 1975) 255.

The grace of the most Holy Spirit does not confer wisdom on the saints without their natural intellect as capacity to receive it; nor does he give the gift of knowledge where there is not a natural rational ability to receive it; nor does he give faith without total certainty of intellect and reason regarding future realities; nor does he give charisms and healings where there is no natural love for our neighbour, nor any one of the other charisms where the conditions are not right and there is no matching ability to receive them. In any case, no one will ever come to possess any of the gifts we have mentioned through any natural ability whatever, but only through the divine power that confers them.[8]

Charisms and natural talents are never "separated," but neither are they ever "confused."

2. Seven Gifts, or Seven Charisms?

In saying all this about the present verse of the *Veni Creator,* it seems that we have lost sight of the title with which it started, that said that the Spirit is "sevenfold in his gifts." For that, in fact, refers clearly to the theme of the "seven gifts" of the Holy Spirit. In the generally-accepted interpretation, these seven gifts do not belong in the charismatic sphere but to the area of sanctification in the strict sense, for they are not given to certain people only but offered exactly the same to everyone. The traditional view of the nature of "gift" has been summed up like this: "A gift is sanctifying and ordered towards the perfecting of its recipient, while a charism is a disposition granted for the benefit of others. The difference between gift and charism is the same as the difference between grace that is *gratum faciens* and grace that is *gratis data.*"[9]

This is one of the points that most clearly bring to light the effects of the fact that the biblical teaching on the charisms has been blurred for such a long time. It will help to run quickly through the history of the theme of the seven gifts of the Holy Spirit. The text from which it takes its rise is Isaiah 11:1-3. In the Hebrew original six gifts are listed, and the last, fear, is mentioned twice: wisdom, understanding, counsel, fortitude, knowledge, and fear of the Lord.

---

[8] Maximus the Confessor, *Various Chapters,* IV.13 (PG 90.1308–9).

[9] X. Ducros, *Charismes,* Dict. Spir. 2, col. 506.

The Septuagint and the Vulgate substitute piety for one of the mentions of fear of the Lord, and so bring the total to the classical number, seven.

Present-day exegesis is unanimous in seeing this text as listing the charisms that would characterize the ideal sovereign, the Messiah who was to come. Wisdom and understanding indicate shrewdness and skill; counsel and fortitude indicate prudence in governing and military valor; knowledge and fear of the Lord indicate a right religious attitude based on the knowledge and veneration of God that the Sovereign would spread around him.[10] The presence of all these gifts in the ruler would ensure a kingdom where right would triumph and the poor would be treated with justice (Isa 11:2-4). These are the Messianic charisms.

The gifts listed are, therefore, in the line of the charisms that bring about the ability to carry out specific tasks for the good of the community, as, for instance, to build and embellish the Temple, to win battles, to see that justice is equitably done to all, and to prophesy. They are not principally intended for the individual good of the one who receives them, for his personal sanctification; they are given, rather, for the direct benefit of the entire people and so given in fact to all of them collectively.

These charisms soon lost their particular reference to the ideal sovereign and to just government. Treatises on the pastoral government and the ideal of the good shepherd took a different path, as we can see in writings such as the *Pastoral Rule* of Saint Gregory the Great, *On Consideration* by Saint Bernard, and *The Seven Wings of the Seraphim* by Saint Bonaventure. Instead, the seven gifts began to be seen as applying to all believers and to each individually. Saint Gregory the Great says that we rise to God's level through the seven gifts in an order opposite to the order in which the Holy Spirit gives them:

> For by means of fear we rise to piety; through piety to knowledge; through knowledge we gain fortitude; from fortitude we come to counsel; with counsel we progress towards understanding and with understanding we move forward towards wisdom, and thus by these upward stages, through the sevenfold grace of the Spirit, the door to eternal life is finally opened to us.[11]

[10] See H. Cazelles, *Saint Esprit*, DBSuppl., fasc. 60, 1986, 141–2.
[11] Gregory the Great, *Sermons on the Eucharist*, II.7.7 (CC 142, p. 322).

Development in the eastern Church took the same direction. Saint Maximus the Confessor writes:

> These spiritual gifts work in particular ways: by fear, we reject evil; with fortitude, we do good; with counsel, we are able to discern what is against us; through piety we gain a genuine knowledge of what we rightly should do; with knowledge, we come to an actual understanding or perception of the virtues, that is, of what is divinely right; understanding brings a transport of the whole soul towards the things that are known; and wisdom leads to that union with God that is wholly beyond comprehension although, in those who are found worthy of it, the desire for it already becomes the fulfilment.[12]

And so we see how the formula emerged that was to become the traditional one: "The sevenfold power of the Holy Spirit,"[13] the "sevenfold gift"[14] *(septiforme munus)* mentioned in our hymn, and the "sacred septenary" *(sacrum septenarium)* of the Sequence for Pentecost. The seven gifts were often seen in relation to the seven spirits of the Apocalypse (see Rev 1:4) and to the eight beatitudes.[15]

Through the whole patristic era, however, down to the emergence of Scholastic theology, no one had ever thought of the seven gifts as a "third kind" of distinct entity, taking a middle position between the sanctifying grace and the charisms. The gifts were seen as only a discernable "branch" within the vast universe of charisms: those in which the aspect of "particular gift" prevailed over the aspect of gift "given for the common good." As we saw, Maximus the Confessor defined them as "spiritual gifts" whose purpose was the acquisition of virtue. Moreover, certain of these gifts, for instance, wisdom and knowledge, are found in the list of the charisms that Saint Paul writes about, and another, counsel, is not very different from the gift of discernment of spirits listed among charisms (see 1 Cor 12:8ff.).

This was the stage reached in the development and this was the significance of the title *septiformis munere,* "sevenfold in your

---

[12] Maximus the Confessor, *Various Chapters,* III.38 (PG 90.1276).

[13] Origen, *Homilies on Leviticus,* 8.11 (SCh 287, p. 66); Origen, *Homilies on Numbers,* 6.3 (SCh 415, p. 150).

[14] Hilary of Poitiers, *Commentary on Matthew,* 15.10 (PL 9.1007).

[15] Augustine, *Exposition on the Psalms,* 150.1 (CC 40, p. 2192).

gifts," as it was used in the *Veni Creator*. In another work by the same author, to which we have referred a number of times, we read: "The Holy Spirit is called 'sevenfold' on account of the gifts that, without dividing himself, he gives to each one according to each one's ability to receive them."[16]

Some hundreds of years were to pass before the theme of the seven gifts of the Holy Spirit entered into a new phase of development in which it came to lose all reference to the charisms and began to be seen as a category apart. We will have an insight into the reason why the development took this course if we are aware of the question that gave rise to it: Are the gifts of the Holy Spirit the same as virtue, or are they something different? The great masters of Scholastic theology came to the conclusion that the gifts were not the same as the moral virtues but of a higher order than virtue. They are permanent dispositions of the soul, given by God to make the soul docile to the inspirations of the Holy Spirit. They are in the same order as the infused (freely given, not acquired) theological virtues, lower than they and given to prepare us for them.

One can say that, from that time onward, there has not been a spiritual writer who has not touched on the gifts of the Spirit at least briefly if not at some length. And so it was that, up to the very eve of the Second Vatican Council, any lively and creative reflection on the Holy Spirit in the Western Church took place within the ambit of the theme of the seven gifts. The theme lends itself to a speculative approach, and for that reason it is open to a myriad of variations, depending on the spiritual experience and the theological views that come into play. For instance, in the Thomist school the primacy among the gifts belongs to understanding, the gift that is most aligned toward knowledge, whereas in the Franciscan school the primacy is given to wisdom, the gift most aligned toward the experience of God and delight in him.

There are some who have tried to show that there is a parallel between each of the seven gifts and the seven verses of the *Veni Creator*,[17] but it is a well-known fact that the hymn had originally

---

[16] Rhabanus Maurus, *On the Universe*, I.3 (PL 111.24); see Isidore of Seville, *Etymologies*, VII.3.13 (PL 82.269).

[17] See H. Lausberg, *Der Hymnus "Veni Creator Spiritus,"* JAWG (1969) 33.

six verses: the seventh *(Deo Patri sit Gloria . . .)* is a doxology from the repertoire added later.

I am not about to go step by step through the very extensive development of the theme of the seven gifts.[18] Enough, here, to note that Saint Thomas's teaching on the seven gifts is summarized in a way that is clear and easy to follow in Pope Leo XIII's encyclical on the Holy Spirit, where we read:

> The just person, who already lives the life of grace and who goes about his work with the aid of the virtues, just as the soul with the aid of its powers, also has need of these seven gifts that are properly called the gifts of the Holy Spirit. By means of these gifts, we are given greater flexibility and at the same time greater strength the more easily and promptly to follow as God leads. These gifts are so efficacious that they are able to spur us to the very heights of sanctity. . . . With these gifts, then, the Holy Spirit encourages us and supports us on our way to experience the beatitudes of which we learn in the Gospel.[19]

The point in all this development that I think gives rise to the most significant consequences for us is the fact that where the gifts of the Holy Spirit were at one time seen mainly in the ambit of the charisms, we now see that they are in fact part of what the New Testament calls "the sanctifying action of the Spirit."[20] They even represent the more elevated aspect of this sanctifying action, pertaining to contemplation and the mystical life. The gifts of the Holy Spirit are seen as the crowning perfection of the whole spiritual life. Along the way that leads us from grace to the fruits of the Spirit, that is to Christian virtues, no mention is made of charisms, their place being taken by the seven gifts. This can be clearly seen in a discourse given by Paul VI on Pentecost 1969. He distinguishes two areas in which the Holy Spirit is at work: that of "individual souls" and that of "the community, or the visible body of the Church."

> The first area is the inward reality of our life, our I: the breath of the Spirit reaches to this deep centre of our being, mysterious

---

[18] See C. Bernard, *Dons du Saint-Esprit,* Dict. Spir. 3, cols. 1579–641.

[19] Leo XIII, *Divinum illud munus,* in the *Acts of Leo XIII,* vol. 17 (Rome, 1898) 141; see Thomas Aquinas, *Summa Theologiae,* I-II, q. 68, a. 3.

[20] See 2 Thess 2:13; 1 Pet 1:2.

even to ourselves. It pervades our soul with that first and greatest charism that we call *grace,* which is like a new life, and at
once it gives us the ability to act in a way that is beyond the capacity of our natural powers. That is, it confers the *supernatural
virtues* on us, spreading through all the ramifications of the
human psyche with those impulses that we call *gifts,* moving
us to easy and courageous action, and it fills us with those
amazing spiritual effects that we call *the fruits of the Spirit.*

Then, moving to the second area of the Spirit's action, his work
in the community as a whole, Paul VI says:

Surely the "Spirit breathes where he wills" (John 3:8), but, in the
economy that Christ has established, the Spirit follows the channel of the apostolic ministry. God has created the hierarchy—the
ministerial priesthood—and thus has more than sufficiently provided for the needs of the Church until the end of time.[21]

What conclusions should we draw, in the light of all that we
have said on the theme of the seven gifts of the Holy Spirit? The
immense body of literature on the theme still has some validity
for the ascetical and mystical doctrine that finds expression in it.
But it is clear that it needs radical rethinking. Two facts point up
the necessity for a thoroughgoing revision. The first is the fact
that the new understanding of Isaiah 11 means that the old theology of the seven gifts really does not have any biblical basis. The
second, and more important, is the rediscovery of the authentic
biblical teaching on the charisms. The doctrine of the seven gifts
was something that developed in the void left by the eclipse of the
theology of the charisms.

It follows, then, that a correct reading of the "sevenfold gift" as
we find it in our hymn will not be found by following the route we
have followed in looking at other titles. There we stretched the
meaning of the title to have it embrace developments of understanding that came after the hymn had been written. Here, however, we need to go back to the way the title had been understood

---

[21] Paul VI, *Discourse on Pentecost,* 25 May 1969, in *Insegnamenti di Paolo
VI,* Tipografia Poliglotta Vaticana, vol. VII, pp. 308–10. The closing sentence is
taken from J. A. Moehler (*Theologische Quartalschrift,* 1823, p. 497) who, however, cited it in order to criticize it.

before the composition of our hymn, when the seven gifts of the Spirit were not experienced as anything other than the charisms.

3. Vatican II: The Rediscovery of the Charisms

In one of the most important documents of the Second Vatican Council we read:

> It is not only through the sacraments and the ministries of the Church that the Holy Spirit makes holy the People, leads them and enriches them with his virtues. Allotting his gifts according as he wills (see 1 Cor 12:11), he also distributes special graces among the faithful of every rank. By these gifts he makes them fit and ready to undertake various tasks and offices for the renewal and building up of the Church, as it is written, "The manifestation of the Spirit is given to everyone for profit" (1 Cor 12:7). Whether these charisms be more remarkable or more simple and widely diffused, they are to be received with thanksgiving and consolation, since they are fitting and useful for the needs of the Church.[22]

To give due value to the renewing impact of this text, we need to know what happened to the charisms after their tumultuous appearance at the beginnings of the Church. The charisms did not disappear from the *life* of the Church. If we run through the history of the Church with the New Testament listing of charisms in mind, we have to come to the conclusion that, with the possible exception of "speaking in tongues" and of "the interpretation of tongues," not one of the charisms was lost. Church history is full of charismatic evangelizers, of the gifts of wisdom and knowledge (one needs think only of the Doctors of the Church), of stories of miraculous healings, and of individuals endowed with the gift of prophecy or of discernment of spirits, not to speak of gifts such as visions, raptures, ecstasies, illuminations, all of which are counted among the charisms.

History is also full of instances of charismatic "awakenings," that is, of periods when the manifestation of the gifts and works of the Spirit was particularly intense: the age of the martyrs, the burgeoning of monasticism (which, as a phenomenon, is charismatic more than it is ascetic), the first evangelization of Europe,

---

[22] *Lumen Gentium* 12.

the mission to the Slavic peoples noted for the abundance of the charisms in evidence, the Franciscan movement and the incredible growth of religious orders, each one of which is rightly committed to live out the "charism" of its founder. Pius XII was therefore right when he said that the Church had never lacked, nor could ever lack, "prodigiously gifted" members.[23] Just as no one can prevent the wind from blowing where it wills, no one can prevent the Spirit pouring out his gifts where and when he decides.

If that is so, what is new? What allows us to speak of a reawakening of the charisms in our own time? What was previously missing? The charisms had been progressively removed from their proper sphere which is the community, the common good and the organization of the Church, and confined more and more to the sphere of the purely private and personal. They were no longer allowed any impact on the basic functioning of the Church, for the Church considered itself "more than sufficiently assured of continuity by the existence of a sacred hierarchy."

The identity of Jesus as a person as we see him in the Gospels is the outcome of two basic relationships: his relationship as Son to his Father, where the outstanding characteristic is obedience, and his relationship with the Spirit, from whom he receives his authority, freedom, and power to carry out his mission.[24] The Spirit conferred on Jesus the Messianic anointing so that he could bring the Good News to the poor and heal broken hearts, gave him power to drive out demons, and filled him with joy in his prayer. We see clearly, then, that the charismatic action of the Holy Spirit was not an "optional extra" in his life; the Spirit was essential to Jesus, constituting him Messiah and empowering him in his mission.

In the life of the primitive Christian community it is clear, too, that the charisms were not private concerns, something over and above the necessities, or a luxury. The charisms worked in close unison with the apostolic authority to produce the actual structure of the community. The community as a whole lived by the same two fundamental relationships as Jesus: with the Father and with the Spirit. The community, however, does not look to Jesus only as

[23] Pius XII, *Mystici Corporis,* AAS 35 (1943) 200.
[24] Dunn, *Jesus and the Spirit,* 90.

a model to follow in its own experience of these relationships: it depends on him totally, living, moving, existing in him and so sharing in his own unique relationship with the Father and the Spirit.

Some have taught that in the very early days of the Church the community was predominantly charismatic. The role of the apostles, they say, was limited only to maintaining discipline in the exercise of the charisms, while the charisms themselves prompted individuals to work together and provided what was necessary for the growth of the community. This view cannot be sustained, for it is the result of a fundamental error of method in the reading of the New Testament. It isolates the charismatic elements of the primitive community as described by St. Paul and then it goes on to judge all the subsequent development of the Christian community as a progressive abandonment of Paul's view, a gradual weakening of the charismatic character to the point where it is supplanted by the "proto-Catholicism" of the pastoral epistles.

Having said that, we have to admit that at an early stage, and for various reasons, the interplay of the two components of community life, charism and office, began to get out of balance, and the imbalance favored office. From then on, charism was seen as something conferred along with ordination, to be exercised by the ordained ministry. One of the factors that led to this change was the emergence of false teachings, especially those of the Gnostics. It was on the pastors, those who held office, that the responsibility of guarding against false doctrine largely fell, and this tilted the balance more and more toward them. The crisis brought about by the spread of the Montanist movement in the second century in Asia Minor was another factor that served even more to shift the emphasis away from charisms.

This imbalance is the fundamental fact from which follow all the negative consequences for the charisms. The charisms came to be relegated to the fringes of the Church. There is evidence that some of them persisted here and there for a time. Irenaeus, for instance, says that in his day there were still "many brothers in the Church who have the prophetic charisms, who speak in many tongues, who reveal the secrets of men's hearts to their benefit, and who explain the mysteries of God."[25] But it is a phenomenon that

---

[25] See Irenaeus, *Against the Heresies*, V.6.1.

was gradually fading out. The charisms that were chiefly exercised in worship and in the assembly were the ones that disappeared almost completely: the inspired or prophetic word and praise in tongues. Prophecy came to be seen as exclusively the charism attached to the teaching office of the Church, the magisterium, to ensure infallible and authoritative interpretation of revealed truth.

Another inevitable consequence of the imbalance was that the charisms became "clericalized." Because the theological view had linked them with personal holiness, they came eventually to be associated almost exclusively with those normally thought to be living holy lives: pastors, monks, religious. The charisms had moved out of the ambit of *ecclesiology* into the area of *hagiography.*

4. Pentecost Is Today!

I believe that, having said all this, we are now able to understand what it was that the recent council once again brought to light and what was so new in the text on the charisms that we quoted. The charisms are brought back to the very center of the Church. The document that speaks of them is the Dogmatic Constitution of the Church! This shows clearly that they are an essential part of the very nature of the Church that is both hierarchical and charismatic, institution and mystery: the Church that lives not by *sacrament* alone but also by *charism.* The two lungs of the Church body are once again working together in full accord. The Holy Spirit breathes into the Church from two directions, and both are now again fully recognized: *from above,* channeled through the sacraments that Christ instituted and entrusted to the apostolic ministry, and *from below,* channeled through each cell of the body, that is, through all the members of the Church.

The entire Church, living organism that it is and bedewed by the Holy Spirit, consists of these two channels together and is brought into being by grace at work in both these directions. The sacraments are gifts given to the community as a whole for the good of each of its members; the charisms are gifts given to individual members for the good of the whole community.

The text of Vatican II has not remained nothing more than a document put out by the magisterium. The charisms typical of Pentecost have come back, not only as a subject for theologians to consider, but also into the life of the Church. We could try to explain what a charismatic event means, by reading an actual account of one of the many little local Pentecosts now taking place in the Church. A young African layman wrote to one of his personal friends:

> Last month we organised a "New Life in the Spirit" seminar. Those who attended were mainly university students and several nuns. At a certain point the participants were filled with the Holy Spirit in a way that we have never seen before. There were some who wanted to ask God to hold back a little because they were afraid they would never sleep again for the overflowing joy that filled them. Some lay flat on the floor, some cried like babies, others danced like angels in heaven. The people were overcome by the love God was pouring into their hearts. On Pentecost Sunday, two of our group were invited by the celebrant to say a few words. One of them began by saying, "Today is Pentecost Sunday, but we do not want only to remember the Pentecost of two thousand years ago. We want today to be truly Pentecost!" When, a little while later, I stretched my hands over the congregation (there were about a thousand people there) and began to pray, saying, "Come, Holy Spirit!" the Spirit answered the call immediately and hundreds of people, from the strongest to the most frail, fell to the ground as they were given the experience of resting in the Spirit. Others were set free from bondage to the occult and demons. Some were healed of physical ailments. Many renounced sin and turned their lives to God. I have never known such an abundant outpouring of the Spirit of God.

According to one theory, often put forward from the time of Saint John Chrysostom down to our own day, certain charisms are said to have been given only to the Church in its "nascent state" and to have ceased when that was over, as they were no longer necessary for the life of the Church.[26] The council, as we know, abandoned this theory. Now, however, we need to watch that we do not fall into the opposite excess of believing that the charisms can and ought to manifest themselves in the Church, always, everywhere, and in the same way. This would contradict another equally essential truth. If the Spirit breathes *where* he wills and distributes his gifts *as* he wills, it follows that he will do it *when*

---

[26] See G. B. Montini (later Paul VI), *Discourse,* 17 May 1959, in "Rivista della diocesi Milanese" (1959) 417.

he wants to. We cannot deny the Spirit the freedom to breathe in certain places and in certain epochs more than in others or in a different way than he did before. There are times when the presence of the Spirit is more intense and more visible. The age of the Prophets in Israel was one such time. There is a time to create, and a time to put in order! There are various "movements"— mosso, forte, fortissimo, adagio, calmo—even in the great symphony written by the Holy Spirit in the history of salvation; each one has its own beauty, and each one plays its part in the harmony of the whole.

Just as charisms are adapted to the temperament of the one who receives them, so also to the temperament of the age and culture into which they are given. Charisms therefore do not need to be manifest in every age and in every culture in the same form as they came in the beginning. There is no need to try to "standardize" the Holy Spirit. The past was not right in that it thought the only charisms were the "spiritual" ones, intended for our sanctification; it would be wrong of us in the present to think that the only charisms are the ones we call "Pentecostal," intended for the mission: speaking in tongues, healings, prophecy, and so on.

5. Exercise of the Charisms

Jesus said something that rings like an alarm-bell for charismatics: "On that day many will say to me, 'Lord, Lord, did we not prophesy in your name, and cast out demons in your name, and do many deeds of power in your name?' Then I will declare to them, 'I never knew you; go away from me, you evildoers'" (Matt 7:22-23).

Three different charisms are mentioned in this text! The warning gives rise to the question of the proper use of the charisms, and this brings us to the point where we need to move beyond theology and look at the practical issues of life. How are we to make sure that the charism that the Spirit has given us works for the building up of the Church and serves the common good? How are we to make sure that our charism does not become a threat to the unity of the body of Christ and a danger to our own soul?

The answer lies in the relationship between charism and sanctity. It is true that a charism is not given to a person because of his or her holiness; yet it is also true that the charism will not be exercised in a healthy way if it is not planted in the healthy ground of personal holiness.

> Just as it is not possible to keep a lamp alight if it has no oil, so also it is not possible to keep the light of the charisms burning if you do not have an attitude capable of nurturing the good by behaving suitably, in speech, in manners, in dress, in your work and in your thoughts as well. For in fact every charism of the Spirit requires in us an attitude suitably attuned to it and which ceaselessly pours into it, like oil, the spiritual fuel it needs if it is to remain available to the one to whom it has been given.[27]

Let us look briefly at certain of the dispositions or virtues that help more directly to keep the exercise of a charism healthy and make it useful to the good of the community.

The first virtue is *obedience*. The norm for the charisms, ultimately, is Jesus Christ. In him we see obedience to the Father perfectly reconciled with freedom in the Spirit. Two things ruled his life: the *command* received from the Father, once only but for all time, when the Father sent him into the world, and the *inspiration* of the Spirit as it came to him moment by moment. His authority flows from these two sources conjointly. When the moment came for him to be supremely obedient to the Father's will (obedience even to death!), Jesus did not turn to the charisms; he did not call for twelve legions of angels, he did not strike out against his enemies with the same "finger of God" he had used when he drove out demons, but said, "Unless a grain of wheat falls into the earth and dies . . ." (John 12:24).

In our case we are speaking mainly of obedience to the institution, to the ones who serve in authority. The real prophets and charismatics in the history of the Catholic Church, also in its recent history, have been those who were prepared to wait, in obedience and in silence, before they saw their suggestions received or their criticisms heard by the institution and so, in some cases, become the basis for Church renewal.

Charism and institution are like the two arms of the cross. The charismatic, often, is a cross to the institution, and the institution is often a cross to the charismatic. Nevertheless, neither can do

---

[27] Maximus the Confessor, *Various Chapters,* IV.8 (PG 90.1340C).

without the other. Charisms without the institution result in chaos; the institution without the charisms becomes stagnant.

The institution does not kill the charisms; on the contrary, it assures them of a future and also a . . . past. That is, the institution prevents the charisms becoming burned out quickly, like straw, and makes available to the charismatics the experience of the Spirit of all generations that have gone before. By God's blessing, the charismatic renewal in the Catholic Church experienced, from its very beginnings, a strong urge to remain in communion with the hierarchy, and by his blessing too, the papal magisterium recognized it as "a chance for the Church," and as "the first signs of a great springtime for Christianity."[28]

The second virtue is *humility*. Gregory the Great writes: "There are certain characteristic signs that make it evident that a soul is filled with the Holy Spirit. When the charisms and humility are in perfect harmony, it is a sure sign that the Holy Spirit is present."[29]

I would like to put forward two things that illustrate this point: first, how humility takes care of the charisms; second, how the charisms take care of humility.

Humility guards the charisms. The charisms are works of the Holy Spirit, sparks from the very fire of God, given to us for the Church. What can we do to prevent this fire from burning out, and what can we do so that we do not burn our hands with it? This is where humility comes in. Humility makes it possible for this grace of God to come in and to spread out over the Church and into the whole of humanity without becoming scattered and lost and without picking up impurities in the spreading. The higher the voltage or the potential of an electric current passing through a conductor, the greater the resistance of the insulator needs to be to prevent the current running to earth and shorting out the circuit. The great insulator in the spiritual life is humility. It permits the divine current of grace to pass through a person without losing its power, and without provoking sparks and flashes of pride and rivalry, which would be far worse.

---

[28] See Paul VI, Address of 19 May 1975, in *Insegnamenti di Paolo VI*, vol. XIII, p. 538; John Paul II, in "L'Osservatore Romano," 14 November 1996, p. 8.

[29] Gregory the Great, *Dialogues*, I.1 (PL 77, 156).

It is easy, then, to become aware of the way humility works to guard and preserve the charisms. But in what sense is the converse also true, that the charisms protect and preserve humility? The fact that there is "a variety of gifts" means that not everyone has all the gifts; not everyone is an apostle; not everyone is a prophet, and we could go on, through the whole list. Very clearly this shows that none of us is everything, but only a little fragment. God alone is everything, and only the Church possesses the fullness of the Spirit (see Eph 1:23). Thus, self-sufficiency is cut off at the root. According to Saint Paul, a charism is "the particular way the Spirit is given to each person, for a good purpose" (see 1 Cor 12:7). Each is, so to say, a tiny detail in an immense mosaic.

The third virtue (but first in the order of importance) is *love*. Saint Augustine offers us an enlightening thought where he comments on Paul's teaching on the charisms. He says that someone, hearing the awesome list of them (prophecy, wisdom, discernment, healing, tongues), may feel a little sad, a little left out, thinking perhaps that he has none of these. But pay attention to this, Augustine continues:

> If you love, it is no small thing that you possess. If you love the unity, all that is in it and everything that belongs to anyone is your possession too! Cast out envy, and all that is mine becomes yours, and if I cast out envy, all that is yours is mine. Envy causes division but love unites. Of all the organs of the body, only the eye can see, but does the eye see for itself alone? Not at all, it sees for the hand and for the foot and for all the members. . . . Of all the body, only the hand can work at things, but obviously it does not work for itself alone, but also for the eye. If a blow is aimed at your face, does your hand say, "I am not moving, because the blow is not aimed at me"?[30]

Here we see, clearly revealed, the secret of why love is "a better way" (1 Cor 12:31): Love makes me love the Church or the community in which I live, and within that unity all the charisms, and not a few only, are "mine." There is more besides. If you love the unity more than I do, the charism that is given to me is more

---

[30] Augustine, *Commentary on the Gospel of John*, 32.8.

yours than mine. Let us suppose that I have the charism of proclaiming the Gospel. I may grow complacent about it, or pride
myself on it (by no means an abstract hypothesis!) and so become
"a cymbal clashing" (1 Cor 13:1); the apostle warns me that my
charism "will do me no good whatever." But to you who listen to
me, it will not cease to do good, in spite of my sin. Because you
love, you possess without any danger to yourself what another
possesses at great risk. Love in very fact multiplies the charisms,
for it makes a charism of one the charism of all.

Let us end this reflection with this beautiful prayer to the Spirit,
giver of the charisms, that we find in the Office for Pentecost used
in the Syriac rite:

> *Spirit, dispenser of charisms to everyone;*
> *Spirit of wisdom and knowledge, who so loves us all,*
> *you fill the prophets, perfect the apostles,*
> *strengthen the martyrs, inspire the teachers with teaching!*
> *To you, our Paraclete God,*
> *we send up our supplication along with this fragrant incense.*
> *We ask you to renew us with your holy gifts,*
> *to come down upon us as you came down on the Apostles in the upper*
>   *room.*
> *Pour out your charisms upon us,*
> *fill us with knowledge of your teaching;*
> *make us temples of your glory,*
> *let us be overcome by the wine of your grace.*
> *Grant that we may live for you, be of one mind with you, and adore you,*
> *you the pure, you the holy, God Spirit Paraclete.*[31]

---

[31] *Pontificale Syrorum*, in E.-P. Siman, *L'experience de l'Esprit* (Paris,
1971) 309.

XI

Finger of God's Right Hand

The Holy Spirit brings the power of God to us

Everyone has seen, at least in reproduction, the fresco of the creation of man by Michelangelo in the Sistine Chapel: God the Father, right hand stretched out with finger extended, almost touches the outstretched finger of Adam who lies on the earth on his back, facing up to God. On the one side life and energy, and on the other, pure inertia, rest, and waiting. It was a new way of representing, in art, the moment when, in the words of the Bible, God "breathed" the breath of life into his creature, and Adam, an inert image in clay, changed into a living being (see Gen 2:7).

Of all the visual images one might match with the title "finger of God's right hand" given to the Holy Spirit, this one is surely the best. It takes us from the idea of the Spirit as the *breath* of God to the idea of the Spirit as God's *touch.* In this chapter we will see how we have come to understand that what the outstretched "finger of God" represents is in fact nothing other than the person of the Holy Spirit. Above all we will discover how it is possible for us today to be that Adam who, though weak and "down on the ground," holds up his hand in anticipation of the energy and vitality that God will give him.

There is a profound theological intuition behind this picture representing the Spirit as the touch of the finger of God's right hand. It says that the Holy Spirit is the "place" where God meets with God's creatures, where the Trinity reaches *ad extra,* beyond itself, the place where God "comes out" to share himself with the world. The Holy Spirit is the one that makes a certain "spiritual contact" with the divine a real possibility. This idea was to find its most profound and inward dimension in the mystics who, when they attempted to describe how God communicates himself to the human spirit, spoke of "the ineffably beautiful touch of the Spirit of God."[1] But, even in the sense in which the mystics use it, the

---

[1] Julian of Norwich, *Revelations,* 74.

expression is derived from the biblical definition of the Holy Spirit as "finger of God." One of the well-known mystics writes:

> The human spirit is lifted up into union with the Spirit of our Lord, and each of these two spirits *touches* the other with love . . . . The *touch* is a work of God, the upwelling spring of all grace and every gift and the final intermediary between God and his creature.[2]

Let us go now to discover the biblical and patristic basis of this aspect of revelation concerning the Holy Spirit that the author of the *Veni Creator* has drawn together in the title "finger of God's right hand."

1. It Is through the Finger of God That I Cast out Devils

To call the Holy Spirit the "finger of God" is something that goes back to Jesus: "If it is by the *finger of God* that I cast out the demons, then the kingdom of God has come to you" (Luke 11:20).

Matthew repeats the same incident, with a variation: "But if it is by the *Spirit of God* that I cast out demons . . ." (Matt 12:28). We may ask which of these two expressions records the original words that Jesus actually said. There are arguments in support of both of them, but on balance it is more likely that Luke's account reports the original words, for it is in fact easier to think of reasons for which Matthew might have felt the need to use the more explicit "Spirit of God" rather than the metaphorical "finger of God" than it is to think of reasons why Luke might have done the opposite. This little uncertainty, however, detracts not at all from the importance of the text. This kind of question actually serves to confirm and make even more explicit the fact that in the Bible "Spirit of God" means exactly the same as "finger" (or more often "hand") "of God" (see Ezek 3:14; 8:3).

Either expression tells us that God's action in the world is action with power, or it indicates the power itself of his action. Using that expression, Jesus is clearly affirming that his exorcisms are carried out in the power of God. It was in the same sense that the expression is used by the Egyptian magicians who, when they saw the amazing things that Moses and Aaron were

---

[2] J. Van Ruusbroec, *The Seven Seals* (CM 102, p. 176).

doing, cried out, "This is the finger of God!" (Exod 8:19), meaning that the power of God was at work.

There is another context in the Bible in which the metaphor finger of God is used. It is the passage where we are told that the two stone tablets of the Law given to Moses were "written with the finger of God" (Exod 31:18), but in this instance the link identifying the finger of God with the Spirit of God is more complex. Jeremiah was to say that in the New Covenant God would "write" the law in the hearts of the people (Jer 31:33). According to Ezekiel, this would take place when God put his Spirit in our hearts (Ezek 36:26–27). And finally, Paul would take the next step where he says that the community of the New Covenant is "a letter of Christ, . . . written not with ink but with the Spirit of the living God, not on tablets of stone but on tablets of human hearts" (2 Cor 3:3). It became common practice in the Church, in this context of the law, to see the Spirit of God and the finger of God as meaning exactly the same thing. There is a text from the second century in which we read, "Moses received from the Lord the two tablets written in the Spirit by the finger of the hand of the Lord," and in a document written at a later date, "The commandments of God are written on the soul and on the tablet of the heart by the finger of God, that is, by the Holy Spirit."[3]

In the Fathers we find the theme of the Paraclete, "finger of the hand of God," developed in two contexts: one concerning the divine nature of the Holy Spirit, in the discussions on the subject of the Trinity, the other in the discussions concerning the law and grace at the time of Saint Augustine. We will be looking into this second development of the theme when we come to reflect on the line "pour love into our hearts," so for the present we will look only at the theme as developed in the other context, which, as we shall see, explains the place that the title "finger of God's right hand" is given in our hymn.

We will be looking only at the Latin sources, for they served directly as the basis of the tradition to which the author of the *Veni Creator* was heir, even though these sources were influenced in their development by the older Greek tradition. Ambrose writes:

---

[3] *Letter of Barnabas,* 14.2; Pseudo-Pionius, *Life of Polycarp,* IV.2 (Funk, vol. 2 [1913] 294).

> The kingdom of the divinity is, so to say, a body that, whole and entire, represents the unity of the Godhead, the right hand represents Christ, and the finger of that hand represents the Holy Spirit. . . . We use the word "finger" to draw attention to the Spirit's power at work *(operatoria virtus)*, since the Spirit too, like the Father and the Son, is author of the works of God.[4]

The title "finger of God's right hand," as we have just seen, came to be used more to show that the Three Persons were of *one nature* than to show that they were distinct Persons. Augustine makes use of another explanation. The Spirit is called "finger of God" because "through him the gifts of God are given to the saints" and, in the context of the human body, "it is especially when looking at the finger that one gets the idea of a certain distinction."[5]

Now we can see how these various voices of Tradition harmonize together in the title "finger of God's right hand" as we find it in the *Veni Creator*. Rhabanus Maurus writes:

> The Gospels tell us clearly that the Holy Spirit is the finger of God. . . . Besides, the Law too was written by the finger of God fifty days after the lamb had been killed, and fifty days after the Passion of our Lord Jesus Christ the Holy Spirit came. And so, he is called the finger of God, meaning that the power at work *(operatoria virtus!)* in him is the power he holds in common with the Father and the Son. And for this reason Paul says, "All these are the work of one and the same Spirit, who distributes different gifts to different people just as he chooses" (1 Cor 12:11).[6]

The *Veni Creator* is in truth a wonderful "strainer": as various streams and currents flow to us from the Bible, through the Tradition, it catches them up for us and transforms them into prayer.

Some have seen in the title "finger of God's right hand" the author's intention to confirm and teach the doctrine of the *Filioque,* that is, that the Holy Spirit proceeds from the Father and the Son: as the finger grows from the arm and the arm from the body, so

---

[4] Ambrose, *Commentary on Luke,* VII.92–3 (CC 14, p. 245); *On the Holy Spirit,* III.3.11–19; Didimus of Alexandria, *On the Holy Spirit,* 20 (PG 39.1051).

[5] Augustine, *Catechesis for Beginners,* XX.35 (CC 46, p. 159).

[6] Rhabanus Maurus, *On the Universe,* 1.3 (PL 111.25); see Isidore of Seville, *Etymologies,* VII.3.21 (PL 82.269–70).

the Spirit proceeds from Father and Son.[7] We do come across this interpretation at a later stage in history, for example in Bonaventure,[8] but there is no evidence that would allow us to attribute it also to the author of the *Veni Creator*. We need to look at the context in which the author uses the title (the verse on the gifts and the charisms), and at the explanation that, as we have seen, he gives elsewhere. On that basis we must conclude that the author keeps to the meaning of the title most clearly supported by the Bible, and intends "finger of God" to indicate the working power of the Holy Spirit as it is made manifest in actions that are out of the ordinary, like casting out demons and working miracles. This is how a medieval writer, paraphrasing the *Veni Creator*, correctly interprets the title:

> The Spirit is *Paraclete* when he comforts the timid,
> *living fountain* when he refreshes those who are thirsty,
> *love* when he unites in faith and practice people of various
>   cultures,
> *fire* when he inflames with love,
> *soul's anointing* when by anointing them with heavenly chrism
>   he makes believers fervent,
> *finger of God* when he distributes the gifts that shine forth
>   among the faithful.[9]

2. To Another Is Given the Gift of Working Miracles

The title "finger of God's right hand," therefore, opens up for us a perspective, in the history of salvation and of the Church, on that particular manifestation of the charismatic Spirit which is "the working of signs and wonders." Miracles are yet another of the important elements that have accompanied divine revelation from its very beginning to its final accomplishment, and this links them too back to the action of the Holy Spirit. Along with the gifts that have to do with leadership and the word, Paul mentions a particular charism of the Holy Spirit that consists in "the working of miracles [literally *dynameis*]" (1 Cor 12:10), and the author of the

---

[7] See H. Lausberg, *De Hymno "Veni Creator Spiritus,"* in *"Nachrichten der Akademie der Wissenschaften zu Göttingen,"* I, Philol. hist. Klasse (1976) 391.

[8] Bonaventure, *On the Gospel of Luke*, XI.46 (Quaracchi, VII, p. 292).

[9] *Speculum Virginum* (later than 1140), 11 (CM 5, lines 626ff.).

Letter to the Hebrews writes that God confirmed the salvation wrought by the Lord "with signs and marvels and miracles of all kinds, and by freely giving the gifts of the Holy Spirit" (Heb 2:4).

It is very probable that what the apostle calls "the gift of faith" refers to the same manifestation of the Holy Spirit, as Cyril of Jerusalem explains very clearly:

> There is only one faith, but it comes in two kinds. For there is faith with regard to the dogmas . . . which is necessary for salvation. . . . But there is another kind of faith, and it is a gift from Christ. For it is written . . . , "and another (may have) the gift of *faith* given by the same Spirit" (1 Cor 12:8-9). This faith, given freely by the Spirit as a gift, concerns not only the dogmas, but is also the cause of those marvels that are beyond all the abilities of humankind. The one who has such faith will be able to say to this mountain, "Move from here to there, and it would move" (Matt 17:20).[10]

The fact that the Spirit works wonders is one of the aspects of the life of Jesus and of the early Church most widely witnessed and confirmed. The people of Jesus' day probably saw him more as a worker of miracles than as a prophet. The Acts of the Apostles describes Jesus as a man "attested . . . by God with deeds of power, wonders, and signs that God did through him" (Acts 2:22). Jesus himself presented this fact as proof that he was the Messiah: "The blind see again and the lame walk, lepers are cleansed, and the deaf hear, and the dead are raised to life" (Matt 11:5). Jesus attributes his ability to cast out devils and to work miracles to the presence of the Holy Spirit in him (see Luke 4:8), and the apostles, after him, were equally convinced of it (see Acts 10:38ff.). Saint Basil says that the Spirit "was inseparably with him when he worked his miracles."[11]

Reading the Acts of the Apostles we see very clearly how important "miracles and marvels" were in the infant Church. The difference now is that the apostles and early Christians attributed all these wonders to the Spirit *of Jesus;* they were all worked in the name of Christ, and never by the individual in his own name or on his own authority, as Jesus alone had done. Jesus is not

---

[10] Cyril of Jerusalem, *Catecheses,* V.10–11.
[11] Basil the Great, *On the Holy Spirit,* XVI.39 (PL 32.140C).

merely the first in a line of miracle workers or a model for all the rest; he is the only one, and *all* wonders are worked through him.

Paul, as we have seen, uses the same expression, "works of power," indicating this whole array of manifestations of the Spirit that most clearly bear the imprint of the power of God. He frequently refers to the decisive role that these prodigies played in his own mission as an apostle. Christ, he says, was at work in him, not only in his words but also "by the power of signs and wonders, by the power of the Spirit of God" (Rom 15:19; see 1 Cor 2:4).

3. Why Miracles?

What are we to think of this phenomenon? What do we make of the miracles that have taken place throughout the whole of salvation history and that continue to occur in the life of the Church today? Miracles belong within the ambit of faith, and our attitude toward them must be the attitude of faith. This does not mean that in faith we have to accept every incident claimed to be a miracle and reported as one, but simply that in faith we admit that miracles are possible. Scripture, as well as telling us of miracles, gives us also the criteria by which we judge whether they are authentic and their purpose in the economy of salvation. A passage in the prophecy of Isaiah will help us to grasp the purpose of miracles in God's plan:

> The Lord said:
> Because these people draw near with their mouths
>   and honor me with their lips,
>   while their hearts are far from me,
> and their worship of me is a human commandment learned by
>   rote;
> so I will again do
>   amazing things with this people,
>   shocking and amazing.
> The wisdom of their wise shall perish,
>   and the discernment of the discerning shall be hidden
>   (Isa 29:13-14).

God, then, uses miracles in his designs with us to shatter our *routine,* to prevent us from falling into a repetitive and ritualistic religiosity that reduces everything to the level of "human commandment, learned by rote." God uses miracles to jolt our minds to be open to higher realities, to preserve in us that sense of awe that is essential in our relationship with God. A miracle that happens now helps us to become aware of, to appreciate, the on-going miracle of life and of existence, for though we are always immersed in that miracle, we find it so easy to trivialize it or to forget it altogether.

At the same time, miracles serve also to upset "the wisdom of the wise" and to confound "the discernment of the discerning," that is, to bring to a salutary crisis our pretence that by human reason alone we can explain everything, and our attitude that says if we cannot explain something, it does not exist. God's plan, then, is to break down and get rid of both dead ritualism and arid rationalism. Understood in the biblical sense, therefore, miracles serve to enhance and uplift, not to abase, the quality of our religion.

A miracle in the Bible, moreover, is never an end in itself, and much less does it ever serve to elevate the status of the one through whom it is worked or draw attention to any extraordinary powers of his own. Miracles are an incentive to faith and the reward of faith. A miracle is a *sign* (John in fact prefers to call them signs) and its purpose is to raise our mind to what is *signified*. It was for this reason that Jesus was saddened when, though he had multiplied the loaves, his disciples still did not understand the sign.[12]

But in the Gospel itself we see that miracle can be ambiguous. At times it is something positive, and at times something negative. It is positive when the miracle is received with gratitude and joy and when it serves to build up a person's faith in Christ. It is negative when it is asked for, or even categorically demanded, as a condition for believing: "Unless you see signs and wonders you will not believe" (John 4:48), "Jews demand signs" (1 Cor 1:22).

The same sort of ambiguity carries on, in other forms, in today's world. On the one hand there are those who want to see miracles at whatever cost: they are always on the hunt for whatever is out of the ordinary, they cannot move beyond miracles but get mired in their immediate benefit, like the people who went looking for Jesus because he had given them enough to eat once and they wanted to eat again. On the other hand there are those who would prefer not to

[12] See Mark 8:17-21; Matt 16:5ff.

allow any room for this charism of the Holy Spirit in the life of the Church, and they carefully avoid any association with it as though it were an indiscretion, beneath them, lowering the caliber of their religion. What these people do not realize is that, in acting as they do, they are setting out to teach God what true religion is supposed to be. In our own day too miracles have a providential and beautiful purpose when they are accepted from God with gratitude as signs of his love for us and as an incentive to grow in faith, but they are ambiguous when we cannot get beyond the miracle itself.

Lessing formulated an argument that, although not acceptable in all its premises, does help us to appreciate the permanent role of miracles in Christianity. Basing his view on Leibnitz, he says that it is not possible to give a rational and definitive proof of the truth of Christianity, because historical truths which are *occasional* cannot serve as proof of a truth that is rationally *necessary*. In other words, you cannot base the proof of a universal on the particular, and in this matter the person and the coming of Jesus would be an occasional event, a particular truth. But is it in fact possible for a particular actual individual to be, at the same time, universal and absolute?

The only proof of the truth of faith that could be convincing is the manifest demonstration of the divine power at work in miracles, signs, and wonders. But if these things are meant to concern others besides the immediate eyewitnesses alone, they lose their validity as soon as they are related to others, because for the others who were not eyewitnesses, the miracles themselves become matters of faith. Instead of serving as proof of something, they themselves need proving. And so, concludes Lessing, Christianity should produce in every age new signs and wonders as "showing forth the Spirit and his power."[13]

What Lessing did not notice was the fact that the Spirit has never stopped providing the Church with this proof, for there were miracles in his own time too just as there are miracles today. However, we need to recognize them, and for this we need not credulity, but a basic disposition to believe. This is a testimony concerning the Spirit who is at work in signs and wonders in the world of today, just as the Spirit was in the days following the first Pentecost:

[13] See G. E. Lessing, *Über den beweis des Geistes und der Kraft* (On the Proof of the Spirit and the Power), in *Works*, vol. 13 (Berlin, 1968).

In one parish, some hundreds of people gathered every Wednesday, and in another there was a gathering of about two thousand people in the church every Thursday. Every week there were first-hand reports of extraordinary healings: a man's numb, stiff hand became normal; a paralyzed woman who had been carried to the meetings for several weeks suddenly, during a time of praise and adoration, jumped up on her own feet, healed; a little later in the week a boy of 15 years, who had been born crippled and never walked, got up and began to walk. But perhaps the greatest miracle of all is that the priests and the bishop actually support this work of the Spirit.

It is true, however, that miracles convince us if we see them, not if we hear someone tell about them. The effect of the miracles mentioned in the testimony we have quoted on the people who saw them or who experienced them in their own body was very different from the effect they have on us in another continent who read about them.

4. In the Power of the Spirit

We should now have a clearer view of the background to the title "finger of God's right hand" in the Bible and in the Church Fathers. The time has come for us to open ourselves up to the possibility of experiencing, in a personal way, the "touch" of the Holy Spirit that we spoke of at the outset.

What could we expect of this "touch"? The gift of being able to work signs and wonders ourselves? This does not depend on us, and in any case it would be wrong to ask for it. What we expect to experience, rather, is the "power from on high" (Luke 24:49) that Jesus promised to his disciples. Signs and wonders are not all that the power of the Holy Spirit at work can achieve. They are simply the accented high notes in a song whose melody contains lower notes too; they are lights that surprise us in order to show us what sort of energy is at work in a quieter way everywhere in our everyday life.

The Church too needs this touch of the finger of God if it is to show forth, in the work it does, the "power" and the "authority" that was so obvious in the deeds and the words of Christ, and that made the people ask in amazement, "Where did the man get the power?

Where did he get such authority?"[14] When Jesus gave a command, or when he laid his hand on someone, something always happened; those in suffering were comforted, those in bondage were set free, demons were cast out. When he spoke it was not only words; his words were "in the power of the Spirit of God."

This is what we need most of all: supernatural power and effectiveness in serving the reign of God. The main problem that the Church is facing is the same as the problem facing the world as a whole, but on a different level. It is the question of the supply of energy. How do we make sure of energy supplies sufficient to sustain life? Where will we find this energy, from below or from above? In the case of physical energy, to seek it from below means to drill wells for oil, but we know that oil not only is not a renewable resource, but that its use also causes all sorts of pollution. For these reasons, we are searching anxiously for power "from above," in this case, how to harness solar energy. The energy that comes to the earth in the form of light is thousands of times better than the energy we get from burning fossil fuels. It has been calculated that the energy of the sun's rays falling during one year on the roads and streets of America alone could deliver twice the energy derived from all the world's consumption of fossil fuels in the same length of time. There is no comparison between the one form of energy and the other; the energy "from heaven" is immeasurably more powerful than the energy "of the earth."

But on the spiritual level too, we stand before a choice: Do we look for the energy we need "from below," in ourselves and the resources of our intelligence and our entrepreneurial spirit, or do we look for it "from on high," from the risen Christ, the Sun of Justice? The world is frantically trying to convert from one source of energy to another, from fossil fuels and nuclear resources to solar power which is infinitely cleaner and also free. The Church is constantly in need of the same "conversion."

"Not by might, nor by power, but by my spirit, says the Lord of hosts. What are you, O great mountain? Before Zerubbabel you shall become a plain!" (Zech 4:6-7). The "mountains" facing us will be laid low, not by any human might or power, but by the power of the Spirit. Those whose duty it is to carry out any office, the Scripture warns us, must do it "as stewards responsible for the

[14] See Mark 1:27; Matt 13:54.

graces received from God" to whom alone all power belongs (see
1 Pet 4:11), and not try to do it in any strength of their own.

What do we need to do, to know the touch of the finger of God
on us, as in the beginning it was stretched out to touch Adam?
That finger, in fact, is reaching out today to each one of us, to
every member of the body of Christ, to give each one of us the energy that pours forth from the Risen Christ. No longer does it
offer us only the energy of creation, but now also the power of the
Redemption. "Put your finger here. . . . Reach out your hand
and put it in my side" (John 20:27), said the Risen Jesus to
Thomas. He placed his finger, held out his hand, and from that
contact with Christ received such a salutary "shock" that all his
doubts fell apart and disappeared. That is exactly the kind of
paschal contact that the Paraclete is bringing about in the Church
today, because the Holy Spirit is the power of the Risen Lord.

Saint Augustine speaks of a "spiritual contact" *(contactus spiritalis)* that is brought about when the human will is in accord with
the will of God.[15] How is it possible to be in contact, to touch,
something that is in the heavens and cannot be seen on earth?
"The one who believes, touches."[16] Believing, consenting, abandoning ourselves to the Spirit in unquestioning docility, we touch
the Spirit and are touched by the Spirit.

In Michelangelo's great fresco we see the finger of God reaching out to communicate God's vital energy to his creature. We
need to be reaching up, as we see Adam do in the fresco, holding
our finger out in faith to receive that vitality.

Let us draw this reflection to a close as we repeat the prayer
that the first Christian community prayed to God in a time of trial.
They asked God to work "miracles and wonders," and God re-
sponded by pouring out the Spirit again, just as at Pentecost.

---

[15] Augustine, *Against the Donatists*, 20.26 (CSEL 53, p. 125).
[16] See Augustine, *Sermons*, 243.2 (PL 38.1144).

Sovereign Lord, who made the heaven and the earth, the sea, and everything in them, it is you who said by the Holy Spirit through our ancestor David, your servant:

"Why did the Gentiles rage,
and the peoples imagine vain things? . . ."

Grant to your servants to speak your word with all boldness, while you stretch your hand to heal, and signs and wonders are performed through the name of your holy servant Jesus.[17]

---

[17] Acts 4:24-25, 29-30.

XII

The Father's Solemn Promise

The Holy Spirit enlivens our hope

1. The Spirit "Already" and "Not Yet"

In this chapter we will be reflecting on the line of the *Veni Creator* that calls the Holy Spirit "the Father's solemn Promise" (*Tu rite promissum Patris*).[1]

In ancient times there was almost no development of the theme of the Holy Spirit as "promise." To make up for this, biblical theology of our own time has given it a great deal of attention. The reasons for this are easy to see. The Fathers of the Church, in tune with the Greek culture in which they lived and worked, were interested only in the titles that conveyed something about the being or the nature of the Spirit. "Promise," however, is not a notion that relates to nature but rather to history, nor does it relate to being as much as it does to becoming. On the other hand, modern thought is more interested in the *history* of things than in their *nature,* and so it has discovered unsuspected depths in the term "promise," and has come to consider it one of the keys to appreciating the dynamism that pervades the whole history of salvation. The tension between *promise* and *fulfillment* is at the very heart of the relationship between the Old and the New Testaments, between law and grace. It follows, then, that "promise" is a term containing a wealth of possibilities that will help us understand the place of the Holy Spirit in the history of salvation.

---

[1] In Latin, *promissum Patris* is taken directly from the text of Luke 24:49 in the Vulgate, and there is no reason to suppose that the text of this line of the hymn as we have it is the result of a copyist's error. The usage that places an adverb, *rite,* before the noun, *promissum,* rather than an adjective, as would seem grammatically more correct, was not unusual in church Latin; its explanation is found in the fact that *promissum,* the noun, is used here in an active or verbal sense. The phrase, then, has two shades of meaning and aptly conveys both the substantive sense, "the Father's solemn promise," and also the verbal sense, "solemnly promised by the Father": see H. Lausberg, JAWG (1969) 28.

Once more, the words of the *Veni Creator* are seen to be "open structures." Because they are taken from the Bible, they share in that characteristic of the word of God of being able to enrich itself rather than to become worn out by the passage of time. The same succession of awaiting and accomplishment, prophecy and realization, promise and fulfillment, which throws so much light on the person and the work of Christ, will also give us new light on the person and the work of the Paraclete.

Just as Jesus was first promised in the Scriptures, then made manifest in the flesh, and is awaited finally in his return at the end of time, so too the Spirit. At one time "what the Father has promised" (see Luke 24:49), the Spirit was given at Pentecost, and now is once again awaited and called upon "with groans and deep sighs" by humankind and by the whole of creation. Having tasted the Spirit's first-fruits, we now await the fullness of the Spirit's gift. As the reign of God is *already* present among us but *not yet* realized in all its fullness, so too with the Holy Spirit; the Spirit has *already* been poured into our hearts, but nevertheless is *not yet* at work except as a pledge of what is to come (see 2 Cor 1:22).

In this space between Pentecost and the Parousia, the Second Coming, the Spirit is the power that urges us forward, that keeps us going on like pilgrims and strangers, and does not allow us to become comfortable with our present condition and "settle down" in it. The Spirit is the one who instills the onward urge in us and, so to speak, gives our hope wings. We will discover, in this, that there is a connection between the Spirit and *hope* that is as close as the connection between the Spirit and love.

First, we will take a brief look at the biblical sources and the work of theologians relating to the Spirit "promised by the Father," as these will enable us to go on to our usual next step and see how to apply the truth we have learned to our spiritual life.

2. The Spirit and the Promise

Two of the New Testament writers, Luke and Paul, speak of the Holy Spirit as a promise. It will be useful to have all the texts together in one place where we can readily see them:

> And see, I am sending upon you *what my Father promised* (Luke 24:49).

While staying with them, he ordered them not to leave Jerusalem, but to wait there for the *promise of the Father.* "This," he said, "is what you have heard from me; for John baptized with water, but you will be baptized with the Holy Spirit not many days from now" (Acts 1:4-5).

Being therefore exalted at the right hand of God, and having received from the Father the *promise of the Holy Spirit,* he has poured out this that you both see and hear (Acts 2:33).

You will receive the gift of the Holy Spirit. For *the promise* is for you, for your children, and for all who are far away, everyone whom the Lord our God calls to him (Acts 2:38-39).

[This was done] in order that in Christ Jesus the blessing of Abraham might come to the Gentiles, so that we might receive the *promise of the Spirit* through faith (Gal 3:14).

In him you also, when you had heard the word of truth, the gospel of your salvation, and had believed in him, were marked with the seal of the *promised Holy Spirit* (Eph 1:13).

To what was Luke referring when he called the Holy Spirit "what the Father promised"? Where exactly did the Father make such a promise? The whole of the Old Testament, we might say, is a promise of the Holy Spirit. The work of the Messiah is constantly presented as coming to its climax in a new and universal outpouring of the Spirit of God on the earth. Luke shows that he was thinking in particular of the prophecy of Joel: "In the last days it will be, God declares, that I will pour out my Spirit upon all flesh" (Acts 2:17; Joel 3:1-5).

But not only of that text. How could he not have had in mind also what is to be found in the other prophets? "Until a spirit from on high is poured out on us" (Isa 32:15); "For I will pour my Spirit upon your descendants" (Isa 44:3); "I will put my Spirit within you" (Ezek 36:27).

When it comes to the *content* of the promise, Luke lays stress, as he usually does, on the charismatic aspect of the gift of the Holy Spirit, and especially on prophecy. The Father's promise is "power from on high" that will make it possible for the disciples to take the message of salvation to the ends of the earth. Yet Luke is clearly also aware of the more profound aspects of the work of the Holy Spirit: those sanctifying and salvific aspects seen, for instance, in the forgiveness of sins, the gift of the new law and the

New Covenant. Luke shows this by linking the events of Sinai and of Pentecost. Peter's words, "The promise is for you" (Acts 2:39), refers to the promise of salvation and not only to the promise of a gift such as prophecy or another charism.

Turning now to what Paul says about the Spirit as promise, we find ourselves moving into a new perspective, theologically of a much deeper order. Paul mentions various objects of the promise: justification, our being made children of God, our inheritance. But the object of the promise par excellence is precisely the Holy Spirit, and Paul refers to this sometimes as "the promise of the Spirit" and sometimes as "the Spirit of the promise."

Paul has introduced two new ideas into the concept of promise. The first is that what God has promised does not depend on keeping the law, but on faith and therefore on grace. God did not promise the Spirit to those who kept the law, but to those who believe in Christ: "Did you receive the Spirit by doing works of the law or by believing what you heard? For if the inheritance comes from the law, it no longer comes from the promise" (Gal 3:2, 18).

Paul, in fact, uses the concept of the promise to place the theology of the Spirit at the heart of his teaching, and in turn the concept of the promise serves as the concrete proof of that teaching. Christians know very well that it was as a result of their hearing and believing the Gospel that they came to experience the Spirit, and not as a result of any efforts they might have made in the usual way to observe the law. The apostle could simply refer them to a fact of their own experience.

The second new idea Paul introduces is a little disconcerting in a way. It seems as though Paul quite unexpectedly is dousing the flame with a dash of water, seeming to say, "But the promise is not yet fulfilled—at least, not yet entirely fulfilled!" Here too, it will help to have before us the texts in which these terms referring to the Holy Spirit are found:

> We ourselves, who have the first fruits of the Spirit, groan inwardly while we wait for adoption, the redemption of our bodies (Rom 8:23).

> It is God who establishes us with you in Christ and has anointed us, by putting his seal on us and giving us his Spirit in our hearts as a first installment (2 Cor 1:21-22).

> He who has prepared us for this very thing is God, who has given us the Spirit as a guarantee (2 Cor 5:5).

What is it that the apostle is saying by speaking in this way? That the fulfillment of the promise as we see it in Christ does not exhaust the promise itself. Using an unusual juxtaposition of contrasts he says that we "possess . . . while awaiting." We possess, and we also still await. What we possess is not the ultimate completion but only the first-fruits, a foretaste, and this is the reason why hope is born in us. And so desire, expectancy, and yearning are more intense than they were before, because now they know what the Spirit is. The coming of the Holy Spirit at Pentecost, far from dashing water on the flame of human desire, has fed it fuel.

The same, exactly, holds true of Christ. His coming fulfilled every promise, yet it has not put a stop to our waiting in anticipation. The sense of anticipation surges up anew, this time in the form of waiting for his return in glory. The title "the Father's promise" places the Holy Spirit at the very heart of the Christian understanding of the final end of the world. We do not entirely agree with the thesis that the ancient Jewish Christians saw the Spirit primarily as the power of the *future,* the world to come, while the Hellenist Christians saw the Spirit primarily as the power of the world *above.* Paul shows that the two concepts are not necessarily opposed one to the other, but can actually be seen together. For him the Spirit is at the same time the reality of *the world above* and also the power of *the world to come.*

In the transition from the first-fruits to the fullness, the first are not discarded to make way for the second; rather, they themselves become the fullness. We will retain what we already possess and acquire what we do not yet have.

The theological principle "grace is the beginning of glory," applied to the Holy Spirit, means that the first-fruits are the beginning of the fulfillment, the beginning of final glory, part of that glory. That being the case, it is not necessary to translate *arrabona* (in 2 Cor 5:5) as pledge, but simply as seal *(arra).* For to give a pledge is not the same thing as to start the actual payment. A pledge is given as a token, an assurance, that payment will be made; once the payment has been made the pledge is given back. But a seal is different. It is not given back, but rather completed when payment is fully made. The seal is part of the payment itself.

If God, through his Spirit, has given us love as a pledge, will that pledge perhaps be taken away from us when the whole reality is given to us? Of course not; what he has already given, he will fulfill. It follows then that we ought not to call it a pledge, but rather a seal.[2]

The love of God, of which, thanks to the seal or mark of the Spirit upon us, we have a foretaste here below, is therefore of the same *quality,* though not of the same *intensity,* as the love we will experience in eternal life. Saint Simeon, called The New Theologian, had a vision one day. He was sure he had looked on God and, so certain that he could never see anything greater or more glorious than what he had just seen, Saint Simeon said that after his death he would be satisfied with that alone. The Lord then said to him: "You must really be quite small-hearted if you would be satisfied with something like that, for what you have seen, compared to the good things to come, is like a picture of the sky drawn on a piece of paper compared to the sky itself."[3] We should say the same about our possession of the Holy Spirit.

A profound change has come about, as we have seen, in the meaning of the feast of Pentecost. In the beginning Pentecost was the festival of the first-fruits,[4] that is, the day when the people came to offer to the Lord the first-fruits of their harvest. Today it is still the feast of the first-fruits, but they are now the first-fruits of what God is offering to humankind in the Spirit. The roles of donor and beneficiary have been exchanged, and this is in perfect harmony with what has taken place, in every area, in the transition from the law to grace, and from salvation as something we strove after by our own effort to salvation as pure, free gift from God.

This explains why the old feast of Pentecost, as the feast of the first-fruits, had, oddly enough, almost no corresponding development among Christians. Saint Irenaeus makes a tentative move in that direction, saying that on the day of Pentecost "the Spirit of-

---

[2] Augustine, *Sermons,* 23.9 (CC 41, p. 314).

[3] Simeon, the New Theologian, *Second Prayer of Thanksgiving* (SCh 113, p. 350).

[4] See Num 28:26; Lev 23:10.

fered to the Father the first-fruits of all the nations,"[5] but it led to almost no further development in Christian thought.

3. The Spirit, God's Future

We noted earlier that, concerning the title of the Holy Spirit as promise, the patristic era has almost nothing to offer, in strong contrast to what it provides on almost all of the other titles. We noted too that the reason for this was that the Fathers took less interest in the historical and eschatological perspective than they did in the ontological. Saint Basil writes:

> Even in the moment of the awaited return of the Lord from the heavens, the Holy Spirit will not be absent. . . . The very crown of the just itself is grace of the Holy Spirit. . . . And so, therefore, those who have been sealed with the seal of the Holy Spirit for the day of redemption and who have preserved intact and undiminished the first-fruits of the Holy Spirit that they have received, will be the ones to hear, "Well done, good and faithful servant . . . you have been faithful in little things; I will now place great things in your charge" (Matt 25:21).[6]

What, however, does he mean by this? Only that the Holy Spirit will have an active part in the final act of human history when time will be over and all will pass into eternity. What is missing is a reflection on what the Spirit is now already doing, in time, to urge humankind on towards the fulfillment: a reflection on the Holy Spirit as the élan, the urge, the propulsive power in the people of God on the way to the Father's home.

The Spirit prompts believers to be on the watch, in expectation of Christ's coming. The Spirit teaches the Church to say, "Come, Lord Jesus" (Rev 22:20). When the Spirit says *Marana-tha* with the Church, it is as it is when the Spirit says *Abba* in the heart of the believer: It means that the Spirit *gives* the Church the *ability to say*; the Spirit makes himself the voice of the Church. In and of himself, in fact, the Spirit cannot say, "Come, Lord" *(Marana-tha)*, because

---

[5] Irenaeus, *Against the Heresies,* III.17.2; also Eusebius of Caesarea, *On the Easter Solemnity,* 4 (PG 24.700A).

[6] Basil the Great, *On the Holy Spirit,* XVI.40 (PG 32.141A).

Christ is not "Lord" of the Spirit, and in the Creed we profess that the Spirit is also "Lord." Jesus, speaking of the Paraclete, says, "He will tell you of things to come" (John 16:13), that is, he will open our awareness to the new order pervading all things as a result of the paschal mystery.

The Holy Spirit is therefore the wellspring of Christian faith, forward-looking toward the final end. It is the Spirit who keeps the Church reaching toward the future, toward the Lord's return. And this precisely is what the biblical and theological reflection of our own time is seeking to bring to light. The Holy Spirit raises us up to a new level of existence which is itself already an eschatological existence, without having to wait for the final moment of the parousia. By the power of the Spirit our existence is the beginning of a life the fullness of which will be manifest only when the way of life, determined by the Spirit, is fully established and no longer hostage to the limitations of the flesh. The Spirit is "promise," not only in a static sense, but dynamic, as power of the promise: The Spirit is the one who makes us see the possibility of being wholly set free, who makes the chains upon us feel even heavier and more intolerable and urges us therefore to break them.[7]

Some have tried to show a relationship between this action of the Spirit unfolding in human history and the place of the Spirit in the Trinity:

> The mutual interaction of Father and Son is always *presence,* and from this presence, as it were a perpetual surprise, the Holy Spirit proceeds as a *future.* He is what comes of the love of Father and Son, what that love involves, always more than what appeared possible in their reciprocal intimacy, a love ever more new, ever more youthful, more fruitful in God. And we cannot doubt that when created time was set in motion, the fact of rising above the present in openness to the future is a potent image of the Holy Spirit.[8]

The idea is helpful and worthy of being kept in view, even though it comes in terms that are valid primarily to the Western, Latin vision of the relationships within the Trinity. Saint Paul writes that "all of us who possess the first-fruits of the Spirit . . .

[7] See J. Moltmann, *Der Geist des Lebens* (München, 1991) 20, 86–7, 176.
[8] H. U. Von Balthasar, *Spiritus Creator* (Einsiedeln, 1991) 132–3.

groan inwardly as we wait for our bodies to be set free"; as a matter of fact "the creation waits with eager longing . . . [to be] set free from its bondage" (Rom 8:19ff). From this we can deduce that the Holy Spirit renews the face of the earth and makes all things new (see Rev 21:5) not only at the very end, at the last moment when time ceases and all enters into eternity, but mysteriously even now.

This aspect of the theology of the Holy Spirit as the power that opens up toward the future has had, as we could well have expected, a particular echo in liberation theology:

> The Holy Spirit is at the root of the cry of the poor. The Spirit is the power given to those who have no power. He guides the struggle for the emancipation and for the full realisation of oppressed peoples. The Spirit is at work in history by means of history. He does not put himself in the place of history, but pervades history by means of the men and women who carry history forward.[9]

4. The Holy Spirit Gives Us Abundant Hope

The title "the Father's promise" is written into the verse of the *Veni Creator* that speaks of the Spirit, giver of the gifts and charisms. It was in fact Luke who, in the Acts of the Apostles, saw the fulfillment of "the Father's promise" especially in the Pentecostal gift of prophecy. But we have seen that Paul sees a wider scope in the title, applying it to all the works of the Spirit and especially to his work of sanctification and salvation. In this light, we want now to draw attention to the relationship between the Holy Spirit and the theological virtue of hope.

In Paul's teaching, all three of the theological virtues have their origin in the Holy Spirit. He writes: "For through the Spirit, by *faith,* we eagerly wait for the *hope* of righteousness. For in Christ Jesus neither circumcision nor uncircumcision counts for anything; the only thing that counts is faith working through *love*."[10]

His insistence on the point, and the regularity with which he raises it, cannot be merely accidental. He is telling us that the

---

[9] J. Comblin, *O Espirito Santo e a libertação* (Petropolis, 1987) conclusion.
[10] Gal 5:5-6; see Rom 5:5.

Holy Spirit is the wellspring and the power of all the three theological virtues. The Holy Spirit is the one who, in particular, makes it possible for us to "abound in hope": "May the God of hope fill you with all joy and peace in believing, so that you may abound in hope by the power of the Holy Spirit" (Rom 15:13).

Hope has often been called the "poor relation" in the family of the theological virtues. It is true that there was a period of intense reflection on the theme of hope that eventually gave rise to a genuine and proper "Theology of hope." Yet it still lacked a reflection on the link between hope and the Holy Spirit. It is in fact not possible to understand the very special nature of Christian hope and the difference that sets it apart from every other kind of hope if we do not appreciate its intimate connection with the Holy Spirit. It is the Spirit that makes the difference between hope as a "principle" and hope as a theological virtue. We call the virtues of faith and love and hope "theological" because God is not only their object but also their cause. They are caused by God, infused into us by God.

Hope is a necessity to us if we are to continue living, and the Holy Spirit is a necessity to us if we are to have hope! The poet Péguy tells us that it is relatively easy to believe; God is so evident in the universe in so many ways! Even to love is comparatively easy; we are all unhappy, and so it ought to be easy for us to show compassion for one another. Hope is the difficult one. It is so easy to fall into despair and we are so inclined to do it; this is the great temptation.[11]

Who will help us climb this hill? Only the Holy Spirit! What persuasions will the Spirit use? None whatever! He will do it simply by being present in us, for he himself is "promise." That is the reason for his efficacy. When the Spirit is present, it is impossible not to "abound in hope."

We can distinguish two types of faith: the faith that is *believed* and *believing* faith; that is, the truths that we believe and our personal act of believing. So too we can distinguish two types of hope. There is an objective kind of hope that means the end we hope for (our eternal inheritance); there is a subjective kind of hope that is our personal act of hoping for something. This sub-

---

[11] C. Péguy, *The Threshold of the Mystery of the Second Virtue*, in *Oeuvres poétiques complètes* (Paris: Gallimard, 1975) 538.

jective hope is the strength that moves us forward, the inner urge, the reaching out of our very soul, an opening up of our self to the future. "A loving movement of the spirit towards that which it hopes for," says one of the ancient Fathers.[12]

> Faith sees only what is,
> and hope sees what is to be.
> Love loves only what is,
> and hope loves what is to be.[13]

One of the great dangers in our spiritual walk is that we become discouraged because we fall into the same sin again and again, and it seems that we will never be able to keep to our resolve to avoid it. It is hope that saves us. Hope gives us the strength to start again from the beginning, to believe every time that this time we will succeed, this time we will really be converted. This moves the heart of God to come to our help with his grace.

Another great obstacle in our life's journey is the troubles we face. Here too we make a new beginning only through hope, which is a fruit of the Holy Spirit. "We also boast about our sufferings, knowing that suffering produces endurance, and endurance produces character, and character produces hope, and hope does not disappoint us, because God's love has been poured into our hearts through the Holy Spirit that has been given to us" (Rom 5:3-5).

The Holy Spirit assures our spirit that we are children of God and that God loves us, and in this way the Spirit gives us the strength not to give in in the face of our many troubles and crosses. There is a close link between trouble and hope, but it is a one-way and not a two-way link. If it is possible to say that the more we experience troubles, the greater our hope becomes, it does not follow that if our hope increases, our troubles will increase too. It is not hope that causes troubles to come upon us, but our troubles that give us opportunity to hope.

Nor should we be content to hope merely on our own account. The Holy Spirit wants to make us sowers of the seed of hope. There is no more beautiful calling than to spread hope in our home, in our community, in the parish, in the Church as a whole.

---

[12] Diadocus of Photike, *On Spiritual Perfection*, Preamble (SCh 5, p. 84).
[13] Péguy, *The Threshold of the Mystery*, 539.

Hope in human life is like an effective modern air-freshener: it clears the air, lends fragrance to the surroundings.

There is a text on hope in the Bible that seems to be endowed with an almost sacramental efficacy, able to bring about what it says. It sees hope giving eagle-wings to those who hope:

> Even youths will faint and be weary
>   and the young will fall exhausted;
> but those who wait for the Lord shall renew their strength,
>   they shall mount up with wings like eagles
> they shall run and not be weary,
>   they shall walk and not faint (Isa 40:30-31).

5. The Promise Is for You!

There is a practical aspect to this teaching on the Holy Spirit as promise: a real difference it makes to us. Peter spoke to the crowd on that first Pentecost morning: "The promise is for you, for your children, and for all who are far away, everyone whom the Lord our God calls to him" (Acts 2:39). What we need to do is to be fully aware that we ourselves are that "you." We are the ones whom the Lord has called in our turn, we follow those first believers, and so the "Father's promise" of the Holy Spirit is for us too!

The most important thing about a promise is not that of studying the documents or analyzing the terms, but rather the fulfillment of the promise and our taking possession of it. And this is something that depends on us. Christianity, in our own time, has experienced wave after wave of the Holy Spirit being poured "on all mankind" (Joel 3:1). They have given rise to numbers of Pentecostal and charismatic movements. For millions of people the prophecy of Joel is no longer a well-sounding text that Peter quoted on Pentecost day, but a reality taking place before their own eyes. They are ready to bear witness that in these days the Lord has "poured out his Spirit on all": on boys and girls, young people and old, even on serving men and serving women.[14]

The wind of Pentecost, the breath of the Holy Spirit, is again blowing strongly throughout the Church. In the midst of all the

---

[14] See Joel 3:1ff.; Acts 2:17ff.

immense difficulties in the way of proclaiming the faith in these times, this move of the Holy Spirit in our own day is the single greatest reason for us to have hope. The Holy Spirit continues to be "the power from on high." The longing that Moses expressed so long ago is now being fulfilled: "Would that all the LORD's people were prophets, and that the LORD would put his spirit on them!" (Num 11:29).

Now, if the promise is for us, what do we need to do to obtain it? What Paul has said about the promise is of great comfort to us here. "The Spirit of the promise" does not come as a result of our observance of the law, but only by faith. In other words, there is no need for us to wait until we have "fulfilled all justice" and managed to observe all the commandments perfectly before we can hope to receive the promise. All we need to do is believe and open ourselves to receive the Spirit as a free gift and not as something owed to us. The apostles did not receive the Spirit because they had become "fired up" with zeal; they became zealous and full of fervor because they received the Spirit. For if we are to "put to death the deeds of the body" (Rom 8:13), the only power by which we will be able to do this is the Holy Spirit. The first step is to pray. Our Father in heaven will "give the Holy Spirit to those who ask him!" (Luke 11:13).

But even as we start to ask this, the Holy Spirit "help us in our weakness; for we do not know how to pray as we ought, but that very Spirit intercedes with sighs too deep for words" (Rom 8:26). Through the Holy Spirit we ask for the Spirit; in the strength of the first-fruits, we ask for the fullness.

In the writings of the Greek Fathers we find a eulogy to the Holy Spirit that reminds us very much of the *Veni Creator,* not only because of its inspired lyricism, but because of the range of its themes and of the titles it uses, among them "seal" and "assurance of eternal good." It is with that extended song in praise of the Paraclete that we close this reflection.

> *He is the divine Name, all powerful and worthy of all honour,*
> *remembered with the Father and the Son, to whom we give glory.*
> *He makes us holy, gives us life, and shares with us the light of*
>   *heaven.*
> *He keeps alive the desire in us all to go forward in oneness of*
>   *heart;*

It was he who inspired the prophets and apostles,
who gave the martyrs the strength to stand firm in the face of
the tyrant's cruelties;
who, as Lord, renews us and sets us free,
who, as Spirit of adoration, makes us children of God;
who puts the armies of demons to flight
by the light he gives in baptism,
and who shields us from shameful Satan, the adversary;
he opens the gates of heaven to us and guides us to the haven of
salvation;
he lets us share in the fellowship of the angels and join in their
singing;
and to us he is the way that takes us to the God and Father of
the heavens,
all because of his coming to us, sovereignly free and generous.

He is the fruitful and infinite power of salvation,
the person incomparable and most holy,
whom no measure can span,
purest, unstained glory,
grace of God giving strength where we are weak,
goodness, ineffable and eternal,
inexhaustible wellspring of charisms,
upholder of every good thought,
revealer of things hidden and things to come,
seal of salvation, divine anointing,
present share and assurance of eternal good.
By him every creature, visible and invisible,
rational and irrational, is sustained in being;
Through him we receive rebirth from on high,
remission of our faults and forgiveness for our sins,
union with God and the crown of the just,
possession of all good and our dwelling-place in heaven,
life without end and an eternal inheritance in the kingdom of
God.[15]

---

[15] Didimus of Alexandria, *On the Trinity*, II.1 (PG 39.452–3).

XIII

Gifting Lips with the Word to Say

The Holy Spirit gives power to our proclaiming

1. Spirit and Word

The verse of the *Veni Creator* that sings of the Holy Spirit acting in the charisms closes with a line that highlights the group of charisms linked to the word: "Gifting lips with the word to say" *(sermone ditans guttura)* or, more literally translated, "endowing mouths with the word."

The Spirit and the Word, *ruach* and *dabhar:* These are the two great powers that together create the world and keep it in motion: "By the *word* of the Lord the heavens were made, and all their host by the *breath* of his mouth" (Ps 33:6). "He shall strike the earth with the rod of his mouth, and with the breath of his lips he shall kill the wicked" (Isa 11:4).

The prophets themselves were seen sometimes as men of the word and sometimes as men of the Spirit. Sometimes we read that the word "came" upon them and made them prophets, and sometimes the task was given them by "the Spirit of the Lord." "My *spirit* that is upon you, and my *words* that I have put in your mouth, . . . from now on and forever" (Isa 59:21).

In this line of the hymn, these two creative powers are shown in their relationship to one another, like two great spotlights, each casting light on the other and both together lighting up the whole of revelation. A whole new horizon opens up before us in these two words. The Spirit is the one who gives the word, and who himself is given in the word. Between these two realities there is a perfect reciprocity that, as we shall see, has its roots in the Trinity itself. The Spirit proceeds "through" the Son, but the Son himself is generated "in" the Spirit. In *revelation* the Spirit gives us the word; in fact, "men and women moved by the Holy Spirit spoke from God" (2 Pet 1:21). But then it was this same Word, that is, the Scriptures, that give us the Holy Spirit when we read them with faith; *inspired by* the Spirit, they work to *inspire us* with the Spirit.

In *redemption* we see the same reciprocity flowing full circle: in the Incarnation the Holy Spirit gives us the living Word of God who is Jesus "conceived by the Holy Spirit." In the paschal mystery it was the Word made flesh who, from the cross, poured out the Holy Spirit upon the Church. This reciprocity explains why theological reflection on Christ (christology) cannot proceed without theological reflection on the Holy Spirit (pneumatology), and vice versa. "Without the word, the Spirit is blind; without the Spirit, the word is dead."

For the author of the *Veni Creator,* Pentecost was the moment when the Holy Spirit put the word on human lips. That moment, in fact, saw the fulfillment of "the Father's solemn promise" of which the previous line had spoken, and of which the visible sign was the gift of words.

But to what, precisely, is he drawing our attention in this line? To the way the apostles spoke in tongues as soon as they had received the Spirit, that is, to the gift of glossolalia? Not only to that. The perspective is a great deal deeper. On Pentecost day there were various manifestations of the Spirit that had to do with language and with human speech. The apostles "began to speak in foreign languages as the Spirit gave them the gift of speech" (Acts 2:4). A little further, the manifestation of the Spirit was seen in the gift of prophecy which was considered the fulfillment of the Father's promise: "In those days I will pour out my Spirit; / and they shall prophesy" (Acts 2:18). And then the gift of the word is seen clearly manifest in Peter's preaching (see Acts 2:22ff.).

It is probable that, at this point, the author of our hymn drew inspiration from a Pentecost hymn by Bede the Venerable, one of the verses of which says:

> In the tongues of fire that appeared
> he who is the tongue's Creator
> came down on believers gathered as one
> and gave them the gift of the word.[1]

---

[1] Bede the Venerable, *Hymn for Pentecost,* VII.8 (CC 122, pp. 424–5): *"ver-bique donum contulit."*

The rest of Bede's hymn shows that he too was not thinking only of "speaking in tongues," but also of the gift of *teaching:* "Those who had received the tongues of flame brought clarity to the minds of their neighbors by causing Christ to resound among them." He was thinking, surely, of the gifts of *preaching* and of *praise.*

When the Bible speaks of God placing his word in a person's mouth it is always linked with prophecy. Of the prophet who was to succeed Moses, God said, "I will put my words in the mouth of the prophet" (Deut 18:18), and to Isaiah and to Jeremiah he declared, "I have put my words into your mouth."[2] It may also be that the saying "You put the words into our mouth" lends greater breadth to the Gospel passage in which Jesus says that the Holy Spirit would give to his disciples, when the time came, "an eloquence and a wisdom" which their adversaries would not be able to resist.[3]

2. Glossolalia and Singing in Tongues

The Acts of the Apostles describe in a narrative style those manifestations of the Spirit that have to do with the use of the tongue. In Saint Paul's writings we find them again, considered in a more reflective way, contrasted one with another and with love, all forming part of his teaching on the charisms. Among the charisms that Paul lists there are many that belong in the category of charisms of the word. We will review them briefly, taking a little more time to look at those that are more evident in the actual experience of the Church in our own day.

Linked to the tongue is first of all *glossolalia.* Saint Paul refers to it by other names as well: "various languages," "the gift of tongues," or "speaking in tongues." It is the gift to which the apostle often returns, giving it particular attention not because it is more important than the others (in fact, it comes last in his list of the gifts), but because it is the one that most needs to be disciplined (see 1 Corinthians 12–14). Oddly enough, although it is the most elementary of the gifts, it is the one that in our own day attracts most attention and is most often the subject of discussion.[4]

[2] Isa 51:16; Jer 1:9.

[3] See Luke 12:12; 21:15.

[4] See J. Sherill, *They Speak with Other Tongues* (New York: McGraw-Hill, 1965).

But let us see in what this gift consists, and how in actual fact it occurs. If we take as a starting point the way in which this same gift has once again been made manifest among Christians of our own time, we need to note that it is experienced in two forms: either in the form of utterances proclaimed in the assembly, or in the form of prolonged personal prayer in private. In either case it involves words and sounds that in the normal course do not belong to any existing language but are made up on the spur of the moment. The one who speaks in tongues is not aware of *what* he or she is saying, but is only aware of *saying* it. The person who speaks in tongues, in other words, is in control, able to decide when to start and when to stop, and not automatically carried away by the gift.

When someone is moved to give a message in tongues in the assembly, it should always be followed by an *interpretation of the tongues,* just as a prophetic message should always be followed by a discernment.[5] The interpreter does not "translate" the message in tongues, but rather is moved to say something (a word of encouragement or a word from Scripture) that he or she and the assembly as a whole feel is linked to the message and that conveys its general meaning.

Those who use the gift of tongues, especially in the context of personal prayer, all without exception affirm that it opens the way to a deeper level of prayer, a more immediate experience of contact with God, from which great benefits flow. At times the exercise of the gift serves to give expression to praise and adoration, and at other times it takes the form of powerful intercession. Those who pray this way experience a new sense of wholeness, of being wholly united in the depths of their personal being, open to God in every way, body, soul, and spirit all in harmony. An actual personal testimony will help us more than any description to form for ourselves an idea of this gift. Let us look at the testimony of a well-known Scripture scholar and teacher.

> As I knelt there, hearing the voices of those praying over me, I began to feel a bubbling inside. It was just there and I didn't know what to do with it. One of the ways in which I sought to release it was by finishing the last three chapters of a book I was writing—and I did it in less than three days. But the bubbling

[5] See 1 Cor 12:10; 14:27-28.

was still there. On New Year's day, as I drove to the ranch to visit my family, I felt moved just to relax and let the bubbling come out however it would. It came out in a melody without words. Three days later, words came to fit the melody: "The Spirit of the Lord has touched my soul. . . ." Far from being spent by the song, the bubbling was still there. It seemed to go beyond what I could put in either melody or words. . . . I went to my room, closed my door, knelt down—and let go. . . . So that's tongues! Praising God by letting the Spirit do it in you, for you and with you! Since then, my life has been so different, so rich, so full of inexplicable events. I have witnessed physical healing. I have witnessed the powerful inner healings of soul and spirit—the healing of marriages and families, the healing of long-festering hatreds. But my greatest witness to the Lord's deep healing is myself. I have found a new strength and vitality, a greater willingness to risk for the Lord, a greater ability to cope with stress and chaos.[6]

We may be a little perplexed at times to note that this phenomenon is encountered also outside of Christianity, for example, in the trance state sought in certain pagan rites, and also in certain non-Christian forms of worship. But this fact does not necessarily mean that the gift of tongues is something brought about by suggestion or arising from trance states artificially induced. It does mean, however, that the charism has a basis in the natural religious propensities of human nature, which the Holy Spirit uses not in the natural human way but in the Spirit's own way.

At times every one of us experiences a desire to be able to say more than the ordinary structures of our words and concepts allow. For these do place restrictions on our urge to express the things that move us, limiting what we can say to the words and ideas we have pigeonholed and ready at hand. Inevitably our heart's urge is caught like a bird in a net, unable to fly free. There are two ways of escape from these constraints: in silence or by transcending words as in glossolalia. It is obvious that somewhat the same sort of need has been felt in the artistic world. There is a type of modern poetry that makes use of words and sounds that have no logical links among themselves but express only a harmony: a type of poetry

---

[6] G. T. Montague, *The Spirit and the Church,* comp. and ed. Ralph Martin (New York: Paulist Press, 1976) 172.

that sets out to suggest a state of mind rather than to describe it. Dreaming of a voyage, himself and God alone in a little boat, the poet Tagore says:

> In that shoreless ocean, at thy silently listening smile
> my songs would swell in melodies, free as waves,
> free from all bondage of words.[7]

Certain modern painters, too, have felt the need to move beyond image and give their inspiration free reign in playing with pure color. Why then should something similar not take place in the religious sphere, where not simple "inspiration," but the Holy Spirit in person is at work?

Having said that, however, it is as necessary today as it was in Saint Paul's day to follow the "yes" with a "but." That is to say, we need to be on guard against the danger of overvaluing the gift and using it without discernment. Among Pentecostals, speaking in tongues is often considered a necessary and sufficient sign, the initial evidence, that a person has in fact received the Spirit. We need to respect this conviction, for it is based on an experience of the Holy Spirit that, on other accounts, is shown to be powerful and authentic. Yet we cannot neglect to notice that it does give rise to serious problems, when we view it in the light of what we read in the New Testament. Paul says, "Another [may have] various kinds of tongues. . . . Do all speak in tongues?" (1 Cor 12:10, 30).

Just as not everyone is an apostle and not everyone works miracles, so too, according to Saint Paul, not everyone speaks in tongues. To make that gift the only obligatory charism for everyone would be to give it a status of its own and remove it from the ambit of the charisms which, by definition, are gifts that God gives "to whom he wills and when he wills." If we do look upon it as necessary for everyone, are we not attributing to speaking in tongues the prerogative that Saint Paul accords to love? Speaking in tongues, just like many other supernatural phenomena, can be counterfeited by Satan; only love can not.

I believe that we ought certainly to encourage people to be open to this gift, and to use it, especially in the area of personal prayer, "for their own benefit" (see 1 Cor 14:4). But if someone,

---

[7] R. Tagore, *Gitanjali,* 42.

after having tried several times, is still not quite certain that the gift is given and that therefore an attempt to pray in tongues would be without real conviction, there is no need to place any insistence on it. A person in that position should not feel disadvantaged or overlooked, and especially should not on that account doubt that he or she has received the Holy Spirit at all. Should anyone confront you with the question, "You have received the Spirit. Why then do you not speak all languages?" answer quite peacefully, with Saint Augustine, "Of course I speak all languages. For in fact, through love, I belong to that body, the Church, that speaks all languages and in every one of them proclaims the mighty works of God."[8]

While we are on the subject of speaking in tongues, we need also to mention *singing in tongues:* "I will pray with the spirit, but I will pray with the mind also; I will sing praise with the spirit, but I will sing praise with the mind also" (1 Cor 14:15).

From the context we understand that "singing praise with the spirit" is a kind of praying in tongues that is expressed in a musical way. It is a kind of singing using words and melody that are not known in advance but, produced under inspiration as one goes along, a sequence of sounds that follows the inward prompting of the Spirit. Saint Paul often makes reference to this kind of singing inspired by the Spirit: "Be filled with the Spirit, as you sing psalms and hymns and spiritual songs among yourselves, singing and making melody to the Lord in your hearts" (Eph 5:18-19).

To judge by our present-day experience in Pentecostal and charismatic gatherings, this is a gift quite beautiful in its simplicity. It allows us to transcend the limitations of set words and known melodies, and so doing, it creates a real unity of heart and soul throughout the entire assembly. It is a wonderful expression of adoration, praise, rejoicing, and thanksgiving to God, majestic in its tranquility. As the last note of a familiar hymn fades, or even perhaps in the midst of a time of silence, a rustle of voices grows little by little, swelling and fading, rising and falling, becoming at times loud and strong and at others soft and worshipful as though an unseen conductor were directing it, and as if at a given sign, it spontaneously comes to an end. Of all the charismatic phenomena,

---

[8] See Augustine, *Sermons,* 269.2ff. (PL 38.1236–7).

this is often the one that most impresses strangers, for instance those who attend some great gathering as part of their job, like journalists, or those who operate the TV cameras.

There is no need to imagine that there is anything miraculous at work in all this. It is well known that a certain atmosphere of unity and spiritual fullness can and does produce effects of this kind. Nonetheless, it is clearly one of the ways the Spirit edifies the community and makes his presence felt: it is, in short, a charism. The best explanation of the dynamics that lead to singing in tongues is the one given by Augustine:

> "Shout for joy. . . . Sing a new song" (Psalm 33:3). What would this song of joy mean? It means something that cannot be explained in words: it is what the heart is singing. In fact those who start singing while reaping the harvest or gathering in the vintage, or while they are eagerly carrying on some other work, start with the words of a song to express their joy, but then it is as though they are overcome with such happiness that words no longer can express it and they leave out the words and simply give themselves over to sounds of jubilation. Jubilation is a certain kind of sound that points to the fact that the heart wants to tell of something that cannot be said in words. And to whom is this jubilation most fittingly addressed, if not to God who is ineffable? For in fact that which is ineffable is what not only cannot be expressed in words but also cannot be passed over in silence, and so, what can one do but jubilate? For in jubilation the heart opens up to joy without words, and that joy widens out immeasurably beyond the utmost reaches of our words.[9]

In the Gregorian chants we often find a number of bars of pure melody following the note that carries the last syllable of a line. Should we not see these extended chants of pure melody as also a "singing in tongues," at very least in the moment when they arose in the heart of the composer? The author of the earliest biography of Saint Francis of Assisi tells that, whenever he was full of fervor and needed to give vent to the fire of love in his heart, "as if drunk in the Spirit," he would sing in French.[10] It was Saint Francis's way of singing in tongues!

---

[9] Augustine, *Exposition on the Psalms,* 32.II.8 (CC 38, p. 254).
[10] Celano, *First Life,* 7.16 (ED, I, p. 194); *Second Life,* 8.13 (ED, II, p. 252).

However beautiful, "singing in the Spirit," or singing in tongues, is not the only form of singing that comes under inspiration. Ordinary singing, or "singing with the mind" as Saint Paul calls it, is in all of its many forms a specially favored vehicle of the Spirit. When Paul uses the phrase "spiritual songs,"[11] that is, songs inspired by the Spirit, he does not mean singing in tongues only, but every form of singing that Christians use in their assemblies, when they sing with faith and with heartfelt participation.

Because of its ability to inspire, to set free and to uplift the heart and mind, its rhythm and its harmony, song is perhaps the most expressive and "connatural" means by which the Holy Spirit can touch us; song, certainly, is the least inadequate way of speaking of God or to God. This shows why the verb we translate as "to sing," along with its various derivatives (like song, singer, canticle) is one of the words that occurs most frequently in the Bible (no less than 306 times in the Old Testament and 36 in the New).

Song melds a number of different voices into one single act of praise and worship. Saint Basil describes what an impression it made on him when he heard his community singing:

> The sea is so beautiful that it moves us to offer our praises to God, but how much more beautiful is this assembly, in which the sound of many voices together is like the gentle washing of waves on the shore. One single voice rises from men and women and little children all together in the midst of the prayers that we send up to God. Deep calm keeps this choir in peace.[12]

Song softens hearts and disposes them to accept God's truths and God's will. When Ambrose was bishop of Milan he encouraged sacred singing in his church, and Augustine tells us of the tremendous impression this made on him at the time of his conversion:

> How many tears flowed while listening to the melodious words of the hymns and the canticles that resounded so sweetly through your Church! How deeply I was stirred! Those words

---

[11] Col 3:16; Eph 5:19.
[12] Basil the Great, *Hexaemeron,* IV.7 (SCh 26, pp. 274–5).

> flowed on the melody into my ears and distilled truth into my
> heart, stirring it to warm sentiments of devotion.[13]

The Church, in both the Greek east and the Latin west, at a
very early stage recognized the irreplaceable function of sacred
music and accorded it a place of primary importance in the liturgy. In the Constitution on the Sacred Liturgy the Second Vatican Council says that "the purpose of sacred music . . . is the
glory of God and the sanctification of the faithful.[14]

3. Other Charisms Linked to the Word

As for the author of the Acts of the Apostles so too for Paul, the
place of honor among the charisms of the word is given to *prophecy*. Paul teaches emphatically that it is more important than
speaking in tongues:

> Pursue love and strive for the spiritual gifts, and especially that
> you may prophesy. . . . On the other hand, those who proph-
> esy speak to other people for their upbuilding and encourage-
> ment and consolation. Those who speak in a tongue build up
> themselves, but those who prophesy build up the church. . . .
> But if all prophesy, an unbeliever or outsider who enters is re-
> proved by all and called to account by all. After the secrets of
> the unbeliever's heart are disclosed, that person will bow down
> before God and worship him, declaring, "God is really among
> you" (1 Cor 14:1, 3-4, 24-25).

If we are to go by the rediscovered experience of this gift in the
Church today, we have to say that it takes the form of words, spoken under inspiration, by a person in the assembly who feels
moved to say them to the whole assembly. When Paul reminded
Timothy of the "words spoken over him *by the prophets*" (1 Tim
1:18), he was probably referring to inspired messages of this
kind, spoken over Timothy while the community was praying for
him either when he was baptized or when he was appointed to his
office, and which revealed God's plans in his regard.

At such times the sense that it is God who is speaking is so strong
that the prophet delivering the message has no hesitation in using

[13] Augustine, *Confessions,* IX.6.14.
[14] *Sacrosanctum Concilium* 112.

words such as "it is the Lord who speaks," or even more coura-
geously, "I say to you, 'I have loved you.'" In such cases it is clear
that the "I" does not refer to the one who is actually pronouncing the
words, but to God. When the prophecy is authentic, the assembly
becomes aware of the presence of God in a way that cannot be mistaken: the light of truth is cast on some particular situation and at
times also on "the secrets of the heart." In that situation a person is
moved irresistibly to proclaim, "God is here!" or if an unbeliever,
"God is among you!" The preference that Paul shows for this charism arises from the fact that more than any other it serves to "build
up" the community, so fulfilling the very definition of charism.

In its exercise, the charism of prophecy should normally be accompanied by the charism of *discernment of spirits:* "To another
is given the gift of prophecy, to another the discernment of
spirits" (1 Cor 12:10).

In the history of Christian spirituality, discernment has taken
on a variety of meanings and has been applied in a number of different ways. But its original sense, as Paul appears to have intended it, seems to be very specific and precise. It concerns the
receiving of prophecy itself, its evaluation by one or several of the
members of the community who themselves are gifted with
the prophetic spirit. However, this evaluation is not something
that takes place on the basis of a rational analysis, but rather under
the inspiration of the same Spirit. The meaning of "to discern" *(di-
akrisis)*, therefore, is somewhere between "to distinguish" and "to
interpret": to distinguish whether the one speaking was the Spirit
of God or some other spirit either human or malign, and to interpret what the Spirit has wanted to say in this concrete situation.
When he wrote his well-known admonition, Paul was referring to
this gift of discernment: "Do not quench the spirit. Do not despise
the words of prophets, but test everything; hold fast to what is
good; abstain from every form of evil" (1 Thess 5:19-22).

If here too we need to take present-day experience into account,
we should think that this charism consists in the ability of the assembly, or of some people in it, to respond actively to a prophecy.
They would do this by exclaiming, "I confirm that" or by giving
other signs like a nod of the head or some other expression in ap-
proval of the prophetic word that has just been heard, or else by indicating a negative judgment, either by silence or by shifting the

attention of the meeting to something else. In this way, whether a prophecy is true or false is judged by the "fruits" it produces or does not produce, as Jesus in fact recommends (see Matt 7:16).

Yet another charism linked to the Word is the gift of *teaching* (see Rom 12:7). Those who have this gift are given the title teacher.[15] Teaching is different from prophecy. Through prophecy God speaks a new word, but through teaching God gives the capacity to bring to light new implications of a word that is already known, either from the Old Testament or from the sayings of Jesus. This is the charism that shines out brilliantly, for example in certain of the more influential spiritual and exegetical writings of the Fathers. Another pair of gifts relating to teaching are the "utterance of wisdom" and the "utterance of knowledge," or "preaching with wisdom" and "preaching instruction" (see 1 Cor 12:8). The difference between them is that knowledge or instruction is concerned with the elementary truths of Christianity, and wisdom relates to deeper insight into the truth, revealed to those who are mature in the faith.[16] (Among Pentecostals and charismatics today, the "word of knowledge" is used rather to mean a revelation of what the Lord is actually doing in a particular case, given normally to a person who is engaged in a ministry such as that of healing, who then makes it known to the assembly.)

I have sought to describe and draw attention to the charisms that are more directly linked to the Word, because it is directly to those that the *Veni Creator* is referring in the line "gifting lips with the word to say." The influence of the Spirit on the word, however, is not limited only to the area of charismatic experience, but embraces all aspects of the life of the Church. The Holy Spirit

> puts the revealed word onto the lips of the sacred writers, and we have the Scriptures;
> puts praise on the lips of the Church, and we have the liturgy;
> puts the words of definition on the lips of the Fathers, and we have dogma;
> puts the word of teaching on the lips of pastors, and we have the magisterium;

---

[15] See 1 Cor 12:29; Eph 4:11.
[16] See 1 Cor 2:6-16; Heb 6:1.

puts on the lips of the preacher the phrase, "Jesus is Lord!"
and we have evangelization;

puts the words of consecration on the lips of the priest, and
we have the Eucharist;

puts on the lips of children the cry, "*Abba,* Father," and we have
Christian prayer;

puts words of fire on the lips of inspired people, and we have
prophecy;

puts songs of jubilation on the lips of those who savor the "new
wine," and we have singing in tongues.

4. Something Appeared to Them that Seemed like Tongues of Fire

There is a common element that binds together all the charisms
we have been considering: in each one of them the Breath of God
mysteriously enters human language, giving it an entirely new
quality. The Spirit continues to do what he did when he inspired
the Scriptures, though of course no longer in a normative and canonical way: "When men spoke for God, it was the Holy Spirit
that moved them" (2 Pet 1:21).

It is chiefly in the proclamation of the kerygma, Jesus Christ
who died and is risen, "in Spirit and in power," that this work of
the Holy Spirit continues. What is it, actually, that happens? At a
certain point while the preacher is speaking, quite apart from any
decision of his, he becomes aware of an intervention, as though a
signal on another wavelength were coming through his voice. He
becomes aware of this because he begins to feel deeply stirred,
invested with a strength and an extraordinary power of conviction
that he recognizes clearly is not his own. His words come out in-
cisive, with greater assurance.

He experiences a touch of that "authority" that all recognized
when they listened to Jesus speaking. If he is speaking of sin, for instance, he feels such zeal for God, such indignation, that it is as
though God himself had appointed him his advocate to the sinful
world. It seems to him that in that strength he would be able to stand
up to the entire world and truly "make mad the guilty and appall the
free."[17] If he is speaking of God's love, or about the sufferings of

---

[17] W. Shakespeare, *Hamlet,* act II, scene 2.

Christ, his voice resounds with something of the very *pathos* of God. Paul gives a very clear description of this experience:

> My speech and my proclamation were not with plausible words of wisdom, but with a *demonstration of the Spirit and of power,* so that your faith might rest not on human wisdom but on the power of God (1 Cor 2:4-5).

> Our message of the gospel came to you not in word only, but also in power and in the Holy Spirit and with full conviction (1 Thess 1:5).

The apostle is speaking not only of his own experience, but of one shared by the whole community. In fact, when it is the Spirit who puts the words on the preacher's lips, the effects, even though wholly spiritual in their nature, are quite evident and easily seen. The listeners are brought to a point of total concentration into which no other voice can reach; they too feel "touched," and shivers often go through their bodies.

In a moment like this, the human speaker and the human voice fade out of the picture, to make place for another voice entirely. "The true prophet, when he speaks, remains silent."[18] The prophet is silent because, at that moment, it is not he who speaks, but another. A mysterious silence comes about within him, as when, for instance, somebody stands respectfully aside to allow the king to pass. The prophet himself is fascinated by the word he is speaking, and if for human considerations he tries to keep a certain thought from being spoken out loud, he seems to feel a fire burning in his heart, imprisoned in his bones (see Jer 20:9). He simply cannot restrain it, and he says those words with even greater emphasis. God says to his prophets, poor sinful human creatures, "You shall serve as my mouth" (Jer 15:19), and the thought of it makes his messenger tremble.

Of course, this is not sustained at the same level of intensity through the whole time that the prophet is speaking or preaching. There are special moments. God needs only one phrase, one word. The speaker and the listeners have the feeling that drops of fire mingle at a certain point with the preacher's words as they are spoken, and the words become white-hot and shining. Of all im-

---

[18] Philo of Alexandria, *Quis rerum,* 266, in *Les oeuvres de Philon d'Alexandre,* vol. 15 (Paris, 1966) 300.

ages, fire is the one that is least handicapped in expressing what the Spirit does in this kind of situation. So it was that at Pentecost he showed himself as "tongues, as of fire" (Acts 2:3). We read that "Elijah arose, a prophet like fire and his word burned like a torch" (Sir 48:1), and in the book of the prophet Jeremiah God declares, "Is not my word like fire, says the Lord, and like a hammer that breaks a rock in pieces?" (Jer 23:29).

5. From Babel to Pentecost

All of this leads us to understand one thing: We really do need to allow the fire of the Holy Spirit to enter into every word that we speak. If not, our words may well make a good deal of sense, but they will be devoid of power; it may be that they will explain something, but they will move nobody. They will be ineffectual, idle, fruitless. In that sense, they will be "careless." Jesus himself said, "I tell you, on the day of judgment you will have to give an account for every careless word you utter" (Matt 12:36).

There has been a great deal of discussion about what a "careless word" might be. But if we read this text in the light of the parallel passage on the false prophets (see Matt 7:15-20), perhaps the obscurity will disappear. The exact meaning of the word *argon* in the original text does not convey the passive sense of baseless, unfounded, a calumny, but rather the active sense of that which achieves nothing. Exactly the opposite of the word of God which by definition is *energes,* full of energy, totally effectual.[19]

The ineffectual words of which we shall have to give an account are not, therefore, any and every idle word we say; they are the empty, fruitless, purely human words spoken by those whose duty it is to proclaim the living, life-changing words of God, inspired words. They are the idle words of the false prophets, that is, the words of those who want us to believe that they speak to us in God's name, but in fact are simply putting forward their own ideas. They do not draw what they say from the heart of God, but merely think it up themselves.

If our words are to be efficacious words, we need the Holy Spirit. Saint Ambrose, commenting on the verse of the psalm,

---

[19] See Heb 4:12; 1 Thess 2:13.

"The floods have lifted up their voice" (Ps 93:3), wrote to one of his fellow bishops,

> There is a river that runs down on God's holy people like a torrent. . . . Whoever receives this river will raise their own voice. And like the apostles who, with mighty voices made the Gospel message resound to the utmost ends of the earth, they too will begin to spread the joyful news of the Lord Jesus. Accept, then, this river from Christ, so that you too may proclaim the message with power.[20]

But it should not be necessary to stress the obvious fact that, without the Holy Spirit, there can be no authentic proclamation or mission. I believe we are all quite convinced of this by now. We need rather to be working at the practical problem of how to be so in tune with the Holy Spirit that he is able to "give our lips the words to say."

We find a very important piece of practical advice in the actual account of the first Pentecost. It is well known that Luke wanted to draw a contrast between Pentecost and Babel. What happened at Pentecost was the undoing of all that had resulted from Babel. And so it was that Luke laid so much stress on the fact of the speaking in tongues. That was exactly the point of contrast and the parallel: At Babel everyone started out speaking the same language, but at a certain point no one could understand anyone else any longer; at Pentecost the people at first were divided into many language-groups (Parthians, Elamites, and so on), but at a certain point they all began to understand one another. Why so? The people of Babel had set about building a tower, saying to one another, "Come, let us build ourselves a city, and a tower with its top in the heavens, and let us *make a name for ourselves;* otherwise we shall be scattered abroad upon the face of the whole earth" (Gen 11:4).

What they wanted was to "make a name for themselves." They were concerned above all with their own desire for power and to ensure their own dominant position. But turn now to Pentecost. Why was it that they all began to understand one another? We find the answer in what the people were saying to one another: "In our own languages we hear them speaking about *God's deeds of power*" (Acts 2:11).

[20] Ambrose, *Letters,* VII.36 (CSEL 8.2, p. 4).

They all understood the apostles, because the apostles were not speaking about themselves, but about God. They had set out not to make a name for themselves, but for God. They had learned "a new song"! A short time before, they had been discussing among themselves who would be the greatest, but not anymore. They had experienced what is the greatest conversion: away from self, toward God. They were dead to any glory of their own. That is why the Spirit was able to put effective words in their mouths. It is simply not possible for the Spirit to become an accomplice in our vanity or to put himself at the service of our own ambition.

Enthusiastic praise of God, admiration and awe at his works are some of the clearest signs that the Spirit of God has visited our soul. When the Spirit overshadowed Mary and the power of the Most High came upon her, she sang her *Magnificat*. When the Church received the power from on high at Pentecost it did the same. The "marvels of God," the great works of God that the apostles were proclaiming, match very closely the "great things" of which Mary sang (see Luke 1:49). "Of all creatures, we humans are the only ones that are able to praise."[21] The Holy Spirit, therefore, is the one who gives us the ability to become gifted at praising, who not only gives us a duty to praise, but puts a desire, a passion, for the praise of God in our hearts. The believer says to the philosopher, "You reason, I admire!"[22]

The Fathers had many profound things to say about Babel, but on one point they were mistaken. They thought that the people who set out to build the Tower of Babel were atheists, titans who wanted to challenge God. But that is not the way it was. They were pious and religious people. The tower they wanted to build was simply one of those famous temples of stepped terraces, called *ziggurat*. The ruins of several of them can still be seen in Mesopotamia today. Where, then, was their sin? They wanted to build a temple *to* God but not *for* God. It was their own glory that they were seeking, not God's. They thought that, by building a temple higher than any other in that region at that time, they would be able to deal with God from a position of strength and so coax favors and victories from God.

---

[21] Augustine, *Sermons,* 29.1 (CC 41, p. 373).

[22] Augustine, *Sermons,* 27.7 (CC 41, p. 366).

At a stroke, this brings the whole affair close to us. Babel and Pentecost are two construction sites still open and still working in our own history. Augustine based his great work, *The City of God,* on this fact. In the world people are busy building two cities. One is Babylon, and its foundation is self-love pushed to the extreme of despising God. The other is the City of God, the new Jerusalem, and its foundation is love of God taken to the extreme of disregard for self. Each one of us is called to choose: we must be working in one or the other of these building sites. Pastoral initiatives, missions, religious undertakings, no matter how holy, may be an effort for Pentecost, or they may be an effort for Babylon. They are for Babylon if those involved are seeking to affirm their own reputation and make a name for themselves; they are for Pentecost if those involved are seeking only God's glory and the coming of his kingdom. And this holds a message for us today. If we really want the Spirit to place words on our lips, we need to live constantly in an attitude of death to our own glory, seeking only the glory of God.

Let us end by making our own the beautiful prayer of Gregory of Narek, an Armenian mystic who lived in the early years of the second millennium, and who has had a major influence on the spiritual life and poetry of his people even to this day:

> *I bow as suppliant before your immutable and all-powerful*
> *   sovereignty,*
> *oh mighty Spirit:*
> *send down the dew of your gentleness.*
> *You, who consecrate the apostles, inspire the prophets, teach*
> *   the teachers,*
> *who make the dumb to speak and open the ears of those that*
> *   cannot hear,*
> *give to me too, sinner though I am, the grace to speak with*
> *   sureness*
> *of the life-giving mystery of the good news of the Gospel. . . .*
> *When I set out to speak your word in the assembly,*
> *may your mercy go before me*
> *and at the right moment prompt me from within*
> *to say what is fitting and helpful and pleasing to you,*
> *to the glory and praise of your Godhead*
> *and wholly for the edification of the universal Church.*[23]

[23] Gregory of Narek, *Book of Prayers,* 34 (SCh 78, pp. 210ff.).

XIV

Kindle Your Light in Our Minds

The Holy Spirit guides us to the fullness of truth

1. The Spirit Works in the Individual Believer

We come now to a new verse of the *Veni Creator,* and it takes us into a new category of ideas. Let us look at a literal translation of this verse:

> Kindle your light in our minds,
> pour love into our hearts,
> all that is weak in this body of ours
> with enduring strength make strong.

The verbs, like those in the first verse, are again in the imperative (perhaps we should say the *impetrative,* because they express a plea rather than a command). While contemplation of the Spirit was the characteristic of the second and third verses, we pass now to invocation of the Spirit which will be sustained through all the rest of the hymn. Also, where the two preceding verses were in the form of a eulogy, a litany of praise ("you who are . . ."), the hymn now takes on the form of an *epiclesis,* that is, a calling-down.

So far we have looked at form. As to content, too, this verse opens up for us a new field of activity of the Spirit. In the first verse we viewed the action of the Spirit against the limitless background of the cosmos and of history, that is, the Spirit's action as the Spirit of creation and as the Spirit of redemption and grace. The second and the third verses focused on the Church, for it is in the Church that the Spirit works as the "Spirit of grace." Following the line of thought as it develops in the hymn, we have been able to contemplate, always in the context of Church, first the sanctifying work of the Holy Spirit, and then the charismatic action of the Holy Spirit through which the Spirit guides and governs the "organization of the Church."

Our attention is now shifted, so to say, from the outside to the inside: we have been looking at the created universe, history and the Church, but now we look at the individual person. In a wonderful way the hymn now brings to light what the action of the Holy Spirit achieves in each believer, the Spirit's relationship with each one of us.

The author of the hymn "frames" the work of the Paraclete in much the same way that a good TV cameraman goes about it. The usual approach is to open with a "wide-angle" shot, or to "pan" the scene, showing us a general view of the situation in which the action develops. The camera then takes us closer and zooms in, narrowing down the field to take in only the actor. Finally, the picture frames only the face of the actor, up close. In the first verse the author gave us a wide-angle view of the Spirit, allowing us to see the Spirit against the whole sweep of history and of the world. In the second and third verses he narrowed the focus and showed us the action of the Spirit in the framework of the Church. In the fourth and fifth verses he zooms in and shows us the action of the Spirit in the individual human person. In the last verse he will go back to a "wide-angle" view, this time, however, no longer of the world and its history, but of the Trinity.

In order to describe the way the Paraclete works in each individual person, the author first of all draws as it were a filigree pattern of human nature, an anthropology. He looks at the human person above all as a rational being, endowed with intellect. The word "sensus" *(accende lumen sensibus)* is used here in its meaning, common in ecclesiastical Latin, of "the mind," the faculty of perception, and not in its narrower meaning which refers to the external senses—sight, hearing, etc.—(see, e.g. 1 Cor 2:16: "Who has known the *mind* [Vulgate: *sensum*] of the Lord?" The plural *sensibus* does not suggest the plurality of the external senses, but meets the needs of meter and rhyme, making *sensibus,* "our minds," match *cordibus,* "our hearts," in the next line.

Next the author looks at the human person as endowed with the faculty of will and with feeling—the human dimension that the Bible often refers to as the *heart*.

Finally, he looks at the human being also as *body,* seeing the body not merely as an element extraneous to the human person (as it is seen in Platonism and other dualistic philosophies), but as itself a work of the Creator Spirit and, by operation of grace, also the temple of the Spirit. "Brother body," as Saint Francis of Assisi called it, has every right to be within the field of the Spirit's action, for the Spirit is the friend of the body too!

Let us take note of certain characteristics of this way of looking at the human person. Although it recognizes all three components in the human makeup, it is not quite the same as the trichotomism of Greek philosophy. That used to distinguish three human components: body, soul (understood as the intermediate principle of life), and *nous,* the highest of the three elements. In our case, in keeping with the traditional Christian view, two basic elements are distinguished in the human person: body and soul. Intellect and will, or mind and heart, are only two *faculties* of one of these two elements, soul.

Note another characteristic. Certain of the Church Fathers understood the Holy Spirit as that divine element that comes to perfect the human person on the supernatural level, linking with that part that is highest in human nature, the intellect, and through the intellect having his effect on the rest of the human person. Our hymn gives us an insight into a different and more biblical perspective: The Holy Spirit acts directly and not through any mediation on the whole human person: the mind, the heart, and the body. For in fact in each of these areas we look to the Holy Spirit for the gifts appropriate to each: light for the mind, love for the heart, and health for the body. The basic christological principle is: "That which is not assumed by the Word is not saved" *(quod non est assumptum, non est sanatum).* The same principle can be applied, in an analogous way, to the Holy Spirit: "If anything is not reached by the Holy Spirit, it is not sanctified." In our reflection, the next three chapters will be looking, in turn, at each one of these three zones of our being, starting with the mind.

2. The Holy Spirit as Light, in the Bible and in the Fathers

Light, unlike the other natural symbols—wind, water, fire, and oil—is never used in the Bible to refer directly to the Holy Spirit. Nevertheless, we see that light plays a very important part in the writings of the Church Fathers on the Holy Spirit. What basis did the Fathers have for this? Is it perhaps a case of a theme that has no foundation in Scripture?

Light, as we know, is widely used throughout Scripture as a way of speaking of God, right up to Saint John's declaration "God is light" (1 John 1:5). It took a little time for the infant Church to come to certainty on the point that the Holy Spirit is God by the same right and title as Father and Son are God. Once this certainty had been reached, the Fathers, just as they had done earlier in relation to the Son, consistently recognized as belonging to the Spirit all that pertained to the nature of God, and in particular, the attribute of light. The entire line of argument that leads to belief that the Spirit is God also serves as basis for the understanding that all the prerogatives and all the titles attributed to God in the Bible are also, rightly, to be attributed to the Holy Spirit. It was in this kind of context that we find, in the earliest writings on the Holy Spirit, discussion of "light" as a title appropriate to the Spirit.[1]

Though Scripture may not specifically attribute the natural *symbol* of light to the Holy Spirit, it often does in fact attribute the spiritual *reality* to which the symbol relates: The Scriptures do represent the Spirit as the principle of knowledge, the source of truth. The Paraclete will teach and prompt the disciples and call to their mind everything that Jesus has taught; the Spirit is "the Spirit of truth," who is going to lead them "to the complete truth" (John 16:13).

Saint Paul too speaks of the Holy Spirit's work of revealing and giving knowledge. When he has spoken of "the things that no eye has seen and no ear has heard, things beyond the human mind," he adds, with an air of triumph:

> These things God has revealed to us through the Spirit; for the Spirit searches everything, even the depths of God. For what human being knows what is truly human except the human spirit that is within? So also no one comprehends what is truly God's except the Spirit of God. Now we have received not the spirit of the world, but the Spirit that is from God, so that we may understand the gifts bestowed on us by God. And we speak of these things in words not taught by human wisdom but taught by the Spirit, interpreting spiritual things to those who are spiritual (1 Cor 2:10-13).

[1] See Ambrose, *On the Holy Spirit,* I.16, 140–51.

This, therefore, is the biblical basis for applying the title "light" to the Spirit. As always, the evidence from the Bible is supported by that other great factor that enriches our knowledge of the Holy Spirit, the *Church's experience*. The Church knows by experience what it is to receive "the illuminating power" of the Paraclete, just as experience shows too, what it is to be touched by his "power to sanctify." Athanasius in fact sees this as the very definition of the Holy Spirit: "power that sanctifies and enlightens."[2] Saint Basil develops the same theme, with telling imagery:

> The Holy Spirit, power that sanctifies and light that gives understanding, himself grants to every rational creature the kind of clarity needed to discover the truth. . . . Just as one on whom the sunlight shines rejoices in it as if he alone were touched by it, even though it lights up all land and sea and sky, so too is the Spirit present to each one able to receive him as though he were the only one, yet he continues to send forth grace in the same undivided abundance to everyone. . . . Enlightening those who are freed from every stain of sin, he makes them spiritual beings by means of their communion with him. And just as something that is clear and transparent shines when a ray of light strikes it, and begins itself to give off light, so too the souls indwelt by the Spirit shine because of him, and made spiritual, begin to pour out grace upon others.[3]

In the writings of this Father of the Church, light is the image that recurs most often. He has had a decisive influence on all the subsequent development of the doctrine of the Holy Spirit in the eastern Church. If by sin we extinguish this light of the Holy Spirit in our soul, everything falls back into darkness.

> If at night you put out the light, your eyes cannot see, other faculties become inert, values become indistinct, you would easily place no worth on a thing of gold, thinking it to be iron. In like manner, in the spiritual order, without the Holy Spirit it is quite impossible to live a life properly in conformity with the law.[4]

---

[2] Athanasius, *Letters to Serapion,* I.20 (PG 26.580A).

[3] Basil the Great, *On the Holy Spirit,* IX.22–3 (PG 32.108–9).

[4] Ibid., XVI.38 (PG 32.137C).

Cyril of Jerusalem too, bears testimony to the same sort of lived experience, where he speaks of the Holy Spirit as "the great doctor of the Church":

> Shining rays of light and of understanding precede his coming. He comes with all the love of a true teacher. For in fact he comes to save, to heal, to teach, to admonish, to strengthen, to console, to enlighten the mind. These effects he produces above all in the soul of the one who receives him, and then, through that soul, he comes upon others too. If someone has been in the dark and suddenly comes into the light of the sun, his bodily eye will keep the light and he will see clearly what he could not see before. In a similar way, someone who has been made worthy to receive the Holy Spirit will retain that enlightenment in his soul and in a way that transcends human nature will see things that could not be seen before.[5]

In the theology of the Holy Spirit of the eastern Church, the theme of light plays a role comparable to that of the theme of love among the Latin Fathers. If at first the symbol of light was used to say something about the divine *nature* of the Holy Spirit, it was not long before it began to be used as a way of understanding something about the hypostasis, that is, the Spirit as *divine person*. In relation to the symbol of water, the Church Fathers used to distinguish three things: the source, the river, and the stream; in relation to light they distinguished the sun, its shining, and its ray.[6] The sun is the Father, the ongoing shining forth is the Son, and the ray channeling the shining is the Holy Spirit. Saint Gregory of Nyssa also makes use of this Trinitarian imagery, but seeks to save it from running the risk of suggesting that there are ranks of importance in the Trinity, as if the Son were inferior to the Father, and the Spirit in turn inferior to the Son and the Father. After he has made his comparison of the Father to the sun and the Son to the light that flows forth from him "like another sun," he extends the image to the Holy Spirit, saying:

> And there is another, similar light that in the same way does not come after the light that is generated but that spreads in virtue of it, yet drawing the source of its personhood from the

---

[5] Cyril of Jerusalem, *Catecheses,* XVI.16.
[6] See Tertullian, *Against Praxeas,* VIII.6; XXII.6 (CC 2, pp. 1168, 1190).

first light. This light itself, just as the one we first spoke about, shines and illumines and accomplishes all the other things that light can do.[7]

The Holy Spirit as light is equal to the Father and the Son, even though the Spirit's light is spread through the Son (the generated light), and draws his origin from the Father (the first light). Light, thus, serves to affirm both the unity of essence and the distinction of the Persons in the Trinity.

Light, as a symbol, usually carries with it the idea of the trans-figuration of a person: to total bathing of the person in clarity both inward and external. Light, in all of these ways, is the symbol used most frequently by the Eastern writers when they describe mystical phenomena. The loveliest example is found in the life of Saint Seraphim of Sarov. One day he was teaching a disciple about the coming of the Holy Spirit. It was a snowy winter day and the two of them were out in the open, busy chopping firewood. Suddenly, the holy man told the disciple to look him in the eye. He looked, and what did he see? A bright shining light that lit up the space all around them and glittered on the snow that covered the ground and on the snow that kept on falling. Seraphim the monk appeared like a man talking, but his face shone like the sun at midday.[8] This is what the coming of the Spirit brings about.

In the Orthodox tradition, the bright cloud that came down upon the disciples on Mount Tabor was nothing other than the Holy Spirit. Also, the "Tabor light" that plays such a great part in Eastern Christian spirituality and iconography was intimately linked with the Holy Spirit.[9] A text in the Orthodox daily Office says that, on Pentecost day, "by grace of the Holy Spirit, the entire world received its baptism of light."[10]

Among the Latins too, we find wonderful appreciation of the Holy Spirit as light. Saint Hilary, using an expression very close to the words of our hymn, says that the Paraclete is "light of minds,

---

[7] Gregory of Nyssa, *Against Eunomius,* I (PG 45.416); see also Gregory Nazianzen, *Sermons,* XXXI.31–2 (PG 36.169).

[8] Conversation with Motovilov, in G. P. Fedotov, *A Treasury of Russian Spirituality* (New York: Sheed and Ward, 1948).

[9] Gregory Palamas, *Homily 1 on the Transfiguration* (PG 151.433B–C).

[10] Sinassarion of Pentecost, in *Pentecostaire* (Parma, 1994) 407.

and splendour of souls." He goes on to say, "It is within the capacity of the soul to know God, but until, through faith, it has in fact received the gift of the Holy Spirit, the soul lacks the light it needs to actually know him."[11] A prayer, predating the composition of the *Veni Creator* but still in use in the liturgy today, says: "Lord, we pray, may the Paraclete who proceeds from you bring light into our minds, and lead us, as your Son promised, into all truth."[12]

The equally ancient prayer for the feast of Pentecost, which we still often use when we want to invoke the Holy Spirit before setting about some task, says: "Oh God, *by the light of the Holy Spirit* you have taught the hearts of your faithful; grant that by the same Spirit we may be always truly wise and ever rejoice in his consolation."[13]

The Sequence for the Pentecost Mass, which often echoes the themes of our hymn, asks the Holy Spirit, the "light of hearts," to send "a ray of his light" from heaven, and asks him, as "light most beautiful," to "fill the inmost hearts of his faithful."

Yet the theme of the Holy Spirit as "light," as it developed among the Latins, did not serve the same function as it did among Eastern Christians. The reason for this is that in the West, following Augustine, "light" was taken to correspond with doctrine, with intellect, and with knowledge, and as a title was consequently by preference reserved to the divine Word. Western writers generally found the category of love the most helpful for developing an appreciation of the Spirit. Wisdom was attributed to the Son and power to the Father, and to the Holy Spirit, goodness, inasmuch as the Spirit proceeds as love from Father and Son.[14] Among the mystics, too, the theme of light was extensively developed in the West, but almost exclusively in relation to the Word, to the Essence of the Divine, as we find for instance in the Rhineland mystics.

---

[11] Hilary, *The Trinity,* II.1.35 (CC 62, p. 71).

[12] *Sacramentarium Gellonense* (8th century), (CC 159, p. 139, n. 1044): *"Mentes nostras, quaesumus Domine, Paraclitus qui a te procedit inluminet, et inducat in omnem, sicut tuus promisit Filius, veritatem."*

[13] Ancient prayer for the Mass of Pentecost: *"Deus qui corda fidelium Sancti Spiritus illustratione docuisti, da nobis in eodem Spiritu recta sapere et de eius semper consolatione gaudere."*

[14] See Thomas Aquinas, *De Veritate,* q. 7, a. 3.

3. What Light Does the Spirit Kindle, and What Does It Light Up?

Christian thinkers have been able to distinguish diverse kinds of light, and various ways of bringing into the light. There is natural light, the light of faith, the light of grace, and, in eternal life, the light of glory. The human faculty of reason is natural light. The *light of faith* makes it possible for us to come to know things that are beyond the scope of reason—it is like a new eye opened on the world of God and on things that are invisible. The *light of grace* is similar to the light of faith, but wider in its scope: It is a supernatural light, to which we human beings cannot attain unless it is infused, poured into us, "through the freely-given help of God moving us inwardly from within."[15] The soul, enlightened by grace, is like the sky lit up by the rays of the sun. Finally, in eternal life, the light of faith and of grace is succeeded by the *light of glory,* by which we will see God "face to face" and by which we will be transformed "from glory to glory."[16]

To which of these kinds of light does the light belong that the Holy Spirit "enkindles" in our minds? It is not simply the same as the gift of faith, by which we believe revealed truth, but it gives us a new capacity to penetrate more deeply into the mysteries, to see how they relate to each other and to our spiritual life, and intuitively to perceive what profound sense they make. It allows us, in short, to be touched by the "splendor of the truth" and to taste its intimate delight. It is in fact a light both of faith and of grace together. All that theology has helped us see regarding the gifts of understanding and of wisdom finds here its rightful application.

The Holy Spirit is poured out upon us "so that we may understand the gifts bestowed on us by God" (1 Cor 2:12). To *understand,* here, is more than just to take in as knowledge; it means also to admire in gratitude, to see with clarity, to taste, to possess. The Spirit makes us share in the joy that comes from being certain. We live in a culture that rates *veracity* ahead of *truth* as the highest human ideal, and simple *sincerity* ahead of *certainty.* We tend to look on a believer who claims that he is utterly *certain* as more than a little presumptuous. Here too, the Holy Spirit has taught us the right attitude: to remain humble in our certainty, and

[15] Thomas Aquinas, *Summa Theologiae* I-II, q. 79, a. 3; q. 109, a. 6.
[16] Thomas Aquinas, *De Veritate,* q. 5, a. 3, ad 10.

certain in our humility. Luther wrote: "The Spirit is not a sceptic. What he impresses upon our hearts is not doubts or opinions but truth more certain and sure than life itself, more certain than any fact of experience."[17] Karl Barth adds that nevertheless "there is no more intimate friend of sound human reason than the Holy Spirit."[18]

But, in actual fact, what does the light of the Holy Spirit show us? Paul says that it enables us to see the "depths of God," the "secrets of God," and teaches us to "understand the gifts that he has given us" (see 1 Cor 2:10-12). According to the sense of the term in the New Testament, the "depths of God" are in the first place the Trinity of Persons, and the divine life in the intimate relationships of Father, Son, and Spirit. The last verse of our hymn in fact prays, "Through you may we the Father know, and through you know the Son as well."

The primary focus, so to say, of the revelation brought us by the Paraclete—as we shall see when we come to comment on the last verse—is the *Person of Jesus and his works*. The Holy Spirit enkindles the light of Christ in our minds, making present to us the one who said, "I am the light of the world" (John 8:12). "We have been given the ability to think so that we may know Christ; desire, so that we may run towards him; and memory, so that we may carry him in ourselves."[19]

The Holy Spirit also casts light on our destiny. The Letter to the Ephesians gives us a prayer to the Father, asking him to enlighten the eyes of our mind with a spirit of perception of what is revealed, so that we may "see what hope his call holds" for us and "what are the riches of his glorious inheritance among the saints" (Eph 1:17-18).

However, the experience of the Holy Spirit enkindling light in our minds comes to us when we are reading Scripture more frequently by far than in any other circumstance. The Holy Spirit continues, among the members of the Church, the work of the Risen Christ who, after his resurrection, "opened their minds to understand the Scriptures" (Luke 24:45).

[17] Luther, *De servo arbitrio* (WA, 18, p. 605).

[18] K. Barth, *Church Dogma*, IV.4 (Zürich, 1967) 31.

[19] N. Cabasilas, *Vita in Christo*, VI.10 (PG 150.680).

"'The Law, of course, as we know, is spiritual' (Rom 7:14); yet not everyone knows what spiritual realities the Law wants to teach, but those only to whom the grace of the Holy Spirit has been given."[20] The immensely rich tradition of "spiritual reading" of the Scriptures is based on this conviction. "Scripture," we read in the Constitution on Divine Revelation of Vatican II, "must be read and interpreted with the help of the same Spirit through whom it was written."[21] To read the Bible without the Holy Spirit is like opening a book in the dark.

It happens that over a period of time you may read a particular passage of Scripture, and perhaps even preach on it, without experiencing any special feelings about it. Then, one day, you may read that same text in an atmosphere of prayer and faith, and quite unexpectedly it is lit up, it speaks, it makes you see some circumstance of your life in a whole new light, and it shows you clearly what is God's will in the situation. And not only that once, but every time, even after a long time, when you read that passage again, you are touched in the same powerful, enlightening way. What causes this change, if not the enlightening touch of the Holy Spirit? The words of Scripture, by the action of the Holy Spirit, are transformed: they glow, they bathe you and your situation in light.

Of all the experiences to which the coming of the Holy Spirit into a soul gives rise, this in fact is one of the most common, most powerful. The Scripture comes alive. Every sentence seems to be written especially for you, to the point of sometimes leaving you breathless, as though God were there speaking to you with tremendous authority but at the same time very, very gently. The words of the psalms keep surprising you: how new and fresh they seem, and what views they open up of unending horizons, and what deep echoes they awaken in your soul. At times like this, you can feel how true it is that "the Word of God is living and active" (Heb 4:12).

This is an experience that comes to everyone, even the most simple. People who have no schooling in the Scriptures whatever often go right to the heart of a text, but the learned may ponder it for years, to much less effect, though they have all the research and

[20] Origen, *On the Principles*, Pref. 8 (SCh 252, p. 86).
[21] *Dei Verbum* 12.

commentaries and dictionaries to help them. This again is the Holy Spirit revealing the secrets of God to the little ones (see Matt 11:25).

The link between the word of God and the work of the Spirit enlightening us was one of the points of greatest concern to the Reformers. The views taken were sometimes radical, going as far at times as to exclude any role of the Church whatever, on the basis of the doctrine of "free interpretation." Every Christian, strengthened by the Spirit's "inward witness," is able to understand the Scriptures without any outside help. Calvin writes:

> The Spirit of God is so closely connected with and bound to the truth that he has expressed in Scripture, that when the Word is received with proper veneration, his power is fully made manifest. . . . The Word is definitively guaranteed to us only if it is confirmed by the inward witness of the Spirit. The Lord has with mutual bonds coupled together in one the certainty of his Spirit and of his Word, in order that our mind should receive the Word with obedience because it accords with the light of the Spirit, which is light given us to see in it the face of God.[22]

Discussions today, in a more serene atmosphere, are leading us to recognize that there can be no opposition between the inward, personal witness, and the external, apostolic witness of the Church, when both truly come from the Holy Spirit. We also recognize that neither, without the other, is enough. At the same time we need to acknowledge that the insistent call of the Reformation was for many reasons very necessary at the time, and that it has brought great benefit to the whole Church.

4. Be Cleansed So As to Receive the Light

In this reflection we come, as always, to the point where we need to pass beyond our consideration of principles, and see how this line too of the *Veni Creator* urges us to action.

Paul, after he has told us that we have received the Spirit of God so that we may understand the gifts that the Spirit has given us, goes on straight away to say that the Spirit encounters obstacles

---

[22] Calvin, *Institutions of the Christian Religion,* I.9.3.

that prevent us doing that: "Those who are unspiritual do not receive the gifts of God's Spirit, for they are foolishness to them, and they are unable to understand them because they are spiritually discerned" (1 Cor 2:14).

The unspiritual person (literally, *psychikos,* "possessing a life-principle," in Latin *animal*) is one who allows himself to be driven by his instincts, thoughts, and desires. If this obstacle is not removed, and if one does not get beyond the "animal instinct" stage, everything remains obscure. The tremendous realities that the Spirit wants to reveal to our minds remain forever beyond our mind's reach. God needs to carry on mournfully repeating, "My thoughts are not your thoughts" (Isa 55:8). What then do we need to do to get rid of this obstacle? The Fathers sum up the answer: Be cleansed!

> Be cleansed of the filth with which sin has covered you, and find again your natural beauty, as you would restore an image to its original condition by cleaning it, and it becomes possible for you at last to come to the Paraclete. . . . The carnal man, whose mind is not trained to contemplation but is sunken rather in the muddy pit of carnal thoughts, cannot raise his eyes to the spiritual light of the truth. This is why the world, that is, life enslaved to carnal passion, does not receive the grace of the Spirit any more than an eye that is diseased can look on the light of the sun.[23]

This idea comes up again and again, whenever the Greek Fathers speak of the enlightenment that the Holy Spirit brings. When they speak of cleansing or purity, they mean in the first place cleansing from bodily passions. In this they echo the Greek thinking of the time. This used to see in the bond between the soul and the corruptible body the greatest obstacle to the contemplation of truth. The intellect as such relates to the divine and tends naturally toward truth; the body, on the other hand, keeps the mind earthbound. Consequently the first necessity is to "overcome the desires of the flesh," to be purified from them, until the mind is able to take in the divine light: "If the human intellect, having abandoned its dwelling in darkness and impurity, is made clean by the power of the breath of the Spirit, it becomes light-filled, one with the purity

[23] Basil the Great, *On the Holy Spirit,* IX.23; XXII.53 (PG 32.109, 168).

that is true and sublime, allowing that purity to shine through unspoiled and so becoming itself a light."[24]

Purity and knowledge of God are linked so closely together that it is possible to say, "Knowledge is given to everyone in the measure of each one's purity."[25] Should we regard all of this as nothing more than a problem arising out of the dualism of Greek thought, and of no concern to Christianity? No. For the opposition of flesh to the spirit is a theme that recurs often in the New Testament, though it is true that we cannot simply reduce it to the opposition of spirit to matter as the Greeks understood it. We would, however, make a serious mistake if we were to fail to see that the wider opposition, *spirit/flesh,* expressed in the New Testament still includes the narrower opposition, *spirit/matter,* taught by the Greeks. The term "flesh" means more than only "sexual," but it is certainly evident that the sexual occupies an important position in the sphere of the flesh. Before any of the Fathers, the Bible itself underlines this for us: "For a perishable body weighs down the soul, / and this earthy tent burdens the thoughtful mind" (Wis 9:15).

Paul's cry, "this body of death," is certainly a warning against more than simply the woundedness of human sexuality, yet it does include that. The human body, created good by God as everything else in creation, once it had lost its inward balance as a result of sin, became a "body of flesh" (Col 2:11), "this sinful body" (Rom 6:6).

Yet it is not "brother body" that bears the guilt. What is said of the whole of creation applies in a special way to the human body: "It was not for any fault on the part of creation that it was made unable to attain its purpose," subject to the fall. It is the fault of the human mind, and more so of the human will, that once having severed their subjection to God's will, subjected everything else to "slavery to corruption" (see Rom 8:19-20). The human mind and will now are blackmailed by the slave whom they themselves taught how to rebel. It is a fact of experience that disorder in the area of sexuality irremediably distorts the faculty of reason, and so darkens the mind that it becomes opaque to the light of God who is Spirit.

[24] Gregory of Nyssa, *On Virginity,* XI.4 (SCh 119, p. 390).

[25] Arethas of Caesarea, *On the Apocalypse,* 39 (PG 106.684C); see also Origen, *Against Celsus,* V.42 (SCh 147, p. 126); Ibid., VII.30 (SCh 150, p. 82).

What, then, is the practical consequence of all of this? If we want to experience the wonderful enlightenment that the Spirit brings (giving us intimate knowledge, as we have been saying, of God, of Christ, of the Scriptures, of our eternal destiny), we need to take the struggle to live in purity very, very seriously: "Blessed are the pure in heart, for they will see God" (Matt 5:8). Almost every time that Saint Paul speaks of purity, he speaks of it in relation to the Holy Spirit. He says, for example, that if someone indulges in fornication, he sins against his own body, and therefore against the Holy Spirit, because the body is the temple of the Spirit.[26] Living in purity is one of the very sure ways of coming to experience the Holy Spirit.

Yet we know how sensitive this question is, and how difficult it is to be truly pure of heart. What does one do so as not to give in and fall? There is a whole gamut of negative ways (don't do, don't say, don't look, don't touch), but the Scriptures and the Fathers have shown us a powerful, positive way that unfortunately is often neglected: Fall in love with genuine beauty, choose carefully the "body" with which you want to become as one. This is the direction in which the Spirit urges us in the real situation of our life, where we cannot simply rely only on the negative means. For the "flesh" has all sorts of ways to get at us, and it assails us everywhere, from within and from without. The little defenses are no longer enough; we need a grand strategy, one that will resolve the problem. Saint Paul suggests one where he writes: "Do you not know that whoever is united to a prostitute becomes one body with her? For it is said, 'The two shall be one flesh.' But anyone united to the Lord becomes one spirit with him" (1 Cor 6:16-17).

There is tremendous power, often unrecognized, in this last little sentence. No one who has repeated it quietly in his heart has ever failed to experience its efficacy. There is in our fallen selves a proclivity toward the material and the fleshly, but God has given us a remedy worthy of his wisdom: the risen body of the Lord. That is the place where the tension between flesh and spirit is finally overcome and where the body has already attained that freedom from slavery to decadence for which the whole of creation yearns. It is like an anchor of safety firmly lodged beyond the

[26] See 1 Cor 6:18-19; 1 Thess 4:8.

reach of the storms we endure or the struggles we wage. More-over, the body of the risen Christ is a real body, though living "ac-cording to the Spirit"; we can join ourselves to that body, in intention, by faith, and sacramentally in the Eucharist. One with the body of Christ, the purity of that body is ours too. The Jews in the desert, bitten by snakes, were healed when they looked upon the bronze serpent; we, bitten by sensuality, are healed when we run to look on him who, for this very purpose, was lifted up on the cross for us (see John 3:14-15).

In this way, there is no need to deny the beauty of the body or to regard human sexuality as something vile. This way, rather, is "from beauty to Beauty." As one of the ancient Fathers has said, "A man may know that his heart is pure when he is able to look on all that is beautiful and see nothing as impure."[27]

After we have pondered upon the action of the Holy Spirit on the human mind, as we have tried to do in this chapter, a good practical step would be to consecrate our mind to the Paraclete. "Consecrate" means "to entrust to, to hand over to, to reserve solely for." Decide that, from this moment on, we will use our mind to know only what is true and for the glory of God. For, whatever may have befallen the human mind, it remains the best, the most noble of all that has been given us, the closest reflection of God's own mind, and the one reality in this world with which God remains most closely in touch.

That is a consecration that we would do well to renew every morning. One of the ancient Fathers has said that our mind is like a mill: it will grind away all day at the first grain that we put into it in the morning. We would do well to be quick to put in, very first thing in the morning, God's good clean grain—good thoughts, God's words—for if we do not, the demons will not miss their chance to feed it with tares.[28]

Let us end with this prayer to the Spirit in the words of a hymn written not many years after the *Veni Creator,* which seems to be commenting on the line we have been considering:

> *Spirit most Holy, bringing light to us all,*
> *dispel from our minds all horrors that lurk;*

---

[27] John Climacus, *Ladder of Paradise,* VII.18 (PG 88.825A).
[28] See John Cassian, *Conferences,* I.18 (CSEL 13, p. 27).

by your love, Spirit, fill us
with good, clean thought.

Pour out within us the salve of your mercy,
ever cleansing our minds from the stains of our sin;
heal the eye deep within us
by evil made dim.
Allow us to gaze on the Father Almighty
whom only the eyes of the pure heart may see,
as the Gospel assures us,
the wisdom of Christ.[29]

---

[29] Notker Balbulus, *For the Day of Pentecost* (PL 131.1012–3).

XV

Pour Love into Our Hearts

The Holy Spirit draws us from love of self to love of God

1. Light and Love

The more one ponders on this fourth verse of the *Veni Creator,* the more one discovers what extraordinary depths are hidden in its simplicity. On the one hand it offers us an all-embracing view of human reality in all three aspects of mind, heart, and body— that is, intellect, will, and bodiliness. On the other hand it offers us an awesome synthesis of the action of the Holy Spirit in our human soul, in which we see it as the principle of knowledge, and conjointly as the principle of love.

Achieving this, the author of the hymn has grasped a pivotal aspect of the revelation and tradition concerning the Holy Spirit that we find clearly represented in some authors of the Middle Ages. William of St. Thierry writes of the Holy Spirit as the one "who enlightens the intellect and is the origin of affection."[1] Another author writes:

> Virtue consists entirely of the truth of love and the love of truth. As truth, it enlightens us so that we may know; as love, it inflames us to love. As in fact knowledge without love becomes puffed up, so too love without knowledge is off track, deceptive. In the warmth and the brilliance of fire the Holy Spirit was given to the disciples because, as shining light he would guide them to the fullness of truth, and as warmth he would make them fervent with the fullness of love.[2]

Yet another writer says that the Holy Spirit works "in the mind, giving intelligence, and in the heart, giving love; intelligence to overcome ignorance, and love to overcome greed; intelligence to

---

[1] William of St. Thierry, *The Enigma of Faith,* 100 (PL 180.440C).
[2] Isaac of Stella, *Sermons on Pentecost,* I.14 (SCh 339, p. 72).

give light to us who are blind, and love to give strength to us who are weak."[3]

This is also how the Bible sees it. In the Scriptures we find two great affirmations about God: "God is light" (1 John 1:5) and "God is love" (1 John 4:8, 16). Moreover, it was also something intuitively perceived in a less spiritualized form outside the Bible. Scholars have distinguished two types of religious expression in classical Greek culture: one based on order and measure, called apollonian (from Apollo, the sun-god), and one based on verve, excess, and passion, called dionysian (from Dionysus, god of the Bacchanalia). The first favored the rational aspect of God; the latter, those elements of the divine that are beyond reason and in that sense irrational.

In an earlier chapter I referred to Mahler's symphony based on the text of the *Veni Creator*. In that symphony two lines of the hymn, "kindle light in our minds" and "pour love into our hearts," are cast in relationship to the two great themes of Goethe's *Faust*: the desire to gain knowledge and salvation through love. The first part, which follows the text of the *Veni Creator,* is followed by a second, still of the same symphony (in significant if questionable juxtaposition) that follows the text of the closing scene of Goethe's masterpiece. It is as though the composer wanted in this way to point out a sort of fulfillment in response to the cry that goes up in the *Veni Creator*.

These two characteristics of the Holy Spirit are not found in the same way or with the same degree of emphasis in all the writers. Biblical scholars have noted that even within the New Testament there are differences. John emphasizes the "Spirit of truth," and Paul, the "Spirit of love."[4] This difference of emphasis carries through into Tradition. For it is evident—and we will in fact see it in the course of this chapter—that just as the Orthodox teaching on the Spirit has cast the Spirit as "light" in stronger relief, the Latin teaching has given greater emphasis to the Spirit as "love." This difference is sharply drawn in the two works that most strongly influenced the development of the two theologies of the Holy Spirit. Saint Basil the Great, in his work *On the Holy Spirit,*

---

[3] Walter of St. Victor, *Sermons,* III (CM 30, p. 27).
[4] See E. Cothenet, *Saint-Esprit,* DBSuppl, fasc. 60 (1986) 377.

gives the theme of love no role, while the theme of the Spirit as light is pivotal. On the other hand, Saint Augustine's work *On the Trinity* makes no reference to the theme of the Spirit as light, but gives the pivotal place to the theme of the Spirit as love.

The same differences of emphasis are found within each of the two traditions. Among the Latins, the Thomist school is characterized chiefly by the search for truth; it considered the "gift of understanding" to be the highest of the gifts and held that our ultimate beatitude would consist in the vision of God. In contrast, the Franciscan school (and the Augustinian tradition in general) is characterized chiefly by the importance it accords to love, holding the "gift of wisdom" as primary among the gifts and holding that our ultimate beatitude would be in loving God and rejoicing in him. In the Thomist tradition, we have the development of the mysticism of light (for example, among the Rhineland mystics), and among those who follow the Franciscan tradition the mysticism of fire and of the "folly" of the cross. Saint Bonaventure notes in a nutshell the difference between the two schools, where he says, "The one is interested primarily in speculation and sees the anointing as secondary, and the other is interested primarily in the anointing and sees speculation as secondary."[5] Dante links the two basic attitudes back to the respective founders, Francis of Assisi and Dominic Guzman, saying that:

> The one was all seraphical in ardour;
> The other by his wisdom upon earth
> A splendour was of light cherubical.[6]

One renowned for fervor, the other for splendor of light; the biblical symbol for one the seraphim, for the other, the cherubim. In times past writers often sought to contrast these two views one with the other and argue about which of the two was the more correct. How very good it is, then, in the light of the *Veni Creator* to discover that these are two ways, complementary and inseparable, that the Holy Spirit uses to manifest himself to us! They are to us as our two eyes: each eye focuses on what we see from a

[5] Bonaventure, *The Hexaemeron,* XXII.21 (Quaracchi, V, p. 440).

[6] Dante Alighieri, *Paradiso,* XI.37–9 (trans. by H. Wadsworth Longfellow): *"L'un fu tutto serafico in ardore, / L'altro per sapïenza in terra fue / Di cherubica luce uno splendore."*

slightly different angle, and when we look at something with both, we have a far better perception of depth.

But in order to see clearly how immensely rich and original are these two modes of approaching the reality of the Holy Spirit, we need to ponder carefully the present line of the *Veni Creator,* "pour love into our hearts."

2. Love, the Christian's New Law

The phrase "pour love into our hearts" clearly takes its inspiration from Paul. "God's love has been poured into our hearts through the Holy Spirit that has been given to us" (Rom 5:5).

In the Latin tradition this passage is linked very closely with the theme of the Holy Spirit as the new law. In order to discover why this is so we need to go back once again to the Pentecost event. There we find that the coming down of the Holy Spirit is intentionally linked to the theophany on Sinai. This is because at the time when Luke was writing the Acts of the Apostles, the Jewish feast of Pentecost was understood precisely as a commemoration of the giving of the Law and the Covenant on Sinai. By that time Pentecost had come to be seen, not so much as a feast linked to the cycle of *nature* (the gathering of the harvest and the offering of the first-fruits), but much more as linked to the *history* of salvation. This is enough to show why Luke did not see the Holy Spirit only as "power of the prophetic word and strength in the work of mission," but already also as an essential agent in the divine work of salvation, even though he does not develop this aspect as clearly as Paul or John. The Holy Spirit not only *carries* the message of salvation to the "ends of the earth," but the Spirit *is* salvation: he is the principle that makes the New Covenant effective and puts it into operation.

There are deep biblical roots for seeing Sinai and Pentecost as related in this way. When we read in the book of Jeremiah (31:31) that God will make a "new covenant" with the people, saying, "Deep within them I will plant my Law, writing it *on their hearts*" (Jer 31:33), it is clear that he intends, already at that stage, to highlight the newness of the law of the New Covenant in relation to the law of the covenant of Sinai, which was written on *tablets of stone* by God (Exod 31:18). Ezekiel took the next step and identified the new law as the Spirit of God: "I will put my spirit within you" (Ezek 36:27). Paul puts the finishing touch to the contrast and makes it quite explicit. He calls the Christian community "a letter of Christ, prepared by us, written not with ink but with the Spirit of the living God, not on tablets of stone but on tablets of human hearts" (2 Cor 3:3). He also speaks of "the law of the Spirit" (Rom 8:2), meaning the "the law which is the Spirit."

Augustine draws the final conclusions from all these premises. He starts off by remarking on a coincidence. Fifty days after the Jews offered the first Passover and marched out of Egypt (the number of days corresponds to the data of biblical reckoning), the law was given on Sinai, written on tablets of stone, to the people of Israel and the people entered into a covenant with God. And fifty days after the celebration of the new Passover and the sacrifice of Christ on the cross, the Holy Spirit came. The meaning of this coincidence is obvious: The Holy Spirit is the New Law, written in truth by the fiery finger of God, this time not on stone tablets but on tablets of living flesh that are our hearts, made clean by the blood of Christ. The message is that the Holy Spirit is the principle of the New Covenant and the one who gives it life.[7] In this sense we can understand Saint Irenaeus when he says, "The Holy Spirit came down on the disciples at Pentecost with power over all peoples to bring them into life and *to open the New Testament to them*."[8]

The Holy Spirit "opens" the New Testament, in the sense that he takes the "new and eternal covenant" brought about by the new Passover, the death and resurrection of Christ, and makes it alive and effective in us.

This interpretation, getting to the depths of the Pentecost event, was taken up by the whole Church. It entered into the Church's liturgical celebration which has kept it alive, even when theologians in their reflections lost sight of it. The Latin liturgy for the vigil of Pentecost has us read chapter 19 of Exodus, which tells in point of fact of the appearance of God on Sinai. In a number of the medieval sequences, the theme of Sinai-Pentecost is central.[9]

---

[7] See Augustine, *Sermons,* 272B.2ff. (PLS 2.253ff.); Augustine, *The Spirit and the Letter,* 16.28ff.

[8] Irenaeus, *Against the Heresies,* III.17.2.

[9] See Adam of St. Victor, *On Pentecost,* AHMA 54 (1915) 243.

The eastern liturgies too, Byzantine and Syrian, highlight the relationship between the theophany on Sinai and Pentecost, but the tendency there is to underline not the contrast of the two events but their affinity. "The upper room corresponds to the mountain, the flashes of fire to the tongues of flame, and the cloud and the trumpet-blast to the violent wind."[10] Pentecost is the day when "the law came from Zion."[11]

The author of the *Veni Creator* presents this rich tradition of the theme Sinai-Pentecost in the form it took in the West with Augustine. Commenting on the title "Finger of God," he writes, "It was by the Finger of God that the law was written fifty days after the slaying of the lamb, and fifty days after the passion of Christ, the Holy Spirit came."[12]

Saint Augustine explains what all of this tells us in relation to the love that the Spirit pours into our hearts: "What is this law of God written in our hearts by God himself, if not the very presence of the Holy Spirit who is the Finger of God and who, by his presence, pours into our hearts that love (Rom 5:5) which both fulfils and ends the law?"[13]

The new law, which is the Holy Spirit, comes into operation through love. Love, then, is not merely the sum of all the law and the prophets, but very much more: love is their complete fulfillment and the achievement of their whole purpose. Only those who love, truly carry out the law, for only in love can the law be fulfilled. Ezekiel ascribes to the gift of the new heart and the Spirit the capacity to put the law of God into practice (see Ezek 36:27).

Love itself is also a "law," that is, a directive principle, that urges us to battle against the flesh and to do or not to do certain things. Love, however does not urge *by constraint* of threats or sanctions as the old law had done and as every written law and directive imposed from without still does, but rather *by attraction*. Filial love, and not servile fear, is the mainspring of all Christian living and doing.

---

[10] See *Pentecostaire,* translated by D. Guillaume (Parma, 1994) 422 (Monday in Pentecost week).

[11] See ibid., 404 (Pentecost, Morning prayer): for the Syriac liturgy see E. P. Siman, *L'experience de l'Esprit* (Paris, 1971) 55.

[12] Rhabanus Maurus, *On the Universe,* I.3 (PL 111.25).

[13] Augustine, *The Spirit and the Letter,* 21.36; see 17.29.

> If the precepts of law are put into practice because of fear of
> punishment rather than because of love of justice, those under
> the law act in a servile way, and not freely, and that is why the
> precepts are often not put into practice. . . . On the other hand,
> when faith is at work through love, it begins to make us *take*
> *pleasure* in the law of God in the very depths of our being.[14]

At the deepest level of the human heart a radical change takes
place. If before we tended to look at God with a suspicious and un-
friendly eye, as a slave would look on his owner, we now look to
him as an ally, a friend, our Father, and on our lips is the spontaneous cry of recognition, "Abba! Father!" (Rom 8:15). The Christian's entire way of acting is changed; it is truly "deified" because it
is now moved by the Holy Spirit: "All who are led by the Spirit of
God are children of God" (Rom 8:14). God intends the Christian
life to be lived that way, in the Holy Spirit, directed by the principle
of spontaneity and freedom. It is the life of those who are "in love."

3. The Holy Spirit Sets Us Free from Self-Love

We have seen how a whole new vision of the Christian life
comes to light as we dwell on the theme of the Holy Spirit as
"light." We begin by seeking to be cleansed of our passions (especially of impurity), because they darken the mind and place obstacles in the way of our receiving the light of the Paraclete. Once
the inward eye has been made clean, we not only become able to
contemplate God, but we also become "transparent": God's light
is able to shine through us, as crystal glows when it reflects the
light of the sun that falls upon it. The life of prayer and discipline
becomes fruitful, and the work we do on ourselves redounds to
the benefit of others.

Now we need also to see how, as we dwell on the theme of
the Holy Spirit as "love," the immense depths of the Christian life
are revealed to us and, at the same time, a whole practical strategy
through which we will be inwardly transformed: in short, we
are given a new spirituality. The same Holy Spirit, who as light
takes us from ignorance to the truth, as love takes us from self-
centeredness to love of others.

[14] Ibid., 14.26.

In what does human sin consist, asks Saint Augustine, and where does it start? He says it is not so much a matter of abandoning God to turn to creatures, as abandoning God to turn, precisely, to our self. Sin consists in that root deflection by which we human beings originally became bent. Our nature was created "straight," upright, aligned on God. It has, however, become "bent toward itself" *(inclinatus ad se ipsum).*[15] The word *perverse* derives, in fact, from *per-versus,* meaning ill-oriented.

This is very much in tune with Saint Paul's thinking. For him the passions of the flesh (which in the context he describes very realistically) are not the cause by which our "empty minds were darkened," but rather the result of that darkening. Humankind turned its back on God, gave God no glory or thanks; they had idolatrously put themselves in God's place. For that reason God "gave them up to degrading passions" (see Rom 1:18ff.).

There have been attempts at times to explain the pessimistic tendency in Augustine's moral teaching as the result of his own negative experience in matters of the flesh. But Augustine's analysis is much deeper than that. He saw the ultimate root of sin in something far beyond the sphere of sexuality: for him it was in the will and in the corruption of love. Man "wanted to take advantage of his free will, so that, not having any master, he could be like God."[16] Saint Francis of Assisi agrees totally with this when, with the intuitive perception of the saints and quite without any rational argument, he said, "That person eats of the tree of the knowledge of good who makes his will his own."[17]

In his book *City of God,* Augustine used this intuitive perception as the principle by which to interpret the whole history of humankind: "Two loves, each the foundation of a city: love of self to the point of despising God brought the earthly city into being; love of God to the point of despising self gave rise to the heavenly city."[18]

There is a kind of love of self that is healthy and good, but that is not the kind we are thinking of now. Love of self becomes bad when it loses its social dimension and becomes *private:* that is,

[15] Augustine, *The City of God,* XIV.13.1 (CC 47, p. 434).

[16] See Augustine, *Exposition on the Psalms,* 70.7 (CC, 39, pp. 966–7) *("sua potestate uti voluit, ut nullo sibi dominante fieret sicut Deus").*

[17] Francis of Assisi, *Admonitions,* 2 (ED, I, p. 129).

[18] Augustine, *The City of God,* XIV.28 (CC 48, p. 451).

when it ceases to be the basis of readiness to be open to others and becomes egotistic, loving self to the exclusion of others. "Two loves, one social and the other private, brought two cities into being among humankind, each one different from the other: a city of the just, and a city of the wicked."[19]

However, Augustine did not stop there. In another and no less important work, *The Spirit and the Letter,* he explains how the move from the one kind of love to the other comes about. It is the Holy Spirit who enables us to pass from love of self to love of God and neighbor, setting us free from our self-centeredness! It is the Holy Spirit who accomplishes the transformation, the "straightening out" that is necessary in the redeeming of us human beings. How does the Spirit do it? To some extent we saw the answer when we were considering the Holy Spirit as the "new law" of the Christian. The Spirit pours love into our hearts, that is, gives us a new capacity to love God and our brothers and sisters, and, so doing, liberates love from the prison of egoism. The Spirit does not impose the *duty* of loving God on us, but rather instills in us *delight* in loving God, and that is what makes us begin to do willingly what God has commanded. The more we become aware that God loves us, the more willing we become to obey God. This is the point at which the decisive transition takes place, from the slavery to sin to the liberty of grace.

To be able to achieve all of this, our human *free will* is not enough. An ascetic, disciplined desire to purify ourselves of our passions will not get us there, and neither will *knowledge* of the truth suffice nor the wisdom to do what is right. Our very will itself needs to be transformed, the entire orientation of the depths of the human heart turned around. Only the Holy Spirit can achieve this, and the Spirit does it by awakening the love of God in us and with it arousing the desire to obey God in all things.[20]

Looking at this from an ascetical perspective, one of the Eastern Fathers wrote:

> Until the outward man is dead to the affairs of the world, and the inward man dead to the persistent memories of ugly things,

[19] Augustine, *De Genesi ad litteram,* XI.15.20 (CSEL 28, 1, p. 348).

[20] Augustine, *The Spirit and the Letter,* 3.5; the theme is taken up by Luther, *Readings on the Letter to the Romans,* 8.3 (WA 56, p. 356).

and until the natural impulses have been humbled and the body wearied almost to death so that the pleasures of sin no longer stir in it, the Spirit will not be able to fill the human heart with his sweetness.[21]

Looking at it from the perspective of grace, Augustine was able to discover the other, and more important, side of the truth: "After he has by his gift justified us, the Spirit of God takes away from us the taste for sin—and this is freedom—just as before his coming we used to find our pleasure in sinning—and that was slavery."[22]

The ascetic says, until we have done the delight of sin to death in ourselves, the Holy Spirit cannot fill us with delight in God. The theologian, with greater precision of thought, says that until the Holy Spirit has filled us with delight in the love of God, we cannot do to death the delight that we take in sin. Grace precedes our effort and makes it possible.

As the developing doctrine of grace brought deeper insight, it brought about a decisive advance in the theology of the Spirit—an advance we cannot ignore without depriving ourselves of an insight fundamental to our understanding of the Holy Spirit and the way the Spirit works in the human soul. The debate between Greek and Latin theologies in the past was often confined to the problem of the procession of the Holy Spirit: whether from the Father alone, or from both Father and Son. This prevented the discovery and appreciation of other points of difference and reciprocal enrichment. Theologians spent a great deal more time in speculations on how the Holy Spirit proceeds in God, a topic way beyond our reach and on which the Scripture is almost totally silent, instead of how the Holy Spirit brings us to new birth in God, a topic vital to us all and on which the Scripture has a great deal to say.

We need, however, to be careful not to give in again to the temptation to regard the two views as opposed one to the other: one insisting that the passions must be stilled and we purified from them before we can come to contemplate God; the other insisting on renunciation of self-love in order to come to love God and neighbor. Both, as we have seen, have solid biblical founda-

---

[21] Isaac of Nineveh, *Ascetical Sermons,* IV, Italian translation by M. Gallo and P. Bettiolo (Rome, 1984) 100.

[22] Augustine, *The Spirit and the Letter,* 16.28.

tions, and there is a clear reciprocity between the two: if the mistaken decision to place self first releases and gives free rein to the passions of the flesh, it is also true that giving in to the passions of the flesh lends strength to our self-centeredness and makes us insensitive to God and to our neighbor. Neither of the two traditions can be sustained without the other. Light and love betoken two equally important works of the Spirit by which the Spirit creates the "new man," as by two radical, healing cleansings. The Spirit's work is *radical* because it brings about the healing and cleansing of the *roots* of evil in the human world—ignorance and self-centeredness—and these, moreover, are so closely linked that when one is attacked, the other is attacked as well.

4. Let Us No Longer Live for Ourselves

What part is there for us to play in all this process that takes us from love of self to love of God? Our part is to work with the Spirit, making use of our own free will to cooperate with grace. We need to pull up the roots we have put down in self and plant them firmly in God: eradicate self and be rooted in God. Many trees have what is called a taproot, one that goes straight down beneath the bole of the tree, deep into the earth. As long as that taproot is secure, unharmed, and firm in the ground, all the lateral roots may be cut off but still the tree will stand secure and nothing will topple it. The tree of our life also has a "taproot"; it is our self-love. As long as nothing stronger comes to "supplant" it, we will not cease to be the "old nature," nor will we become the "new creation"; we will not cease to live according to the flesh and begin to live according to the Spirit. But, as we have seen, the Holy Spirit comes to achieve this "supplanting" in us. By our own strength we could never achieve what the work of the Spirit achieves in us; we can, however, work along with the Spirit, cooperate with the Spirit.

Paul sketches this out as a program for moving from "living for self" to "living for God":

> He died for all, so that those who live might live no longer for themselves, but for him who died and was raised for them (2 Cor 5:15).

> We do not live to ourselves, and we do not die to ourselves. If we live, we live with the Lord, and if we die, we die with the Lord; so then, whether we live or whether we die, we are the Lord's (Rom 14:7-8).

It is a sort of Copernican revolution: not the earth (the ego) any longer at the center, and the sun, like a satellite, orbiting around it to serve it, but quite the contrary. The Holy Spirit was given to us so that we may live no longer for ourselves, but for the Lord! This achievement is the Paraclete's crowning glory. In one of the new Eucharistic prayers, at the invocation of the Spirit we say: "And that we might live no longer for ourselves but for him, he sent the Holy Spirit from you, Father, as his first gift to those who believe, to complete his work on earth and bring us the fullness of grace."[23]

If we are to cooperate with this work of the Holy Spirit in us, we need first of all to learn to recognize "desires" and impulses, and distinguish between those that come from self-love, that is, from "the flesh," and those that come from the love of God, that is, "the Spirit":

> Nature labours for its own interest,
> but grace considers what may be beneficial to many.
> Nature loves ease and bodily repose,
> but grace cannot be idle and willingly gets down to work.
> Nature seeks to have things that are rare and beautiful,
> but grace delights in that which is plain and humble.
> Nature is quick to complain of any want or trouble,
> but grace bears poverty with constancy.
> Nature turns all things to its own ends
> and contends and argues for its own advantage,
> but grace refers all things to God.[24]

If we make up our mind not to live for ourselves—that is, not for our own glory, our own advantage or comfort—the Holy Spirit comes to our aid with grace in a thousand ways. The Spirit helps us to recognize an opportunity to overcome self-love as soon as one arises; the Spirit gives us a certain inner urge to make use of the opportunities; the Spirit gives us also a delight in doing

---

[23] Roman Missal, Fourth Eucharistic Prayer.
[24] *Imitation of Christ*, III.54.

so and joy when we have done it, or makes us feel sad when we look for all sorts of excuses to let the opportunity go by and fail to make use of it.

When we are accused or reprimanded or criticized in some way, or when someone says something hard for us to bear, the Spirit also helps us not to start immediately to defend ourselves, and this is his most effective way of helping us to overcome self-love. For in fact it is impossible to rid ourselves of self-love all on our own without any assistance from others; we might just as well imagine we could operate on our own head to remove a tumor. The Holy Spirit also gives us an inward urge to look well at the company we keep and perhaps make changes.

We can also work along with the Holy Spirit in these matters by the way we pray. Using the words of the Sequence of Pentecost we can say, "Make supple the stiff" *(flecte quod est rigidum)*, or, with another prayer from the liturgy, "Make our hearts obedient to your will however rebellious we may be."[25] Grace really acts in the simple, easy little decisions we make; it is never the automatic result of who-knows-what outward routines we think up and perform mechanically without involving our will, nor does grace ever demand that we look for extraordinary circumstances before it will work in us.

5. A Theology of the Spirit for the Computer Age

I would like to conclude this reflection on the Holy Spirit as love with an observation that will show how very pertinent the theme is in our day. Dominated as it is by technology, our society has a great need to rediscover its heart, for otherwise we will become completely dehumanized and not be able to survive as human beings. Not only religious people, but also persons outside the faith are convinced that we need to give more room to "reasons of the heart" if we want to avoid moving into a kind of ice-age of humanity.

In this area, quite unlike most others, technology is of very little help to us. For some time people have been working to develop a computer that can "think," and many are convinced that

[25] Roman Missal, *Prayer Over the Gifts,* Saturday, fourth week of Lent.

one day they will succeed. But (fortunately!) it seems that no one has so far suggested developing a computer that can "love" or experience emotions or become affectionate toward a human being. Can you imagine using a computer to help you to love, just as we use computers to help to calculate the distances between the stars or the frequency of atomic oscillation or to remember the date of someone's birthday? These days we make use of atomic clocks whose margin of error would be one second in every two million years. We can count precisely how many hundreds of thousands of years it would take to travel at the speed of light to a given point in the universe, even though it is unlikely we will ever get there, seeing that we have only a few dozen years to live. Is technology outpacing life?

The development of the human intelligence and the mind's expanding capacity to acquire knowledge do not proceed at the same pace as the human capacity for love. For this reason it seems to some that that capacity is of very little account, even though we know very well that the happiness we enjoy or the misery we suffer here on earth does not depend on what we know or do not know, but rather on whether we love, and on whether we are loved. It is not difficult to see why we are so keen to widen our knowledge and why we are so little concerned about increasing our capacity for love: knowledge translates directly into power, but love into . . . service.

One of the modern idols most worshipped is the IQ, the "intelligence quotient." There are many ways of measuring the IQ, but fortunately up to now none has proved very reliable. When there is question of selecting a donor of semen to fertilize a human ovum, the donor's IQ is almost always one of the decisive factors. Has anyone ever thought of taking the "heart quotient" into consideration? When all is said and done Paul's words remain true: "Knowledge puffs up, but love builds up" (1 Cor 8:1). Secular culture is no longer willing or able to accept this truth as from its religious source, in Paul's writing, but it is ready enough to accept it when it comes in a literary garb. What else would the ultimate thesis of Goethe's *Faust* be, if not that only love can redeem and save, while science and the thirst for knowledge can lead to damnation?

What then can save our civilization from this slippery slope? Saint Augustine has explained to us that free will is not enough, and neither is it enough to know what the problem is and what we "ought" to do about it. We also need help from outside: outside of ourselves and of our world. That is what the Holy Spirit gives, "pouring love into our hearts." Our great need today is a new openness, a new readiness to approach the Holy Spirit, a reawakened longing for the Spirit. Now that we have knowledge enough to explore the immense horizons of cosmic space in one direction and subatomic particles in the other direction, only the Holy Spirit can give humankind that sustenance of soul, that love which will prevent our humanity from shriveling up altogether as a result of our own knowledge. Only the Holy Spirit's help will make us able to use our technical knowledge not to destroy but to humanize our planet and improve the lot in life of every person.

In Western Christianity one man stands out for what he has done to bring back into the spotlight of attention Augustine's grand theme: the Holy Spirit who takes us from love of self to love of God and neighbor. That man is Luther. He left us his own translation of the *Veni Creator* (which Bach later set to music),[26] but more, he composed two hymns to the Holy Spirit that still play a central part in Protestant worship. In one of them he takes up the ancient Pentecost antiphon, "Come, Holy Spirit, fill the hearts of your faithful and enkindle in them the fire of your love,"[27] and develops it into a chorale. Speaking of it one day, he said that "it was composed, words and music too, by the Holy Spirit himself." Taking inspiration from our present verse of the *Veni Creator,* Luther worked into his hymn the two themes of the Spirit as "light" and as "love." Let us join our Lutheran brothers and sisters in praying this hymn:

> *Come, Holy Spirit Lord and God,*
> *fill full with your own gracious good*
> *the faithful ones' heart, mind, desire;*
> *inflame in them your love, O Fire!*
> *The light you bring, O Spirit, Lord,*
> *gathers now in one accord*

[26] See J. S. Bach, *Komm, Gott Schöpfer, Heiliger Geist* (BWV 631).

[27] See *Corpus antiphonalium officii,* ed. R. J. Hesbert, III (Rome, 1963) 528, n. 5327: *"Veni, Sancte Spiritus, reple tuorum corda fidelium, et tui amoris in eis ignem accende."*

folk from every land and tongue;
your praise, O God, by all is sung.

O holy Light, safe rest from strife,
shape us by the Word of Life;
teach us to know our God aright
and call him Father with delight.
Guard us, Lord, against false creed,
nor let us other masters heed
but cling in faith to Jesus only,
and him with all our might trust wholly.[28]

---

[28] Luther, *Komm, Heiliger Geist, Herre Gott* (WA 35, pp. 165ff.; 448–9); Engl. transl. in Luther's Works, vol. 53 (Philadelphia: Fortress Press) 266–7. (Adjusted in part to current English idiom).

XVI

Infirmity in This Body of Ours Overcoming with Strength Secure

The Holy Spirit prepares the way for the redemption of our body

1. Brother Body and Sister Soul

Saint Cyril of Jerusalem starts one of his sermons to the catechumens this way: "In circumstances like these we have to be careful not to overtire you who are listening, and so we have to keep our enthusiasm firmly under control. For, you see, when one is speaking of the Holy Spirit, it is just not possible to say enough."[1]

There was a time when this used to be said of Mary: *de Maria nunquam satis,* it is never possible to say enough about the Mother of God. The same maxim would apply, with greater reason, to speaking of the Holy Spirit. I need to try to follow the example of Saint Cyril and keep a firm rein on my own enthusiasm, for it would have been easy for these little reflections on the Holy Spirit to get too long.

The verse of the *Veni Creator* we are now considering first shows us how the Spirit relates to our human mind and heart. It now goes on to show how the Spirit relates to our human body. "Brother Body," as Saint Francis of Assisi called it, is not barred from the great banquet of the Holy Spirit! It takes part, and with every right. The Bible does not see the human body as an insignificant adjunct to the human person, but rather as integral to our reality as persons. A human being does not *have* a body; a human being *is* a body. The body was created by God himself, made and shaped by his "own hand"; in the incarnation it was personally *united* to the divine Word and in baptism it has been *sanctified* by the Spirit. It is, as the Scripture tells us, in very truth "the temple of the Holy Spirit" (1 Cor 3:16; 6:19).

---

[1] Cyril of Jerusalem, *Catecheses,* XVII.1.

If we take only a superficial look at what the New Testament, and particularly Paul, have to say about the flesh and the Spirit, there is a risk that we may fall into error. The relationship flesh/Spirit is not merely negative, that is, irreducibly a relationship of conflict; it is also positive, a relationship of cooperation toward a shared goal. The flesh serves the Spirit, and the Spirit sustains the flesh. It is precisely through the body, that is the element that most intimately and directly links us to this world, that the Holy Spirit is manifest in us. We are called, as believers, to give glory to God with our body and in our mortal flesh.[2] The work of the Holy Spirit, then, is to sanctify the flesh, not merely to fight against it, and to enable the flesh to achieve its purpose, not merely to eliminate its influence.

The first one to see the need to find clarity on this sensitive point of revelation was Irenaeus, even though we find in his writings a kind of oscillation between spirit, the incorporeal element of the human composite, and the Holy Spirit properly speaking. The Gnostics in his day taught that the body was the work of a secondary, inferior god and not the God preached by Jesus Christ. Against that teaching he wrote:

> In the complete human being, there are three realities: the flesh, the soul, and the Spirit. One, that is the Spirit, saves and gives stature. Another, the flesh, is saved and is given its stature. Between these two is another, the soul, that sometimes follows the Spirit and in the power of the Spirit is able to rise to the heights, and sometimes follows the flesh and so descends to the level of earthly desires.[3]

To illustrate the way the Spirit relates to the body, Irenaeus uses the example of grafting: the root-stock of flesh is weak, but by the engrafting of the Spirit it receives a new kind of vitality and so it becomes able to bear "spiritual" fruit.[4]

Irenaeus explains that flesh and blood as such are not excluded from the kingdom of God (see 1 Cor 15:50), but only those who live according to the bad tendencies of flesh and blood. To live *in the flesh* is not evil; what is evil is to live *according to the flesh.*

---

[2] See 1 Cor 6:20; Phil 1:20.
[3] Irenaeus, *Against the Heresies*, V.9.1.
[4] Ibid., V.9.2; 10.1.

He goes so far as to say that "to bring the human body to maturity and make it capable of receiving immortality is the visible fruit of the invisible Spirit."[5]

In the beginning, when things were still as God intended them to be, body and soul, spirit and matter, related to each other in this positive way. Now conflict reigns between them but eventually they will be reconciled, for the human spirit and the human flesh are destined to live together for eternity—for good or for ill.

> The body and the soul are like two hands joined.
> And both will go together into eternal life.
> And they will be two hands clasped.
> Or they will fall together like two wrists shackled.
> For an ugly, dread forever.[6]

It was the incarnation of the Word that restored the friendship between human flesh and the Spirit of God to its pristine state and gave it the hope of winning through into eternity. Communion in the Body of Christ is the sign and the pledge of this:

> He gives us the body so that, as we together become one with him, we may have a share in the Holy Spirit. For in fact the reason why the Word of God came to us in a body and, as the Gospel says, was made flesh was that, since we were not able to have a share in him as Word, we might be one with him as flesh . . . . This communion with the Spirit of Christ is the reason why we treat our bodies in an honourable way, as holy (see 1 Thess 4:4) as the members of Christ's own body.[7]

2. The Charism of Healings

But let us look and see what the *Veni Creator* tells us to ask of the Holy Spirit for our body. The request, "infirmity in this body of ours overcoming with strength secure," clearly recalls what Jesus said in the Garden of Gethsemane, "The spirit indeed is willing, but the flesh is weak" (Matt 26:41). It alludes perhaps also to the

---

[5] See ibid., V.12.4.

[6] C. Péguy, The *Threshold of the Mystery of the Second Virtue, Oeuvres poétiques complètes* (Paris: Gallimard, 1975) 580–1.

[7] *Easter Homily,* attributed to Saint John Chrysostom (SCh 36, pp. 91–3).

Holy Spirit who "helps us in our weakness" (Rom 8:26). On this point the author of the hymn is simply applying to the Holy Spirit two lines that Ambrose, in one of his hymns, addressed to Christ in his incarnation.[8]

The attention drawn to the power *(virtus)* of the Holy Spirit puts the finishing touch to another of the brilliant syntheses in this verse of the hymn. Saint Bonaventure explains that the Holy Spirit possesses three special characteristics: The Spirit is at the same time ineffable *truth,* generous *love,* and invincible *power.* From the Spirit as *supreme truth* comes the shining glory of an understanding enlivened by faith which enlightens the human faculty of knowing; from the Spirit as *supreme love* comes the love enlivening a healthy attitude of good will which rectifies the human will; and from the Spirit as *supreme power* comes the strength of a robust consistency which invigorates our human ability to do what is to be done.[9] This is the same truly biblical triad that the author of the *Veni Creator* had in mind when he spoke of the Holy Spirit as *light* for the mind, *love* in the heart, and *strength* for the body.

The Latin word *infirma* in the hymn has two meanings, both retained in our English word *infirm:* weak and sick. We are in fact asking the Spirit for two things to overcome these two kinds of infirmity: strength and healing. The Holy Spirit is not limited to propping us up when we are weak or healing our wounds or plugging the potholes in the road of our physical life. The Spirit does infinitely more than that for "brother body": The Spirit redeems our body from its own precariousness and prepares it for the complete and definitive redemption (Rom 8:23). And this takes us into an eschatological perspective, looking at our ultimate destiny:

> For while we are still in this tent, we groan under our burden, because we wish not to be unclothed but to be further clothed, so that what is mortal may be swallowed up by life. He who has prepared us for this very thing is God, who has given us the Spirit as a guarantee (2 Cor 5:4-5).

When we pray in the words of this verse of the *Veni Creator,* we are asking the Holy Spirit to "transfigure these wretched bod-

---

[8] Ambrose, *Hymn: Veni Redemptor gentium,* Opera Omnia 22 (Milan, 1994) 50: *"Infirma nostri corporis / virtute firmans perpeti."*

[9] Bonaventure, *Sermon 1 on Pentecost* (Quaracchi, IX, p. 331).

ies of ours" into copies of the glorious body of Christ (Phil 3:21), we are asking that one day the Spirit will give life to our mortal bodies (Rom 8:11). However, as long as we are living in this world we do not experience our bodies in that glorious way at all; we are far more aware of our bodily weakness and illnesses, and when the *Veni Creator* uses the word *infirmity,* it is alluding to the way we normally experience our bodily condition.

Once again a huge horizon opens up to our view: the part that the Spirit plays in physical healings. Already in his day, Irenaeus, in the same context to which we referred above, mentions the healings that Jesus had worked and the dead that he had restored to life as proofs that the body too is able to receive the works of the Spirit of God:

> It was the one who made the universe, the Word of God, who in the beginning formed human beings. When he found that his creature had been harmed by evil, he brought healing to every part of us in every way, sometimes restoring the wounded parts to the wholeness they had enjoyed when they were first made, and sometimes all in an instant bringing the whole of us to completeness, preparing the way for the resurrection. What reason could he have had for healing the fleshly part of us, if that part, once healed by him, was not intended to share in his salvation?[10]

In this passage Irenaeus reveals how profound is the theological significance underlying the miracles of healing, although some, in our day, are not comfortable with the idea that miracles are possible, or simply reject them out of hand, as if the notion of anything miraculous simply indicated a primitive, unspiritual kind of religiosity. Let us then take time to consider this aspect of Christ's ministry, to see what it is saying to us today.

Almost one-third of the Gospel tells of Jesus healing the sick and restoring the dead to life. He did not set out to heal to prove a point, but simply because he had come to "save those who were lost" (Luke 19:10), because he had compassion on people and what he wanted for them was life and the liberty to know joy as God's creatures. Alongside of proclaiming the Gospel, care for the sick has a fixed place in the commission Jesus gave to his followers: "He sent them out to proclaim the kingdom of God and to heal" (Luke 9:2).

---

[10] Irenaeus, *Against the Heresies,* V.12.6.

In the Church of apostolic times we find a rite used for the special purpose of taking care of the sick (recognized later on as one of the seven sacraments), based on the conviction that "the prayer of faith will save the sick, and the Lord will raise them up" (Jas 5:15). One of the most important factors in the "mission and propagation" of the Christian faith was precisely its concern for the health of the body as well as the salvation of the soul. Jesus was looked upon as "healer, in his very being, of both body and soul,"[11] and was, therefore, well able to heal both body and soul.

In the lifetime of Jesus it is clear that his miracles of healing were worked in the power of the Holy Spirit. Jesus himself affirms that "the Spirit of the Lord" has been given to him, not only to "bring good news to the poor," but also "to proclaim release to the captives / and recovery of sight to the blind, / to let the oppressed go free" (Luke 4:18). "Power came out from him" (Luke 6:19), and the same Gospel, a little before, has told what that power was: not any magnetism of hypnotic influence or force of suggestion, but "the power of the Spirit" that had come into him at his baptism (see Luke 4:14).

Saint Paul too, shows that he is equally convinced of this close relationship between the power of the Spirit and healings, and he speaks of a special charism in this regard: "To another again [may be given] gifts of healing by the one Spirit" (1 Cor 12:9).

If we go further down the road of history into "the time of the Church," we will notice that this Gospel ministry has undergone an evolution. The gift of healings came to be seen more and more as an extraordinary charism linked to the personal holiness of the one who exercised it; such a person came to be regarded as a *thaumaturge*, a miracle-worker. Miraculous healings came to be looked upon as the prerogative of special people, the saints, or the sort of thing that happens only in special places, such as sanctuaries.

In all of this there is nothing strange, nothing unorthodox, given that though God gives gifts freely "to whom he wills" for the common good, these gifts are not entirely unrelated to the personal holiness of the recipient. It is only to be expected that such gifts will be more manifest, and more powerful, in those whose lives are more deeply rooted in love. Nevertheless, this development has actually resulted in a mistaken conviction that has

[11] Ignatius of Antioch, *Letter to the Ephesians*, 7.2.

caused many to lose sight of the original idea and purpose of charism. Although the link between healings and holiness is strong, it is never exclusive, and extraordinary sanctity has never been a requirement for healing.

However, perceptions did evolve in that way, and the main reason for this was perhaps the fact that the early Church soon lost the natural ambience for the manifestation and operation of charisms: the open assemblies of the primitive Church that were imbued with a powerful sense of the Spirit present and at work and in which every believer was able to exercise his or her own charism (see 1 Cor 14:26). In a similar way many species of living things have become extinct because their natural habitat has disappeared.

Must we then say that the Church has paid no attention to Christ's command, to "heal the sick"? Not at all. Christians in every age have set up all sorts of institutions for good works whose aim was to relieve the sufferings of the sick: hospitals, leprosariums, sanatoriums, places of care of all kinds. Down through the centuries this has been one of the great achievements of the Church. What happened was that the work of healing became "institutionalized," the charisms were transformed into institutions. Though this development was good in its own way, it did mean that something was lost.

We have two ways to face up to our problems, and particularly to the problem of ill health: the way of human nature, and the way of grace. *Nature,* in this sense, encompasses science and technology and all our resources: in short, all that we have received from God in creation and all that we have developed from that by using our intelligence. *Grace* indicates faith and the prayers by which, as God may will, we sometimes obtain healings in a way that goes beyond the scope of human resources. Outside of these two ways nothing is legitimate: no "magic," for instance, or other ambiguous methods practiced by those who profess to be professional "healers."

Against disease and ill-health, a Christian cannot be satisfied to use only the facilities of "nature": to set up hospitals or to work along with the structures of the state to provide care and comfort. Christians have a very special power of their own, given them by Christ: "[He] gave them authority . . . to cure every disease and every sickness" (Matt 10:1). It would be a sin of omission to fail to have recourse to this power and so fail to hold out hope to those to whom science denies all hope.

In our day the Church is undergoing a kind of examination of conscience in regard to this power. After the council there was a revival of the practice of the anointing of the sick and of praying for the sick. The sacrament of the sick is no longer withheld until the moment of death but conferred whenever someone who is seriously sick asks for it, and we now expect from it not only that "the sins of the sick person will be forgiven," but also that "the prayer of faith will save the sick, and the Lord will raise them up" (Jas 5:15). A prayer borrowed from the old ritual mentions the Holy Spirit explicitly in this regard: "We ask you, oh our Redeemer, heal by the grace of the Holy Spirit this person of this sickness."

The most significant fact, however, is that in many Christian churches the charism of healings has reappeared just as Saint Paul understood it: that is, as a gratuitous gift given to some among the believers, not necessarily in relation to any holiness of their own, but for the good of the community, and above all because God faithfully fulfils the promises Jesus Christ has made. This is delicate ground, easily exposed to all sorts of manipulation and abuse, and in which we can never hold in sufficiently high regard the prudence and vigilance of the Church when it seeks to maintain discipline in the exercise of this charism. A guarantee of authenticity in this is to see the balance maintained that we find through all the ministry of Jesus, between the proclamation of the Gospel and care for the sick. Prayer for healing should never be allowed to become an end in itself, detached from the ongoing proclamation. And, thank God, we frequently see the two going hand in hand.

3. From What Does the Holy Spirit Heal Us?

For us, however, it is one thing to know the story of healing or the doctrine of healings, but we are much more concerned to know how to obtain a healing. This is what we are asking for when we ask the Holy Spirit to "overcome the infirmities in this body of ours with strength secure." In *our* body, not only in the bodies of other people. To grasp how we come to experience healing in ourselves, we want to look now at a few of the principal types of "infirmity" that we find in our body, because it is likely that we will recognize one of them as our own.

We are in no sense at fault in the fact that we suffer certain kinds of malady, such as physical defects that may be congenital or acquired, or dysfunction of some organ of the body, defects inherited or arising from trauma in childhood or even in the womb.

Others again can be at least in part the result of our own culpable action: the various forms of dependence on alcohol, drugs, tobacco, or the various eating disorders or the results of abuses in the area of our sexuality.

There are maladies rooted in the unconscious, or in the memories, that would for that reason seem to be more sickness of soul than of body but that nevertheless have a profound influence on our physical well-being: the fear of death, disturbances arising from a relationship with an authoritarian father or a possessive mother, complexes, aggressive behavior, insecurity. Here too, we would rank disorders like the non-acceptance of oneself or of others; depression, chronic discouragement, and sadness; deep-seated grudges and resentment.

There is also that disorder that psychologists single out as particularly to be avoided, and that is the attachment to one's own sickness. For it is in fact possible to take refuge in one's own sickness or neurosis to such an extent that it becomes impossible to conceive of living without it or of doing without the commiseration that we imagine it deserves. Jesus asked the paralytic at the pool of Bethesda, "Do you want to be made well?" (John 5:6), a question that might appear to some a little odd, but it is not really so.

When we are dealing with a deep-seated psychological disorder in which the free will of the sick person is in some way involved, it is necessary for the sick person to cooperate with the action of the Spirit and to get rid of certain obstacles, above all by repenting of personal sins and forgiving others if there are things to forgive. In this situation it is of tremendous importance to approach the *sacraments* with faith. For in the sacraments we are given the opportunity again, in faith, to reach out to Jesus and "touch his cloak" (Matt 9:21). The Gospel tells us "that power came out of him that cured them all" (Luke 6:19): it continues to come, strongly as ever, from the eucharistic body of Christ.

But the *Word of God* too, can be a potent instrument of healing. Speaking of the people of God in the desert, the Scripture says, "Neither herb nor poultice cured them, / but it was your word, O Lord, that heals all people" (Wis 16:12).

There was a man who had come to the last stages of alcoholism. He had made life impossible for his wife and children. One evening they asked him to go to a meeting where there would be readings from Scripture. As he was listening, on hearing certain words he felt something like a wave of heat pass over his body and he sensed that he had been cured. From that evening on, whenever he was tempted to take alcohol again, he quickly went to that passage of the Bible and read those words again, and he always received new strength, and eventually he was totally free, cured of the craving. When asked what precise line had worked so powerfully in him, he was so moved he was unable to speak. The line was the verse in the Song of Songs that says, "For your love is better than wine" (1:4).

4. What about Those Who Are Not Healed?

What are we to say of the many who, for all their deep faith and intense prayer and their taking part in the "liturgies of healing," are not healed? Whose fault is that? Some would say, "They do not really have faith, or those that pray for them do not really pray in faith, for God really wants to heal everybody, always; sickness is the result of sin and it is contrary to God's will that anyone should be sick . . . ."

However, if that is true, then we need to say that many of the saints should be counted among those who have little faith, because they often had to suffer all kinds of sickness. The Church's teaching on this point, sound and reliable, is that the power of the Holy Spirit is not manifested in one way only: The Spirit does overcome evil by healing, but the Spirit also overcomes it by giving people strength to bear, and often joy in bearing, their infirmities with Christ, and in their own bodies "completing what is lacking in Christ's afflictions for the sake of his body, that is, the church" (Col 1:24). Christ has redeemed all, suffering and death included. Suffering is no longer a sign of sin and of sharing in the guilt of Adam's sin; it is now an instrument of redemption and a sharing in the destiny of the New Adam.

Nothing whatsoever is excluded from the sphere of redemptive value; all sickness enters into it, physical and psychological. Christ accepted anxiety and the fear of death and made them instruments of redemption; even those neuroses that are ineradicably part of our natural baggage can become occasions of sanctification. Some saints suffered neuroses, but that did not stop them becoming saints! In those who suffer this type of malady, the action of the Holy Spirit is made manifest in a different way: The Spirit gives the person the ability to live the malady in a new way, with greater freedom bearing it and sharing in it but not shattered by it.

The underlying reality, the profound reason for all this, is that God has decided to overcome evil not simply by annihilating evil as God has the power to do, but by taking it on, in Christ, conquering it and transforming it from within: "He took our infirmities and bore our diseases" (Matt 8:17).

Paul is a shining example in this regard. He asked the Lord repeatedly to free him from a certain "thorn in the flesh," but heard the Lord answer, "My grace is sufficient for you, for power is made perfect in weakness" (2 Cor 12:9).

And at that, he broke out into the great paean of faith: "I will boast all the more gladly of my weaknesses. . . . For whenever I am weak, then I am strong" (2 Cor 12:9-10). The power of the Holy Spirit in confronting the infirmities of our body is seen in the fact that the Spirit gives us strength to bear the evils we suffer in union with Christ even more clearly than it would be seen in setting us free of them by a miracle. Saint Maximus the Confessor says, "The weakness of the flesh in suffering provides a firm working-place for the surpassing power of the Spirit."[12]

The conclusion to draw is this: We are free and able to ask the Holy Spirit at any time to heal us. But if the Spirit does not do it, there is no reason to think that it is because we have no faith, or that God does not love us, or that God is punishing us. All it means is that God is offering us a gift that is far more precious than healing, even though it may be more difficult for us to accept it. If health is recovered, it may one day be lost again, but to have borne suffering with patience is something good that will last for eternity.

However, the reflection on healing does not end here either; we need to note and consider one more point. In the spirit of the Gospel, the most important thing is to be concerned not about our own personal infirmities, but rather about those of our neighbor.

---

[12] Maximus the Confessor, *Various Chapters,* IV.93 (PG 90.1345).

The saints give us an example: Be willing to put up with our own illnesses, but do all we can to help those around us to be well. They were reluctant to pray for healing for themselves though they prayed with great ardor for others to be healed.

The Gospel tells of four people who one day moved some tiles to make a hole in a roof so that they could lower a stretcher. In other words, they allowed no difficulty to stand in the way until they had succeeded in getting their sick friend to Jesus and hearing Jesus say finally, "I say to you, stand up, take your mat and go to your home" (see Mark 2:1-12). We need to follow the example of the zeal of those four friends.

5. A Spiritual Therapy

As we come to the end of this reflection, we need to see things in a wider perspective. The healing power of the Holy Spirit is not limited only to healing the human body. The Spirit's power to heal extends to the whole of the human reality, as it is presented in this verse of our hymn: mind, spirit, and body. The Holy Spirit has come to save, to heal, to teach, to admonish, to strengthen, to console, and to enlighten, first those who receive the Spirit and then, through them, everybody else.[13] To use the expression that is much in favor in our day, the Spirit really does have an "holistic approach"; the Spirit takes into account, all at the same time, all the dimensions and all the needs of the human person. The Spirit would not cure an infection in a finger without noticing that the person's heart or stomach is suffering from some serious defect. The Holy Spirit sets us free from all ills. The liturgy has a prayer that says: "Lord, may the healing power of your Spirit at work in this sacrament turn us from sin and keep us on the way that leads to you."[14]

Irenaeus says that the Holy Spirit is the "innkeeper" to whom the Good Samaritan, Christ, entrusts wounded humanity, asking the Spirit to take care of it.[15] And see what Saint Bonaventure says in this connection:

> The Holy Spirit comes to us, first of all as the most expert of healers, bringing life to both spirit and body. Oh, how wise this

[13] See Cyril of Jerusalem, *Catecheses*, XVI.16.
[14] *Roman Missal*, tenth Sunday in Ordinary Time.
[15] Irenaeus, *Against the Heresies*, III.17.3.

> doctor is! He gives life to those who are dead in body and in spirit and he cures every ill without scalpel and without cautery, not needing any magic words, but by the simple decision of his will alone.[16]

This time the practical application of the doctrine to our life situation will take a slightly different form: We will be using it as a therapy. Based on the Holy Spirit, it ought to be a good one. We have heard of heliotherapy; by analogy, we will call this pneuma-therapy. Heliotherapy consists in going to the beach and exposing your body to the sunlight, rich in ultraviolet rays. Pneuma-therapy consists in exposing our whole person, body, mind, and will, to the invisible but powerful rays of the Paraclete.

This means a great deal more than simply hearing something explained and understanding it. To expose our *mind* to the action of the Holy Spirit means to offer the Spirit our mind in prayer, asking the Spirit to cure all of our many "mental maladies": incredulity, or its opposite, superstition, arid intellectualism, pride, and presumption. It means to consecrate our intelligence to the Holy Spirit so that we may always use it in service of the truth and never of lies or of error. It means always to hold our mind open, exposed, to the word of Scripture, for it is in point of fact through the Word that the light of the Holy Spirit comes to us.

To expose our *will* to the work of the Spirit means to ask the Spirit to heal our many "maladies of the heart": coldness, indifference, rebelliousness, self-love, and the abominable lust for power that have caused so much evil in the world. Origen said, "The Word and its healing power (*therapeia*) are more powerful than all the maladies of the soul,"[17] and we can say the same of the Holy Spirit.

We know already what it means to expose *"brother body"* to the action of the Spirit, for much of this reflection has been listing the various maladies that reside in the body.

There is an Afro-American spiritual with a refrain that consists simply in the repetition of the line: "There is a balm in Gilead to heal the wounded souls." Gilead, or Galaad, is a place often mentioned in the Old Testament and famous for its perfumes and

---

[16] Bonaventure, *Sermon for the Fourth Sunday of Easter,* 1 (Quaracchi, IX, p. 309).

[17] Origen, *Against Celsus,* VIII.72 (SCh 150, p. 340).

unguents (see Jer 8:22). As we listen to this song, it seems at times to make us think of the cry of a peddler walking the streets, calling out his wares and what they are good for. And as we round off this consideration of the healing power of the Spirit, I too would like to be one of those peddlers. The balsam of Gilead was only a dim figure of the balm of the Holy Spirit. The song carries on:

> There is a balm in Gilead
> to make the wounded whole.
> Sometimes I feel discouraged
> and think my work's in vain
> but then the Holy Spirit
> revives my soul again.

And so I take courage and call out: There is a balm in the Church to heal all tired-out spirits, souls sick from sin, to set stony hearts free. Come, buy wine and milk: you need no money. Come, take this oil that comes to you through the Word, the sacraments, and prayer. Take this balm—take it in massive doses! For our world really does need massive doses of the Holy Spirit . . . .

And to end this meditation, let us make our own the beautiful prayer to the Holy Spirit composed by a medieval author in his commentary on the opening lines of our hymn:

> *Come, Holy Spirit, fill the hearts of your faithful.*
> *You, who have already come to make them believers,*
> *come now to make them blessed.*
> *You who came so that with your help*
> *we might glory in the hope of the glory of the sons and daughters*
>   *of God,*
> *come anew so that we might also glory in the possession of that*
>   *glory.*
> *For yours it is to strengthen and make firm,*
> *to perfect and to bring to fulfillment.*
> *The Father created us, the Son has redeemed us:*
> *accomplish now what it belongs to you to do.*
> *Come and lead us into the fullness of truth,*
> *the enjoyment of the supreme Good,*
> *the vision of the Father,*
> *the abundance of all delights,*
> *the joy of all joys. Amen.*[18]

[18] Walter of St. Victor, *Sermons*, VIII.9 (CM 30, p. 70).

XVII

The Enemy Drive from Us Away

The Holy Spirit gives us assurance of victory over evil

1. The Holy Spirit and Spiritual Combat

This chapter takes us to the opening line of the fifth verse of the *Veni Creator,* which reads:

> The enemy drive from us away,
> peace then give without delay,
> with you as guide to lead the way
> we avoid all cause of harm.

The *Veni Creator* in its majestic simplicity is like a masterpiece of Romanesque architecture. Like the best examples of buildings of that style, its beauty resides not as much in the boldness of its individual elements viewed separately, as in its harmony and proportion as a whole. That is why it is important, when we are looking at a line, always to keep in mind not only the content of that particular element but also the underlying design that takes shape through all the elements and unifies them all, and that gives us an awesome, and perhaps unsurpassed, spiritual and theological synthesis on the Holy Spirit.

Let us look, then, at the intent of the verse we are now starting to consider and how it fits into the economy of the hymn as a whole. This verse continues with the contemplation of the *personal* action of the Paraclete, the work the Spirit does in each of us as individual persons as distinct from the Spirit's work in and on the world, its history, and the Church as a whole. But we notice that there is a difference: Where in the preceding verse the consideration focused on the Holy Spirit's action on the particular constitutive elements of the human person (mind, heart, body), here it moves to the Spirit's action on the whole of the real-life situation of each person. The spotlight has moved from essence to existence: from the Spirit's work on the *structural* elements of the human person we move to the Spirit's part in the dialectic of human life.

Without actually proposing it in these exact terms, the hymn provides the means and opportunity to sketch out an essential analysis of the way the Holy Spirit works, and then to draw from it an expression of faith in the Spirit in language that we can understand. It helps us to map out a theology of the Holy Spirit in terms that are meaningful for us who live at the beginning of the twenty-first century.

The verse evokes only two existential situations, but together they serve to sum up the entire spectrum of human experiences. The first is struggle, the second, choice. The first two lines of the verse illustrate the role of the Holy Spirit in our struggle against evil, and the last two lines look at the part the Spirit plays in discernment, in the decisions we are called to make, and hence in our spiritual progress. Looking at the first two lines, one takes us into the dramatic climate of battle ("the enemy drive from us"), and the other takes us into an atmosphere of quiet enjoyment of the prize of victory ("peace then give").

And so we come to the first line of this verse, which will be the subject of our present reflection: *Hostem repellas longius,* The enemy drive from us away. The *Veni Creator* is the only one, among the more significant hymns to the Holy Spirit, that draws into high relief the Spirit's role in the struggle against the spirit of evil.

In Vivaldi's *Four Seasons,* and also in Beethoven's sixth symphony, the *Pastoral,* there comes a moment when the rhythm and the flow of the music is broken. The hiss of a bolt of lightning or maybe a clap of thunder changes the whole atmosphere: there is a sense of a storm about to break. That is exactly the function of the words "the enemy," given its strong position at the very beginning of the verse. It changes the whole climate of the hymn; we step into the storm of life. The same Spirit who led Jesus into the wilderness where he was to meet the tempter is now in us, to drive and to lead us too. But this same Spirit remained with Jesus in the wilderness and gave him power to triumph over the tempter; the Spirit is with us today, too, our constant companion, to "train my hands for war, / and my fingers for battle" (Ps 144:1).

Here again one word is sufficient to evoke a whole world: Page after page of the Bible comes to mind at the mention of the word "enemy." It is not difficult to discover the immediate biblical sources of this expression. The most direct of them is this, from Peter: "Like a roaring lion your adversary the devil prowls around, looking for someone to devour" (1 Pet 5:8).

But we notice too, an echo of what Jesus said, "An enemy has done this" (Matt 13:28). This word "enemy" is not merely a figure for the normal difficulties and confrontations of life, but something a great deal murkier, as Scripture itself warns us: "For our struggle is not against enemies of blood and flesh, but against the rulers, against the authorities, against the cosmic powers of this present darkness, against the spiritual forces of evil in the heavenly places" (Eph 6:12).

However, it would be equally a mistake to reduce the focus entirely to the one personified enemy, the devil. Here the whole gamut of evil is evoked. When Paul speaks of the "adversary," he includes the antichrist, that is, the mystery of iniquity, the impious rebel that goes about its evil work in Satan's power, and of whom Paul says that the Lord will kill him with the breath of his mouth (in the Vulgate translation, "with the Spirit of his mouth") (see 2 Thess 2:4-8).

For Paul, the struggle between flesh and spirit[1] and the opposition between the "Spirit of God" and the "spirit of the world" (1 Cor 2:12) also belong to this spiritual combat. The world, the flesh, the devil: the enemy around us, the enemy within us, the enemy above us. The word evokes the whole of the deathly "triple alliance." The line, "The enemy drive from us away," in the *Veni Creator* occupies the position that the final cry, "Deliver us from evil," fills in the Our Father. In that prayer too, the word indicates at one and the same time both "evil" and "the evil one."

2. I Drive out Devils with the Spirit of God

Let us now look briefly at what Scripture and Tradition have to say to us on this particular theme of "the Holy Spirit and the battle against the spirit of evil." The most important piece of information given us in this regard is what the Holy Spirit does in the life of Jesus. Jesus was "led up by the Spirit into the wilderness

[1] See Rom 8:5-13; Gal 5:16-23.

to be tempted by the devil" (Matt 4:1). It was God, not Satan, that took the initiative. When he went into the wilderness, Jesus did not wander, so to say, into a snare set by the devil; he went, rather, in obedience to an inspiration of the Spirit. Having withstood the test, "Jesus, filled with the power of the Spirit, returned to Galilee" (Luke 4:14). At his baptism it had been made clear that the Spirit was present to him. Not only did the temptations not interrupt this presence; they increased it and strengthened it.

Jesus in the wilderness rid himself of Satan, and so now he is able to free others from Satan. That is what the Gospel writers wanted to show in the stories of freeing the obsessed, beginning with the incident in the synagogue at Capernaum (Mark 1:21ff.). Once when he set a person free, Christ was accused of casting out demons by the power of the prince of demons. In his response on that occasion he made this solemn declaration: "If it is through the Spirit of God that I cast devils out, know that the kingdom of God has overtaken you" (Matt 12:28).

We find the same in Luke: "If it is by the finger of God that I cast out the demons . . ." (Luke 11:20). As we noted in an earlier chapter, it is not easy to be sure which of these gives the words of Jesus as he actually said them, but neither is it absolutely necessary, since we know that, in biblical language, the expressions "Spirit of God" and "finger of God" can have the same meaning. What it was vital for the evangelists to make clear, however, was that Jesus himself was convinced not only that his own power over devils was due to the operation of the Holy Spirit in him, but also that his own victory over Satan was the sign that in him the kingdom of God had finally begun on earth. "In the presence of the Holy Spirit, the devil lost his power."[2] Another point in this regard is what Jesus said when speaking of the Paraclete: "When he comes, he will prove the world wrong about sin and righteousness and judgment; . . . about judgment, because the ruler of this world has been condemned" (see John 16:6-11).

When Jesus had died and had risen again, the Holy Spirit would make it quite clear to the world that Satan had been defeated. He would not merely reveal what had happened in Jesus' death. He would "convince" the disciples in the depths of their

---

[2] Basil the Great, *On the Holy Spirit,* XIX.49 (PG 32.157A).

being that the enemy had been overcome, and so enable them to undertake their own struggle with utter confidence.

Let's pass now to Tradition to see how this basic biblical truth has found concrete expression in the experience of the Church in past times, before we go on to see what form it takes in the experience of the Church today. What the Bible tells us is that the demon has been vanquished "by the power of the Holy Spirit." This fact was given expression first of all in baptism, through rites that varied from place to place. For instance, the Roman ritual that was in use right up to the time of Vatican II called for a pre-baptismal exorcism expressed in the command, "Go out of this child, unclean spirit, and leave place for the Holy Spirit." And the order of the two anointings in the rite, the first with the "oil of exorcism" and the second with chrism or "perfumed oil," pointed to the substitution of one spirit for another: The unclean spirit is driven out and the Holy Spirit comes in. "There is a spirit living in everyone: in some, the Holy Spirit and in others the unclean spirit. . . . There is in fact no way to overcome the unclean spirit except through the pure and holy Spirit of God."[3]

The Tradition came to see this as an invariable: Where the Holy Spirit comes in, the unclean spirit goes out; the two cannot be in any place together. When a view contrary to this was put forward by the Messalians, there was a vehement reaction.[4]

The Church had taken up Christ's command, "Cast out demons" (Matt 10:8), and carried it out by means of exorcisms, evidence of which we find already in the Acts of the Apostles. One of the Fathers of the fourth century, documenting this practice of the Church in his time, writes: "It happened that a demon, whom many had been unable to bind, was overcome by the words of one man's prayer because of the Holy Spirit who dwelt in him. The very breath of the exorcist, though invisible, was like fire to the malign spirit."[5]

During the age of the persecutions, the role of the Holy Spirit in the spiritual struggle tended to be experienced specifically in the support given to Christians facing martyrdom. For it was due to the Holy Spirit that the martyrs were able to bear their torment.[6]

---

[3] *Syrian Didascalia,* XXVI, ed. R. H. Conolly (Oxford, 1969) 246.

[4] See Diadochus of Photike, *On Spiritual Perfection,* 76 (SCh 5, p. 134), cited above (Ch. VII, n. 13).

[5] Cyril of Jerusalem, *Catecheses,* XVI.19.

[6] Irenaeus, *Against the Heresies,* V.9.2; Cyril of Jerusalem, *Catecheses,* XVI.20.

Tertullian, making use of the sporting terminology of his day, said that the Holy Spirit was the martyrs' "coach" and Jesus the "president" of the games who anoints his athletes with the Holy Spirit before sending them to the arena.[7] When the age of the persecutions had passed, there were those who still saw the Holy Spirit as "coach," but now in the context of the ascetical striving for Christian perfection. One of Saint Augustine's sermons is entirely on the subject of spiritual combat; this is how he ends it: "And so it is the Holy Spirit who trains our hands for battle and our fingers for war."[8]

However, in spite of these few significant instances, it does seem that the role of the Paraclete in the spiritual battle has not been given much attention in Tradition. We might say that psychology seems to have taken the wind from the sails of pneumatology; in other words, we have tended to look more at the causes and the dynamics of temptation than at the ally that we have in the Holy Spirit and at the help the Spirit can give. The "spiritual homilies" attributed to Macarius the Egyptian are an exception. In those writings the Holy Spirit is continually mentioned as the decisive factor in the warfare that the saints are called to wage in the world around them and within themselves. The author writes that the suggestions of the enemy are overcome "with the aid of the Holy Spirit together with our personal effort in exercising all virtues"; "without the weapons of the Holy Spirit we cannot make headway in this battle."[9]

3. Does the "Enemy" Still Exist?

Having come this far, we can now ask the usual question: What does this aspect of the doctrine of the Holy Spirit have to say to us in our day? What are we to think when we come to the line in the *Veni Creator* that says, "The enemy drive from us away"? Or, more radically, is there really an enemy?

To answer such questions we need to make a careful distinction. On the level of popular belief there is not much difference between our situation today and the situation in the Middle Ages,

---

[7] See Tertullian, *To the Martyrs*, 3.3–4 (CC 1, p. 5).

[8] Augustine, *Exposition on the Psalms*, 143.7 (CC 40, p. 2078).

[9] *Spiritual Homilies,* attributed to Macarius, 21.5 (PG 34.660A); 23.2 (PG 34.661B).

say from the fourteenth to the sixteenth centuries, well known for the importance people gave to the diabolical and to manifestations of evil. It is true that we no longer have the "trials" of the Inquisition, the stake for the demon possessed, witch hunts, and such things, but practices that have the devil as their focus, either as someone to be cast out or as someone to be worshipped, are even more widespread today than they were then. It has become a social (and commercial) phenomenon of huge proportions. It could incline people to say, in fact, that the more you try to drive the devil from the door, the more he creeps back in through the window; the more he is left out of the ambit of faith, the more prevalent he becomes in the ambit of superstition. Origen in antiquity and Thomas Aquinas in the Middle Ages were the two writers who did most to build up a true "theology" dealing with the devil, and it is interesting that the periods they represent were relatively free of "demonism."

Things are quite different on the level of culture and art. For our present purposes, if we sum up the causes that have led to our present-day situation, we can distinguish three phases. The first was the process that took place in the area of aesthetics that led to divergence from the traditional view. Where before the devil had always been represented in art and in poetry (e.g., in Dante) in an "ugly key," as monstrous and grotesque, from a certain point in history he gradually came to be represented as beautiful, or at least as melancholy in a poetic kind of way. Certain artists show the devil as a handsome young man, more as Lucifer (that is, the Light-bearer, the radiant one) than as the "angel of darkness." Lorenzo Lotto, in a painting kept in the museum at Loreto, shows the archangel Michael driving Lucifer from paradise with one hand while with the other he seems to want to protect him. In poetry too, from the time of Milton, the devil takes on the aspect of fallen beauty.

If in this first phase the enemy comes to be seen as somehow likeable, in the next phase, reaching its acme in the nineteenth century, there was a clear and explicit reversal of roles: The Holy Spirit ("the god of the priests") is now clearly the enemy, and Satan becomes a friend and ally, the one who takes sides with us humans. For us the evil one does not bring struggle, warfare, disquiet, but "peace." The devil has fused into the role of Prometheus, the one who because of his love for humankind was cast out of heaven and banished to earth. Satan comes to be seen as someone who "has wept and loved with man and written his victories in blood." Writers in this intellectual climate composed hymns and poems in celebration of Satan.

We need to note, however, that not all of this was "diabolical," Satanism pure and simple. There were cultural and religious reasons that at least helped to bring about this regression. Just as not all atheism, when you look at it carefully, proves to be "atheistic," so too not all Satanism is really Satanic. Atheism, in many instances, is not a denial of the living God of the Bible but rather of the idols that we have substituted for God in many areas of our thinking and our way of life. In the same way, many instances of Satanism are not really the cult of evil itself but rather what people thought the Church was condemning as evil: science, the freedom of conscience, democracy—in short, modernity. One example of this is Carducci's well-known, if somewhat naïve, verse:

> Hail, oh Satan,
> oh rebellion,
> oh avenging power
> of human reason.[10]

And this brings us to the third phase, our present situation. We can sum it up very briefly: silence on the subject of the devil. This silence, however, is not an indication of prudent discretion but rather of negation. It is supposed to mean that there is no longer any such thing as "the enemy," unless by that we mean what Saint Paul refers to as "flesh and blood," that is, nothing more than the evil that we human beings carry within ourselves. The devil, it is said, is symbol of the collective unconscious, or of our collective alienation, merely a metaphor. Rudolph Bultmann writes: "It is not possible to use an electric light or to listen to the radio, nor is it possible to go to a doctor or make use of clinical remedies when you are sick, and at the same time believe in the world of spirits."[11]

Why is it that many intellectuals today, certain theologians among them, are no longer able to believe in the existence of a

---

[10] G. Carducci, *Hymn to Satan: "Salute, o Satana / o ribellione / o forza vindice / della ragione."*

[11] R. Bultmann, *Neues Testament und Mythologie* (München, 1985) 16.

devil, not merely as a symbol, but as a real, personal entity? One of the reasons, I believe, is that they have looked for the devil in books, while the devil is not interested in books, but in souls. You do not meet the devil in libraries or academic institutions, but in souls, and particularly in certain souls. For the most cogent proof that the devil exists will not be found in sinners or in the obsessed, but in the saints. The devil, it is true, is present and at work in certain more extreme forms of "inhumanity," in the egregious forms of evil, but there he is "at home" and well able to mask himself behind any one of a thousand doubles and look-alikes. He manages the tactic of camouflage very well, as certain insects are able to do, blending in perfectly with their background. Because of this, it is practically impossible in any particular instance to say, with certainty, what is the devil's work and where precisely the dividing-line is between that and the evil that we human beings set in train.

But in the lives of the saints the situation is quite different. There the devil is obliged to come out into the open, to stand out "against the light"; his activity stands out in clear contrast, black on white. In the Gospel itself the clearest proof of the existence of evil spirits is not found in the many accounts of freeing the obsessed (in many of which it is not easy to say with certainty what part was played by the beliefs of that time regarding the causes of certain forms of sickness), but actually in the episode of the temptations of Jesus. All the saints give testimony, some more, some less, to the struggle they had to wage against this obscure reality. It is simply not possible to suggest with any honesty that they were all deluded, knowing the intellectual stature of some of them. Nor is it possible to think they were victims of the prejudices of their times. Francis of Assisi broke with almost all the common assumptions of his day, but he did not break with this one. To one of his companions he once confided, "If the brothers knew how many trials and how great are the afflictions the demons cause me, there would be not one of them who would not be moved to pity and compassion for me."[12]

Some have researched extensively all the phenomena that are traditionally considered to have something to do with the devil (possession, pacts with the devil, witch-hunts and such things),

[12] *A Mirror of the Perfection,* 99 (ED, p. 346).

and the conclusion they draw is that it is all a matter of superstition and that the devil does not exist. These people are a little like the Soviet astronaut who came to the conclusion that there is no God because, he said, he had been in the heavens for a good long time and he had not seen any sign of God anywhere. Both were looking in the wrong place.

There is another misunderstanding that it would be well to mention here. Theologians and secular thinkers enter into discussion with each other on whether or not there is a devil, assuming that they share the common ground necessary for such a dialogue to take place. What they do not seem to take into account is that a secular culture that excludes faith cannot possibly believe in the existence of a devil, and rightly so. It would really be a tragedy if a person excluding all belief in God found it possible to believe in the devil. That would surely be a desperate situation. What can anyone know of Satan who has never had to deal with the reality of him, but only and exclusively with the idea of a devil and various representations of the devil in the different ethnological traditions? People in that position, with certainty and great self-assurance, usually dismiss any question of that kind as nothing more than another example of "medieval obscurantism." But such certainty is baseless, like the certainty of the man who boasts that he is not afraid of lions because he has seen many photographs of lions but none has ever frightened him.

The magisterium of the Church has taken a very cautious line in the matter of the teaching on the devil, and some claim that this is an indication that the Church itself, if it has not actually given up believing in a devil, at least does not know any longer how to handle its traditional doctrine in this regard. But it is simply not so. Paul VI very strongly reaffirmed the biblical and traditional teaching on this "obscure and inimical agent who is the devil." He has much to say, this included: "Evil is not only a deficiency, but something active and efficient, a living, spiritual being, perverted and perverting. Terrifying reality. Mysterious and to be feared."[13]

In times past, it is true, there was exaggeration in speaking about the devil. People saw him where he was not, and a great

---

[13] See Paul VI, Sermon on "Deliver us from evil," 15 November 1972, in *Insegnamenti di Paolo VI,* vol. X, Tipografia Poliglotta Vaticana, p. 1969.

deal of wrong was done and many injustices committed under the pretext of combating him. The truth is that we really do need to be very prudent and to act with great discretion in this regard, precisely in order not to fall into playing the enemy's game. To see the devil everywhere is no less a deviation from the truth than see him nowhere. Augustine says, "The devil delights in being blamed for something. In fact he actually wants you to blame him. He is more than willing to listen to all your recriminations, as long as they keep you from making your own confession!"[14]

But all of this notwithstanding, the truth remains clear that the Bible speaks of the devil as a "personal" power with intelligence and will, against whom Christ had to struggle and whom Christ overcame definitively on the cross, but who is still at large, "making war on the saints" for their purification, and who tries by all and every means to "seduce" men and women.

It is sometimes said that belief in the devil was something of secondary importance that was introduced into the Bible at a later stage as a result of contact with other religious cultures. Those who put this view forward forget that the idea of an "enemy" and of a continuous battle without quarter between him and humankind up to the moment of his final, total defeat was there in the Bible from the very first page, in the story of the original fall (Gen 3:15).

However, the demythologization that has taken place in this area has not been in vain, and it has produced some positive fruit. Now that the dust-clouds of imagery around the devil have dissipated, we are in a better position to rediscover the heart of what the Bible would have us believe in this regard and the profound existential impact it has on our life. Stripped of all the folklore, the devil is seen as an important element in the explanation of the mystery of human existence. There are many today, even among the intellectuals, who admit that human life has not actually become more peaceful, more rational, as a result of having left the devil out of the picture. The result, on the contrary, has been to make us less likely to perceive what is wrong, and more likely to accept the horrors of evil as normal.

---

[14] Augustine, *Sermons,* 20.2 (CC 41, p. 264).

4. The Devil and Anxiety

The devil, then, has been "sent into retirement"; he is no longer allowed any place in the intellectual world. But he had taken care to "lay his serpent eggs" in the world of the human mind, and the hatchlings undergo a change of form, and we call them fear and anxiety. It is significant that the first philosophical treatise on anxiety, Kierkegaard's *The Concept of Dread,* was also the first philosophical treatise on the "demonic," and that the focus of the work is divided between the two themes in almost equal shares.

Dread or anxiety has been defined as the "evil of the era." The cry that goes up in the *Veni Creator,* "the enemy drive from us away," can therefore be taken in yet another sense: We can understand it as a plea to the Holy Spirit to free us from all our fears, from the anxiety that besets us. For there is clearly a link between the devil and fear, and we find it reflected already in Scripture. The Letter to the Hebrews says that the devil holds us enslaved all our life long by the fear of death (Heb 2:15), that is to say, by the very thing that underlies every form of fear and anxiety and which itself is the single most intense expression of anxiety.

The saints and the mystics tell of many experiences that bear witness to this link between the devil and fear. The Blessed Angela of Foligno had a vision one day in which she saw what seemed to be one of the saints. She was not immediately aware that it had actually been the devil masquerading, but she was at once aware of a strange disquiet of soul that would not leave her for ten days. Her soul was filled with sadness and perplexity and she could no longer pray or recollect herself.[15] Anxiety is the devil's "element," just as the Holy Spirit's is peace. Hence it is that in our hymn the invocation "the enemy drive from us away" is followed immediately by "Peace then give without delay."

As I have said, in our modern age the nexus between anxiety and the demonic has become a subject of reflection even for philosophy, and in order to give present-day content to the line we are now considering, it will be quite useful to highlight some of the conclusions Kierkegaard reached in this matter. We find a definition of the concept of anxiety using, as starting-point, the biblical

[15] Angela of Foligno, *Complete Works,* trans. by P. Lachance (New York: Paulist Press, 1993) 169.

account of Adam's fall: "Dread is in reality human liberty viewed as something possible to achieve. . . . The prohibition gave rise to anxiety in Adam, because it was the fact of the forbidding that awakened in him the awareness that he might possibly be free."[16]

In his innocence, still unaware of his ability to do good or evil, Adam was unaware of his freedom. But God forbade him something, and that immediately opened the way to anxiety within him. For now he knew that he had the power within him to commit evil if he willed to do so. Anxiety is that state in which a person resists the attractive and at the same time is attracted by what is resisted. It is a prelude to sin, but it is not yet sin; what separates anxiety and sin is the mysterious leap from indecision to decision, from innocence to guilt.

In the philosophical analysis, the category of the "demonic" is presented more as a result of sin than as its cause. Once we have fallen into the false liberty of sin the object of anxiety changes: It is no longer evil but the good that gives rise to fear in us. And this is said to be the essence of the demonic: that state in which the possibility of good fills us with anxiety. On this account, we are told, the Gospels show demons revealing themselves particularly when Christ is present, because he is the one who represents the possibility of the good and of salvation.

There is something missing from this analysis. It allows no role for the serpent-tempter or for temptation. There is reference in passing to this element of the Genesis story, but it is dismissed as irrelevant on the basis of James: "God . . . tempts no one. But one is tempted by one's own desire" (1:13-14).

But this text is ruling out the possibility that we may be tempted by God to do evil, and it does not in any way exclude the possibility that we may be tempted by the devil. A little later in his letter James says, "Resist the devil, and he will flee from you" (4:7), and what would there be to resist if the devil did not attack us?

We cannot use the account of an event in the Bible as the basis for a definition of anxiety if we neglect an element that, for the Bible, is central to that event, and that element is the temptation. At a later stage Scripture was to comment, "It was the devil's envy that brought death into the world" (Wis 2:24). What caused

---

[16] S. Kierkegaard, *The Concept of Dread,* 1.5.

Adam to fear and awoke in him the possibility of disobeying God was not, at least according to the biblical teaching, the simple fact that God forbade him to do something, but the interpretation that the tempter insinuated he should place upon that forbidding: It was not the prohibition itself alone that moved him, but linking the instigation with it.

The appearance of the devil on the horizon is what gives rise to the most dreadful kind of fear that the saints can know, and the reason is this: The devil gives present and concrete reality to the possibility that they too might, if they so willed, rebel as he did. And since, for the saints, to lose God is to lose everything, and to fall back into something that is even more terrifying than to cease to exist altogether, they experience their reaction to the devil as a form of anxiety. Satan reawakens in them "an awareness that it is possible to lose God." His presence alone is enough to open wide the abyss of nothingness before the spot on which they stand and make them feel the terrifying vertigo that comes from looking into the depths of their own freedom. When a great ship sinks, it drags down with it everything around it in the vortex of its descent. Satan is somehow like a sinking ship, always inevitably "plunging into the depths."

All of those who have tried to explore the concept of anxiety in an existential sense have intuitively perceived its very close link with the sense of emptiness and nothingness. It would be of tremendous help, in this matter, to take account of the way certain mystics have described the experience of dread and how they passed through "the horrifying, terror-inducing" dark night of the soul.[17] For their experience not only confirms the mysterious bond between dread and nihilism, but helps us also to understand why nothingness is so terrifying to us human beings. The reason is that nothingness is not at all—as a certain existentialist philosophy would have us believe— "the very foundation of all being," that from which we emerge and into which it is our natural destiny to return, but rather the result of the loss of the All and of our failure as creatures. Only the saints, and among them in a special way the mystics, know truly what anxiety really is. It is the feeling of one who believes that he has lost God irretrievably and through his own fault.

---

[17] John of the Cross, *The Dark Night,* I.8.2.

To admit the existence of a tempter and of temptation is by no means to deprive human freedom of all value, for it remains a fact that "everyone is tempted by his own wrong desire," that is, by himself or herself. Adam himself was the principal cause of his fault, not the tempter. Otherwise there would have been no justice in God passing judgment not on the serpent alone, but on Adam and Eve also. No temptation, of itself, can induce anyone to an evil act unless the free will cooperates with the temptation. One of the Desert Fathers was asked, "In what way is it possible for the demons to do anything against us?" He answered with a fable:

> The cedars of Lebanon said one day, "Though we stand so strong and tall, a little piece of iron can fell us! But if we did not give the iron a little bit of ourselves, even though it is iron it would not be able to fell us." For of course men need some wood to make the axe that they use to cut down the tree. Our souls are the trees. The devil is the iron, but the handle is our own will. That is what makes us fall.[18]

After the coming of Christ,

> The devil is bound, like a dog on a chain. He cannot bite anyone unless, having no concern about the danger, they go too close. . . . He can bark, he can whine and entice, but he can bite only those who go close and let him. In fact it is not in any way by forcing us, but simply by enticing us that he is able to harm us. He cannot force our consent, but only try to solicit it.[19]

5. The Holy Spirit Frees Us from All Fear

Happy news ends this chapter too, though it has had to deal with such a murky subject. The Holy Spirit frees us from all fear, all anxiety! This is the hope of our age, the "era of anxiety." Today, as much as ever before, Jesus continues to cast out devils "by the finger of God," that is, by the Holy Spirit.

One of the most significant documents of Vatican II opens with the words, "The joy and the hope, the grief and the anguish" of the people of our time, whom it goes on to describe as "hovering

---

[18] *Lives of the Fathers,* VII.25.4 (PL 73.1049).
[19] Caesarius of Arles, *Sermons,* 121.6 (CC 103, p. 507).

between hope and anxiety."[20] Thanks to the presence of the Holy Spirit, we know which one of these two opposites, hope and anxiety, will prove the stronger and will eventually triumph. The Spirit is the great "liberator." The apostle declares: "For you did not receive a spirit of slavery to fall back into fear, but you have received a spirit of adoption. When we cry, Abba! Father!' it is that very spirit bearing witness" (Rom 8:15-16).

The Spirit brings about the reality of this interior change by bearing witness to our spirit that we are children of God (see Rom 8:16). The Spirit makes us know, in the depths of our being, that God is our Father and that God is on our side, not an enemy, not against what gives us joy and not against our coming to realize ourselves as human beings, as the tempter is only too ready to insinuate. There was a time when "sin" (and, by means of sin, Satan) used the commandments ("thou shalt") or the prohibitions ("thou shalt not") as pretexts in order to give rise to desire in us, and along with desire, to sin (see Rom 7:7ff.). Now, after the advent of the grace of Christ, he is no longer able to use this pretext because God does not tell us what to do or not to do, but actually enters into the doing or the refraining from doing with us.

That is the reason why "where the Spirit of the Lord is, there is freedom" (2 Cor 3:17). The freedom this speaks of is no longer the "liberty of innocence" based on "ignorance" of good and evil, as it was before the Fall (and for that very reason open to anxiety), but freedom of another kind altogether: It is freedom redeemed. Perhaps the most profound of the works of the Paraclete in us (as we have already had occasion to note when speaking of the Spirit who "pours love into our hearts") is that the Spirit enables us to move from a state of being where what attracts is predominantly evil, into a state where the attractive is predominantly the good. In other words, the Spirit leads us out of our slavery to sin and into the liberty of grace. In the terminology of the philosopher we mentioned earlier, he takes us away from the demonic "anxiety on account of the good" and into that fear "that saves through faith."[21]

The Christian certainty of victory over the "enemy" rests entirely on faith in this grace. If it were to depend in any way on us,

---

[20] *Gaudium et Spes* 1, 4.
[21] See S. Kierkegaard, *The Concept of Dread*, V.

we would have no certainty at all. One of the fourth-century Fathers had this to say about the certainty that comes from the Holy Spirit: "In God we have a great ally and protector, the great teacher of the Church, our great defender. That is why we do not fear the devil or his demons, because the one who fights with us is so much greater than they."[22]

The Christian life is a spiritual battle. The charismatic experience of the Spirit does not place believers above or beyond the reach of this conflict but actually makes it more intense, because it makes us aware of living between two worlds, equally real but always in contention one against the other. The Spirit asks us to live "according to the Spirit" while we are still living "in the flesh."

The confidence that we enjoy in the midst of this conflict is such, thanks to the Holy Spirit, that it is not lessened even in the face of defeat. We read in the stories of the Desert Fathers of a certain monk who often, in the dark of night, gave way to sins of the flesh, but for all that he did not give up praying, and prayed with great intensity after every fall. Once, no sooner had he sinned than he got up and started praying the daily office, whereupon the devil, "astonished at his persistent trust," appeared to him and asked whether he was not ashamed to appear before God in his present condition. The monk answered him, "I swear that I will not tire of asking God to help me against you until you stop your attacks on me, and we will see who wins: you, or God." The story continues, "And the devil stopped tempting him from that very moment, because he saw that the temptations served only to increase the monk's crown."[23]

Experience shows that the struggle against the spirit of evil is won in the same way that Jesus won in the wilderness, using the Word of God to strike the blows. For the Word is in truth the "sword of the Spirit" (Eph 6:17). Anyone tempted by the spirit of pride could try answering, "I do not seek my own glory" (John 8:50) or, "What do you have that you did not receive?" (1 Cor 4:7). If it is the spirit of impurity that tempts, let the word of Christ echo

[22] Cyril of Jerusalem, *Catecheses,* XVI.19.

[23] *Apophthegms* from the Coislin manuscript, 126, no. 582, in L. Cremaschi, *Detti inediti dei Padri del deserto (Unpublished sayings of the Desert Fathers)* (Qiqajon: Comunità di Bose, 1986) 226–7.

loudly within you, "Blessed are the pure of heart" (Matt 5:8), or, "It is the Spirit that gives life; the flesh is useless" (John 6:63), or some other word that has helped you in the past, and keep to that word. You will soon be convinced that you have an invincible weapon at your disposal.

We end this reflection with a resounding invocation by one of the great writers of Eastern Christendom, Simeon the New Theologian, whose great love was to sing the praises of the Holy Spirit. His prayer, like our hymn, helps us see clearly how powerful is the work of the Paraclete against the enemy:

> *Come, true light. Come, eternal life. Come, mystery concealed.*
> *Come, treasure unnamed. Come, reality outreaching all telling.*
> *Come, oh you whom our minds cannot grasp.*
> *Come, everlasting joy. Come, light that casts no shadow.*
> *Come, hope of all the redeemed. Come, you who raise the dead.*
> *Come, you only, to the lonely. Come, my breath and my life.*
> *Come, my soul's consoler.*
> *Come, my joy, my glory, my everlasting delight.*
> *Shining vesture, searing to demon touch,*
> *cleansing bath, bathe me in purest tears most holy.*
> *Stay with me, oh Sovereign, alone do never leave me:*
> *for so, when those enemies of mine shall come*
> *who always seek to devour my soul,*
> *it is you they will see, dwelling in me, and at once they will flee,*
> *able to do nothing to me, finding you, most powerful of all,*
> *enthroned within the poor home of my soul.*[24]

---

[24] Simeon, the New Theologian, *Hymns to the Divine Loves* (SCh 156, pp. 150–2).

XVIII

Peace Then Give without Delay

The Holy Spirit gives us the wonderful peace of God

1. The Dove of Peace

The theme of this reflection will be the line in which we ask the Holy Spirit to give us peace: *Pacemque dones protinus!*—"peace then give without delay."

In the Bible and in Christianity, peace is one of the words that recurs most frequently and is most pregnant with meaning. The liturgy of the Mass is punctuated with the word from beginning to end: "Peace on earth to those who are God's friends"; "Peace be with you"; "Give us peace"; "Go in peace." Every Christian life begins, in baptism, with the greeting of peace and ends with the prayer *"requiescat in pace,"* may he or she rest in peace. On ancient sarcophagi and on modern tombstones in Christian cemeteries, the line we most often see is "In the peace of Christ."

But peace is a word that also expresses one of the most universal and most deep-seated desires of every human being. "The storm still seeks its end in peace when it strikes against peace with all its might."[1] In a similar way human history, through all its wars and all its tangled ways, is engaged in the quest for peace. A Christian thinker in ancient times had already said that all things without exception were in motion toward peace. Some argue against this, saying that there are many who strive against peace, actually taking delight in conflict and confusion, change and sedition. But those too are held to their aims by the desire for peace, although their idea of it is misconceived and they choose mistaken methods to achieve it.[2]

---

[1] R. Tagore, *Gitanjali,* 38.

[2] See Pseudo-Dionysius the Areopagite, *The Divine Names,* XI.5 (PG 3.953A).

In the Christian mind, peace occupies more or less the same place as nirvana for the Buddhist: It points to the ultimate outcome of all things, the supreme achievement of the adventure of life and time. It would be very instructive to deepen this comparison, taking proper account, of course, of the religious world with all its associations and definitions to which each of these two concepts belongs and from which it cannot be detached. Nirvana is interpreted as negation and the end of all suffering, the exhaustion of all passion; peace (which derives from the same root as appeasement) does not point to the extinction of desire but to the fulfillment of all desires; peace says affirmation, not negation. However, the two ideals are not necessarily incompatible nor are they so mutually exclusive as to make a fruitful debate impossible. Nirvana points to the negative aspect of peace, and peace points to the positive aspect of nirvana. The similarity is even greater if we accept Gandhi's interpretation of nirvana as an extinction only of what is vile or evil in human nature and as "the living peace and conscious happiness of a soul which has found rest in the heart of the Eternal."[3]

The *Veni Creator,* in this simple line, states firmly that there is a necessary link between the peace for which we all long and the Holy Spirit, and as this hymn constantly does, it invites us to explore that link in the Bible and in Tradition. And so we see yet another important area, not only of faith but also of human life, drawn back into the ambit of the Holy Spirit's action and clarified by the Holy Spirit's light. It is significant that the Holy Spirit and peace are indicated by one and the same symbol, the dove. We read in Tertullian:

> After the flood, which was a kind of baptism of the whole world, washing it clean of the old human wickedness, the dove was sent out from the Ark and it returned with an olive twig. So it was that the dove became the messenger bearing tidings of peace and of the end of God's anger: a symbol of peace, this, that in time became familiar to all the nations. With the same purposes at heart, but in a spiritual sense, the dove of the Holy Spirit, sent out from heaven upon the Church, prefigured in the Ark, rests now upon each one who comes up out of the baptismal flood in which all of the sins of the past have been left behind, bringing back God's peace.[4]

[3] M. K. Gandhi, *Buddhism and Theosophy,* The Navajian Trust, 1962.
[4] Tertullian, *On Baptism,* 8.4 (CC 1, p. 283).

One of the psalmists says, "O that I had wings like a dove! / I would fly away and be at rest" (Ps 55:7). And how should we not associate this dove too, with the Holy Spirit who leads our soul to peace? One of the ancient spiritual writers says:

> When God created Adam, he gave him no physical wings like he had given to the birds, but he prepared him for the wings of the Holy Spirit by which he would be lifted up and fly to find rest where the Spirit pleased. . . . Let us pray God that he will give us the wings of the dove that is the Holy Spirit, so that we too may fly and find rest close to him.[5]

In the most ancient phase of revelation, as in the book of Judges, the Holy Spirit is often cast as an agent in bellicose enterprises and deeds of violence. The Spirit of God comes upon a person, who then raises an army, wages a war, and routs an enemy.[6] But these texts refer to warlike encounters where the conflict was not only clearly defensive in nature and explicitly not sought, but that arose only as a result of the extreme need of the situation.[7] Not even in this primitive phase, therefore, can the Holy Spirit be considered to be in any way a "spirit of war," but always a Spirit of succor who helps even in situations of war.

Leaving aside the veiled reference to the dove of peace, it is not difficult to identify the immediate biblical background on which the author of the *Veni Creator* draws in the appeal to the Spirit for peace. It is the same as for the preceding line. Mark's Gospel says that after he had repulsed the devil's assault, Jesus "was with the wild beasts; and the angels waited on him" (Mark 1:13), wanting in that way to show that in Jesus the Messianic ideal had in fact been realized: The peace that all creatures had shared in paradise had returned (see Isa 11:6-9). When we pray, "the enemy drive from us away. Peace then give without delay," we are asking the Holy Spirit to give effect in our life to what the Spirit brought about in Christ: to help us gain the victory in the struggle, to overcome temptation,

---

[5] *Spiritual Homilies,* attributed to Macarius, 2.3; 6.11 (PG 34.465A; 516C); see also 30.6; 47.2 (PG 34.725B; 797B).

[6] See Judg 3:10; 6:34; 11:39.

[7] M. Welker, *Gottes Geist. Theologie des Heiligen Geistes* (Neukirchen-Vluyn, 1993) 65.

and to allow us, already in this life, a little foretaste of that eternal peace that will be fully revealed in heaven.

We understand right away that we are not asking the Spirit for the kind of peace that is merely living free of disturbance, the false peace that Jesus said he had come to destroy, not to establish, on earth (Matt 10:34). What the Spirit brings is rather a peace that sustains us in time of trial, and a peace that we enjoy after we have passed through the time of trial: "in the midst of labor bringing rest" *(in labore requies)*, as we read in the Sequence for Pentecost. Neither is this peace for the individual alone, but for the whole community: "That olive-twig and that Ark were symbols, of peace and of the Church, to show that though the world all around may be in ruins, the Holy Spirit brings profound peace to his Church."[8]

2. The Fruits of the Spirit

The titles chosen and the words used in the *Veni Creator* are open structures in the widest sense; they gather together, every time, all that the Bible has to say on a particular theme. Here, the author has in mind all of the passages in the Bible that show a link between peace and the Holy Spirit:

> To set the mind on the flesh is death, but to set the mind on the Spirit is life and *peace* (Rom 8:6).
>
> The kingdom of God . . . [means] righteousness and *peace* and joy in the Holy Spirit (Rom 14:17).
>
> The fruit of the Spirit is love, joy, *peace,* patience, kindness, generosity, faithfulness, gentleness, and self-control (Gal 5:22).

Each one of these texts shows peace as a "fruit of the Spirit," and this gives us an opportunity to dwell a little on this theme too, so very relevant as it is to the Christian life and to an understanding of the way the Holy Spirit works. We come to understand what the "fruits of the Spirit" are as we analyze the contexts in which the idea is put forward. In the letter to the Galatians as well as in the letter to the Romans, the context has to do with the tension, the struggle, between the flesh and the spirit, that is, between the principle that regulates human life in the "old order"

---

[8] Ambrose, *Commentary on the Gospel of Luke,* II.92 (CC 14, p. 74).

heavily weighted with carnal and earthly desires, and the principle that regulates human life in the "new creation" according to the pattern of the Spirit of Christ.

Paul lists the manifestations that are proper to the one and to the other. He calls one set "the works of the flesh" and the other "the fruits of the Spirit." In fact, the original text (Gal 5:22) says *karpos,* fruit, in the singular. One author says that this is intentional, as though Saint Paul wanted to make it clear that life according to the Spirit calls for an attitude that is undivided, coherent, every one of its elements springing from the one and only root which is love, whereas life according to the flesh is characteristically a chaotic multiplicity of vices.[9] However, there is no reason to insist too much on this detail, given the fact that in other places where he is speaking of the same reality the apostle uses expressions in the plural, for instance, "the things of the Spirit" (Rom 8:5), or "the armor (*ta opla,* plural) of light" (Rom 13:12).

The list of the fruits of the Spirit has value simply as providing examples; it is not intended in any sense as exhaustive. For elsewhere in similar contexts other virtues are mentioned, for instance purity.[10] The expression itself, "fruits of the Spirit," is only one of many images used to express the same reality. At other times the opposition between works of the flesh and fruits of the Spirit is expressed as opposition between "the works of darkness" and "the armor of light."

This should be enough to dissuade us from wanting to develop a theory to justify, at whatever cost, the use of the specific word "fruit," taking as basis the fact that "the fruit, and the sweet flavour of fruit, in the natural order is what the plant produces when it has developed to its perfection."[11] It is more useful to look at the word, for instance, in relation to what Jesus said about the good tree that produces good fruit and the bad tree that produces bad fruit (Matt 7:16ff.). In this instance, the flesh would stand for the bad tree that can produce nothing but bad fruit, and the Spirit for the good tree that simply cannot produce bad fruit but only good.

There is a much more relevant theological question about the fruits of the Spirit: Are the fruits of the Spirit to be identified with

---

[9] See J.-P. Lemonon, *Saint Esprit,* in DBSuppl. fasc. 60 (1986) 252–3.

[10] See 2 Cor 6:6; Jas 3:17.

[11] See Thomas Aquinas, *Summa Theologiae* I-II, q. 70, a. 1, ad 2.

the virtues? Saint Thomas Aquinas says that the fruits are acts, not habits, and therefore they are distinct from the virtues. The fruits do not arise, as the virtues do, in the process of the right use of reason; the fruits come directly from a higher principle which is the Holy Spirit. They must then belong within the order of the works of the Spirit.[12] However, a better understanding of the biblical sources is available to us today, and it obliges us to reexamine the way Aquinas viewed these things. In the expression "fruits of the Spirit," the word "Spirit" may perhaps be taken to refer to the person of the Holy Spirit, but in a stronger sense it refers to the Holy Spirit as principle of the new creation, or even the human spirit that is open to the guidance of the Holy Spirit (and so it would be equally correct to write "spirit" in "fruits of the spirit" with a lower-case "s"). It is as if Saint Paul were saying to us that a person who lives according to the flesh does this sort of thing, but one who lives according to the Spirit will produce these fruits.

The subject, the primary agent, is certainly the Holy Spirit, but not simply the Spirit alone. The fruits are distinct from the *charisms,* which are quite clearly works of the Holy Spirit alone, who decides when and on whom to bestow them. The *fruits,* on the other hand, are the result of the cooperation of human freedom and grace. The fruits are produced when the garden of our liberty receives the dew of the Holy Spirit. They are, then, exactly what we mean today by the word *virtue,* if we mean virtue in the biblical sense of habitual behavior "moulded in the pattern of Christ" or "according to the Spirit," rather than in the Aristotelian sense of action "according to right reason." Paul's purpose, in the texts we have looked at, is precisely to encourage Christians to live by virtue: love, humility, purity, obedience (see Romans 12–14).

The fruits are also distinct from the gifts of the Spirit, in that the charisms differ from person to person, but the fruits are the same for everyone. Not everyone in the Church can be apostles, prophets, evangelists, but all without exception or distinction, from the first to the last, can be, and ought to be, loving, patient, humble, peaceful.

The fruits of the Spirit are "christological" fruits; that is, they are signs of the closest relationship with Christ. Jesus said, "Those who abide in me and I in them bear much fruit" (John 15:5), and

[12] Loc. cit.

again, "My Father is glorified by this, that you bear much fruit and become my disciples" (John 15:8). For Paul, to produce the fruits of the Spirit, to be of "the same mind . . . that was in Christ Jesus" (Phil 2:5), and to "put on the Lord Jesus Christ" (Rom 13:14) were all ways of expressing one and the same basic reality. Jesus Christ is the vine; his disciples are the branches; the Holy Spirit is the life-giving sap by virtue of which the branches, the disciples, bear much fruit. One of the ancient spiritual writers says that Christ as a gardener tends the soul so that it may produce "the good fruits of the Spirit." His gardening tool is the cross, and he uses it to break up the hard soil of the arid soul, to prepare it and to plant in it the Holy Spirit's garden of delights, to grow all kinds of fruit, sweet and most pleasing to God.[13]

3. Peace Is God!

Now that we have had a look at the fruits of the Spirit in general, we can move on to reflect more directly on that special fruit which is peace.

What in fact is peace? The classical definition was framed by Saint Augustine: "Peace is the tranquility of order."[14] Saint Thomas Aquinas used this definition as the basis for his comment on Christ's words, "Peace I leave with you; my peace I give to you. I do not give to you as the world gives" (John 14:27):

> There are three kinds of *order* in man: the way a man is ordered within himself, the way he is ordered towards God, and the way each of us is ordered towards our neighbor. And so it is that, for man, there are three kinds of peace: interior peace, in which a person is at peace with himself and his faculties are not in a state of turmoil, the peace by which a person is at peace with God, subjecting himself utterly to God and to God's plans for him, and peace in relation to his neighbor, by which we live in peace with all men.[15]

---

[13] See *Spiritual Homilies,* attributed to Macarius, 28.2 (PG 34.712B).

[14] Augustine, *City of God,* XIX.13 (CC 48, p. 679).

[15] See Thomas Aquinas, *Commentary on the Gospel of John,* XIV, lect. 7, n. 1962.

The peace that Jesus gives differs from the worldly peace on a number of counts. It is different in regard to its *intention,* for worldly peace is ordered toward undisturbed and peaceful enjoyment of temporal goods, but the peace of the saints is ordered toward eternal good. It is different also in regard to its *reality,* for the world looks for outward peace and that can be misleading, but the peace of Christ is true, never deceptive, and it assures peace within ourselves and in our relationships and surroundings.[16]

This is the vision of peace that comes to us through Tradition. Rich as it is, we need today to integrate into it certain new insights that have come to us through advances in the study of the Scriptures. In the Bible "peace" *(shalom)* says more than just the tranquility of order. It does include that state in which we live in harmony with God, within ourselves, and with our surroundings, but it says more: It includes well-being, repose, security, success, and glory. At times it gathers together and points to the totality of the Messianic blessings and is synonymous with salvation and with all good:

> How beautiful upon the mountains
> are the feet of the messenger who announces *peace,*
> who brings *good news,*
> who announces *salvation* (Isa 52:7).

The New Covenant is called "a covenant of peace" (Ezek 37:26) and the Good News "the gospel of peace" (Eph 6:15), as though the word "peace" summed up the whole content of the covenant and of the Gospel.

In the Old Testament we often find peace coupled with "justice" (also variously translated as "virtue" or "righteousness": see Pss 72:7; 85:11), and in the New Testament with "grace." In the greetings that the apostles write at the beginning of their letters, "grace and peace" are almost invariably linked together to indicate the same fundamental reality: the sum total of all the good that comes through the redemption that Christ has achieved. When Paul writes, "Since we are justified by faith, we have peace with God through our Lord Jesus Christ" (Rom 5:1), it is clear that "we have peace with God" is pregnant with all the wealth of meaning that we find "in the grace of God."

---

[16] Ibid., n. 1964.

Yet Scripture wants to lead us to discover still higher reaches of meaning in the word *peace* when it speaks of "the peace of God" (Phil 4:7) and of "the God of peace" (Rom 15:33). In these texts, peace indicates not merely something that God *does,* but also what God *is.* Peace in the truest, fullest sense is that which reigns in God. In one of its hymns, the Church calls to the Trinity as "ocean of peace," and this is not merely poetry. Almost all of the religions that grew and flourished outside the Bible speak of divine worlds always in a state of war. The world-myths or cosmogonies of Babylon and Greece tell of deities constantly at war among themselves, trying to destroy one another. In some of the mythologies the elements of this world are supposed to be the result of such squabbles, the place of exile of deities conquered and banished from the heavens, or even the remains of vanquished deities killed, dismembered, and scattered throughout the universe. Even in the heretical Christian Gnosis there was no peace between the supreme divine Being and the celestial "aeons" that emanate from him, and the material universe was supposed to be the result of some mischance or disharmony among these beings of the higher order.

Against this backdrop of comparative religion, we are better able to grasp the absolute novelty and the total otherness of the doctrine of the Trinity as a perfect unity of love in plurality of Persons. The author who best celebrated this divine peace rooted beyond history was Pseudo-Dionysius the Areopagite. Peace, he said, is one of the "names of God":

> Above all, therefore, we praise divine peace, principle of unity, in hymns of peace. For it is peace that brings all things together in unity and is the wellspring of harmony and the source of every harmonious work and the accord of all that is. And so it is that all things aspire to that peace that holds their diverging multiplicity together in all-embracing unity and changes the inward urge to battle, in all the universe, into unruffled togetherness. . . . God is the author of that peace in himself.[17]

Nor is this divine peace something that is present only when all is at rest; it prevails also in activity. All things in motion, and life itself, are spurred on by the desire for this peace. The peace that

[17] Pseudo-Dionysius the Areopagite, *The Divine Names,* XI.1–2 (PG 3.948–9).

Christ brought about on the cross is seen against this cosmic background as the reflection of the peace of God prevailing in the universe.[18]

Though peace is an attribute of all three Persons of the Trinity, it is ascribed in a special way to the Holy Spirit. Peace is "tranquility of order" in the relationship between a number of persons, and the Holy Spirit is the one through whom many, though many, are of one heart and one soul. He is *con-cord,* heart-unitedness, personified. Of the multitude of persons in the Church he makes one "mystical person," and in the Trinity he is the "bond of peace" between Father and Son.

> It is not through any intervention from without but in virtue of the essence of what they are in themselves, not by gift of anything outside of themselves but by the gift proper to themselves, that the Father and the Son conserve their unity in the Spirit through the bond of peace.[19]

When the Scripture urges us to "maintain the unity of the Spirit in the bond of peace" (Eph 4:3), it is urging us to preserve unity in and through the Holy Spirit.

4. In His Will Is Our Peace

We may call the peace we have been describing up to this point *objective* peace, in the sense that it exists in the real order independently of us human beings and can be communicated to us. This peace is beyond any merit of ours, and it is the peace proclaimed in the Angels' song at the moment of the birth of Christ: "Glory to God in the highest heaven, / and on earth peace among those whom he favors!" (Luke 2:14).

An older translation says, "Peace to men of good will," *eudokia.* The "good will" in virtue of which this peace comes down is not our good will but God's; peace is given us purely because it pleased God to give it.

When we as believers receive this peace of God, or peace of Christ, it becomes conjoined, like grace, with our free will and it

[18] Ibid., XI.5 (PG 3.953).
[19] William of St. Thierry, *The Enigma of Faith,* 98 (PL 180.139C).

works, or achieves its effect, through the operation of our free will, as is the way with every "fruit of the Spirit." Thus we can speak of a real *subjective peace:* the "virtue" of peace, or that habitual quality that distinguishes the person who is meek and peaceful. This is the peace in which we too have to play our part. We know it as peace of heart or peace of soul or interior peace.

In this sense the theme of peace is woven into the whole history of Christian spirituality in the West and in the East as well. The great Orthodox tradition of *hesychasm* (quiet, tranquility) is in fact a pursuit of the same ideal of inward peace, sought after by means of guarding one's thoughts, silence, and sobriety. "Sweet *hesychia*" is defined as "the blessed state of the soul freed of fantasy," and it can be achieved by consistent effort to develop "the virtue of attentiveness which is the custodian of the intellect, vigilance, and perfection of heart."[20] However, besides the stress on the need for human effort, the indispensable need for the action of the Holy Spirit is highlighted: "As the sea, when it is stormy, tends to quieten if oil is poured on the troubled water . . . , so too our soul calms down serenely when it receives the oil of goodness of the Holy Spirit."[21]

This state of *hesychia* or of peace of heart is something that we can indeed experience but cannot ever describe. It is not something that depends on the absence of all confrontation, temptation, and struggle. It is in fact found at a level deeper than any of these things. Jesus tells us that we will have both peace and tribulation at the same time: "I have said this to you, so that in me you may have peace. In the world you face persecution. But take courage; I have conquered the world!" (John 16:33).

The true nature of the peace of the Spirit can be misinterpreted, just as at times the freedom of the Spirit has been misinterpreted. A Christian in whom the Holy Spirit dwells is not exempt from having to experience struggle, temptations, disorderly desires, rebellious feelings, because what we have received are only "the first fruits of the Spirit" (Rom 8:23). The difference between such a person and a "carnal" man is that the former experiences all these things as coming upon him against his will, while the latter

---

[20] Hesychius Presbyter, *To Theodulus,* II.13 (PG 93.1116B).
[21] Diadochus of Photike, *On Spiritual Perfection,* 35 (SCh 5, p. 104).

feels no concern about such desires and is not bothered in the least by them. "The world thinks of peace as a situation where evil is cut away and removed from the person . . . . But Christ does not give us that kind of peace; he cuts the person away from evil, not evil from the person."[22]

The peace of the Spirit is also, most times, "quiet after the storm," in the sense that, as for Jesus in the wilderness, the experience of peace comes after some or other struggle has been won or temptation overcome or attack withstood. The saints can be joyful sometimes and at other times sad; these experiences come and go, but not the experience of peace in the depths of the heart. That is like a deep-ocean current, always flowing steadily regardless of the winds and waves on the surface. In times of trial, the just feel that they are in difficulties on all sides but never cornered; they see no answer to their problems but they never despair (see 2 Cor 4:8).

God's enemy is able to counterfeit just about every good experience and every condition of soul, even including ecstasies and visions of Christ, the saints, or the angels. The one thing that Satan is utterly unable to counterfeit is peace of heart, and for that reason the surest criterion we have for discernment in such matters is what their effect is on that inner peace: Do they give it, or do they destroy it? Peace is the one totally incontrovertible sign that God is present.

The most important point regarding this peace of heart is that we should discover how to acquire it and how to have it grow ever deeper in us. Spiritual writers have given us an endless array of practical advice on this subject.[23] Yet it is possible to tie it all back to two great principal means: Keep your will fixed on God and follow the example of Christ. The Holy Spirit leads us to the place of our rest, and that place is God's will for us. The Spirit is that "place":

> Our rest, and our place, are the same. It is love that takes us there. . . . In good will is our peace. Every body, by force of its own weight, tends towards its proper place. . . . My "weight" is the love that is in me: that is what takes me wherever I go.[24]

The secret of peace is to find the place of our repose, our point-of-rest. For the human soul that point is God. For in fact God has

---

[22] Luther, *Sermon on Pentecost* (WA 12, p. 576).

[23] See *The Imitation of Christ,* II.3; III.25, 28.

[24] Augustine, *Confessions,* XIII.9.10.

made us "for himself"; there is a force of gravity in us that will always draw us toward God, and it is the reason for the dis-quiet, the lack of peace, we will continue to feel as long as we do not seek and find our rest in God.[25] It is a little bit like the rock rolling down the mountain that will not stop until it has reached the lowest point that it can reach, the point closest to the center of the earth, or like the stream that will not stop until it reaches the ocean. Dante Alighieri gathered all of this together in the line that many judge the most beautiful in all of his *Divine Comedy:* "And in His will is our peace."[26]

From all of this we can see that inward or subjective peace is ours in the measure in which, already in this life, we cling fast in faith and in abandonment to the will of God. And so, in the *Veni Creator,* when we ask the Holy Spirit to give us peace, we are, by implication, asking the Spirit to help us, moment by moment and in everything we think and do and undergo, to cling to the will of the Father for us, just as Jesus did. Our every response to God our Father, "let your will be done" in me, translates into a deepening of that peace within us. "Those of steadfast mind you keep in peace" (Isa 26:3). Peace is the child of trust in God. Psalm 131 sings of the peace of the soul that rests tranquil and serene in the holy will of God, "like a child in its mother's arms."

This great road to peace, this clinging to the will of God, has become something more concrete and more accessible to us because of Jesus and the life he lived among us. For us, now, to do the will of God means to follow the example of Jesus: "Learn from me, for I am gentle and humble in heart, and you will find rest for your souls" (Matt 11:29). The outcome is always the same: rest, peace.

A stele from an archaeological site in Asia Minor shows the Emperor Augustus celebrating the peace he had established on earth as "the fruit of victories" *(parta victoriis pax).*[27] Jesus too teaches us that peace is the fruit of victories; however, not victories over enemies, but over ourselves. We find peace when we deny ourselves, when we succeed in overcoming our own pride and harsh temper

---

[25] Ibid., I.1.1.

[26] Dante Alighieri, *Paradiso,* III.85 *("e 'n la sua volontade è nostra pace").*

[27] *Monumentun Ancyranum,* ed. Th. Mommsen, 1883.

and anger. On the cross he taught us how to make peace: "Destroying in his own person the hostility . . . restoring peace through the cross" (see Eph 2:15-16). Destroying the "enmity," not the enemy; destroying it "in his own person," not in anyone else!

5. How Happy the Peacemakers!

Yet, we must ask, having seen all that, is there not a danger of reducing peace to an intimate, private little affair, that is, to peace of the heart and nothing more? Another of the more recent developments on the theme of peace concerns its social dimension. Peace is for the whole of humankind; it is "peace on earth," that is, peace for the world, for the whole of creation, showing, as we like to say these days, that there is a link between peace and the ecology.

The Church's magisterium has been giving attention to this in several important encyclicals, in the messages for the World Day of Peace, and on many other occasions. We will find in these documents a justified insistence on the link between this peace in society and justice, following the word in Isaiah that defines peace as the fruit of justice: "The effect of righteousness will be peace" (Isa 32:17). There can really be no doubt that this opens up the true width of the horizon of peace in the biblical sense and of the work of the Holy Spirit in establishing that peace. Peace in society is also a "fruit of the Spirit" in the sense that it is the cumulative effect of the decisions taken in their free will by all individuals spurred and aided by the action of the Spirit. Wherever peace is achieved in any sense, or wherever there is an end to apartheid in any form, the Holy Spirit is at work in some way. But, precisely because this peace is something to be realized in the broad picture as a whole, it has to be realized first in the individual heart. Peace, fruit of the Spirit, flows on into the Gospel beatitude, "How happy are the peacemakers" (Matt 5:9).

Billions of drops of dirty water will never make a clean sea, and billions of hearts at war will never make up a humanity at peace. "Those conflicts and disputes among you, where do they come from?" asks James. "Do they not come from your cravings that are at war within you?" (Jas 4:1).

One does not make peace in the same way as one makes war. To have a war extensive preparations are needed: alliances must be sought, armies recruited, plans made, strategies prepared, all to get ready to launch an attack. Ruin awaits the soldier who would want to start all on his own; his campaign would certainly end in disaster. But to have peace we need to go about it in exactly the opposite way. No need to wait until we can all agree on a peace program or a plan to achieve it. No need to recruit large numbers of supporters and get them all to move together to mount an action for peace. If we try it that way, we will soon be faced with dozens of different suggestions on how to go about it, and as each one comes up we will need to start the whole process all over from the beginning. No. Peace is in fact brought about by individuals, here and there, on their own, starting right away, where they are, without waiting. It takes only two people, a man and a woman, to generate a human life, while all the people in the world, discussing human life, will never achieve the same thing. Likewise, it takes only two people to start peace. Peace spreads like an avalanche. As it continues, it takes with it everything in its path. But how is it started? With a tiny movement, a fistful of snow slipping on the high mountainside, and drawing along with it all the snow it meets on its way down.

And this brings us to the third dimension of peace. Peace is a *gift of God* and it is also a *fruit of the Spirit,* but in the Gospel peace is also a *beatitude.* As a gift it is in the order of *grace;* as a fruit it enters into the order of *virtue;* as a beatitude it is in the order of *duties,* as a task to be carried out: "Blessed are the peacemakers, for they will be called children of God" (Matt 5:9).

How does one become a peacemaker? One way, significantly important in itself, is not to be a spreader of evil: Don't be an agent of the accuser, don't be a sower of darnel or bad seed, don't spread news of evil. We need to be "the end of the track," the terminus, for any gossip that we hear, for any ugly word, hostile judgment, criticism. The terminus is the place where the train or the bus stops and goes no further. We need to be like "black holes" for evil, vortices that swallow everything and allow nothing whatsoever to pass by and continue on its way. Of course, to be a peacemaker means more than just that; it means to take the initiative in the matter of peace, to do what you can to promote justice. But we must be careful not to let these aspects obscure the other, the simpler and narrower strategy of "don't spread evil," which is always open to everyone.

Francis of Assisi is an outstanding example of what one man alone is able to achieve in promoting peace. To him is attributed the prayer in which he asks the Lord, "Lord, make me an instrument of your peace." And God truly did make him an instrument, or rather a channel, of his peace. Wherever he went, peace flourished: between one city and another, between factions within the same city, between civil authority and religious authority, and also between human beings and the rest of creation. To his brothers he gave this counsel: "As you announce peace with your mouth, make sure that greater peace is in your hearts."[28]

He wanted them all to use as their greeting, "May the Lord give you peace." And because many thought this unusual form of greeting a little embarrassing, one of the brothers complained to him about it one day. Francis answered, with words that have proved prophetic, "Do not be embarrassed, for one day the nobles and princes of this world will show respect to you and the other brothers because of a greeting of this sort."[29] *Pax et bonum,* "Peace and the good," has become the motto of his order. Assisi itself has become, because of him, a crossroads of peace, especially since Pope John Paul II in 1986 chose Assisi as the place to hold history's first encounter for peace among the religions of the world.

An important chapter in the history of peace is being written today in the emerging peace between religions, and especially between the various Christian churches. It is the Church herself, in her totality, that ought to be the great crossroads for peace among the nations. But how can a Church preach peace to the nations if she herself is inwardly torn apart by divisions and conflicts that are anything but peaceful? Jesus on the cross became our peace; he has "broken down the barrier which used to keep us apart" and made "the two into one," "to create one single new man in himself out of the two" (Eph 2:14-15). "The two," at the time of Paul's writing, were the Jews and the Gentiles. Not only does that particular barrier, by right removed, still have to be removed in fact, in spite of recent advances in this respect, but in the meantime other barriers have been erected, this time between Christian and Christian.

The start of the new millennium may be a unique opportunity to stop this tendency to tear ourselves apart and to set in train a

---

[28] *The Legend of Three Companions,* 58 (ED, II, p. 102).
[29] *The Assisi Compilation,* 101 (ED, II, p. 205).

process of reconciliation around the cross of Christ. What a marvelous gift it would be for Jesus if the major schisms and divisions among Christians could be brought to an end, and we could all go forward into the new millennium together, as one "new man in Christ." In the middle ages there was a custom on special occasions to make a bonfire of the vanities: all the people of the town would come together and, in public, burn the things that they had used for evil ends. Let us get ourselves ready to make a bonfire of all our hostilities. We cannot simply burn all our doctrinal divergences that need to be resolved, with great patience, in the forums where such matters are properly dealt with, but each one of us can begin now to get rid of, to burn away, our hostility. Recent experience has shown that doctrinal differences can be dealt with and leveled out much more readily when there is no hostility between those who participate in the discussion. At times they simply fall away on their own, because it becomes possible to see that they were nothing more, in fact, than an inability to hear and to understand the other point of view.

As a fruit of the Spirit peace is the result of grace and of our own free will working together. But the contribution of our free will doesn't consist only in our personal and collective efforts to establish peace. We always have another weapon at our disposal, and that is prayer. In the Mass, before communion the liturgy calls for the priest to pray this heartfelt plea for peace: "Lord Jesus Christ, you said to your apostles, 'I leave you peace, my peace I give you.' Look not on our sins, but on the faith of your Church, and grant us the peace and unity of your kingdom where you live forever and ever."

The Jesus who, in the supper room, bade farewell to his disciples, saying to them, "I leave you peace. My peace I give to you," is risen and alive. He carries on giving his peace with the same incessant loving care with which he carries on breathing on his disciples and saying, "Receive the Holy Spirit" (John 20:22). When it is Jesus who says, "Peace be with you" (John 20:19), it is not merely a greeting. His words are words of power: they bring about what they mean. On his lips the word *peace* is not a benevolent intention, but an active and creative reality. It is something that, if the hearers deserve it, is able to "remain" in them; if the hearers don't deserve it, it will return to the one who spoke it (see Matt 10:13). It is something very concrete, an almost palpable presence.

It is of course true that as long as we are in this world we cannot expect to find ourselves in a state of peace that is absolute and definitive. Saint Paul writes to the Christians at Rome: "Live peaceably with all" (Rom 12:18).

It is not always possible, then, to live at peace with everyone. Peace, like holiness and unity, is one of the good things that will come at the end of time, a blessing of the heavenly Jerusalem that one of the Church's hymns—harking back to a supposed etymology of that name—calls, "blessed vision of peace" *(beata pacis visio)*.[30]

In this life we can discover the ways that lead to peace (Luke 19:42), and we can "guide our feet into the way of peace" (Luke 1:79). We can, in moments of special grace, have a foretaste and a pledge of the peace we hope to enjoy in heaven. Once on a Pentecost Sunday Saint Teresa of Avila experienced an ecstasy: she saw a dove come down and rest on her head, its wings like flakes of mother-of-pearl glowing brightly. But far from upsetting her, as such visions often do, she writes that her spirit "was filled with great peace and began to rejoice in sweetness and quiet."[31] Peace comes down on a soul in the presence of the Spirit as quiet comes down on the field of battle after the enemy has fled.

We end this chapter on peace with the Sequence of Pentecost,[32] which speaks of the Spirit as our rest in the midst of labor and tears:

> *Come, Holy Spirit,*
> *send from heaven*
> *the rays of your light.*
>
> *Come, father of the poor*
> *come, giver of gifts,*
> *come, enlightenment of hearts.*
>
> *Of consolers, very best,*
> *of the soul the sweetest guest,*
> *you sweet refreshment are.*

---

[30] *Urbs Jerusalem Beata,* Vespers of the common office of the Dedication of a Church.

[31] Teresa of Avila, *Autobiography,* 38.9–10.

[32] Known as the "Golden Sequence," it is now commonly attributed to Stephen Langton, Archbishop of Canterbury († 1228), (translator's English version).

In midst of labour bringing rest,
tempering the summer heat,
soul's ease in midst of tears.

Oh, most happy-making light
fill to the very depths the hearts
of all who believe in you.

Of your divinity bereft
all humankind is empty left
and nothing harmless is.

Wash the filthy,
water the dry,
heal the wounded.

Make supple the stiff,
warm what is cold,
give direction to the stray.

Give to your faithful
who trust in you
the sevenfold sacred gift.

Deserts to virtue lend,
bring us to salvation's end,
give joys that never end.

XIX

With You as Guide
We Avoid All Cause of Harm

The Holy Spirit is our guide in spiritual discernment

After the struggle against evil, the second of the two broad fronts opened up by this verse of the *Veni Creator* is, as we said, decision or choice. In the modern concept of human existence choice plays a definitive role. If we refuse to accept that we exist as human beings according to the model and design defined by the Word of God, our humanity becomes something that we have to define over and over again, a design that is totally open ended. Like a river, people hollow out their own beds as they go along. Human beings are what they make of themselves by the exercise of their own autonomous will. This is the source of the anxiety that goes hand in hand with this secularized view of human existence. For to choose is necessarily also to renounce, and if there is no objective criterion for any choice, every choice becomes a reason to be anxious.

But this all holds true, though in a different way, in the spiritual arena for a person of faith, and from the attention given in recent times to the question of choice we can, as always, gather something that will help us to new discoveries in the Word of God itself. Though we may have come to know God's design for us and decided to live our life in accordance with it, we are still faced with the never-ending need to discern what is in accordance with that design and what is contrary to it or less in accordance with it. For progress in the spiritual sense depends on that discernment.

That is the reason why the apostles in their teaching were so insistent on the point. In the Letter to the Hebrews we read, "Solid food is for the mature, for those whose faculties have been trained by practice to distinguish good from evil" (Heb 5:14). Paul wanted his faithful to be "wise in what is good and guileless in what is evil" (Rom 16:19); he therefore exhorts them to "hold fast to what is good; abstain from every form of evil" (1 Thess 5:21), thinking before they do anything so that they will always be able to distinguish what is the better.[1]

We now turn to the two lines of the verse that help us to discover what role the Spirit plays in our journey toward Christian maturity. If Jesus Christ is the way *(odòs)* that leads to the Father, the Holy Spirit is our guide along that way *(odegòs)*.[2] Ambrose greets the Spirit in words that closely match in meaning these two lines of our hymn: "The Spirit is our guide and leader *(ductor et princeps)* who directs our mind, strengthens our affection, draws us where he wants us to go and steers our steps to the upward way."[3]

1. The Spirit as "Guide," in Scripture and Through Tradition

The theme of the Holy Spirit as guide is found expressed in Christian Tradition by a symbol that is particularly meaningful: that of the "bright cloud" or "pillar of fire" that accompanied the chosen people on their way to the Promised Land.[4] On Tabor the bright cloud, that is, the Holy Spirit, had at last reached the goal toward which the people were being led; that goal was Christ.[5] The title itself, "guide," *ductor*, seems to be linked with this tradition. A medieval author writes: "The symbol of this mystery was the pillar of fire that went ahead of the people of God on their journey towards Jerusalem; it stood for the Holy Spirit who is the guide *(ductor)* of all those who are on the way to Christ."[6]

This significant patristic tradition does have a biblical basis, although it is indirect. In the book of the prophet Isaiah, the whole journey of the people in the desert is ascribed to the guidance of

---

[1] See Phil 1:10; Rom 2:18.

[2] Gregory of Nyssa, *On Faith* (PG 45.1241C); *Spiritual Homilies*, attributed to Macarius, 1.3 (PG 34.453A); see Pseudo-Athanasius, *Dialogue against the Macedonians*, 1.12 (PG 28.1308C).

[3] Ambrose, *Apologia for David*, 15.73 (CSEL 32.2, p. 348).

[4] Ambrose, *On the Holy Spirit*, III.4.21; see Ambrose, *The Sacraments*, I.6.22; Ambrose, *The Mysteries*, 3.33.

[5] See Theophanes Cherameus, *Homily 59 on the Transfiguration* (PG 132.1037A).

[6] Paschasius Radbertus, *Commentary on the Gospel of Matthew*, II.2 (CM 56, p. 153).

the Spirit. "The Spirit of the LORD gave them rest" (Isa 63:14); God endowed Moses with the Spirit, and when the people rebelled against Moses it was the Spirit that they grieved (Isa 63:10-11). Paul says that "all were baptized . . . in the cloud and in the sea" (1 Cor 10:2). Now, how is it possible to link the cloud with baptism or understand the meaning of the expression "baptized in the cloud," except in reference to baptism "in water and the Spirit" or "in the Holy Spirit and fire"? Not many lines later Paul himself says, "In the one Spirit we were all baptized" (1 Cor 12:13).

The symbol of the cloud aside, the New Testament explicitly attributes the function of guide to the Paraclete. Jesus himself was "*led* by the Spirit out into the wilderness"; as a Christian you are no longer subject to the Law "if you are *led* by the Spirit" (Gal 5:18).

The Acts of the Apostles conveys the same idea in a descriptive way, telling the story of a Church that is "led by the Spirit" each step of the way. Luke's very purpose in compiling the Acts as a sequel to his Gospel was to show that the same Spirit who, moment by moment, was guiding Jesus during his earthly life is now, as the Spirit "of Christ," also guiding the Church. Did Peter go to Cornelius and to the pagans? It was the Spirit who ordained that it should be so (see Acts 10:19; 11:12). When the apostles met together in Jerusalem, did they make far-reaching decisions? The Holy Spirit was the one who prompted them (see Acts 15:28).

The guidance of the Holy Spirit is given not only for the great decisions that have to be taken, but even for the smallest. Paul and Timothy wanted to preach the Gospel in the province of Asia, but the Holy Spirit told them not to; when they wanted to go to Bithynia, "the Spirit of Jesus did not allow them" (Acts 16:6-7). We can see the reason for such insistent guidance: The Holy Spirit drove them onward in this way because he wanted the newly-emerging Church to branch out from Asia and plant itself in a new continent, Europe (see Acts 16:9). Paul, because he had chosen willingly to be guided in this way, came eventually to describe himself as a "prisoner" of the Spirit (Acts 20:22).

The Second Vatican Council sums up this deep-seated biblical and traditional conviction when it speaks of the Church as "the people of God, who believe that they are guided by the Spirit of the Lord."[7]

---

[7] *Gaudium et Spes* 11.

2. *Where the Spirit Provides Guidance:*
   Conscience and the Church

Where does the Paraclete's role as guide actually touch us? What, if we may use the expression, are the organs through which the Spirit fulfils this function? The first arena of guidance is the *conscience*. There is a relationship between conscience and the Holy Spirit that we have not yet fully explored. What exactly is the famous "voice of conscience," if not a kind of "receiving-set" through which the Holy Spirit speaks to us? Paul, speaking of his love for his own people, the Jews, says, "My conscience confirms it by the Holy Spirit" (Rom 9:1).

The guidance of the Holy Spirit, given through the workings of conscience, extends beyond the Church and reaches every human being. The pagans "show that what the law requires is written on their hearts, to which their own conscience also bears witness" (Rom 2:15). It was because the Holy Spirit uses the way of conscience to speak to every rational being that Maximus the Confessor says, "Even among the barbarians and the nomads we see many individuals adopting a good and decent way of life in spite of the savage customs that from the beginning have reigned among them."[8]

Conscience itself is also a kind of law that is intrinsic to us, not written, different from, and of a lower order than that which is in the believer by virtue of grace. But conscience and grace are not at loggerheads, given that both proceed from the same source, the Spirit. One who possesses only the "inferior" law of conscience but obeys it is closer to the Spirit than one who possesses the higher law that comes through baptism but does not live in accordance with it.

In believers the inner guide of conscience is, so to say, empowered and raised to a higher order by the anointing that "teaches everything" (1 John 2:27), and so it is an infallible guide, if we listen to it. It was in fact when commenting on this very point that Saint Augustine formulated the teaching on the Holy Spirit as "the teacher within." What, he asks, does it mean, to say, "You do not need anyone to teach you" (1 John 2:27)? Could it mean that the individual Christian already, on his own account alone, knows

---

[8] Maximus the Confessor, *Various Chapters*, I.72 (PG 90.1208D).

everything and does not need to read or to seek instruction or to listen to anyone else? If that were the case, what point would there be in the apostle having written his letter at all? The truth is that we do need to listen to teachers and preachers other than ourselves, but only the one to whom the Holy Spirit speaks inwardly will grasp and be able to profit by what the others are saying. This explains why many can listen to the same sermon and the same teaching, but not all will understand it in the same way.[9]

And what consoling assurance we can find in all of this! The word that was spoken one day, "The Teacher is here and is calling for you!" (John 11:28), resounds today for every Christian. The very same Master, Christ, who spoke then, speaks now through his Spirit and he is within us and he is calling us. Saint Cyril of Jerusalem phrased it very accurately when he called the Holy Spirit "the Church's great teacher *(didascalos)*."[10]

In this intimate and personal area of conscience, the Holy Spirit guides us by means of those "good inspirations" and "interior illuminations" that every one of us has experienced at some time or other. They are appeals to us to follow the good and to flee from the bad; they are inward inclinations or propensities of the heart that it is simply not possible to explain in any natural way, because they often lead in a direction that nature would not be inclined to take. Moments of light or desires that arise as one listens to the Word of God or is confronted with some or other good example. It is in moments like these, above all, that one becomes aware of the Spirit as a breeze that blows where it wills; one hears its sound, but does not know where it comes from or where it is going (see John 3:8). It is only later that the fruits of the impulse will tell that it was the Holy Spirit who was there.

Up to this point we have been looking into the first of the ways, the way of conscience, in which the Holy Spirit guides us. There is a second way, and it is the *Church*. The witness of the Holy Spirit within each of us needs to match and merge with the outward, visible and objective testimony which is the apostolic commission to teach, the magisterium. In the book of Revelation, at the close of each of the seven letters, we hear this admonition:

---

[9] See Augustine, *On the First Letter of John*, 3.13; 4.1 (PL 35.2004–5).

[10] Cyril of Jerusalem, *Catecheses*, XVI.19.

"Let anyone who has an ear listen to what the Spirit is saying to the churches" (Rev 2:7ff.).

For the Spirit speaks to the Church too, and to the community, and not only to individuals. In the Acts of the Apostles, Peter brings together the two forms—the inward and the outward, the personal and the public—of the Spirit's witness. He had spoken to the crowds of Christ put to death and risen, and his hearers were "cut to the heart" (Acts 2:37). He later said the same things to the rulers and members of the Sanhedrin, and they were infuriated (Acts 4:8ff.). The same sermon, the same preacher, but the outcome very different. Why? The explanation is given in what Peter himself said in that very situation: "We are witnesses to these things, and so is the Holy Spirit whom God has given to those who obey him" (Acts 5:32).

The two testimonies need to come together so that faith may be released: the testimony of the apostles who proclaim the Word, and the testimony of the Spirit that enables the listener to receive the Word. John's Gospel sets out the same idea where Jesus, speaking of the Paraclete, says, "The Spirit . . . will testify on my behalf. You also are to testify" (John 15:26).

In the case of the Sanhedrin, the inner testimony of the Spirit was missing, because God gives the Spirit "to those who obey him," and they had not shown themselves willing to obey.

It is equally fatal to pretend to do without one or the other of the two forms of guidance of the Holy Spirit. When we neglect the inner witness, we fall very easily into legalism and an authoritarian attitude; when we neglect the outward, apostolic witness, we fall into subjectivism and fanaticism. In the early days of the Church the Gnostics rejected the apostolic, the official, witness. Against their view, Saint Irenaeus made the well-known statement:

> The Gift of God was entrusted to the Church just as breath was given to the new-formed body . . . . Those who do not enter the Church and live accordingly, do not share in that breath . . . . Separated from the Church, they become busied with every form of error and allow themselves to be jerked about by error; they interpret the same thing now this way and now that, and retain no consistent thought about anything.[11]

[11] Irenaeus, *Against the Heresies*, III.24.1–2.

If everything is reduced to the individual's personal, private hearing alone of what the Spirit is saying, the way is opened to an unstoppable process of divisions and subdivisions, because each person believes that his or her own view is the right one. The very multiplicity of denominations and sects, often divided on essential points, is proof that the same Spirit of truth cannot be speaking in them all, for if that were the case the Spirit would be contradicting himself.

This, we can see, is the risk to which the Protestant world is most exposed, having made the "inward testimony" of the Holy Spirit the only criterion of truth prevailing against any external or ecclesial criterion whatever, apart from only the written Word.[12] Certain fringe groupings go so far as to detach the inner guidance of the Spirit even from the Word of Scripture; the result is the various movements of "enthusiasts" and "enlightened" that have peppered the history of all the Church, Catholic, Orthodox, and Protestant alike. This tendency to concentrate all attention on the inward testimony of the Spirit usually ends up in the Spirit coming gradually to be deprived of the capital "S" and taken to mean nothing more than the human spirit alone. That in fact is what happened among the rationalists.

However, we need to be aware that there is also the opposite risk; that is, of making the external and public testimony of the Spirit absolute and ignoring the individual witness that operates in the individual conscience in the light of grace. In other words, reducing the guidance of the Spirit to nothing but the official magisterium of the Church and in that way impoverishing the Spirit's many and varied ways of acting. In this kind of situation, it is very easy for the human element to usurp control, to organize and to institutionalize. It opens the way for the laity to be marginalized and for the Church to become excessively clerical.

The Vatican Council II affirmed the priority of the value of freedom of conscience and also, indirectly, of the witness of what the Spirit is saying to each individual. Moreover, the Church has always believed that there is a *sensus fidelium,* a sound understanding on the part of the community as a whole concerning the matters of faith, the capacity to judge soundly, conferred specifically by the

---

[12] See J.-L. Witte, *Esprit Saint et Églises séparées,* in Dict. Spir. 4, col. 1318–25.

anointing of the Spirit. However, in practice this "sound sense of the faithful" has often been disregarded or reduced merely to an assumed agreement with whatever the Church magisterium teaches.

In this case too, as always, we need to rediscover the integral truth, the synthesis, that is the criterion of what is genuinely "catholic," that is, universal. The ideal is a healthy harmony of tension between listening to what the Spirit says to me as an individual, and to what the Spirit says to the Church as a whole and through the Church to all individuals. What we need is a reciprocal sort of listening, by which each one of us is ready and willing to hear what the Spirit is saying to us through the Church, and the Church is ready and willing to listen to what the Spirit is saying through individuals, without, if possible, waiting until the individuals concerned are dead.

3. The Spirit Helps Us Discern the Signs of the Times

Now that we are clear as to the principles, we can try to see how they apply to our life. In our own lives and in the affairs of the world, how are we to recognize when the Spirit is truly moving, and how do we distinguish that from moves that are not authentic or that are the activity of other spirits?

Paul mentions a specific charism in this regard and calls it discernment of spirits (1 Cor 12:10). The meaning of this expression was originally very specific: It meant the gift which made it possible to distinguish, among the inspired or prophetic messages spoken during a Christian assembly, those that came from the Spirit of Christ from those that came from other spirits, such as the spirit of man or a demonic spirit or the spirit of the world.

This is the basic sense for Saint John too. Discernment consists in putting inspirations to the test: "Do not believe in every spirit, but test the spirits to see whether they are from God" (1 John 4:1). The fundamental criterion of discernment for Paul is confessing Christ as Lord (1 Cor 12:3); for John it is confessing that Jesus "has come in the flesh" (1 John 4:2), that is, the Incarnation. In John discernment had already taken on a theological function, as the criterion by which to discern true teaching as distinct from false, orthodoxy from heresy, and in later development this would become its central function.

There are two areas in which the Holy Spirit carries out this work of guidance: the ecclesial and the personal. In consistency with that we need to exercise this gift of discernment of the voice of the Spirit in the same two areas, the ecclesial and the personal.

In the ecclesial area, discernment of spirits is carried out in an authoritative way by the magisterium that needs, however, to take into account the "sound sense of the faithful" as one of the criteria. In the actual situation today, where a peaceful dialogue is taking place among the various religions, discernment is of vital importance. In the area of religious standpoints and of the way the Christian life is actually lived, the gift of discernment allows us to distinguish when a popular religious standpoint or a new devotion or a private revelation is from God and will enrich the faith, or when on the other hand it will compromise the faith by adding too many divisive and secondary elements.

But I would like to dwell on a particular point: the discernment of the signs of the time. The council declared:

> At all times the Church carries the responsibility of reading the signs of the time and of interpreting them in the light of the Gospel, if it is to carry out its task. In language intelligible to every generation she should be able to answer the ever-recurring questions which men ask about this present life and of the life to come, and how one is related to the other.[13]

The collegiality of the bishops is an important factor in carrying out this task, and the council itself laid significant stress on this. Together the bishops are charged "to settle conjointly, in a decision rendered balanced and equitable by the advice of many, all questions of major importance."[14] By the effective exercise of collegiality, the bishops would be able to bring discernment to bear and find a solution to the problems arising out of the great variety of local situations, points of view, different ways of understanding and diversity of gifts, that burden every bishop and every pastor.

We have a moving example of this very thing in the first "council" of the Church, in Jerusalem. That meeting allowed ample opportunity to both of the opposing points of view, those who wanted to keep to the Jewish way and those who were in favor of being

---

[13] *Gaudium et Spes* 4.
[14] *Lumen Gentium* 22.

open to the pagans. The "discussion went on for a long time," but it did enable them in the end all to agree in decisions that they announced using this extraordinary formula: "It has been decided by the Holy Spirit and by ourselves . . ." (see Acts 15:28).

From this we can see that the Spirit guides the Church in two different ways: sometimes directly and in a charismatic way, through revelations and prophetic inspirations; at other times in a collegial way, through the difficult process of opposing views considered patiently until a point is reached where all parties to the discussion and all points of view can be brought together in agreement. The way Peter spoke on the day of Pentecost and when he was in Cornelius's house was very different from the way he spoke later to justify what he had decided (Acts 11:4-18; 15:14).

This work of bringing people who are different and free to agree together as one, "united heart and soul" in a common purpose (see Acts 4:32), is an intrinsic characteristic of the Holy Spirit. This is not submission to a decision imposed on them, mechanically and passively accepted, but an accord in which all have taken part. As different notes must sound together to form a chord, accord is achieved as a harmony of different standpoints. This characteristic is an outflowing of the special role of the Spirit in the Trinity and in the Church. The Spirit is "one person of two persons" (as distinct from Jesus who is "one person of two natures"); the Spirit is, as it were, a kind of divine "We" spoken by Father and Son together.

We need, therefore, to have trust in the ability of the Spirit eventually to achieve that accord, even if at times it seems as if the whole process is getting quite out of hand. Whenever pastors of the Christian churches gather together, whether locally or worldwide, to discern or to make important decisions, each one needs to hold in his heart the confident certainty that the *Veni Creator* has summed up in the two short lines, "With you as guide to lead the way, no risk for us to go astray."

4. Discernment in Our Personal Life

Over the centuries there has been a significant evolution in the way the charism of discernment was understood. Originally, as we have seen, the gift served to discern the inspirations of those who had spoken or prophesied in an assembly. Later it came to serve mainly to enable individuals to discern their own inspirations. This was no arbitrary change: It was in fact the same gift though it was used for different purposes. A great deal of what the authors have written about the "gift of counsel" applies just as well to the charism of discernment. Through the gift or charism of counsel the Holy Spirit helps us to evaluate situations and to direct our choices, not only on the basis of human wisdom and prudence, but also in the light of the supernatural principles of faith.

The first fundamental discernment is that which lets us distinguish "the Spirit of God" from "the spirit of the world" (1 Cor 2:12). Paul gives the same objective criterion of discernment that Jesus gave: the fruits. The "works of the flesh" show that the sinful desire giving rise to them comes from the old nature, and "the fruits of the Spirit" show that the desire from which they spring comes from the Spirit (see Gal 5:19-22). "For what the flesh desires is opposed to the Spirit, and what the Spirit desires is opposed to the flesh" (Gal 5:17).

However, there are times when this objective criterion is not enough, because the choice is not between good and bad, but between one good and another good, and the question is to know what God wants in that particular situation. Saint Ignatius Loyola developed his teaching on discernment mainly as a response to the needs of such a situation. He suggests that we take note of one thing in particular: our own inward dispositions, the intentions (the "spirits") that underlie our choice. In that, he was aligning himself with a tradition already established. A medieval author writes:

> How can a person examine intentions and see whether they come from God, unless discernment has been bestowed on him by God in such a way as to make him able to judge the thoughts, dispositions and intentions of the spirit precisely and with right judgement? Discernment is, as it were, the mother of all virtues, and necessary to everyone to guide ourselves, or others, in the way we live. . . . This then is what discernment is: the conjunction of right judgement and virtuous intention.[15]

[15] Baldwin of Canterbury, *Tracts*, 6 (PL 204.466).

Ignatius Loyola suggested practical ways to apply these criteria.[16] As an example, when two possible choices are open to you, it is good to settle on one of them as though that were without question your choice and to stay with that for a day or more; then stop and evaluate how you really feel in your heart about that choice. Are you at peace about it, is it in harmony with all the other choices you have made, do you feel inwardly encouraged to follow that route, or on the other hand does it leave you under a veil of disquiet? Repeat the process with the other choice open to you. Do it all in an atmosphere of prayer, of abandonment to God's will and openness to the Holy Spirit.

When you come right down to it, it is simply a question of putting into practice the advice that Jethro gave to Moses: Put the questions to God, and wait in prayer for God's answer (see Exod 18:19). A deep-seated habitual disposition to do God's will whatever the situation puts you in the best position to discern well. Jesus says: "My judgment is just, because I seek to do not my own will but the will of him who sent me" (John 5:30).

A danger in some modern ways of practicing discernment is that the psychological aspects may be accentuated to such an extent that the primary agent in every discernment, the Holy Spirit, is forgotten. Saint Ignatius Loyola too recalls that in some cases it is only the anointing of the Holy Spirit that will permit us to discern what we are to do.[17] There is a profound theological reason for this. The Holy Spirit is substantively the will of God, and when the Spirit enters into a soul, "he shows himself as the very will of God for the one in whom he dwells."[18]

This renewed attention to the role of the Holy Spirit is the freshest note that the Pentecostal and Charismatic movements have brought to the question of discernment of spirits. We are experiencing a return to its original meaning and purpose. Discernment, when all is said and done, is neither an art nor a technique but a charism, that is, a gift of the Spirit! Its psychological aspects are of great importance, but they remain always in the second place. One of the ancient Fathers wrote:

[16] See Ignatius Loyola, *Spiritual Exercises,* Fourth Week, ed. BAC (Madrid, 1963) 262ff.

[17] Ignatius Loyola, *Constitutions,* 141.414 (ibid., pp. 452, 503).

[18] See William of St. Thierry, *The Mirror of Faith,* 61 (SCh 301, p. 128).

Only the Holy Spirit can purify the mind . . . . We need, therefore, by every means possible and especially by peace of soul to have the Holy Spirit come and "rest" upon us, so that we will always have, close by and kindled, the light of conscience. If that light is continually shining in the recesses of our soul, not only will our mind be able to see all the devious and dark demon assaults quite clearly, but they will be unmasked, deprived of any force, as they always are in that glorious light. That is why the apostle says, "Don't extinguish the Spirit" (1 Thess 5:19).[19]

The Holy Spirit does not normally shed this light in our soul in a way that is out of the ordinary or miraculous, but simply through the Word of Scripture. The most significant discernments in the history of the Church happened in that way. It was when Saint Anthony was listening to the Gospel and heard the words, "If you want to be perfect, . . ." that he understood that he was to go and live in a way that proved to be the beginning of monasticism. It was in the same way that Saint Francis of Assisi received the light to go and start his movement of return to the Gospel; in fact, we read in his *Testament:* "After the Lord gave me some brothers, no one showed me what I had to do, but the Most High himself revealed to me that I should live according to the pattern of the Holy Gospel."[20] It was revealed to him during the Mass, while he was listening to the Gospel passage where Jesus tells the disciples to go to the world taking nothing for the journey: neither staff nor haversack nor bread nor money and no spare tunic (Luke 9:3).[21]

I remember an example of the same sort of thing. During a popular mission a man came to me with a problem. His eleven-year-old son had not yet been baptized. He said, "If I baptize him there will be trouble in the family, because my wife has become a Jehovah's Witness and will not hear of him being baptized in the Church. If I do not baptize him my conscience will simply not leave me in peace, because when we were married we were both Catholics." This was a classic case for discernment. I suggested he come back the next day, to give me time to pray and reflect. Next day he came looking radiant and said, "I found the answer,

[19] Diadochus of Photike, *On Spiritual Perfection,* 28 (SCh 5, p. 87ff.).
[20] Francis of Assisi, *Testament* (ED, I, p. 125).
[21] Thomas of Celano, *First Life,* 22 (ED, I, p. 201).

Father. I was reading in the Bible about Abraham, and saw that when he went off with Isaac to offer him in sacrifice, he said nothing about it to his wife!" The Word of God had done more for him than any human counsel could ever have done. He brought the boy to me to baptize him, and the moment was one of great joy for everybody.

If we are looking for an answer from God and we feel inwardly moved to open the Bible at random, there is no reason we should not do it. God has often spoken to people in this way. But it would not be good to make a habit of it, for that would expose us sooner or later to unhappy consequences. The gifts of the Spirit are never intended to become a mechanical routine. There is also the idea of "putting out a fleece before the Lord" (see Judg 6:36-40), that is, to ask God to give us specific signs. Sometimes we may do it, and if we do it in a truly humble way and in submission to God's will the fruits are good. But we need great discretion in this, for the practice can so easily turn into "putting God to the test."

5. Allow the Holy Spirit to Guide Us

The practical outcome of this reflection ought to be a new sense of resolve to entrust ourselves in every way and for everything to the inner guidance of the Holy Spirit: to allow the Spirit, so to say, to be our "spiritual director." It is written that, "Whenever the cloud was taken up from the tabernacle, the Israelites would set out on their journey; but if the cloud was not taken up, then they did not set out until the day that it was taken up" (Exod 40:36-37). Nor should we start anything or do anything at all unless we have first consulted the Holy Spirit, and unless the Spirit, of whom the cloud was a figure, is the one who moves us to start. We have the most shining example of this in the way Jesus himself lived. It was with the Holy Spirit that he went into the wilderness; it was in the power of the Spirit that he returned and began his preaching; it was "in the Holy Spirit" that he chose his apostles (Acts 1:2); it was in the Spirit that he prayed and offered himself to the Father (Heb 9:14).

At the beginning of this reflection we noted the tendency among us in our day, secularized as we have become, to set out to guide ourselves without help, as flowing water washes out its own stream-bed. One of the great philosophers tells a fable to illustrate where this leads us. A rich man once bought two splendid horses, thoroughbreds, and decided that he would train them himself. He actually knew nothing about horses, however, and he would drive them as they showed they wanted to be driven. The result was that in a very short time they looked like the two most miserable horses imaginable: sleepy-eyed, no style to their pace at all, full of whims of their own, skittish at the slightest excuse, always sluggish, and ready to stop at any moment. Eventually the man decided to take them to the king's own coachman. It took him just a month. No finer pair of horses could be seen in all the land: with beautiful, high-stepping pace, heads held so proudly, and such fire in their eyes, they were ready to set off at a gallop and not pause for seven miles. The expert knows how to drive horses as horses should be driven, not as they want to be driven.

Our faculties are the horses, and we are the owner who thinks he knows how to drive horses. The king's coachman is the Holy Spirit. "Oh, if only we could see how wonderful it is for us when the king's own coachman himself takes up the reins!"[22]

But we "believers" too, need to be on our guard against the temptation: We often want to guide the Holy Spirit instead of letting the Spirit guide us. "Who has directed the spirit of the LORD, / or as his counselor has instructed him?" (Isa 40:13).

The Holy Spirit directs all and is directed by none; the Spirit guides and is not guided. We have a subtle way of telling the Holy Spirit what to do with us and how to guide us. For in fact we make our own decisions at times, and then pretend with casual confidence that they come from the Holy Spirit.

Saint Thomas Aquinas speaks of the inner guidance of the Holy Spirit as a kind of "instinct proper to the righteous": "As in life on the physical level, the body does not move unless it is moved by the soul that gives it life, so also in the spiritual life every movement of ours ought to come from the Holy Spirit."[23]

---

[22] See S. Kierkegaard, *For Self-Examination,* III, First day of Pentecost (Samlede Vaerker, XIII, pp. 337ff.).

[23] Thomas Aquinas, *On the Letter to the Galatians,* c. V, lec. 5, n. 318; lec. 7, n. 340; see also *Commentary on the Gospel of John,* VI.5.3.

This is how the "law of the Spirit" works; it is to this that the apostle is pointing us when he says, "If you are led by the Spirit . . ." (Gal 5:18).

Once I asked a little five-year-old girl what she thought obedience was, thinking that she would answer me something like, "to do what mommy tells me" or "to do what daddy says." I would never have expected her to answer as she did: "Obedience is like this: the Holy Spirit says to Jesus, 'Let's do this,' and he says, 'OK!' The Holy Spirit says to you, 'Let's do this,' and you say, 'OK!'" I have no idea who could have possibly suggested this answer to her, but this is certain: Her answer reveals the secret of true "spiritual" obedience.

We need to hand ourselves over totally to the Holy Spirit, abandoned to him like the strings of a harp to the hand that strums them. Like good actors we need to keep our ear attentive to the voice of the hidden prompter, so that we may recite our part faultlessly in the play that is life. This is actually easier than we might think, for our prompter actually speaks within us, teaches us everything and is our instructor, our trainer, in every facet of our life. All we need is a simple inward glance, a movement of the heart, a prayer. Melito of Sardis was a saintly bishop who lived in the second century; of him we read this beautiful eulogy, and would it not be wonderful if it could be said of each one of us after we die: "Everything he did in life, he did in the Holy Spirit."[24]

Let us ask the Paraclete to guide our minds and lead us through the whole of our life, using these richly anointed words of a medieval author:

> *Holy Spirit, direct our mind,*
> *fill our heart, be words on lips that we open to you.*
> *You tell the festive bell to ring*
> *and prompt the singer of psalms to sing,*
> *Holiest of the holy,*
> *God of gods,*
> *joy, light, healing draught and life:*
> *praise be to you, with Father and Son,*
> *Spirit life-giver so kind. Amen.*[25]

---

[24] Eusebius of Caesarea, *Church History,* V.24.5.
[25] Rupert of Deutz, *Hymn to the Holy Spirit,* 13 (CM 29, p. 380).

XX

Through You May We the Father Know

The Holy Spirit enables us to cry out, Abba, Father!

1. From History to the Trinity

We come now to the last verse of the *Veni Creator* and start out on the final stage of our exploration of the Spirit. This is the verse:

> Through you may we the Father know,
> and through you know the Son as well,
> and may we always cling in faith
> to you, the Spirit of them both.

Up to now our meditations have been horizontal; this verse shifts the focus into the vertical plane. We are no longer looking at history or at the Church; we are not speaking of the enemy or of dangers or of the choices we have to make. In this last verse we move from the history of salvation (in the language of the Fathers, the *oikonomia*) onto the Trinitarian plane, the intimate life of God (the *theologia*). From what the Holy Spirit does in history, we pass to what the Holy Spirit is in the Trinity.

Our hymn does not follow the order of being in which the Spirit exists, but rather the order in which the Spirit becomes known to us. In the order of reality, first there is the Holy Spirit in his relationships within the Trinity; but in the order of the Spirit's manifestation, the Spirit's action in history comes first, and only then can we come to discover the Holy Spirit in the Trinity. The *Veni Creator* follows this historical order which is also the order we see in the Bible. In this regard, the author's approach comes across as particularly "modern."

What is new in the *Veni Creator,* however, is that even on this Trinitarian plane we are not left out; the character of the hymn as prayer is maintained, and in that we ourselves are involved, in a very deep way, in the relationships of the three divine Persons with each other. "Through you may *we* the Father know," and "through you may *we* know the Son as well." We are drawn into a triangle of relationships: the Holy Spirit, we, and the Father; the Holy Spirit, we, and the Son. There has been no cold, abstract speculation anywhere in this hymn, and neither is there any in this last verse either.

We are asking the Holy Spirit for something that Scripture tells us the Spirit accomplished in the first beginnings of the Christian faith. How, in fact, did the early Christian community come to believe in the Trinity? Some have put forward the theory that that belief grew under the influence of Hellenism and that the Trinity emerged as a product of the Greek way of thinking quite foreign to the Bible. But that view is utterly false. Belief in the Trinity was born out of experience. Christian believers, by grace of the Spirit, experienced God as Father and Jesus as Lord. It was the Holy Spirit within them, teaching them to speak to God as *Abba,* Father, and to know Jesus as *Kyrios,* Lord, who gave them the impetus to be open to this new idea of God as a communion of love between three Persons, Father, Son, and Holy Spirit.[1] An experience of that kind does not materialize out of thin air; it grew as a result of what Jesus had revealed concerning the Father and the Paraclete. In this matter John complements Paul.

In our own day we are taking part in the same process. Wherever the Holy Spirit's presence is felt in a new and powerful way, for example in what is called the baptism in the Spirit, those involved never fail to come to a new discovery of the Trinity. And that discovery is experiential, vital, and not any matter of abstract theology. Prayer becomes Trinitarian: The Father leads us to the Son, the Son sets us again on the way to the Father, and the Holy Spirit teaches us, like people who somehow have forgotten their mother-tongue, once again to say, *Abba* and *Marana-tha.* We have the feeling that we have been accepted into a family, that the members of the family love us, and that they really are eager to introduce us to all the others and that everyone has no end of happy things to tell of one another. It is a most moving experience, and it is shared by just about everyone who comes under the anointing touch of the Spirit.

---

[1] See J.G.D. Dunn, *Jesus and the Spirit* (London, 1975) 326.

Our aim in these, our last three reflections, would be nothing other than this: to abandon ourselves totally to the Holy Spirit so that the Spirit may lead us into this reality so alive and so throbbing with life that is the Trinity. But we, as Gregory Nazianzen said when he was preparing to speak on the Father and the Son, "are setting out in tiny little boats on the long voyage to the heavens, and of ourselves we have only tiny little sails to help us."[2] More than ever we have need of the help of the Holy Spirit.

2. The Holy Spirit Leads Us to Know God as the "Father of His Son Jesus Christ"

The New Testament makes a clear distinction between two different meanings of the word "father" when used in relation to God: "our Father" and "the Father of our Lord Jesus Christ"; or as Jesus expressed it, "my Father and your Father" (John 20:17). Both of these meanings are present in this line of the *Veni Creator.* In it we ask the Spirit to do two things: to make us know God as the Father of our Lord Jesus Christ, as "the eternal Father," and to make us know God as our "daddy," that is, to instill in us the kind of loving, confident relationship toward God that little children have toward their fathers. These two meanings of Father are linked; it is not possible to separate one from the other but neither can we confuse one with the other. We will, then, consider them one at a time, beginning with the Trinitarian meaning of the word.

In the New Testament the one prerogative of the Son that stands out above all others is that he knows the Father. Jesus again and again affirms, "I know the Father"[3] and he says too that "no one knows the Father except the Son and those to whom the Son chooses to reveal him" (Matt 11:27). How then can we ever think of asking the Holy Spirit to make us know the Father instead of asking Christ the Son directly? The answer is that it is the Holy Spirit who makes us know simply what the Son has revealed about the Father! He enables us to grasp and understand what Jesus has said about the Father. He takes the "outward" revelation that comes through the Word and makes it "inward" in us.

---

[2] Gregory Nazianzen, *Theological Poems,* 1 (PG 37.397).
[3] See John 7:29; 8:55; 10:15.

This answer is there already in the Gospel, and Tradition has served only to make it more explicit. When Jesus said that the Paraclete would teach the disciples "everything" (John 14:25), it is quite clear from the context that Jesus was referring, in the first place, to what he had been saying about the Father. One phrase stands out as especially significant: "The hour is coming when I will no longer speak to you in figures, but will tell you plainly of the Father" (John 16:25). When would he be able to speak to them in plain words, if those were among the last few words that he would be speaking to his disciples on earth? Only after Easter, when he would be speaking to them through his Spirit! In the same context he says clearly, "I still have many things to say to you, but you cannot bear them now. When the Spirit of truth comes, he will guide you into all the truth" (John 16:12-13).

Here too we see how "all the truth" refers in the first place to the complete revelation of the Father. The knowledge of the Father that the Paraclete will give is knowledge of a very special kind: It not only lets us "know" the Father, but it also places our very "being" in the Father: "We can know that we abide in him and he in us, because he has given us of his Spirit" (1 John 4:13). To know the Father in this way is "eternal life" itself (see John 17:3).

Paul too, speaks of this role of the Spirit in relation to our knowledge of God, though in other terms:

> The Spirit searches everything, even the depths of God. For what human being knows what is truly human except the human spirit that is within? So also no one comprehends what is truly God's except the Spirit of God. Now we have received not the spirit of the world, but the Spirit that is from God so that we may understand the gifts bestowed on us by God (1 Cor 2:10b-12).

Now among these "depths" or "secrets" of God, it is quite easy to see that the first and greatest of them all is the intimate life of God himself, the mystery of the Trinity. There is, says the apostle, an inviolable area of our being that no one can enter by any means whatever, unless we ourselves by our own free choice open the way from within. It is the same for God: The secret of his inward life is known only to the Holy Spirit who is within God, and can be revealed by him alone.

Let us turn now to see how this role of the Spirit regarding the knowledge of the Father has been understood and experienced in Tradition. Saint Irenaeus writes, "The Holy Spirit gets us ready to receive the Son of God, and the Son then takes us to the Father."[4] Saint Basil takes up the idea and develops it in a way that will influence all the Church's subsequent reflection:

> The way of the knowledge of God proceeds from the one Spirit through the only Son to the one Father; and in the other direction the goodness of nature, sanctification that follows on nature and the royal dignity that is conferred, all proceed from the Father, through the Only-begotten, to the Spirit.[5]

At times this biblical idea took on the Platonic tinge prevalent in the cultural ambience. This is evident in Basil himself, where he writes: "The Paraclete, like a sun lighting up the view for a healthy eye, will show you in himself the Image of the invisible, and as with great delight you contemplate that Image, you will see the inexpressible beauty of the Archetype."[6]

In this philosophical view, the Spirit is seen above all as the movement of return to the One, and himself constitutes that return, in as much as it is the Spirit that gives knowledge of the Father. Creatures "receive from God the Spirit through whom they know God."[7]

This line of thought traces a clear path in Tradition and is represented in the West by Hilary, Ambrose, and others,[8] and we can see that the author of the *Veni Creator* also followed it, in the line that we are now considering. But on this point too, the words he has used in the hymn prove to be "open structures." On the one hand they recall the whole biblical and patristic tradition and sum it up neatly, but at the same time they succeed in giving them new shades of meaning.

---

[4] Irenaeus, *Against the Heresies,* IV.20.5.

[5] Basil the Great, *On the Holy Spirit,* XVIII.47 (PG 32.153).

[6] Ibid., IX.23 (PG 32.109).

[7] Marius Victorinus, *On the Letter to the Galatians,* II.4.9 (CSEL 83.2, p. 146).

[8] See Hilary of Poitiers, *The Trinity,* II.1.35 (CC 62, p. 71); Ambrose, *On the Holy Spirit,* II.12.130.

What are we, today, asking of the Holy Spirit when we ask him to make us know the Father? The things that are our chief concerns are no longer the same as those that preoccupied Saint Basil and other Fathers. For them the main problem was how to show that the three divine Persons were three in one nature and that the Holy Spirit was a divine Person ("If he is able to make us know the Father, it can only be because he is of the same nature as the Father"). A more radical problem faces us today: Will we maintain the Trinitarian perspective of the Christian faith, or will we fall short of it? There are fairly strong and widespread tendencies in theology today to marginalize the Trinitarian dimension on the pretext that its derivation is Hellenist, or as a means of facilitating dialogue with other monotheistic religions.

The re-awakening of Christians to the reality of the Spirit is also a Trinitarian revival. This in fact highlights the most reliable standard by which to gauge the quality of a theology of the Spirit: Is it open or is it closed to the Trinitarian perspective? In some of the smaller churches and sects the teaching on the Spirit seems at times, at least in language and in practice, to show signs of a latent binitarianism: Jesus Christ and his Spirit and that is all. The Father, to all intents and purposes, is out of the picture.

We face yet another problem today concerning the Father in which the Holy Spirit will help us to a peaceful resolution, and it is in the use of the very term "father" in reference to God. As we well know, this usage is energetically contested by the feminist movement. If we know how to read it, this sign of the times can, as always, be an opportunity for a great enrichment of our theological insight and it need not end up in sterile polemics. At the very least it can spur us on to clear the term of the residue of masculinism with which the influences of the dominant cultural mindset have inevitably loaded it. We in our day have a clearer awareness that the word "father" should not be taken in the strictly literal sense when we use it to refer to God. If we could invent a term that in one word conveyed the meaning of both "father" and "mother" at the same time (as the Greeks invented *huiospator* to describe a divine being who is both "son and father"),[9] there would be no reason why, in principle, we should not use that term to translate the biblical word

[9] See G.W.H. Lampe, *A Patristic Greek Lexicon* (Oxford, 1968) 1426.

"father." God comes before any distinction of male and female, and God cannot in any sense be said to be the *synthesis* of mother and father. God is, rather, the transcendent *source* of both realities.

The Holy Spirit, we see, is also using the feminist movement to guide the Church a little farther along in its ceaseless journey toward "the whole truth" about God the Father. The problem aside, the principle remains: If it should one day be necessary or opportune to put some other word in place of the biblical "father" (the ongoing evolution of Christian faith-awareness will determine that), it remains true that even now, in the way we "translate" or understand the biblical word, we cannot ignore the understanding that is evolving in the modern cultural context without being unfaithful to the original and profound sense of the term.

Saint John, speaking to all Christians, said:

> I write to you, children,
>   because you know the Father.
> I write to you, fathers,
>   because you know him who is from the beginning
>   (1 John 2:14).

In his view, the most beautiful gift that could be given, to the young or to the mature, to children or to human parents, was to know the one who above all was "Father," the one "from whom every paternity in heaven and on earth takes its name" (see Eph 3:15). In the words of the *Veni Creator,* this is what we are asking the Holy Spirit to do: to carry on making the parents and children of our own day know God in this way. While Jesus was on earth Philip asked him, "Lord, show us the Father, and we will be satisfied" (John 14:8). We, today, need to be asking the Holy Spirit to do the same for us.

3. The Holy Spirit Helps Us to Know God as "Our Father"

Saint Paul has a number of ways to describe the new life that bursts into being from Christ's Passover. For him, however, the central element, the pivotal reality, is always the work that the Holy Spirit accomplishes in the depths of our human heart when the Spirit leads us to discover that God is our own Father and that we are God's own children. "Because you are children, God has sent the Spirit of his Son into our hearts, crying, 'Abba! Father!'"[10]

The work of the Holy Spirit in this is simply the continuation of what the Spirit did before in Jesus of Nazareth. For it was in fact in the Holy Spirit that Jesus, as man, came to discover and to experience his own relationship as Son with the Father more and more and with deeper insight. When he was baptized in the Jordan and the voice proclaimed him, "My Son, the beloved," the Holy Spirit came down in that same moment, "descending like a dove and alighting on him" (Matt 3:16-17). It was always the Spirit who moved Jesus Christ in the depths of his human heart to cry *Abba*. The Gospel itself assures us that it was so, where it says, "Jesus rejoiced in the Holy Spirit and said, 'I thank you, Father, Lord of heaven and earth . . .'" (Luke 10:21).

The Holy Spirit continues now to carry out in the members what the Spirit did in the Head, but with an important difference. The members also come to experience that they are children of God, but this experience of theirs is not exactly parallel to that of Christ: rather, it depends on Christ's and it is something that Christ shares with them. In other words, believers experience God as their Father in the sense that he is the Father of Jesus with whom, in the Holy Spirit, they have a share in this relationship with the Father as his Child. The "Spirit of God" prompted the experience of sonship in Jesus; the "Spirit of Christ" prompts now in us the experience of our relationship as children of the Father.

How can we say that the Spirit, coming into, can cry *Abba* to God the Father? The Spirit is not "begotten" of the Father, but rather "proceeds" from God. How then can the Spirit call God "Father"? The explanation is simple: The Spirit cries *Abba* because when the Word became Flesh, the Spirit became the Spirit of the Son. As the Spirit of the Son in his human nature the Spirit is, if we may so say it, "acclimatized" to human existence and now comes to us through Christ's paschal mystery. The Spirit acts "as would a mother, teaching her baby to say, 'daddy,' and she repeats that name to her baby until the baby becomes so used to calling 'daddy' that it can call even in its sleep."[11]

---

[10] Gal 4:6; see Rom 8:15-16.
[11] Diadochus of Photike, *On Spiritual Perfection*, 61 (SCh 5, p. 121).

As the wife and not the child of her husband, the mother would not be able to say "daddy" on her own account. But she identifies with her baby and teaches and encourages it. And that is what the Paraclete does for us.

The knowledge of the Father that the Holy Spirit gives us in this way is knowledge of a very special kind. It is the kind that was meant by the word "knowledge" in the Bible. For the Greeks, the knowledge of God meant pure contemplation in the highest degree of abstraction, but for the Jews it consisted essentially in a concrete mutual relationship with God: to experience in time what God wants for human beings, to listen, and to obey God's commands.

To know God as Father, therefore, consists in a recognition, an awareness, an experience of God as our real Father. We know well what the term means in an expression like, "He knew his wife," or, "Know the loss of a child" (see Isa 47:8). Something of the same sort holds true here. In the order of nature it is the prompting of the blood-relationship that makes a little child recognize its own father in a crowd of thousands. In the spiritual order, it is the prompting of the Spirit. And an experience of "knowing" in this way usually goes along with a surge of "exultation," a happy trembling to the roots of one's being, as we know happened to Jesus from the text we saw earlier.

"Blessed are those who know the Father," exclaimed Tertullian when he was commenting on the opening words of the Our Father.[12] Such knowledge does in fact make one blessed and happy, feel secure and invincible. It makes a radical change to the way one feels about oneself; it gives one a whole new identity as a daughter or son of God. We have a most moving example of this in the life of Saint Margaret of Cortona. After her conversion she went through a period of terrible desolation. It seemed to her that God was angry with her, and at times God brought back memories to her, one after another, of every painful detail of all the sins she had ever committed, until all she wanted was to disappear, to cease to be. One day after holy communion she quite unexpectedly heard a voice saying within her, "My daughter!" She who had been able to stand the vision of all her sins could not sustain the sweetness of this voice and was rapt in ecstasy. And those

[12] Tertullian, *On Prayer,* 2.3 (CC 1, p. 258).

who were there and saw what happened tell that while she was in ecstasy, she said, over and over, quite beside herself with joy, "He said I am his daughter! Oh, infinite sweetness of my God! Oh word that I have for so long longed to hear! So tenaciously prayed for! Word whose delight is greater than all delights! Ocean of joy! 'My daughter': that is what my God said, 'My daughter'!"[13]

This will give us some idea of what the experience of knowing that we are a child of God will mean, if we live it to the full. The saints show us full-blown and fast-flowering what is happening in every believer, even though in us its bloom may be weaker and the pace of its unfolding slower.

In an earlier chapter when we were speaking of the Holy Spirit as the "new law," we gave a theological explanation of this work that the Spirit does in us. As long as we live under the rule of sin, subjects of the law, God seems to us to be a severe taskmaster; we look on him as one who does not want us to know the satisfaction of fulfilled desire, and makes it clear with his peremptory commands, "Thou shalt" and "Thou shalt not." As long as we are in that condition we do not want to listen and a dark, underhand resentment against God grows in the depths of our heart. It seems to us that God is quite against us being happy, and if it were up to us, we would be content if God ceased to exist.[14]

The first thing that the Holy Spirit does upon coming into us is to make us see God in a different way. The Spirit shows us the true face of God. The Spirit leads us to discover that God is on our side, a friend, one who, for our sake, "did not withhold his own Son" (Rom 8:32), in fact a most loving father. The true childlike attitude blossoms in us, and spontaneously we give expression to it in the cry, *Abba!* Father! As though to say, "I didn't know you. I thought I did but it was only hearsay. Now I know you. I know who you are, and that you really love me, and that you really do have my own good at heart." Where there was a slave before, there is now a child of the family. Where there was fear, there is now love. And this is in fact what happens, in a real, personal and existential way, in those who are "reborn in the Spirit."

---

[13] Giunta Bevegnati, *Life and Miracles of St. Margaret of Cortona,* II.6, ed. Vicenza (1978) 19.

[14] See Luther, *Sermon of Pentecost* (WA 12, p. 569).

In our day a new and difficult field has opened up, a need that cries out for this secret, inward work of the Holy Spirit. That "underhand resentment" against God has spread like a contagion among us on a global scale. No longer because of the law that God imposes, but because of the suffering that God allows. There are many who say that after Auschwitz we no longer have any reason for calling God "Father." Nothing short of the Holy Spirit working in a powerful way will enable us in this modern age to get over this kind of obstacle that no theological reasoning seems able to move. This is the greatest of the healings that we should expect from the Holy Spirit through the wind of Pentecost blowing again in our day. Our minds are not merely "inadequate" to grasp the realities of God, but the very mindset of our age is hostile, in rebellion against God.

We already have an indication of how the Holy Spirit is answering this need: by revealing to believers that God is suffering too! As the Bible reveals to us a God who in the very depths of his being is love, it reveals at the same time "that God suffers the pains of love."[15] God suffers because of the very nature of love, for to love is to be vulnerable. "There is no living in love without some sorrow."[16]

This is a new chapter that theology is only beginning to explore, one that cannot be seen except in conjunction with the work of the Paraclete. It is the way the Holy Spirit is working in our day at his task of leading us into the "whole truth" concerning the Father. It is significant that the first mention of the theme of "God's suffering" in the documents of the magisterium is found in an encyclical on the Holy Spirit, and that its revelation is explicitly attributed to the action of the Paraclete who "convinces the world of sin."[17]

The Holy Spirit is not confined merely to correcting our knowledge of the Father where it has become distorted by sin and the way we are inclined to look on the suffering of the innocent. The Spirit does more, by giving us access to the intimate mystery of God, drawing us in, in a way, into the intimate circle of relationships of

---

[15] Origen, *Homilies on Ezekiel*, 6.6 (GCS 1925, p. 384).
[16] *The Imitation of Christ*, III.5.7.
[17] See John Paul II, Encyclical *Dominum et Vivificantem*, 39.

Father, Son, and Spirit. By him, "your life is hidden with Christ in God" (see Col 3:3). The mystics assure us that it is so.[18]

4. Make Us Know the Father's Love!

Finally, what is it that we ask of the Spirit when we pray, "Through you may we the Father know"? This, above all, is what we ask for: "Make us know *the Father's love!*" This is the Paraclete's most special and important task: to pour the love of God into our hearts; to give us not just an abstract knowledge of that love but to make us feel it and really live it. Of all the prayers that we could pray to the Spirit, this is the most important, the most essential: "Let us know how much the Father loves us, and we will need nothing more!"

In the language of the Bible, to know God always means, as we have seen, to fulfill God's requirements, to listen and obey God's commands. And therefore, when we ask the Spirit to make us know the Father, we are also asking the Spirit to "make us know *the Father's will!*" For it is in fact through the Holy Spirit that God's will is made known to us (see Eph 1:9).

> The mystery of the will of God is the most sublime of all mysteries. . . . It is not merely something that belongs to God, but it is precisely God himself, in as much as it is the Holy Spirit himself who in substance is the will of God. . . . Therefore, when the Holy Spirit enters into a person, he reveals himself as the will of God for the person to whom he manifests himself, and he does not manifest himself anywhere except where he himself is present.[19]

It follows, then, that no one at all really knows the will of God for me except the Holy Spirit who has been given to me, and it is from the Spirit alone that I must come to know it. In order to do that, I must take properly into account all the criteria, subjective as well as objective, that are needed for a true spiritual discernment.

By the Holy Spirit's action in us the Spirit gives form to every aspect of our relationship with the Father, and not only to our

---

[18] See John of the Cross, *Spiritual Canticle,* A.38.

[19] William of St. Thierry, *The Mirror of Faith,* 61 (SCh 301, p. 128).

obedience to God's will. Just as obedience to the Father becomes an obedience in the Holy Spirit, so too does our suffering become a suffering in the Spirit, our adoration becomes an adoration in the Spirit, our contemplation becomes a contemplation in the Spirit, and our prayer becomes prayer in the Spirit.

On this matter of prayer we may ask why it is that among all that we ask for in the Our Father the Holy Spirit does not figure. There is so evidently a gap there that, in ancient times, there was an attempt to remedy it by inserting, in place of "may your kingdom come," the words, "may your Holy Spirit come upon us and purify us." Several manuscripts have it in that form, and so do several of the ancient Christian writers.[20] However, there is a simpler explanation. We do not ask for the Holy Spirit because the Spirit is the one who prays all the petitions! Paul tells us that it is only by the Holy Spirit coming into us that we can say, *Abba,* Father! And what is that, if it is not the opening cry of the Our Father? It is, then, the Holy Spirit who starts the Our Father in us every time we say that prayer.

The Spirit is the only one who can lead us into the mystery of this prayer, taking us beyond the mere mouthing of words. In the first of these reflections we were looking at the Holy Spirit as the mystery both "tremendous and fascinating," of power and of tenderness. Through the Our Father the Spirit opens us to know God the Father as the mystery of utter transcendence and also of intimate closeness. The opening words of the Our Father show us God as our dad who loves us most tenderly, one to whom we can turn with all the uninhibited confidence of little children. But the next phrase, reminding us that the Father is "in heaven," makes us aware that God is all-powerful, great, holy, as far above us as the heavens are above the earth (see Isa 55:9), in whose care we may know that we are absolutely protected, utterly safe. Father, but omnipotent; omnipotent, but Father: this shows us the true, complete Christian concept of God. A God who is as "fatherly" as can be, but quite the opposite of a softy or a sweetie-pie.

That is what the Holy Spirit led Jesus himself to experience when he was prompted to cry out, "I thank you, Father, Lord of heaven and earth" (Luke 10:21). "Father," but also "Lord of heaven

---

[20] See K. Aland, *Synopsis Quattuor Evangeliorum* (Stuttgart, 1967) 86 *(apparatus criticus).*

and earth!" The Our Father is simply the ever-widening ripple of the prayer of Jesus Christ himself spreading through the ages, spreading over the sea of humankind, from the head to every member of the body. In the *Veni Creator* we ask the Holy Spirit to give us knowledge of the Father: All of that knowledge is summed up in the Our Father.

Saint Ignatius of Antioch, on his way to Rome where he knew he was to suffer martyrdom, wrote, "I feel within myself a living water, murmuring and saying, 'Come to the Father!'"[21] That is the way the Holy Spirit goes to work, bringing about the "return of all creatures to God," drawing them to the Father, giving rise in them to a longing for him, putting into the hearts of the redeemed a burning desire to see his face. The Holy Spirit is "the ladder of our ascent to God."[22]

A few pages earlier we recalled the words of the medieval author, William of Saint Thierry. Let us end this reflection with his magnificent cry of praise to the Holy Spirit, where he emphasizes especially the role of the Holy Spirit in bringing us to the knowledge of God:

> *Hurry, then, to have a share in the Holy Spirit.*
> *He is present when you call on him,*
> *and if you call on him it is because he is present in you.*
> *He is the rushing river that brings joy to the city of God.*
> *He will show you what God the Father keeps hidden*
> *from the learned and the wise of this world.*
> *God is Spirit and those who adore him must adore in spirit and*
>   *in truth,*
> *so too it is fitting that those who long to understand him and to*
>   *know him*
> *must seek in the Holy Spirit alone*
> *the insight of faith and the meaning of Truth pure and simple.*
> *In the darkness and ignorance of this life, to the poor in spirit,*
> *he is light that enlightens,*
> *he is love that enraptures,*
> *he is gentleness most moving,*
> *he is our access to God,*
> *he is the love of the one who loves,*
> *he is dedication, he is devotion.*[23]

---

[21] Ignatius of Antioch, *Letter to the Romans*, 7.2.

[22] Irenaeus, *Against the Heresies*, III.24.1.

[23] William of St. Thierry, *The Mirror of Faith*, 71–2 (SCh 301, p. 138).

XXI

Through You May We Know
the Son As Well

The Holy Spirit teaches us to proclaim that Jesus is Lord

In the Sacred Scriptures, the Holy Spirit never puts himself forward proclaiming his own name; the Spirit is always revealing, telling of, the Father or the Son. The Spirit does not teach us to call on him, *Ruach,* by his own name, but rather to cry, *Abba,* that is, Father, or *Marana-tha,* that is, Come, Lord Jesus! The Spirit is revealed by making the other two Persons known. The Spirit, the Unknown, is the one who makes everything known. In this we see how the symbols of wind and light are particularly apt as expressions of the characteristics of the Spirit. We cannot see the wind itself, but we do see what it does: it bends the trees, whistles through the branches, stirs up waves on the sea. Light, too: though it is by means of light that we see all that we see, we do not see light itself: that remains hidden. Again, if the lamp is at our shoulder, a little behind us, we see things very well, but if the lamp is in front of our eyes, we see nothing; it dazzles us.

The Holy Spirit, if we may say so, is "God behind the scenes"; the Spirit prompts, reveals, but remains out of sight. But it is precisely by working in this way that we gain an understanding of who the Spirit is. Saint Basil, with penetrating insight, offers this explanation: You see the reason why you are able to see, in the very act of seeing what you see. When the Spirit reveals the Son to us—who is the image of God and the splendor of God's glory—the Paraclete is revealed.

> It is not possible to see the image of the invisible God except by the light of the Spirit. When we fix our gaze on an image, it is simply not possible to separate out the light, because we must necessarily see that by which we see at the same time as we see what we see. Thus it is by the illumination of the Spirit

that we are able to see in a clear and accurate way the splendour of the glory of God![1]

And so, when we pray, "and through you come to know the Son
as well," we are asking the Spirit to carry out this task in us, giving
the light that will let us see the face of Christ with our own eyes.

1. He Will Bear Witness to Me

Let us see first of all what the New Testament has to say about
the Spirit as the principle, the source, of our knowledge of Christ.
Before we read any explicit statements referring to it, this role of
the Spirit is evident in the actual events. When the Spirit came at
Pentecost, the meaning of the whole life and work of Christ suddenly became clear, and immediately Peter was able to proclaim
Jesus "both Lord and Messiah" (Acts 2:36).

Paul declares that it was by the work of the Holy Spirit that Jesus
Christ, in his resurrection, "was declared to be Son of God with
power" (Rom 1:4). No one is able to say, "Jesus is Lord," except by
the inward enlightening of the Holy Spirit (1 Cor 12:3). According
to what we read in the Letter to the Ephesians, it is to the Holy
Spirit that Paul attributes the knowledge of the mystery of Christ
that has been given to him and to all the holy apostles and prophets
(Eph 3:4-5). It is only "through his Spirit . . . that you may have
the power to comprehend, with all the saints, what is the breadth
and length and height and depth and to know the love of Christ that
surpasses knowledge" (Eph 3:16-19).

In John's Gospel Jesus himself tells of this work that the Paraclete will do in his regard. The Spirit will take what belongs to
Christ and proclaim it to the disciples; the Spirit will remind them
of all that Jesus has said; the Spirit will lead them into the fullness
of truth concerning his relationship with the Father; the Spirit will
bear witness to Christ. This last point will in fact, from Gospel
times and forever, be the main criterion by which we may know
whether we have to do with the true Spirit of God or with some
other spirit: Does the Spirit prompt and empower us to acknowledge Jesus come in the flesh? (see 1 John 4:2-3).

---

[1] Basil the Great, *On the Holy Spirit,* XVI.64 (PG 32.185).

Already in the pages of the New Testament we see the patterns emerging of two kinds of knowledge of Christ, or two different ways in which the Spirit works. We can come to know Christ in an *objective way,* becoming aware of his being, his person, his mystery. We can also come to know him in a more inward, personal, and *subjective way:* a kind of knowledge that has more to do with what "he does for me" than with what "he is in himself." These two kinds of knowledge are inseparable and we are often aware of both at the same time, but nevertheless they are distinct. Paul usually focuses on the knowledge of what Christ has done for us, on the way he works in us, and in particular on the paschal mystery. John, on the other hand, is more concerned with the knowledge of what Christ is: the eternal Logos who was with God, who is of one being with the Father, and who came to us in the flesh (John 10:30).

Yet it was only as a result of later developments that these two tendencies stand out clearly. We will sketch the way the development took place as briefly as we can, because it will help us appreciate what the Holy Spirit is doing in our own day for the Church in this regard.

In the patristic era, the Holy Spirit was seen above all as the guarantor of the apostolic tradition concerning Jesus, against the innovations of Gnostic teaching in his regard. Saint Irenaeus says, "The gift of God which is the Holy Spirit was entrusted to the Church: all those who with their false doctrines deviate from the truth preached by the Church have no part in that gift."[2] Tertullian says that the apostolic churches could not have erred in what they preached as truth, for to think otherwise would be the same as saying "that the Holy Spirit, for whom Jesus asked and whom the Father granted as teacher of the truth and who was sent by Christ for that very purpose, the one who speaks and acts for Christ and who carries forward the work of Christ, could not have been adequate to fulfill his own task."[3]

In the era of the great disputes on points of dogma, the Holy Spirit was seen as the guardian of the orthodox teaching on Christ. The acts of the ancient ecumenical councils show that the Church

---

[2] See Irenaeus, *Against the Heresies,* III.24.1–2.
[3] Tertullian, *Prescription Against the Heretics,* 28.1 (CC 1, p. 209).

has the unshakable certainty of being "inspired" by the Spirit in its formulations of the truth concerning the two natures of Christ, the unicity of his Person and the complete perfection of his humanity. The stress is clearly on the kind of knowledge of Christ that is objective, ecclesial, and able to be expressed in dogmatic formulas.

This tendency remained predominant in theology until the time of the Reformation, yet with a difference. When they were first formulated these dogmas were vital questions, fruit of a very lively participation and closely bound up with the whole life of the Church and especially with the liturgy. Once the formulas had come to be accepted and passed on as normal teaching, they tended to lose the bite of urgency and to become merely formal. "Two natures, one Person" had become a neat little ready-made axiom; it was no longer experienced as the final solution to a long and painful struggle. Throughout this time there was certainly no lack of outstanding examples of the experience of an intimate, personal knowledge of Christ, full of warmth and devotion, yet they did not have any great influence on theology.

The Protestant Reformers broke free of this situation and said, "To know Christ means to know the blessings he brings, not to analyze his natures or the ways of the incarnation."[4] The Christ "for me" leapt suddenly into the forefront. The objective, dogmatic knowledge of Christ was contrasted against the intimate and subjective kind of knowledge. Where the main focus had been on the testimony of the Church and of the Scriptures concerning Jesus, the foreground was now taken by the "inward testimony" to Jesus given by the Holy Spirit in the heart of each individual believer. This was a theological novelty that in time also tended to lose its vital urgency and emerge as a Protestant orthodoxy. Periodically movements arose, like Pietism and Methodism, to put new life into what had come to be seen as "lifeless orthodoxy." In these movements true conversion is achieved when, moved by the Holy Spirit, we realize that Jesus "died for me," personally for me, that "I can call the Savior mine."[5]

---

[4] P. Melanchthon, *Loci theologici,* in *Corpus Reformatorum,* XXI (Brunswick, 1854) 85.

[5] C. Wesley, Hymn *Glory to God and Praise and Love.*

To complete this rapid historical tour, we take a look at a third phase in our way of understanding the relationship between the Holy Spirit and the knowledge of Christ, characteristic of the age of Enlightenment of which we are direct heirs. A detached, objective kind of knowledge had come once again into favor: not, however, an ontological kind of knowing as in antiquity, but rather one based on history. In other words, the interest was focused not on who Jesus Christ is in himself (his pre-existence, his natures, his person), but rather on who he was in historical reality. This is the age of research into what the scholars call "the historical Jesus"!

In this, the rationalist phase, the Holy Spirit is no longer considered as fulfilling any role in our coming to know Christ; the Spirit has no part in it at all. The "inward testimony" of the Holy Spirit has come to be identified with the human spirit and with reason. The "external testimony" alone has any importance, but that is no longer considered as having anything to do with the Church's apostolic witness; it is merely a matter of history and we come to it only through the various critical methods available to us. The presupposition common to all efforts of this kind was that, to find the true Christ, we need to look outside of the Church and to cut Christ loose from "the wrappings of ecclesiastical dogma."

We know the outcome of all this research into the historical Jesus. It failed, although this is not saying that it did not produce many positive results. There was, and in this regard there still is, a basic misconception. Jesus Christ and certain other great historical figures, but to a lesser degree, like Francis of Assisi, not only lived in history; they also created a history, and now live on in the history that they created, as a sound carries on in the sound wave it causes. It seems that the rationalist historians set out to separate him from the history he created and to put him back into the common and universal history, though this is like saying that one can better appreciate a sound if you detach it from the wave that carries it. The history that Jesus created, or the wave that he sent out, is the faith of the Church enlivened by the Holy Spirit. This does not do away with the legitimacy of normal historical research about Jesus, but normal human research needs perhaps to be a little more aware of its limitations, and recognize that what it achieves does not exhaust all that can possibly be known of Christ.

2. The Surpassing Knowledge of Christ

In the first fifty years of the twentieth century, theology left aside the so-called historical Jesus in favor of the Christ of dogma and of the Church (Barth), or in favor of the Christ "for me," the Christ of the kerygma (Bultmann). In the second fifty years theology was characterized by the search for continuity between the Jesus of history on the one hand and the Christ of the faith on the other.

All saw the chief cause of the difficulty in the weak and unsatisfactory state of the theology of the Spirit which was not up to the task of bringing light to the theological understanding of Christ and assisting in it. But the difficulty was in how to overcome that weakness. At the end of his classical work on the history of Christian exegesis, de Lubac concluded that we moderns do not have the means to practice the spiritual reading of the Bible that was typical of the Fathers. We lack the hearty verve of their faith, the sense of the fullness and the unity of the Scriptures that they enjoyed. If we were today to try to imitate their audacity, we would be open to the risk of profanation, since we lack the spirit that sparks such insights.[6] However, he did not entirely shut out the possibility of hope, and in another work he says that "if we want to rediscover something of the spiritual way the Scriptures were interpreted in the early centuries of the Church, we need first of all to set up the same kind of spiritual movement again."[7]

What de Lubac had to say on the matter of the spiritual understanding of the Scriptures applies, for the most part, to the spiritual knowledge of Christ. There is no need to write new and more up-to-date theologies of the Spirit. If we lack the support of a lived experience of the Spirit such as was common in the fourth century when the theology of the Spirit was first developed, whatever we achieve will still be wide of the mark and short of solving the problem. We will not have the conditions needed to lift us to the level on which the Paraclete's tasks are carried out: that daring, that "sober inebriation of the Spirit" of which we can read in almost all of the authors of that time. We will not be able to show forth Christ under the anointing of the Spirit if we ourselves do not in some way live under that same anointing.

[6] See H. de Lubac, *Exégèse Médiévale*, II.2 (Paris, 1964) 79.
[7] H. de Lubac, *Histoire et esprit* (Paris, 1950) 394–5.

Now, in our own time, the great new thing for which de Lubac envisaged the need has actually come about. The twentieth century saw the rise and the immense spread of a "spiritual movement" that has provided the basis for a renewal of the theology of the Spirit rooted in the experience of the Spirit and the Spirit's charisms. The Pentecostal and charismatic phenomenon of our own time has come to be recognized as the spiritual movement of the vastest proportions and most rapid growth ever known in the whole history of the Church. It started less than a century ago, and has grown from zero to involve hundreds of millions of people. In the light of this fact, it is difficult not to recognize the prophetic character of words written by that servant of God, the great Hispanic mystic Conchita, in the years 1916 to 1918, before anyone had spoken of a new Pentecost. It is the Son, Jesus, who says,

> On sending to the world a new Pentecost, I want it inflamed, purified, illuminated by the light and the fire of the Holy Spirit. The last stage of the world must be marked very specially by the effusion of the Holy Spirit. He must reign in hearts and the entire world, not so much for the glory of His Person as for making the Father loved and bearing testimony to me, although His glory is that of the whole Trinity.
>
> He will come, I will send Him again clearly manifest in His effects, which will astonish the world and impel the Church to holiness.[8]

Before Conchita another lady, the Blessed Elena Guerra, had written that, just as once "Jesus had shown his Heart to humankind, so now would he show his Spirit."[9]

In its first fifty years this movement paid little attention to theology and was, in its turn, ignored by theologians. However, when the movement found its way into churches that possessed vast theological resources and had there basically been accepted by the various hierarchies, theology could no longer ignore it. In a work entitled *The Rediscovery of the Spirit: Experience and Theology of the Holy Spirit,* the foremost theologians of the time, Catholic and

---

[8] Diary, 26 January 1916 and 27 September 1918, quoted in M. M. Philipon, *A Mother's Spiritual Diary* (New York: Alba House, 1978) 211–2.

[9] Quoted in D. M. Abrescia, *Elena Guerra: Profetismo e rinnovamento* (Brescia, 1970) 63.

Protestant, set out to examine the significance of the Pentecostal and charismatic phenomenon for a reappraisal of the doctrine of the Holy Spirit.[10] Congar devoted a whole section of his work on the Holy Spirit to it.[11] In various ways almost all who have written on the theology of the Spirit in recent times have done the same,[12] not to mention the innumerable books and articles that have come from within the ranks of the movement itself.

All of this is of interest to us now, only from the point of view of knowing Christ. What sort of knowledge of Christ is emerging in this new spiritual and theological atmosphere? The point of outstanding significance is not any new discovery about Christ—new themes, new insights or methodologies—but the rediscovery of the elementary biblical fact that "Jesus Christ is Lord"! Saint Paul speaks of a kind of knowledge of Christ that "nothing will outweigh"; he calls it in fact the "supreme advantage," and it consists in knowing him and proclaiming him as "Lord" (Phil 3:8). It is that proclamation that, together with faith in the risen Christ, makes a person "saved" (Rom 10:9). And it is the Holy Spirit that makes it possible to know Christ in this way. "No one can say, 'Jesus is Lord' except by the Holy Spirit" (1 Cor 12:3). Anyone, even without the Holy Spirit, can pronounce the words, "Jesus is Lord," but in that case it wouldn't be enough to make a person "saved."

What is special about this affirmation that makes it so decisive? There are several explanations, depending on the point of approach, whether subjective or objective. The *objective power* in the words "Jesus is Lord" comes from the fact that they make history, and in particular the paschal mystery, present to us now. The words state with clarity the conclusion that shines out from two events: Christ died for our sins and he rose from the dead to justify us, and that is why he is Lord. "For to this end Christ died and lived again, so that he might be Lord of both the dead and the living" (Rom 14:9).

The events that led up to it are, so to say, contained within this conclusion, and when it is proclaimed the events are rendered present to us and work their effect in us. "Jesus is Lord" is the

---

[10] See *Erfahrung und Theologie des Heiligen Geistes* (München, 1974).

[11] Y. Congar, *I Believe in the Holy Spirit*, vol. 2, part III (New York, 1983).

[12] See J. Moltmann, *Der Geist des Lebens* (München, 1991) passim; M. Welker, *Gottes Geist* (Neukirchen-Vluyn, 1993) 15.

that deliberately leaves aside all reference to the Holy Spirit cannot attain to anything but the "dead" Jesus of history, and we have seen that this was in fact the case.

On this point I feel I ought to offer my own little bit of personal testimony. I am encouraged to do this by that great poet of the Holy Spirit, Simeon the New Theologian. He said that if a rich man gave a penny to a beggar and the beggar ran off to tell all the others so that they too came crowding to the rich man clamoring for a penny, the rich man would surely be irritated, but with the Lord things are different. The Lord would be irritated if the beggar did not run off and tell all the others, so that they too should come to receive something from him.[14]

So then, let me tell that I used to teach the history of Christian origins at the Catholic University of Milan. My doctoral thesis in theology was on the christology of Tertullian, and the study of the christological doctrines of antiquity continued to be the main focus of my research and my teaching. Yet I became aware of something that made me uneasy. When I was speaking of Jesus in the lecture halls, he became a subject of research. As in all historical research, the researcher needs to master his subject and remain neutral in regard to it. But how could it be possible to "master" *this* subject and how would it ever be possible to remain neutral toward it? How could one reconcile that with the Jesus one called on in prayer and received each morning in the Eucharist?

The discovery of Jesus as "Lord" that came to me along with the baptism in the Spirit wrought a great change that I would never have been able to achieve by myself alone. It seemed to me that I became able to see what lay behind Saint Paul's experience, when all at once he began to consider as "disadvantage" all the things that before he had looked upon as the "advantages" he had enjoyed in life, and as "so much rubbish" everything other than "the supreme advantage of knowing Christ Jesus my Lord." I saw all at once what boundless gratitude, what pride and joy were hidden in that phrase of his, in that pronoun in the singular, "Christ Jesus *my* Lord."

I knew so many things about Jesus: doctrines and heresies and explanations ancient and new. But when I read Paul's exclamation

---

[14] See Simeon, the New Theologian, *Catecheses*, 34 (SCh 113, p. 276).

in this context, "I want to know him" (Phil 3:10), that simple little "him" seemed to me to contain infinitely more than all the books I had ever read or written. For Christ is in fact the living Jesus, the risen one who is alive in the Spirit: not theories and doctrines about Jesus, but Jesus himself.

Later, reflecting on this experience, I remembered that Thomas Aquinas had said, "The object of faith is not the statement, but the reality."[15] I remembered also the reorientation set in train in philosophy early in the twentieth century: "Back to the things in themselves."[16] The "thing," the reality to which we turn in this case is Christ alive in the Spirit, the one and only truly "existing" reality. Sartre's description of the moment of sudden insight into the existence of things, an experience that left him breathless, has become famous.[17] It occurred to me that we need to pass through a similar experience in coming to know Christ if we are to know him truly. We need really to discover that he exists, that he is alive. And this experience is exactly what the Holy Spirit is giving to many ordinary people in our own day. There is a difference between the real, living Jesus and the Jesus you find in books and learned discussions about him; it is the same as the difference between the real sky and a penciled sketch of the sky on a piece of paper.

To know Jesus in this spiritual and existential way does not lead us to care nothing for the objective, dogmatic and ecclesial knowledge of him. On the contrary it gives it new vitality. The Holy Spirit is shown to be "the light of dogma." It is by the grace of the Holy Spirit that revealed truth, like a "precious preserve in a vessel of value, is always itself refreshing and lending fresh value to the vessel that holds it."[18] In my own case, after this experience I went back with new eyes to the study of christology and it led to a new book, *Jesus Christ, the Holy One of God*.

The Holy Spirit, who makes all things new, can renew the dogmas of the Church. The Spirit does not make new things; rather,

---

[15] Thomas Aquinas, *Summa Theologiae*, I-II, q. 1, a. 2, ad 2 (*"Actus credentis non terminatur ad enuntiabile, sed ad rem"*).

[16] "Zu den Sachen selbst": Heidegger's motto to describe Husserl's phenomenology.

[17] See J.-P. Sartre, *La Nausée*, in *Œuvres romanesques*, ed. Gallimard, 105–6.

[18] Irenaeus, *Against the Heresies*, III.24.1.

the Spirit makes things new. The Spirit does not give us new dogmas about Christ, but rather makes the old dogmas new, making
them pertinent reality effectively at work today as much as they
were in ancient times. Kierkegaard wrote: "The dogmatic terminology of the primitive Church is like an enchanted castle where,
locked in slumber, lie the handsomest of princes and the loveliest
of princesses. They only need to be aroused, for them to leap to
their feet in all their glory."[19] The Holy Spirit is the only one who
can wake them from their age-long slumber.

4. Where the Holy Spirit Leads Us to Know the Son

To give our reflection a more practical bent, we must, before
we finish, try to see where the Holy Spirit will give us this new
knowledge of Christ and what means the Spirit will use to do it.

One way, the most common one, is the written Word, the Bible.
The Holy Spirit helps us to discover for ourselves what the Fathers have always affirmed: that the whole Bible speaks to us of
Christ. The Spirit teaches us to read the Bible in a spiritual way,
which is in fact to read it all as in reference to Christ who is its
fulfillment. Once, at a prayer meeting, someone read the passage
of Scripture that tells of Elijah being taken up to heaven and leaving a "double share" (in the official Italian translation: "two
thirds") of his spirit to Elisha (2 Kgs 2:9). After the reading I
heard a lady pray this prayer, "Thank you, Jesus, that when you
went up to heaven you did not leave us only a part of your Spirit
or even two thirds, but your whole Spirit. Thank you that you left
your Spirit not to one disciple only, but to all of us, all humankind!" That was truly a "spiritual" and christological reading of
the Bible, and moreover of the highest quality, and it had been
learned nowhere else but only in the school of the Holy Spirit!

In prayer the Holy Spirit not only leads us to know Jesus, but
also (as we saw in the preceding chapter) puts the Spirit's own
praying into us, sharing his own states of mind, his own intentions,
and his own sentiments with us. The Spirit "transforms" us in
Christ, for the Spirit is the Spirit of the Son praying in us. The very

---

[19] S. Kierkegaard, *The Journals,* IIA.110 (Oxford University Press, 1938)
entry 127.

best way to start a time of prayer is by asking the Holy Spirit to unite us with the prayer of Jesus. Jesus as we see him in the Gospels used to pray at all times of the day: early in the morning, in the evening, at night. When we turn to prayer at one or other of these times, we can simply put ourselves at Jesus' side as he prays and let the Spirit carry on praising and blessing the Father in us. There is a hidden power in all of this that we come to know only when we consistently put it into practice. In prayer, and especially in contemplative prayer, we find that "all of us, with unveiled faces, seeing the glory of the Lord as though reflected in a mirror, are being transformed into the same image from one degree of glory to another; for this comes from the Lord, the Spirit" (2 Cor 3:18).

However, of all times when the Spirit does this work in us, the most potent is the Eucharist. It is the Holy Spirit who makes the body and blood of Christ present on the altar, and it is the Spirit who makes them present to our spirit. It is the Holy Spirit who enables us to comprehend, without any need of words, that this blood is shed "for me"; it is the Spirit who enables us to "discern" the body of the Lord, to penetrate the inexhaustible mystery of redemption that enters into us at every Eucharist. Saint Irenaeus says that the Holy Spirit is "our communion with Christ."[20]

Let us end this reflection with the prayer of a medieval author whom we have already met. We will see that the last few words of his prayer echo the words of our hymn. He asks the Holy Spirit to help us to grasp the whole mystery of Christ, the mystery that the Spirit inspired and brought about in history:

> *Holy Spirit, my Lord and God,*
> *let your saving plan be fulfilled in us all.*
> *You drew God down from heaven and into the Virgin's womb;*
> *You are the love that moved God to become one with our own*
>   *flesh.*
> *You built for God's Son a home in his mother:*
> *built it on seven pillars, your seven gifts.*
> *From the root of Jesse a shoot has sprung:*
> *on it you would one day come to rest.*
> *God, we have heard with our very own ears;*
> *our fathers have told us*

---

[20] Irenaeus, *Against the Heresies*, III.24.1.

the work that you did
when you came in flame-tongues from your throne in the
    Godhead
to make earth a heaven and all of us gods.
From that moment on, as children adopted, scattered through-
    out all the earth,
through you we keep crying Abba, our Father! to God.
How great are your mercies, oh Spirit, oh Lord!
They revive me in hope; through them I entreat you.
faith's seal, of believers the counselor-helper,
light, fire, and wellspring of light,
oh, listen to us who call you, and come!
If you will but guide us
our Father's face we'll see, and also the face of his Son,
and know you too, who flow from them both,
life's fountain and river of peace.[21]

---

[21] Rupert of Deutz, *Prayer to the Holy Spirit* (CM 29, pp. 422–3).

XXII

And You, the Spirit of Them Both, May We Always Believe

*The Holy Spirit gives us light
to know the mystery of his own Person*

The opening line of the *Veni Creator* is a profession of faith in the divine *nature* of the Holy Spirit (the "Creator" Spirit), and the line with which it ends is a profession of faith in the Holy Spirit as a distinct divine *person*. The hymn starts by making clear *what* the Spirit is, and closes making clear *who* the Spirit is. What we need to do now is to make the supreme effort to rise to heights where we will be in touch, not with something that the Paraclete is doing, but with the Paraclete in person in the deepest intimacy of the inaccessible mystery of the Spirit's being. We cannot rise to such heights with our mind, for that is simply impossible, but with faith it is possible. Notice that the hymn does not say, "may we *comprehend*"; it says, "may we *believe*"!

This last chapter of our meditation will be a little different from the others, demanding greater concentration, because of the theological problems involved. But with the help of the Spirit who has guided us up the mountain this far, no one need hold back from this last stage of the climb to the summit.

1. The Problem of the Filioque

We set out now to reflect on the two last lines of the *Veni Creator*. They appear to be so familiar, so simple, but they are in fact more loaded with problems than all the rest of the hymn. In regard to these problems, we need right away to clear out of the way a misunderstanding that could lead to a wrong understanding not only of these two lines, but of the whole hymn. To do that we need to look briefly at the main points of the famous question of the *Filioque*.

What the Church believes of the Holy Spirit was defined, as we know, at the Ecumenical Council of Constantinople in the year 381. The definition reads: ". . . and [we believe] in the Holy Spirit who is Lord and giver of life, who proceeds from the Father and with the Father and the Son is adored and glorified, and who has spoken through the prophets."[1]

If we look at it carefully, we see that this formula contains the answer to two fundamental questions that were being asked about the Holy Spirit. The first question was, "Who is the Holy Spirit?" The answer is that the Spirit is "Lord" (that is, the Spirit is of the uncreated order of being, Creator, and not creature), that the Spirit proceeds from the Father, and that the Spirit is to be adored exactly as the Father and the Son are adored.

The second question was, "What does the Holy Spirit do?" The answer is that the Spirit "gives life" (which sums up all of the inward, sanctifying, and renewing work of the Spirit) and that the Spirit "spoke through the prophets" (which sums up all the work the Spirit does through the charisms).

The achievements of the Council of Constantinople in arriving at this formula, great as they were, represented only a provisional stage. The lacuna that stands out most noticeably in the formula is that it does not yet, at least not explicitly, acknowledge that the Holy Spirit is "God." This reflects the attitude of Saint Basil and others who, though they fully acknowledged the divinity of the Holy Spirit, refrained, for reasons of prudent caution, from explicitly calling the Spirit "God." The first to lament this reticence was Saint Gregory Nazianzen, who said, "Well then, is the Spirit God? Yes, certainly! And so then, is he consubstantial *(homousion)*? Clearly he must be, if it is true that he is God."[2]

No sooner was the council over than he began expressing his disappointment with a formula that still contained an element of compromise and that perhaps was to some extent the result of imperial pressure. The emperor wanted at all costs to avoid any conflict with the party of the Macedonians who followed the contrary view.[3] It was in fact the practice of the Church that tacitly brought

---

[1] DS 150.

[2] Gregory Nazianzen, *Sermons*, XXXI.10 (PG 36.144).

[3] See A. M. Ritter, *Das Konzil von Konstantinopel und sein Symbol* (Göttingen, 1965) 189–91.

the issue to a head: shrugging off the secondary concerns that up to that time had held it back, the Church after the council began to speak of the Holy Spirit as God and to define the Spirit as "consubstantial" with Father and Son.

The "gap" that we have noted was not the only one in the formula. Simply on the grounds of the history of salvation, it should appear peculiar that the only operation attributed to the Spirit was that the Spirit "spoke through the prophets" and that all references to the Spirit's other works, especially the Spirit's action in the life of Jesus in the New Testament, were passed over in silence. In this instance too, the completion of the dogmatic formula arose spontaneously in the life of the Church, as we can clearly see from this epiclesis in what is known as the "Liturgy of Saint James," which attributes the title "consubstantial" to the Spirit:

> Send your most holy Spirit, Lord and giver of life, who is seated with you, God and Father, and with your only-begotten Son, reigning consubstantial and coeternal. He has spoken in the Law, through the prophets, and in the New Testament, and came down in the form of a dove on our Lord Jesus Christ in the river Jordan and remained over him, and who came down on your holy apostles on the day of holy Pentecost.[4]

Another point on which the Creed of Constantinople had remained silent was the relationship between the Holy Spirit and the Son and, in consequence, the relationship between christology and pneumatology. Its only nod in that direction was in the line, "by the power of the Holy Spirit he became incarnate from the virgin Mary," which probably was already there in the credal formula adopted by the council as the basis of its own creed.[5]

On this point the interpretation of the Creed was far less simple. Some of the Greek Fathers spoke of the relationship between the Son and the Holy Spirit, saying that the Holy Spirit proceeds from the Father "through the Son," or referring to the

---

[4] A. Hänggi and I. Pahl, *Prex Eucharistica* (Fribourg, 1968) 250.

[5] See R. Cantalamessa, *Incarnatus de Spiritu Sancto ex Maria Virgine: Cristologia e Pneumatologia nel Simbolo Costantinopolitano e nella Patristica,* in CinSS I, 1983, pp. 101ff.

Spirit as "the Image of the Son" in the same sense as the Son is said to be "Image of the Father."[6]

When the Latin world took up the discussion on the Holy Spirit a new phrase was coined in the effort to express this relationship: the Spirit proceeds "from the Father and the Son." The Latin for "and the Son" is *"Filioque,"* and thus we can see how this word came to take on such overriding significance in the Trinitarian debate between the East and the West. Some say that it was actually "a heretical view that crept into Augustine's theology," but this is simply not true, neither as to the imputation of heresy nor as to historical fact. Augustine did indeed supply his own theological justification of the expression *Filioque,* which has in fact characterized all of subsequent pneumatology among the Latins. But the first actually to formulate the idea that the Holy Spirit proceeds "from the Father and the Son" was Ambrose.[7] Augustine uses expressions like "from them both" *(de utroque)*[8] that are usually pretty well toned down and certainly do not put Father and Son together on the same line in reference to the Holy Spirit, as we see from his well-known affirmation: "The Holy Spirit proceeds principally from the Father *(de Patre principaliter)* and, by the gift that the Father makes to the Son, without any lapse of time, from both at the same time."[9]

The first one to use the expression *Filioque* in that exact form in order to indicate the procession "from the Father and the Son" was in fact Fulgentius of Ruspe. Here, as in other cases too, he was the one who gave final, inflexible form to formulations already in use in the theology of the Latins.[10] He makes no mention of Augustine's precise formulation that says the Spirit proceeds "princi-

----

[6] See Athanasius, *Letters to Serapion,* I.24 (PG 26.585–6); Cyril of Alexandria, *Commentary on the Gospel of John,* XI.10 (PG 74.541C); John of Damascus, *Orthodox Faith,* I.13 (PG 94.856B).

[7] Ambrose, *On the Holy Spirit,* I.120: *"Spiritus quoque Sanctus, cum procedit a Patre et a Filio, non separatur"* (neither is the Holy Spirit to be considered differently, since he proceeds from the Father and from the Son).

[8] Augustine, *The Trinity,* XV.26.45.

[9] Ibid., 47.

[10] Fulgentius of Ruspe, *Letters,* 14.21 (CC 91, p. 411); Fulgentius of Ruspe, *On Faith,* 6.54 (CC 91A, pp. 716, 747): "Spiritus Sanctus essentialiter de Patre Filioque procedit"; Fulgentius of Ruspe, *Book on the Trinity,* passim (CC 91A, pp. 633ff.).

pally" from the Father, and instead insists on saying that the Spirit proceeds from the Son "just as" *(sicut)* he proceeds from the Father, "entirely *(totus)* from the Father and entirely from the Son," and thus placing both relationships of origin on exactly the same level.[11] It was in this undifferentiated form that the doctrine of the procession of the Holy Spirit from the Father and the Son entered into the Church's definitions of faith, starting from the Third Council of Toledo in 589.[12] It is significant that later when Charlemagne set out to make the use of *Filioque* mandatory in the Creed, he referred to a text on the *Filioque* that he thought was from Augustine but was in fact from Fulgentius of Ruspe.[13]

It is thought that Ambrose, when he first formulated the idea of the procession of the Holy Spirit "from the Father and the Son," was influenced by the Latin tradition and in particular by Tertullian. Yet Ambrose was the only Latin author of any note who did not know of Tertullian, or who in any case never quoted him at all, while it is well known that his works show that in his teaching on the Holy Spirit he depended and often drew literally on Saint Basil and even more on Saint Athanasius and Didimus of Alexandria.

It seems to me that Ambrose wanted only to gather together and explain clearly what he understood as the obvious meaning of certain ways of saying things that he read in his Greek sources, as for instance that the Spirit proceeds "through the Son"; the Spirit is "Image" of the Son; the Spirit "proceeds from the Father and receives from the Son"; the Spirit is "the ray" pouring from out of the sun (the Father) and from God's splendor (the Son); the stream flowing from the wellspring (the Father) and from the river (the Son). These forms of expression all draw attention to a certain relationship, however unclear and mysterious, between the Son and the Holy Spirit, within their shared origin in the Father. If "through the Son" means anything beyond a mere unspecified kind of motion, it must mean what Ambrose was trying to say by the expression "and from the Son."

[11] Fulgentius of Ruspe, *Letters,* 14.28 (CC 91, p. 420).

[12] DS 470. In the creed of the First Council of Toledo of the year 400 (DS 188), *Filioque* appears but as a later addition.

[13] See *Libellus Smaragdi,* in *Monumenta Germaniae Historica,* Concilia Carol., t. I, p. I, 1906, p. 238 (PL 98.923): the text in question is Fulgentius of Ruspe, *On Faith,* 6, cited above.

This could perhaps also be a common point of departure from which to work toward reaching a solution to the centuries-old problem that divides the Orthodox East and the Latin West. It was, in any event, the point on which the Fathers of the fourth century, Greek as well as Latin, were all of one accord. If we look at what they wrote about the Holy Spirit and read them one after the other, we will find that they are all in profound agreement and that there is a greater degree of continuity between them than there is now between the two traditions, the Eastern and the Western, that were developed out of their works during the centuries that followed.

Thank God an accord seems now to be not as far off as we used to think. A document issued in 1995 by the Pontifical Council for promoting Christian Unity at the Pope's own urging has been well received by exponents of Orthodox theology. The document says all that can be said, given the present position, in order to smooth the way for an ecumenical accord.[14] The rest depends perhaps to a greater extent on a change of heart and on actual dialogue between the two churches than on any change in their theologies.

What is the position of the *Veni Creator* in relation to the problem of the *Filioque*? It has been suggested that the hymn was composed precisely to defend the use of this expression and its insertion into the Creed at the time of the dispute between Charlemagne and Pope Leo III.[15] But in fact the position of the author of the *Veni Creator* is clearly the same as that taken by the pope of the time. He believed, as did all the Latins, in the procession of the Holy Spirit "from the Father and the Son,"[16] but he refrained from using the hotly debated term *Filioque* in a composition that he intended to be used in the liturgy, choosing instead the expression *utriusque Spiritus,* with which everyone would be perfectly happy. Both Eastern and Western Fathers point to the fact that Scripture refers to the Paraclete at times as the "Spirit of the Father" or "of God" and at times as the "Spirit of the Son" or the

---

[14] See *The Greek and Latin Traditions regarding the Procession of the Holy Spirit,* in "Information Service of the Pontifical Council for Promoting Christian Unity," n. 89, 1995, pp. 88–92.

[15] See Excursus: "The *Veni Creator* and the Doctrine of the *Filioque,*" at the end of this volume.

[16] See Rhabanus Maurus, *On the Universe,* I.3 (PL 111.23).

"Spirit of Christ."[17] The *Veni Creator* wasn't composed in a polemic mood to endorse one view on the Holy Spirit against the other; its situation in the life of the Church *(Sitz im Leben)* was liturgy rather than controversy.

2. New Perspectives on the Origin of the Holy Spirit from the Father

The teaching on the Holy Spirit has, so to say, become stranded on the dry shoals of discussion on the *Filioque* and on the modes of procession, and weighed down as well by the sands of quite extraneous theological issues. It is urgently necessary that it be floated free again.

A truly great renewal of the teaching on the Holy Spirit cannot therefore be a simple agreement on the *Filioque*. It needs to be something that blazes forth from a renewed reading of the Bible, undertaken against a much wider spectrum of questions. This kind of renewed reading has already been going on for some time, and it has already yielded new insight on one very precise point: The Holy Spirit, in the history of salvation, is not only sent *by* the Son, but is also sent *to* the Son; the Son is not only the one who *gives* the Spirit, but also the one who *receives* the Spirit. In the ecumenical document mentioned earlier there is a lovely passage that draws together all of the interventions of the Holy Spirit in the life of Jesus:

> Through love, the Holy Spirit orients the whole life of Jesus towards the Father in the fulfillment of his will. The Father sends his Son (Gal 4:4) when Mary conceives him through the operation of the Holy Spirit (Luke 1:35). The Holy Spirit makes Jesus manifest as Son of the Father by resting upon him at baptism (Luke 3:21-22; John 1:33). He drives Jesus into the wilderness (see Mark 1:12). Jesus returns "full of the Holy Spirit" (Luke 4:1). Then he begins his ministry "in the power of the Spirit" (Luke 4:14). He is filled with joy in the Spirit, blessing the Father for his gracious will (Luke 10:21). He chooses his apostles "through the Holy Spirit" (Acts 1:2). He

[17] Athanasius, *Letters to Serapion,* III.1 (PG 26.625); Augustine, *The Trinity,* XV.26.45.

casts out demons by the Spirit of God (Matt 12:28). He offers himself to the Father "through the eternal Spirit" (Heb 9:14). On the Cross he "commits his Spirit" into the Father's hands (Luke 23:46). "In the Spirit" he descended to the dead (1 Pet 3:19), and by the Spirit he was raised from the dead (Rom 8:11) and "designated Son of God in power" (Rom 1:4).[18]

From one phase of the history of salvation to the next—from Jesus who receives the Spirit to Jesus who sends the Spirit—the moment of transition is defined by the cross.[19]

A broad glance at all the links between Jesus and the Spirit shows the reciprocity of their relationship better than any reasoned argument could do. First of all, in the incarnation the Spirit gives us Jesus, for Jesus was conceived "through the Holy Spirit" (Matt 1:18). Next, in the paschal mystery (and, according to John, already on the cross), Jesus gives us the Holy Spirit. This relationship finds a parallel in the Eucharist. First, in the consecration, the Holy Spirit gives us Jesus (for it is by the power of the Holy Spirit that the bread becomes the body and the wine becomes the blood of Christ); next, in communion, Jesus gives us the Holy Spirit, for "anyone who is joined to the Lord is one Spirit with him" (1 Cor 6:17).

This relationship of reciprocity that can be seen so clearly on the level of history cannot be anything else than a reflection in some way of the relationship that exists already in the Trinity. The document we quoted above draws the following conclusion from the texts that it listed: "This role of the Spirit in the innermost human existence of the Son of God made man derives from an eternal Trinitarian relationship through which the Spirit, in his mystery as Gift of Love, characterizes the relation between the Father, as source of love, and his beloved Son."[20]

But how do we understand this reciprocity in the sphere of the Trinity? This is the field that is opening up to present-day reflection in the theology of the Holy Spirit. The encouraging thing is that theologians of different backgrounds—Orthodox, Protestant,

---

[18] *The Greek and Latin Traditions,* pp. 91–2.

[19] See John Paul II, Encyclical *Dominum et vificantem,* nn. 13, 24, 41; J. Moltmann, *Der Geist des Lebens,* cit., pp. 84–5.

[20] *The Greek and Latin Traditions,* p. 92.

and Catholic—are all moving in the same direction on this point, in a friendly and constructive dialogue. A solution proposed by several authors would be to reformulate the *Filioque* to reflect the reciprocity by following it up with a *Spirituque*. This would lead us to say that if it is true that the Holy Spirit proceeds "from the Father and the Son," it is equally true that the Son proceeds "from the Father and the Spirit."[21] This line of thinking, however, has a serious weakness: Never does the Scripture say that the Son "proceeds" from the Spirit.

Another and more satisfactory way of expressing the relationships seems to be to use the preposition traditionally used in speaking of the Holy Spirit, "in," and not "from." Thus we would say, "the Son is born of the Father *in* the Spirit."[22] This way of solving the issue was taken up and systematically developed in great depth in a recent essay by a Catholic theologian. It was "in the Spirit" that Christ cried out *Abba* while on earth (see Luke 10:21), and it is "in the Spirit" that the Son speaks his eternal *Abba* in his generation by the Father. Here too, what happens in history is an echo of the Trinitarian mystery.[23]

In this line we can go further. One of the fixed characteristics of all the thinking of the Fathers, especially of Augustine, and by which it was all conditioned, was the absence of the notion of reciprocity between the Spirit and the other two divine Persons. We can, they said, call the Holy Spirit the "Spirit of the Father," but we cannot call the Father the "Father of the Spirit"; we can call the Holy Spirit the "Spirit of the Son," but we cannot call the Son the "Son of the Spirit."[24]

In the new perspective we can perhaps overcome the difficulty. It is true that we cannot call God "Father of the Spirit," but we can say that God is "Father *in* the Spirit"; it is true that we cannot call the Son the "Son of the Spirit," but we can indeed call him "Son *in* the Spirit." This is not simply a clever new formula, but the

[21] See P. Evdokimov, *L'Esprit Saint dans la tradition orthodoxe* (Paris, 1969) 71–2; Moltmann, *Der Geist des Lebens*, 84–5; L. Boff, *The Trinity and Society* (New York, 1988) 6, 146–7.

[22] O. Clément, *The Roots of Christian Mysticism* (London, 1993) 70ff.

[23] See T. G. Weinandy, *The Father's Spirit of Sonship: Reconceiving the Trinity* (Edinburgh, 1995).

[24] Augustine, *The Trinity*, V.12.13.

opening up of a whole new way of conceiving the relationships within the Trinity. The Word and the Spirit proceed simultaneously from the Father. We need to be careful to keep away from any idea of precedence between the two, not only in the order of being, but also in the order of knowledge. A precedence was once accepted on the basis of the principle that the Word proceeds from the Father in the order of knowledge, the Spirit proceeds in the order of love, and knowledge logically must precede love. But we can by no means be sure of the validity of such a principle, not even on the level of human knowing and loving. (It is true that you cannot love what you do not first know, but it is also true, on a more profound level, that you cannot truly know what you do not first love!) How then can we be sure that the principle would hold in the order of the divine?

Just as the nature by which all three divine Persons have their being is one, so too the operation which constitutes the Father "Father," the Son "Son," and the Spirit "Spirit" is one and has its source in the Father. Son and Holy Spirit do not come one after the other, or one alongside of the other, but "one in the other." In the Trinity, "generate" and "proceed" are not "two separate acts" but two aspects or two outcomes of one and the same act.[25]

How are we to conceive of and express this infinite and mysterious act out of which the entire mystical flowering of the Trinity blooms? Here we have several suggestions, but the debate is still wide open and that is the way it will always remain. For here we stand before the very heart and center of the mystery of the Trinity, and that is much more accessible to intuition than to any human analogy or description. There is perhaps merit in going back to the old formula that has proved so fruitful through all the changes of theological climate over the centuries—Augustine's the lover, the beloved, and love[26]—and reevaluating it in this new light. This is what Durrwell has done, though he places alongside of this triad the other, begetter, begotten, and begetting: "There are three: the one who generates, the one who is generated, and the generation who is the Holy Spirit."[27]

[25] See Moltmann, *Der Geist des Lebens,* 85; T. G. Weinandy, *The Father's Spirit,* 53–85.

[26] Augustine, *The Trinity,* VIII.14.

[27] F. X. Durrwell, *Le Père: Dieu dans son mystère* (Paris, 1993) ch. 6.

3. The Eternal Anointing of the Word in the Holy Spirit

However, it seems to me that the Orthodox theologian Clément has a more plausible idea to offer in this regard, where he speaks of the Father's "eternal anointing" of the Son through the Spirit.[28] It is the idea that I would like to put forward, especially as it can be shown that the formula "anointer, anointed and anointing" goes back to some of the earliest Fathers of the Church. Saint Irenaeus wrote: "When we use the name Christ, we infer the one who anoints, the one who is anointed, and the anointing itself with which he was anointed. It is in fact the Father who anoints and the Son who is anointed in the Holy Spirit who is the anointing."[29]

Saint Basil repeats this affirmation as it stands, and Saint Ambrose later does the same.[30] At first this was a direct reference to the historical event, the anointing of Jesus at his baptism in the Jordan. Later the anointing came to be understood as having taken place right from the moment of the incarnation.[31] But the Fathers themselves, in their day, had already begun to see the anointing as taking place before history and time. Justin, Irenaeus, and Origen all spoke of a "cosmic anointing" of the Word, that is, the anointing conferred by the Father on the Word in view of the creation of the world, in that "through him the Father *anointed* and made provision for every thing."[32] Eusebius of Caesarea takes the idea still further, and sees the realization of the anointing in the very act of generation. "The anointing consists in the very generation of the Word, through which the Spirit of the Father passes into the Son like a divine fragrance."[33]

The witness of Eusebius alone would not be enough to lend the seal of patristic authority to this affirmation, given his ambiguous position on the question of the consubstantiality of the Son. However, this authority is present in Saint Gregory of Nyssa who

---

[28] See Clément, *The Roots of Christian Mysticism*, 58–9.

[29] Irenaeus, *Against the Heresies*, III.18.3.

[30] Basil the Great, *On the Holy Spirit*, XII.28 (PG 32.116C); Ambrose, *On the Holy Spirit*, I.3.44.

[31] See Cantalamessa, *Incarnatus de Spiritu Sancto*, 120ff.

[32] Irenaeus, *Proof of the Apostolic Preaching*, 53 (SCh 62, p. 114); the texts from these authors are the subject of an extended commentary by A. Orbe, *La Unción del Verbo*, Analecta Gregoriana, vol. 113 (Rome, 1961) 501–68.

[33] Orbe, *La Unción del Verbo*, 578.

devotes a whole chapter to developing the idea of the anointing of the Word, through the Holy Spirit, in his eternal generation by the Father. His point of departure is the supposition that the name "Christ," the Anointed, belongs to the Son from all eternity:

> The oil of exultation stands for the power of the Holy Spirit with whom God is anointed by God, that is, the Only-begotten is anointed by the Father. . . . Just as a righteous person cannot be at the same time unrighteous, so too, one who is anointed cannot not be anointed. Now, the one who is never not anointed has certainly forever been anointed. And everyone ought to see that it is the Father who anoints and the Holy Spirit who is the anointing.[34]

The anointing of Jesus in his baptism in the Jordan is certainly a more convincing biblical basis than the reference to Psalm 45:8, which Gregory of Nyssa takes as his starting point, but this is not what concerns us now. The analogy of *anointing* (because it is always with analogies that we are dealing) adds something new that is not expressed by the more usual analogy of *breathing*. It was common practice in the West to say that the third divine Person was called "Spirit" in that the Spirit is breathed *(spiratus)* and also breathes *(spirat)*. In a short paraphrase of the *Veni Creator* found in a work attributed to Saint Bonaventure, we read:

> The Holy Spirit is called Spirit, from *spirare,* to breathe. In the active sense, in as much as he breathes, as we read in Saint John, "the Spirit breathes where he will" (John 3:8), the name can be applied to all three Persons and is fittingly applied to the Holy Spirit by appropriation. In the passive sense, in as much as the Spirit is breathed, the name belongs properly to the Holy Spirit who proceeds by way of being breathed, or spiration.[35]

From this point of view, the Holy Spirit would be fulfilling an "active" role only outside of the Trinity, insofar as the Spirit inspires the Scriptures, the prophets, the saints. Within the Trinity the Spirit would be only passive, insofar as the Spirit is breathed *(spiratus)* by the Father and the Son. But this absence of an active

---

[34] Gregory of Nyssa, *Against Apollinaris,* 52 (PG 45.1249–50).

[35] Pseudo-Bonaventure, *Compendium of Theological Truth,* 10, in Saint Bonaventure, *Opera Omnia* (Paris, 1866) 68; see also Isidore of Seville, *Etymologies,* VII.3.2 (PL 82.268).

role for the Spirit within the Trinity is seen today, and rightly, as perhaps the most serious gap in the traditional theology of the Spirit. In the perspective of the reciprocity of the Son and the Spirit, the gap is mended. If, in fact, we recognize an active role for the Son in relation to the Spirit, expressed in the image of breathing, we can also recognize an active role for the Spirit in relation to the Son, expressed in the image of anointing. We cannot say of the Word that he is "the Son of the Holy Spirit," but we certainly can say of him that he is "the Anointed of the Spirit."

We might well ask whether we should not understand in a reciprocal way also the appellative "We" that some give to the Person of the Holy Spirit in the Trinity.[36] If the Holy Spirit is the divine "We," in whose breathing the Father and Son are united, the Son would also be the divine "We" in whose generation/anointing the Father and Spirit are united. Without this reciprocity, Mühlen's brilliant insight remains inevitably bound up in the *Filioque* problem, and hence of significance only within the ambit of Latin theology.

Now, however, we need to be careful not to re-create the difficulty we have noted in the other direction, leaving out of the picture the active part that the Son also has in the procession of the Spirit. This shows that it is not a matter of choosing between breathing and anointing, but to encourage theology to continue to use both analogies. The analogy of breathing, in fact, is the one that stands out as more useful than any other to bring the active role of the Son to light, especially if we think of it as a *conspiracy,* Father and Son breathing the Spirit together, with all the shadings of intimacy, shared secrets, loving cooperation in intention and purpose, that the word "conspire" conjures up in our mind, once freed of its usual negative meaning.

If there is a limit beyond which we must not go in affirming full reciprocity between the Son and the Holy Spirit it would be in regard to *mission.* In the history of salvation we find the Holy Spirit being sent upon the Son, but never the Spirit sending the Son. What the Gospels show us is an *impulse* from the Holy Spirit in Jesus (as when the Spirit "drove" him into the wilderness), or the Spirit accompanying Jesus, rather than a *sending* in the strict meaning of the word. We read that the Holy Spirit is sent "in the name" of

---

[36] H. Mühlen, *Der Heilige Geist als Person, Ich–Du–Wir* (Münster, 1963); H.-U. von Balthasar, *Spiritus Creator* (Einsiedeln, 1967) 115.

Jesus Christ the Son (see John 14:26), but never that the Son is sent "in the name" of the Holy Spirit or by the Holy Spirit. This is sufficient to justify the order in which the three divine Persons are traditionally named, the Father, the Son, and the Holy Spirit.

4. We Thank You, Holy Spirit!

And now, to conclude, we go back to the two lines of the hymn with which we started this last chapter: *"Te utriusque Spiritum credamus omni tempore."* Their meaning is not, "let us believe that you are the Spirit of the Father and of the Son," but rather, "may we believe in you who are the Spirit of Father and Son." We are praying to believe not a doctrine (the procession of the Spirit from Father and Son), but a person, the Holy Spirit. The analogy of the previous two lines shows us that this is so, for in one we are asking to know the Father, in the next to know the Son, and so here it is the Spirit we are wanting to know. It is true that when we want to express faith in the divine Persons we usually use the preposition "in": I believe *in* the Holy Spirit. But I think that the absence of the preposition in the Latin text in this place is sufficiently explained by the demands of the meter.

To believe in the Holy Spirit! What does that mean, in the light of the hymn as a whole? Not merely to believe in the abstract existence of the Spirit, to believe that there is a Holy Spirit; neither merely to believe in the Spirit's precise relationships of origin according to the way the Spirit was understood in the Latin tradition. For a faithful disciple of Augustine, as the author of the *Veni Creator* shows himself to be, to call the Paraclete "the Spirit of them both" means a great deal more. It means to say that the Spirit is the mutual love of the Father and the Son, the kiss, their mutual embrace full of joy and happiness in which, thanks to the Spirit, we find ourselves in some way caught up, held close by Father and Son, sharing their kiss.

That is what "I believe in the Holy Spirit" should mean for us too today. It is not merely a question of believing that there is a third Person in the Trinity, but of accepting in faith that the Spirit is present to us, among us, in our very heart. It is to believe in the ultimate victory of love. It is to believe that the Holy Spirit is busy leading the Church to perfect unity just as the Spirit is busy leading the Church to the fullness of truth. It is to believe in the ultimate unity of all humankind, however far off that might seem, for it is the Holy Spirit who is guiding our history and who presides over "the return of all things to God."

To believe in the Holy Spirit means therefore to believe that history and life make sense, and that all human hopes will be fulfilled. It means to believe that our human bodies will be fully redeemed, and also in the redemption of that greater body that is the whole created universe, because it is the Spirit who sustains it and who makes it groan in anticipation as in the pangs of birthing.

To believe in the Holy Spirit means to adore, to love, to bless and praise, and to thank the Spirit, as we want to do now as we come to the end of these pages in which we have dared the adventure of a "full immersion," of a new baptism in the Spirit, the fountain of blessed water:

> *Thank you, Creator Spirit, because you never cease transforming our chaos into cosmos, because you have come into our minds and filled our hearts with grace.*
>
> *Thank you, because you are our consoler, the Father's supreme gift to us, living water, fire, love, and anointing for our soul.*
>
> *Thank you for your infinite gifts and charisms that you, powerful Finger of God, have given to us, you, the Father's promise to us, fulfilled and ever to be fulfilled.*
>
> *Thank you for the word of fire that you never cease to put on the lips of your prophets, your pastors, your missionaries, and of all your people who pray.*
>
> *Thank you for the light of Christ that you have caused to shine in our minds, for his love that you have poured into our hearts, for his healing that you have brought about in our bodies so prone to infirmity.*
>
> *Thank you for being at our side in the struggle, for helping us overcome the enemy, and for the times you have helped us up again when we have fallen.*
>
> *Thank you for being our guide in the difficult choices of our life, and for keeping us safe from evil's allure.*
>
> *And thank you, above all, for having shown us the Father's face and for teaching us to cry, Abba!*
>
> *Thank you that you prompt us to proclaim: Jesus is Lord!*

Thank you that you showed yourself to the Church of the Fathers and show yourself now to the Church of our day. Thank you that you let us see you are the bond of unity between Father and Son, the ineffable outflowing of their together-breathing love, the life-giving breath and fragrance of divine union that the Father shares with the Son, generating him before ever ages began.

Simply because you are, Holy Spirit, may you be thanked, now and for all eternity!

Excursus

The Veni Creator *and the Doctrine of the* Filioque

There is a study on the *Veni Creator* full of useful historical facts and philological data (for which all who love the hymn will always be profoundly grateful to its author), but which, unfortunately, puts forward a thesis that is quite unfounded and compromises the meaning of the whole hymn. The thesis is this: Rhabanus Maurus, who lived from about 780 to 856, was probably the author of the hymn. At that time, in 809 to be precise, a synod was convened at Aachen at the bidding of Charlemagne to discuss and approve the insertion of *Filioque* into the Creed of Nicea-Constantinople, which certain churches had started to sing at the Mass. After the synod a delegation went to Pope Leo III in Rome to seek his support for the addition to the Creed. But, although he fully accepted the doctrine of the *Filioque,* the pope considered its insertion in the Creed inopportune and would not be persuaded to change his mind on the matter.[1]

In this matter the pope was adopting the same position as that of the Greek Church, which had come to a deeper understanding of the article on the Holy Spirit without, for that reason, having had to change the wording of the Creed. The pope's position was that it was not necessary to put into the Creed and into the liturgical formulae all the new implications that theology was discovering, and would go on discovering, in the dogmas.[2]

---

[1] Notes and Documents relating to the synod and the colloquium between Leo III and the delegation from the emperor, in *Monumenta Germaniae Historica,* Concilia Carol., t. II, p. II, 1906, pp. 235–44, and in PL 102.971–6.

[2] There is an antiphon in the eighth-century *Sacramentarium Gellonense* (CC 159, p. 139) that was in use at the time in the liturgy of Pentecost, and that is perhaps a sign of a liturgical reluctance to include the *Filioque:* "May the Paraclete who proceeds from you, Lord, enlighten our minds and lead us, as your Son promised, to the fullness of truth" *("qui a te procedit,"* not *"qui a te Filioque procedit"*!).

The learned study I mentioned linked the composition of the *Veni Creator* to this event in history. It suggested that Rhabanus Maurus wrote it as a kind of "battle hymn" to support the emperor's view. It supposed that the "enemy" in the second-last verse ("the enemy drive from us away") was not the devil, but the ecclesiastics who opposed the *Filioque,* in point of fact the pope himself! It suggested that the intention underlying the words "with you as guide to lead the way, we avoid all cause of harm," was to say that we must avoid false doctrines in the synod we are about to hold, and we must not fall victim to the sort of evil manipulation that is often unleashed in gatherings of that kind. And so on.

Now, within this framework, what would be the significance of the last two lines of the hymn, "and may we always cling in faith to you the Spirit of them both" *(Te utriusque Spiritum credamus omni tempore)*? The literal meaning of the words would be, "may we always believe you who are the Spirit of both Father and Son." But the real sense, the study suggests, was the underlying intent: "Let your procession from Father and Son be put at long last into the Creed!"[3]

This recasting of the hymn's message will not stand up to scrutiny, for the following reasons. Taking for granted that Rhabanus Maurus really was the author, he would have been no more than thirty years old in 809, and it seems very unlikely that at such an age he would have displayed the deep maturity of thought and the uncommon command of the writings of the Fathers that are manifest in the hymn. And again, the *Veni Creator* displays a spiritual grasp so wide, so universal, that it is quite impossible to believe that it was intended only for that narrow little polemical purpose.

But the principal reason is another altogether. These last two lines, which are supposed to be the basis for the reconstruction we have been looking at, simply do not contain anything to support the thesis that the study puts forward. It would be very odd if the author of the hymn, setting out to plead for the inclusion of the Filioque in the Creed, should carefully avoid using it himself. If he had wanted, he certainly would have had no difficulty in fit-

---

[3] See H. Lausberg, *Der hymnus "Veni Creator Spiritus,"* JAWG (1969) 26–58; and a synthesis by the same author in "Nachrichten der Akademie der Wissenschaften zu Göttingen," I, Philol.-hist. Klasse (1976) 389–94.

ting the word into his final doxology, something we often find in hymns of a later period when the word *Filioque* had already been added into the Credo and its use was no longer a topic that gave rise to discussion.[4]

The position taken by the author of the *Veni Creator* is clearly, to the letter, the same as that taken by the pope of the time. He believed, as did all the Latins, in the procession of the Spirit "from the Father and the Son,"[5] but he refrained from using the hotly debated term *Filioque* in a composition that he intended to be used in the liturgy, using instead an expression with which everyone would be perfectly happy.

There is no doubt that, in the period when our hymn was written, the expression *utriusque Spiritus,* the Spirit *of* both, was understood as equivalent to *Spiritus ab utroque,* the Spirit *from* both, and hence in line with the doctrine of the *Filioque.* But the expression itself is one that we have from the Bible, perhaps the most certain of the points that the Bible gives us concerning the Holy Spirit. It was from Scripture that Augustine derived it directly. He writes: "Sacred Scripture in fact tells us that he is the Spirit of them both (*Spiritum amborum*)."[6]

Immediately following this statement, Augustine cites the biblical texts in which the Spirit is called, now "Spirit of God," now "Spirit of the Father," then "Spirit of the Son," or again "Spirit of Christ."[7] The expression *utriusque Spiritus* was therefore not derived from the doctrine of the *Filioque,* but rather, the other way around: The doctrine of the *Filioque* was based on the biblical affirmation of *utriusque Spiritus.*

There is still more, however. On the theme of the Paraclete as the Spirit of both Father and Son we find complete agreement between the Greek and the Latin authors. In the first place Athanasius writes: "Through all of Scripture I will find that the Holy Spirit who is said to be 'of the Son,' is also said to be 'of God.'"[8]

---

[4] See, for example, Adam of St. Victor, *Hymn for Pentecost,* AHMA 54 (1915) 241: *"qui procedis ab utroque."*

[5] See Rhabanus Maurus, *On the Universe,* I.3 (PL 111.23).

[6] Augustine, *The Trinity,* XV.26.45.

[7] See Matt 10:20; Acts 16:7; Gal 4:6; Rom 8:9; 8:14; 1 Cor 2:11.

[8] Athanasius, *Letters to Serapion,* III.1 (PG 26.625).

Saint Basil follows him in the same line of thought (Spirit "from God," and Spirit "of Christ"),[9] and in a marked way also Cyril of Alexandria, who again and again refers to the Spirit as "the Spirit of the Father and the Son."[10]

It is clearly unthinkable, then, that the author of the *Veni Creator* was lining himself up, dagger drawn, at the side of the emperor against the opponents of the *Filioque*. It is equally unthinkable that he actually set out to write the hymn as a way of putting pressure on the pope, for why then would he have used the most "innocuous" word he could find, one that no one would think to dispute? That would have been like trying to dig his way under an open door. Clearly we must reject the whole card-castle of hypotheses built on these last two lines of the hymn and on the supposed close link of the hymn to the argument between the pope and the emperor concerning the *Filioque*. If in any event there is no ultimate certainty about who wrote the *Veni Creator*, how is it supposed to be possible to pinpoint precisely the year when it was written and the circumstances surrounding its composition?

Perhaps influenced by the interpretation we have just been considering, there was a proposal put forward in Germany to provide an "ecumenical version" of the *Veni Creator* to be used in meetings with fellow-Christians of the Orthodox faith. The last two lines were to be changed to "Help us, oh Spirit, to be aware / of you, God dwelling in us."[11] Of course, there is nothing to say that the lines of a hymn should not be changed if they do in fact upset the feelings of our Orthodox brothers. But before we go ahead and change anything, we surely need to make sure that, understood as they were meant to be understood, the lines as they are in the *Veni Creator* actually do offend someone.

The *Veni Creator* as it is, is already "ecumenical," not only in the sense that as it stands it does not canonize any particular thesis about the origin of the Holy Spirit, but especially because of the all-embracing breadth of its vision and the limitless horizons it opens, qualities that so distinguish it and that account for its popu-

---

[9] Basil the Great, *On the Holy Spirit*, XVIII.46 (PG 32.152).

[10] Cyril of Alexandria, *Commentary on the Gospel of John*, IX (PG 74.257A); Cyril of Alexandria, *Dialogue on the Trinity*, VI (PG 75.1056A).

[11] *Gotteslob. Katholisches Gebet-und Gesangbuch* (Stuttgart, 1975): *"und dich erfahren, Gott in uns / dazu hilf uns, o Heiliger Geist."*

larity among Christians of the West right down to our own day. The contributions of the Greek Fathers filtered through its lines are no less than those of the Latins, even though it is through the latter that they entered in the hymn. The *Veni Creator* is no "battle hymn" but a song of peace, no "special occasion" hymn, but one that is linked to the feast of Pentecost. The same author composed hymns for other liturgical feasts in the same sort of way.

Index of Authors

391

Index of Subjects